JOYCE CARY:
THE WRITER AND HIS THEME

A self-portrait lithograph completed by Joyce Cary in the last
year of his life. Reproduced by courtesy of Mrs. D. M. Davin.

JOYCE CARY:

THE WRITER
AND HIS THEME

Barbara Fisher

HUMANITIES PRESS
Atlantic Highlands, N.J.

First published in North America by Humanities Press Inc.
171 First Avenue, Atlantic Highlands, N.J. 07716, U.S.A.

Library of Congress Cataloging in Publication Data

Fisher, Barbara
    Joyce Cary.
    1. Cary, Joyce – Criticism and interpretation
    823′.9′12   PR6005.A77Z/
    ISBN 0–391–01763–2

Printed in Great Britain

TO
TOM CARRIGAN
and his generation

Contents

Foreword and Acknowledgements

The writing of this book began with the award of grants in 1967 from the Leverhulme Trustees and the International Federation of University Women, whose generosity I gratefully acknowledge. The book had been planned as a critical biography since 1963, when I was writing a thesis on Joyce Cary's files and notebooks. The form of the book differs from that originally planned, because the publication of Malcolm Foster's biography in 1968 suggested that a different type of study might be more valuable. The essential biographical facts are here presented as a framework, in the bibliography of Cary's published writing.

Publication has been delayed for several reasons. Meanwhile, many people who spared time to write or talk to me about Joyce Cary may well have decided that their trouble was wasted. Many alas have died. But I record here my gratitude for all the help I have received, in the hope that its nature will be remembered by those still living, and that the acknowledgement will be appreciated by the relatives and friends of those who have died.

I am particularly indebted to Joyce Cary's eldest son, Sir Michael Cary, his cousin Professor Lionel Stevenson, and his brother, Commander John Cary, whose deaths have most regrettably occurred. Other members of his family, on both sides, who graciously responded to my inquiries, are Mrs Howard Cusworth, Dr Dorothy Heard, Mrs Muriel Munro, Mrs T. Thompson, Miss Shiela Cary, Mr Tristram Cary, Mr Cary Clark, and Sir W. Arbuthnot Lane. Lady Ogilvie, widow of Sir Frederick Ogilvie, kindly interviewed me, and Joyce Cary's other brother-in-law, Sir Heneage Ogilvie, sent information shortly before his death.

Others whom I should like to name are: Professor Walter Allen, Mr John Bell, Mr S. M. Bessie, Mrs Alice Dixon Bond, Mr Anthony Borrow, Mr Harvey Breit, Mrs Helena Brett-Smith, Mr A. N. Bryan-Brown, Mr Spencer Curtis Brown, Mr Cass

Canfield, Dr Arthur Melville Clark, Mr and Mrs Dan Davin, Mrs Cecilia Dick, Mr and Mrs Thorold Dickinson, Mr and Mrs Frank Doherty, Mr Tom Driberg, Dr McD. Emslie, Mr Charles Ferguson, Mrs Margaret Morris Fergusson, Mr and Mrs John Fischer, Mrs Matthew Fisher, Ms Katharine Gildersleeve, Mr Max Gissen, Mr Ian Grant, Mrs Sarah Gleason, Mrs Graham Greene, Sir Alec Guinness, Mrs Beulah Hagen, Mrs Sewell Haggard, Mrs Nicky Hahn, Mr Thomas Higham, Mr P. W. S. Hodge (for George Newnes Ltd), Dr Richard Hunt, Mrs Elizabeth Kalashnikoff, Mr J. J. Keaveney, Mr A. H. M. Kirk-Greene, Miss C. R. B. Kirkwood, Miss Olive Kirkwood, Mrs Irene Laune, Mrs Nora Lightburne, Miss Ruth Linnel, Sir Robert Lusty, Mrs Liam McCormick, Mr R. D. McEldowney, Mr Donald Mackie, Professor John Macmurray, Professor M. M. Mahood, Mr T. S. Matthews, Mr S. J. M. McWatters, Mr Charles Napier, Dr and Mrs James Osborn, Mr F. W. Parsons, Mr J. R. Pim, Professor Ritchie Russell, Dr Peter Shillingsburg, Mr Harry Sions, Mrs Edith Stapleton, Dr Enid Starkie, Mr and Mrs James Stern, Ms Aline Talmey, Mr Adam Bruce Thomson, Professor John Dover Wilson, Mr Merrick Winn, Dr C. W. M. Witty, Professor and Mrs Andrew Wright.

I am very appreciative of the use of the James Osborn Collection of Joyce Cary Manuscripts in the Bodleian Library, and for the assistance of the Bodleian Library staff throughout my years of research. I have received equally courteous attention when pursuing research at the Oxford City Central Library; the B.B.C.; the British Library; Goldsmiths' University of London Library; the National Library of Scotland; the National Library, Dublin; the Library of Trinity College, Dublin; the Genealogical Office, Dublin Castle; the Public Records Offices in Dublin and Belfast; St Colomb's Cathedral, Christ Church, McGee College Library, the City Cemetery, and the offices of the *Derry Journal* and the Northern Bank (formerly the Belfast Bank), all in Londonderry; the *Portadown News* office, Portadown, and the *Daily Express* Library, London.

I received generous help with research information from Cary's American publishers, Harper & Row, from Michael Joseph Ltd and Victor Gollancz Ltd in London, and from his first and later literary agents, A. P. Watt & Son and Curtis Brown Ltd.

My particular thanks are due to Professor Lorna Reynolds, Professor A. Norman Jeffares, and Mr Colin Smythe, without whose advice and encouragement the book would not now be published.

Quotations from the unpublished manuscripts in the Bodleian Library are made by kind permission of Mrs Davin, on behalf of the Joyce Cary Estate. Quotations from Joyce Cary's published works are by permission of Michael Joseph Ltd, Curtis Brown Ltd, and Harper & Row.

A Note on References

Unless otherwise stated, all unpublished material, including correspondence, is in the James M. Osborn Collection of Joyce Cary's Manuscripts, deposited in the Bodleian Library, Oxford.

Many quotations are from notes or letters written long ago, in haste, for private use only. Many are somewhat indecipherable, or made obscure by cancellations, contractions, or omissions. They also contain errors in spelling and punctuation. Because this book is concerned primarily with making Cary's ideas known, ease of reading has been the first consideration. Therefore some corrections have been made. But their nature is indicated in a note. Minor typical irregularities or contractions remain, such as 'd' for 'and'; 't' for 'the'. Where any difficulty in interpreting the word is anticipated, it has been expanded in a square bracket. Words of doubtful reading are preceded by a question mark and enclosed in a square bracket. Cancellations are not shown, but punctuation is unaltered. Cary's erratic typescript is reproduced in a simple example on p. 49, showing why 'sic' has been generally omitted. Foliation numbers are given where possible.

The Carfax edition has been used for all quotations from the novels, apart from *Except the Lord,* which has not yet appeared in this uniform edition. For it, the Michael Joseph edition, published in London in 1953, has been used.

Space does not allow any lengthy explanation of the methods by which the dates of manuscripts have been arrived at. They include a comparison with writing of known date, according to the paper, pen, and ink used, and also according to variations in the formation of letters, for Cary's handwriting changed considerably during his writing life. Another method is mentioned in chapter 7, n. 56. A full account of the dating appears in my thesis in the University of London Library.

Oxford   Barbara Fisher
June 1979

1. Introduction

> But all great artists have a theme, an idea of life profoundly
> felt and founded in some personal and compelling experience.
> This theme then finds confirmation and development in new in-
> tuition. The development of the great writer is the development
> of his theme – the theme is part of him and has become the cast
> of his mind and character.[1]

Here Joyce Cary is pointing out what distinguishes the great
writer from 'the yarn-spinner who works merely from happy
thoughts'. He implies that the writer's theme and the cast of his
mind and character are to be discovered from each other, and
that these are the clearest guides in assessing a writer's worth. He
seems also to be saying that a critic should not attempt a final
judgement unless he is satisfied that he understands the writer's
theme. This whole study is based on this criterion.

When Cary set down these words, he had been discussing the
theme of the novelist whom he thought the greatest, and by whom
he had been most influenced: Tolstoy. By going straight on to
speak as he does of a yarn-spinner, he gives a hint that his own
dilemma as a writer is here in his mind. For he knew that to
many readers he was just such a yarn-spinner.

Cary's dilemma may explain why he has gradually suffered
eclipse. 'A Great Author Faces up to Death' was typical of the
public notice he received around 29 March 1957, when he died
from the paralysis, amyotrophic lateral sclerosis, which he had
most bravely fought and endured for two years. His fame owed
something to his courage, but had already been won by his
writing. In his sixty-eight years he had published fifteen novels,
and another would appear posthumously. Four are set in Nigeria,
where he was a soldier and colonial serviceman for six years,
before retiring in 1920 to live, from then on, as a professional
writer, in Oxford. He had previously attended Oxford University,
and numerous subtle references throughout his work indicate the

1

significance of Oxford to it. His later novels, including the two trilogies for which he is best known, have English settings. But between the African and English come two novels of Northern Ireland, to which by family tradition, and sentiment, he belonged. These provide the best clues to his mind and character. He would have continued the first, *Castle Corner*, which is his longest and most ambitious novel, into a trilogy, but was discouraged by uncomprehending reviews. However the other, *A House of Children*, won the James Tait Black prize in 1941, and so marked, for him, his first recognition by the academic world.

His novels had frequently been recommended by the Book Society, and reviews had been generally favourable. But the quality chiefly admired was his zest for life, which strongly suggests 'the yarn-spinner who works merely from happy thoughts'. Certainly he had never been satisfied with the criticism of his books, and he was obviously distressed by the reviews of the American critic Mark Schorer. For in 1951 he found an excuse to write to Schorer, whom he had met earlier in the year, on a lecture tour arranged through his American publishers, Harper & Row. This tour, and another in 1953, ensured Cary a far bigger and more appreciative audience in the United States than he ever enjoyed elsewhere. Understandably therefore, he hoped to win over American critics.

Schorer had just reviewed *Mister Johnson* for the *New York Times Book Review*, and Cary wrote:

Oxford. 13.10.51

Dear Professor Schorer,

I wanted to thank you for a very kind and interesting review and also I want to put a problem to you as a critic. My novels are all about one world – as much so as Blake's poetry is about his world, and I want, like him, to make people *feel* that world which might be described as that of freedom.

By freedom I don't mean the figment that politicians talk about – but *real* freedom – the active creative freedom which maintains the world in being – the activity which is most nearly described by theologians – the source of moral responsibility and of good and evil; but for me also of injustice and love, of a special comedy and a special tragic dilemma which can never be solved.

. . . but of course my theme is far wider than any religious construction. It includes aesthetic and political freedom, the whole problem of the created symbol.

And like others (like Blake again) obsessed with a view of the world which seems to me so obvious, but to other people apparently so dark, I am very anxious to make my world understood and felt.

That is why, unlike Blake who invented his own mythology, to avoid the cliché of worn out definition, I use a quite different method of approach. I do not want to frighten people at the beginning by difficulties or by the idea of instruction. I do not want to start by saying 'this novel is a metaphysical construction based on a comprehensive idea of life' or they will stop entering into my characters' lives and instead treat the book, if they tackle it at all, as a kind of crossword-puzzle, asking what does this character stand for, – or that, – they will imagine an allegory. And I detest allegory – my people are real people in a real world or they are nothing.

In this book the dilemmas of Rudbeck, *making* his road – his wife *creating* her independent life (as she must do for his happiness as well as hers) Johnson creating his personal legend and the careerist making his career – all immersed in the world of creation – of free imagination – of injustice, of change – are those of actual souls faced with personal problems which are also universal ones.

Of course there are all the other elements to be considered to give a true picture – the 'created' elements of society and convention – set-ups which have a temporary stability or rather a slower rate of decay ("The Horses Mouth" largely turns on such constructions of taste – "The Moonlight" with those of marriage and sex); the permanent characters of being itself – such as science examines – without which there would not be anything at all; and the derivative (which crop up in "The Fearful Joy" for instance, in the study of the refugees) such as the family and the social consequences of the family relation; and the sexual relation which obliges us to create with certain given materials.

Thus my problem of form tends to be complex. It is ultimately a moral problem (to give a true experience) – one can't put in the Whole in a single book (nor in a hundred) one has to seek a balance. It is a special and difficult form forced upon me by my material.

An old friend who understood what I was at, was always pressing me to explain the position, but I have always been afraid of killing the books. I know how hard it is to make people enter into a new situation; how easily they push a book into a pigeon hole and turn your meaning into a cliché.

That is why I fought so long even against writing introductions and why, when I gave way, I made them so short and plain in the new edition.

But to you I can be frank. Ought I to go on as I am doing, presenting the books as yarns and letting a few people here and there find out by their own penetration what I am trying to do? creating a homogeneous picture of the world as it is, as perpetual creation of the free soul with all its complex results in art and religion and its politics, its special tragedy and special morality: . . . Or ought I to write a general preface to the whole series under the head (which I once thought of using) "The Comedy of Freedom?" But what worries me is not the reviews of Mr. John but that such theses on my work as I have seen, even a very good job that came to me this week from a Norwegian scholar – are just as much at sea as most of the newspaper notices.

This man has discovered or sensed that the books are all part of one related scheme but he has no inkling of its nature. Perhaps such words as creation, freedom are so utterly worn out by fanatics and cranks, that they no longer carry any of their tremendous meaning.

Yours sincerely

Joyce Cary[2]

This letter has been quoted at length because it contains more direct clues to Cary's mind, character, and work than are to be found in any published form, such as the prefaces to the Carfax edition, which Cary was still writing, and to which he refers. He may have hoped that his references to Blake would rouse interest in Schorer, whose publication, *William Blake: the politics of vision*, had appeared in 1946. But they are justified because Blake had influenced Cary for forty years.

This study then is largely an amplification and interpretation of this letter. It shows that Cary's theme is freedom in the widest sense, and particularly in its moral and religious implications;

that he is in some way a symbolist, yet also treated each novel as 'a metaphysical construction based on a comprehensive idea of life'; and that his difficulty was to make a whole of his poetic and philosophical elements in a form that also included the level at which everyone can see life – as a yarn. For his main object was to be read, in the belief that readers *'feel'*, rather than understand, a work of art. Above all, his books are to be seen as 'part of one related scheme'. Elsewhere he said his books were like chapters of one work.[3]

Another illuminating letter is Cary's reply to Andrew Wright, dated 16 August 1955, in which he agreed enthusiastically to Wright's proposal to undertake a full-length study, but warned, with regard to his work:

> The great difficulty of critics in dealing with it is that it does not reveal any subjective centre. It deals, as far as I can manage it, with the whole landscape of existence; and though that landscape is seen from one point of view, the especial nature of that point of view does not appear in the books. It could not appear anywhere except in a treatise.
>
> It has, of course, been partly stated in my lectures, and I am going to try to give a more complete statement in the Clark Lectures which I am giving next year at Cambridge.

The Clark lectures became *Art and Reality*, the treatise from which our key quotation comes, and this treatise can be regarded as the general preface that Schorer agreed Cary should write. That it is not called 'The Comedy of Freedom' indicates that Cary was more concerned with 'the whole problem of the created symbol', on which the comedy of freedom in fact depends.

His meaning is perhaps clearest in the following passage: 'The most important part of truth is what humanity is suffering, is feeling and thinking at any moment, and this cannot be known, as a totality, to any person. It is not known completely to the individuals themselves. For immediately life takes place in the subconscious, before it is known to reflection; and its sources, the active nature of being itself, are completely beyond the human imagination' (pp. 115–16).

The implications here are enormous. Cary is not only insisting on the subjectivity of truth, whereby all established creeds are challenged; but also saying that we are part of an ever-changing world, which we know directly through our subconscious minds, yet cannot claim to know consciously except by a 'created symbol'. The title *Art and Reality* expresses this conviction: that each one of us knows the world from a unique symbol or image formed from unique experience.

But following the last passage quoted Cary immediately argues against theorists who judge art solely by its coherence and effect on the reader or observer. 'A whole school of criticism, in the twenties, took this view', he says, 'in accord with the general fashion of thirty years ago; it was in reaction against the religiosity of the Victorians before and any belief in real values. It went with atheism, dadaism, Marxism, Freudianism and the rest. It is now old-fashioned and generally on the defensive.' These words suffice to explain why Cary's first novel did not appear until 1932, though he became a professional writer in 1920. He needed confidence in his own convictions to stand aside from this fashion. Here he rejects this 'behaviourist theory' as false, by noting 'a difference between truth of art and truth of revelation. . . . We accept *The Kreutzer Sonata* as a masterpiece of form, but we don't accept its meaning as a general truth. And this sense of revelation certainly appears to be the same as that with which we intuit the real.'

Cary's choice of an example is typical and significant. For by 1920 he had accepted the principles of Tolstoy's theory of art. He noted: 'What can the author, the artist, the novelist reply to the question, Are you doing any good in the world, and what good. He can say that education is the principal force for good in the world and that artists are the chief educators, perhaps the only true educators.'[4] But he soon recognized that Tolstoy's theory of art and morals was confused, and the 'one related scheme' of Cary's work centres on this confusion, with particular reference to *The Kreutzer Sonata*.

For his main point in *Art and Reality* is that 'men live so entirely by feeling that reason has extremely small power over even our most intelligent, our geniuses like Marx and Tolstoy' (pp. 23–24). Tolstoy truly said that art is an infection, by which someone successfully communicates his feeling to others. What Tolstoy communicated most successfully was a clear picture of reality, such as men urgently desire as a guide to life. The last quotation is preceded by this account of it:

Tolstoy's anarchism carried such weight because it was the simplest of all. Tolstoy said in effect, do nothing, leave it all to God, who is found in our own human nature. This fiction carried a unique emotional appeal. It offered a golden age of peace and love and happiness, which was to be attained at once, much sooner than the Marxian. Tolstoy did not promise merely that the State would wither when evil had vanished from the world and all men were always good; he said that if the State were at once abolished, all men would be good, and universal happiness would begin.

Tolstoy propounded this doctrine in *A Confession* and *What I Believe*, which Aylmer Maude introduced to English readers in 1920 with these words: 'if our spiritual leaders believe that there is anything in our existing institutions, industrial, legal, religious, or national, which deserves defence, they should produce some reply to the indictment formulated in this book, and should publish the same before it is here, as already in Russia, too late to save the existing structure.'[5] Cary took up this challenge, but needed to know his own belief, and not merely what he thought he believed. For Tolstoy would have been shocked at the effect of his teaching on the Russian revolution, Maude says. Awareness of this unconscious power of the artist, to communicate feelings unintentionally, is another explanation for Cary's long delay in publishing.[6]

Tolstoy was converted to his own Tolstoyan doctrine in reaction against the orthodox Christianity of his upbringing. His 'Sick Soul' and 'Divided Self' are analysed at length by William James in *The Varieties of Religious Experience*, which Cary desribes in his preface to *The African Witch* as 'one of the most absorbing books in the world. For the fundamental question, the root of all politics, all arts, is what do men live by? What makes them tick and keeps them ticking; and if you answer love and hate, curiosity, ambition, duty and pride, you are already deep, whether you like it or not, in metaphysics, in the science of the soul, or whatever synonym you may choose for that central activity.'[7] Of Tolstoy's conversion James says: 'Tolstoy does well to talk of it as *that by which men live*; for that is exactly what it is, a stimulus, an excitement, a faith, a force that re-infuses the positive willingness to live'.[8] James then begins his next lecture, entitled 'Conversion', with these words: 'To be converted, to be regenerated, to receive grace, to experience religion, to gain an assurance, are so many phrases which denote the process, gradual or sudden, by which a self hitherto divided, and consciously wrong inferior and unhappy, becomes unified and consciously right superior and happy, in consequence of its firmer hold upon religious realities.'

This is the definition Cary has in mind when, in *Art and Reality*, he explains the appeal of new creeds besides Tolstoy's – 'Marxism, Fabianism, Nazism, spiritualism, any new "ism" which offers a complete picture' – and says: 'They set free; they give a coherent set of values, in which emotions formerly in conflict, and therefore frustrated, can suddenly find complete satisfaction' (pp. 22–23). Each may give what James calls a 'firmer hold upon religious realities', but remains a 'fiction', a unique 'created symbol', by which the person concerned lives. This is the dilemma of mankind, who must above all beware of simple, absolute, final answers, Cary urges. For though each of us must try to shape our own coherent symbol, we must be prepared to test it by each renewal of truth, from the reality that is far greater than any form known to human minds.

It becomes clear why Cary's novels have no subjective centre. If the 'sense of revelation' from a novel is to be 'the same as that with which we intuit the real', the novelist must be absent. For the novel has become, for that moment, the reader's symbol of reality. But the author needs his own coherent symbol from which to write. Tolstoy taught Cary to recognize his own divided self, and his writing is the result of an experience that had 'the force of a conversion', he says, making reference to James's account of the term.[9]

Wright says of Cary's theme: 'It stems both from the intuition of man's freedom and from the intuition of grace'.[10] But Cary defined the theme itself as 'my whole view of life',[11] which echoes his words to Schorer, 'one can't put the whole in a single book', and also to Wright, regarding 'the whole landscape of existence'. His theme is primarily the need to reconcile the intuitions of freedom and grace, in a whole view; going beyond this, it is the whole view by which Cary himself reconciled these intuitions, so that it became 'the cast of his mind and character'.

As he explained to Wright, this 'whole' view and subjective centre are revealed in his non-fiction. He was in fact writing a treatise in some form throughout his writing life. It is as though he had to keep his subjective vision clear, and whole, while creating intuitively from his subconscious. In practice, it seems that the creative artist in him worked from a subconscious intuition in writing a novel, and then the philosopher in him clarified and rationalized it. Thus *Power in Men* follows *Castle Corner,* and *The Case for African Freedom* follows *Mister Johnson,* which is his last and most popular African novel. But the treatise would evidently influence the next intuition, as can be seen from the three novels of boyhood that follow *Power in Men.*

The Case for African Freedom has this clue to Cary's 'whole view' in its introduction: 'I do not write as an African expert . . . but as a man . . . who, after ten years of active, thoughtless and various experience in the world, began, rather late in youth, to ask what it amounted to; to dig up all his foundations, to find out exactly what they were; who discovered then, as you might expect, that some of them were mud, some were hollow caves of air, others sand; and who then slowly and painfully rebuilt them, as far as he could manage the task, as a coherent whole, on which to found a new life and a new mind.'[12]

The words 'as you might expect' challenge anyone who has not done likewise. The word *expert* occurs with similar overtones throughout Cary's writing, from his first novel,[13] implying that such men can be dangerous, simply because their views are not whole in Cary's sense. But the key word that Cary used more often than any other is *surprise.* It records a sudden consciousness of intuited truth, which 'is not known completely to the individuals themselves' (p. 5 above). The most obvious example is in the title *Herself Surprised,* but others will be found in this study. Those quoted from his treatises clearly relate to his discoveries, when he began 'to dig up all his foundations'.

Towards the end of his life, Cary was planning another treatise, which he apparently intended to introduce thus: 'The liberal revolution of the last two centuries has ended in confusion and doubt. . . . This book is an attempt to show the real nature of the liberal crisis'.[14] Thus Cary proposed taking the challenge offered by Tolstoy, as a Russian liberal, back to the eighteenth century – to Rousseau, who was Tolstoy's chief inspiration, and Blake's anathema.

But the theme of this treatise had been the theme of his novels. They illustrate the stages by which Cary dug up his foundations, and so understood the nature of the liberal crisis. They are like chapters of one work in recording this process. Their chronology is that of the spiritual experience; a spiritual autobiography. They reveal how Cary came to understand himself, as he looked back, at a later date, at different stages of his development.

He in fact said that an author's own character is revealed in his books, where all the fictional characters are in some way himself.[15] But the most striking thing about Cary's own character as a writer was his ability to enter into the characters of other people. Walter Allen – with reference to Coleridge's description of Shakespeare – called Cary ' "the one Proteus" of the English novel today'.[16] For V. S. Pritchett he was 'the chameleon among contemporary novelists'.[17] Cary himself admitted that inevitably, though not deliberately, he drew characters from life, for: 'I have a "flypaper" memory, I'm always recording – faces, figures, names, actions, sentences, words . . .'.[18] But the way he so convincingly 'becomes' the wide range of characters enumerated by both Allen and Pritchett seems primarily an ability to enter into the lives and feelings of others – above all of other writers. Cary indeed knew that this is the surest way of understanding oneself. People who influenced Cary, therefore, are discussed at some length in this study.

A valuable guide to Cary's characterization lies in the following account of the creative process. The original is in the form of rough notes for a lecture, in Cary's erratic typescript, with additions in his handwriting. As running prose it would read: Writing *begins and continues in intuition* and that is the work of the subconscious. It works, that is, like poetry, with the technique of symbolism, of substitution, association, and the dream. And in the dream you have not only the substitution of one character for another, the melting of experience together, but the reversal of characters. The dwarf becomes a giant, the gentle do murder, and men turn into women. . . . But this does not mean that Dostoevsky, when he intuited the essence of Stavrogin, had actually raped a child. That is a stupid suggestion, which ignores the whole process of imaginative creation. Dostoevsky had only to imagine or dream his normal impulse in reverse. For, as psychologists point out, the primitive imagination (and that is the one that lies closest to intuition) always combines opposite ideas in the same emotion – to love is to think of killing – to imagine the horror of a deed is to understand its attraction for evil.[19] The novelist discovers in himself in this way the primitive impulses that have to be civilized in every human being.

Cary's symbolic method is best approached from what has already been said concerning 'the created symbol'. He regarded words as symbols, by which the novel is built up into a 'total symbol'. His philosophic authority for this view was A. N. Whitehead (who was indeed his chief inspiration in metaphysical ideas).[20] As Cary also called a novel 'living history',[21] he seems to mean that the novel symbolizes reality at a point in time, for its author and then for its reader. For the novel as a work of art is really the reader's state of mind, he maintained.[22]

For this reader, Cary's use of names is highly symbolic, and helps to link the novels as a series. Reasons for so regarding them are given as they occur,[23] but the main argument is on pp. 102, 140 ff. Ordinary words also link Cary's writing, by echoing through it in significant contexts. *Surprise* and *expert* are examples. But, in relation to his theme, the most obvious are *conversion, grace,* and *gift,* and all associations with the verb *give,* including the *given* in philosophical discourse, and the equivalent *datum.* For Cary divided people into essentially life-givers or life-takers;[24] and he summed up his philosophy as 'life is a gift'.

PART I

DEVELOPMENT OF
THE THEME

2. The Child and his Family [1]

Joyce Cary was born on 7 December 1888, in Londonderry. He was to become heir of Castle Cary, a property north of Londonderry, in Inishowen. His family had owned the land since the early seventeenth century, when the founder of the Irish branch of the Devonshire Carys had come from Bristol, during the Protestant settlement of Ulster. This ancestor was the first Recorder of Londonderry, and its member in the Irish parliament. After nearly three hundred years the family had made deep roots in Ireland.

Joyce Cary never occupied his inheritance, however. For the Land Act of 1881, which excused the back rents of Irish tenants, and was intended to strike at absentee landlords, in fact hit hardest at those resident landlords who, like Joyce Cary's grandfather, Arthur Lunel Cary, had allowed tenants to owe their rents. Cary's rents were needed to pay the mortgage on the fine new house he had built on the site of an earlier Castle Cary. Being forced to leave his home, he died soon afterwards, in all ways a ruined man. His family went as exiles to London, to make careers for themselves, leaving only the mother and one daughter in Ireland. Arthur Pitt Cary (Joyce's father) became a civil engineer, and made his home in South-East London when, in 1887, he married Charlotte Louisa Joyce, the eldest daughter of James Joyce, manager of the Belfast Bank in Londonderry. She bore him two sons: Arthur Joyce Lunel (known as Joyce) and John Pitt, who was three years younger. Then, on 1 October 1898, the mother died suddenly, of pneumonia.

Joyce Cary was then nearly ten years old – old enough to remember events clearly. Yet he claimed later that she died when he was eight, and that he had little memory of his mother. [2] Evidence in this study suggests that he was protecting his feelings by such remarks; that his mother's death was a crucial part of the compelling experience from which his theme developed; and that he should have regarded it as the greatest tragedy to have forgotten her.

His sensitivity on this point seems apparent from the preface that he first wrote for *A House of Children*. He wants to stress that his childhood was very happy, he says, because 'it is so often said that I became a writer because of some neurosis – because my mother died when I was eight and after that, I was so much away from home at boarding school or with relations. Or because I was born in Ireland which was then full of trouble, the kind of tensions and neuroses which lie behind the work of the Russians, Dostoevsky, Tolstoy and Tchekov.'[3] There is no evidence that this judgement was often made; but perhaps Cary hoped for understanding of this kind.

Another clue to his feelings comes from an unpublished story about a boy called 'Whick Macarthur'.[4] This boy performs a misdeed close to one ascribed by Cary to himself, in his preface to *Charley is my Darling,* where he is explaining why he understands delinquency. He does so, he says, because he writes as a former gang leader, who can still vividly recall his sense of glory when, at the age of seven, he accepted a dare to drag several doorbells from their sockets; his sense of fear when thereupon forced to hide all afternoon from the police; but above all his sense of relief at the sight of his mother, to whom he rushed, clasping her about the knees.[5] This action of rushing to the mother appears in *Except the Lord*, where Chester says, 'The column of her skirt was like a fortress against all pain'.[6] But in Whick Macarthur's story, the child returns from his daring misdeed to learn that his mother has gone away with another man, and will never be seen by her son again. The father tries to continue the mother's routine, notably of repeating a prayer and hymn at bedtime, but this soon lapses.

Cary's mother had been a devout supporter of the Church of Ireland, and the prayer learnt at his mother's knee had been the most important event in his life, he elsewhere claimed, when speaking plainly of religion.[7] In this prayer he had learnt to ask God's blessing on his father, mother, and self, so acquiring a deep-rooted faith in the family, and in 'one universal person' who wished him well. Reason and events made him subsequently question this basic, unreasoning faith, but had never, he finally discovered, succeeded in destroying it, so that it had sustained him throughout life. The 'personal and compelling experience', in which his theme was founded, was without doubt this prayer and, inseparable from it (as 'Whick Macarthur' suggests), the death of his mother, occurring as it did when he was old enough to question the benevolence of the God who had allowed her to die.

Cary makes Whick Macarthur's mother leave him when he is only six. He shows the child at this age wholly absorbed in egocentric pleasure, ignoring his mother when she asks him to kiss her, and even when she comments that he would not care if she were dead. Yet he runs to her the moment he is thwarted and hurt, and begs her never to leave him – as he seems to sense that she will. She in fact does a few days later, having rushed to the nursery protesting that she will soon return if he is brave. The episode contrasts with that in the second trilogy, where Nina leaves her infant son without even going to his nursery to say goodbye.[8] A main point of this trilogy is that Nina and both male protagonists, Chester and Jim, have all lost their mothers young, and none appears to have learnt that faith in love which Cary claimed to have learnt from his own mother.[9] Chester, like him, recalls praying in his mother's lap (as he also shared the memory of rushing to her protecting skirts). But Chester's mother 'trembled before a god that judged the very heart',[10] and this is not the loving god of Cary's own childhood prayer. Chester's mother dies when he is eight, and he then becomes wild and brutish, much as Whick is supposed to do, until sent to school, at the age of eight.

Such hints in his writing reveal how Cary's personal memories contribute to his view that every child's religion grows from the most primitive level. In his essay entitled 'A Child's Religion', he recalls his attachment at the age of two to a broken wooden horse, as his juju,[11] and the significance of this juju is evident from his use of it in two novels; in one he tells how the child would fight with his mother over it.[12] This symbolizes a struggle between two sides of his nature, on which Cary throws some light in the preface to *A House of Children*.[13] Here he recalls an experience which also occurred 'at about eight years old', when he was seated with three of his father's sisters, behind the lifeboats on the steamer bound for Ireland, defying all laws of both nature and man, since the steamer rolled heavily and they sat where there were no rails, where no other passenger would dare to sit – simply because these Cary aunts, despite a reprimand from the King

himself, chose to smoke. Feelings of fear and glory had com-
pounded, on this occasion, into 'a kind of elated solemn tension',
to live 'for ever, as pure sensation, in my cells', says Cary. With
this he contrasts his 'indescribable' feeling at his brother's
christening, when the baby was given to him to hold. The sensation was equally powerful, and the scene pictured equally vivid.
But imagination could not combine the sensation and the memory
satisfactorily, because Cary, as a child of three, was incapable of
the feeling of love which the occasion was actually celebrating.
He has clearly given the clue to his theme in these two situations.
One reveals an intuition of freedom, derived primarily from
nature itself, for the sea had a 'majesty which belonged only to its
dangerous roaring freedom'.[14] The other was an intuition of
grace, for which his imagination prepared him by recording,
' "that was something important" '. But he could not recognise its
meaning until it could be confirmed in a new intuition, after his
power to love had been educated.

The preface continues with Cary's insistence that 'immediate
experience is of a split between mind and body, spirit and flesh',
which the philosopher must explain as a 'rational whole', drawing
on the experience recorded by the artist. This gives insight into
his own practice, of concurrently writing a treatise as a background to his creative work. As artist, he says here: 'I have only
to give the fact, without comment, that even a small child records
experience from both sides of its being, in its senses and in its
imagination, which can remain separate and yet react upon each
other.'

He then explains that *A House of Children* is disguised autobiography 'because many of the people are living'. The brothers
Harry and Evelyn represent his own divided self and, as Evelyn is
the narrator of the novel, he represents Cary as potential artist.
The earliest incident Evelyn recalled occurred at the age of six,
when he had been briefly separated from his playmates and had
joined a ragged little girl, to become 'tribal allies' as they spied
under a door at a drunken, swearing man, chasing his two
daughters, whose necks he would break, the little girl assured
him, if he should catch them. 'Perhaps this was the first time that
I realized another person', says Evelyn. 'I began to feel very fond
of her. . . . But suddenly we were bored' (pp. 14–15). Here Evelyn
has illustrated Cary's belief that children become individuals and
realize other persons only gradually.[15] He has also illustrated his

belief that boredom, and a desire for change, are basic human characteristics. Above all, he has given a vital clue to Cary's theme: that if freedom and grace are to make a man whole, they must do so within the privacy of family life, where children's observation of adult behaviour will largely determine their own. This incident combines with the one already described on the steamer, which is expanded in the text of the novel. There it shows Evelyn recording the conversation of his three smoking (and therefore emancipated) aunts who, while calmly defying the wild Atlantic, express their contempt for men's treatment of women. In doing so, they personify the unity of body and mind, freedom and grace. Cary's ideas surrounding his article 'The Revolution of the Women' clearly owe much to them.

The significance to him of his brother's christening ceremony was of course that he was being persuaded to accept, lovingly, the challenge of a brother to his hitherto unrivalled place, in the relationship of father-mother-child. This reference suggests that Harry in the novel, the brother who is also himself, is in part Joyce Cary's real brother, Jack. For rivalry between brothers recurs in his novels, and Jack, a gifted sportsman who became a Commander in the Royal Navy, had all the qualities traditionally valued by the Carys. Since his birth challenged the relationship of their parents to his older brother, it is understandable that the latter might have created this role for himself in *A House of Children*, partly to express his acceptance of a brother. There are hints of this personal situation in the novel. For example, in the play they invent, Evelyn wants to be an admiral, wearing a sabre, but in quarrelling over it he nearly kills Harry, and is forced to surrender it. Instead he plays a gamekeeper in a tweed hat, and might be describing the situation in real life. For elsewhere Joyce Cary confesses that, from the age of three, by his own choice, he himself was destined for the Navy, a life at sea appealing to him as the most 'romantic of occupations'. Only short sight prevented him, but when his brother first appeared in naval uniform, at the age of twelve, it 'made him my hero', he says.[16]

Cary found some fulfilment for this lost ambition in writing his long poem *The Drunken Sailor*, which he once described as his best work,[17] partly perhaps because it expresses most satisfyingly for him the reconciliation of artist and man of action, which his brother had expressed in an active life at sea – the life he had himself dreamed of.

The sea is the symbol dominating *A House of Children*. It is also the symbol of the mother, of the collective unconscious.[78] The actual period covered by the novel is from a date shortly before Harry's tenth birthday – that is, when Cary's mother actually died. The boys are terrified by a practical joke in a graveyard, with a hollow voice saying, ' "Your time has come" ' (p. 22). It ends when Evelyn, who has just turned ten, has become reassured of his father's love, in a scene where his father accepts and applauds him, as both a poet and a sportsman – as someone who has begun to reconcile the two sides of his nature. Evelyn then reflects that all children are born poets and singers, and that, whereas he remembers nothing of the sermons heard in his childhood, and the face of only one clergyman, he remembers that clergyman from the musical quality of his voice, 'the very reality of compassion'. He was 'Canon P., who loved my mother, and after she died came to see me at my English school', he says. He fears that the Canon judged, from the response of both Harry and himself, that his journey had been a failure. 'In fact, he had left such a deep mark on my spirit, or whatever you choose to call the living character of a human creature, that his voice and look remained there for ever, and with them, the experience of compassionate love; a true intuition of goodness in its own spirit. He taught us something new about the world; he opened suddenly a way for the sense of my imagination. But I don't remember a word he said, only the vibration of his voice and his affection, his meaning carried directly to my feelings.'[19]

A House of Children symbolizes the world as Cary remembers it, during the period when he was learning to accept his mother's death. When it occurred, her death had struck him as a grim practical joke, unreal except to his outward self. In *Castle Corner* he conveys the confused indifference of this outward self to the mother's death, by the autobiographical treatment of Cleeve Corner, whose mother dies in somewhat similar circumstances, (p. 33 below). Portrayed in such ways, Cary's conflicting feelings bear on his claim, that reason must guide love and goodness.[20] For the cruel reality of his mother's death does raise the question whether, indeed, she behaved responsibly, having died by going out, in dreadful weather, when ill with a cold, in order to interview a maid.[21] Her son might well have felt betrayed in this fact, which would help to explain why he maintained, even late in life, that all women are masochists.[22]

His juju horse is mentioned in *A House of Children* in connexion with Evelyn's fears of injustice from his father. Such fears arise, he suggests, from natural conservatism and the belief that laws rule life, combined with a dread that these laws may somehow fail to apply personally. 'Like most children', he and Harry held very conservative views regarding the family; 'our conservative feelings were that of nature itself, so deep that they cannot be changed by an idea, but only distorted. To us the family was the structure of society, the only one we knew. We felt it sacred as a savage feels the sacredness of earth and water, simply and without thought' (pp. 116–17). Since this sacred structure had been broken by his mother's death, Evelyn's desire for his juju reveals a desire to restore it, or at least to ensure that the father does not fail him.

The brothers are depicted throughout this novel in the company of their cousin Kathy. She and Evelyn have agreed to marry, and Cary's discarded preface shows that at ten he had indeed agreed to marry his cousin Helen – from whom Kathy is drawn.[23]

Helen Beasley was the eldest daughter of Helen, the younger daughter of James and Helen Joyce, their maternal grand-parents. Whenever he stayed with these grandparents, Joyce Cary met his cousin Helen, who lived with them from the age of four. She can be recognized in Nina of the second trilogy, orphaned at four and living with the aunt whom her cousin Jim visits during holidays. Helen lived with her grandparents because her mother's second child, named Harry, was a blue baby, and when a third child was expected the grandparents took charge of Harry, but wanted Helen to keep him company. In *A House of Children,* Helen's sense of responsibility for Harry is depicted in Kathy's concern for Anketel. But the 'Harry' of *A House of Children* is very close to Helen's memories of her cousin Joyce. Throughout his life, he was the king in their family circle, and this came out on the colonial side of his career, she said. In their games he was always the king, or a general. He invented wildly imaginative tales, notably about his namesake King Arthur, who held court, he claimed, above Ravenscliff (the house that became Crowcliff in *A House of Children*), where these cousins spent four or five summer holidays with the Joyce grandparents during the late nineties.

Kathy can be seen as the reconciler of Cary's divided self, and her relation to the brothers Harry and Evelyn suggests a symbol of the soul that modern readers may best appreciate in terms of Jung. But Plato's symbol of the soul also comes to mind, as if Cary were showing its effect on his mind and character.[24] Evelyn fills a role that Plato condemned – Cary elsewhere writes of Plato's fear of the power of art.[25] So, as the potential champion of women's freedom, he represents the later reconciler of Kathy and Harry, the latter's 'platonic' attitude toward women being evident in their childhood games, as Evelyn remembers them.

Cary's links with Ireland continued after his mother's death, when he and his brother spent holidays with one or other of his Irish grandmothers. In essays written towards the end of his life he seems eager to establish the fact that his work can be understood only if he is recognized as an Anglo-Irish writer, in whom the split between spirit and flesh, which every human being must reconcile in himself, was present to an exceptional degree. That was probably the idea behind his discarded preface to *A House of Children* (p. 16 above). For the tensions and neuroses of the Russians whom he mentions are of a similar nature. Geographically they belong to a land mid-way between East and West, while spiritually they are divided between the cultures and values of both.

'They say that tensions make the artist and writer. That is certainly true of the Anglo-Irish writers, and my childhood should have been full of tensions', he wrote in 1950.[26] He describes the 'battleground' of Ireland, which taught him, regarding his grandfather, that a man can be ruined, though well liked, just 'because he represents a class or race'. He himself came to live between two irreconcilable worlds, he says: in East End London, near his father's work, in a small house 'among miles of streets in which all the people seemed equally drab and anonymous'; or on holiday in Ireland, where everyone was intimately known, and 'the background was an historical war of religion and nationality'. 'But even in Ireland I had two different beings', he continues. With his Cary grandmother he was often the only child, in a house full of portraits and books, amidst which he read and dreamed. From her home he 'would wander in the old walled gardens of Castle Cary, with all the appropriate feelings of the banished heir in the romances.' With his Joyce grandmother, however, 'at some holiday house taken for all her grandchildren, I would range over the countryside with a horde of cousins. We went fishing, exploring, stealing rides on other people's horses, sailing on the lough, often for long journeys. We were as free as the mountain slopes, and often in mischief.' Thus he indicates the contrast between the two sides of his nature and ancestry, which had to be reconciled.

In *A House of Children,* he allows Evelyn to write: 'my own name, Evelyn, has always existed for me as a separate word with quite separate meaning from the ordinary girl's name, because mine is inherited, the name of part of my blood, and theirs is a label, put on from outside' (p. 47). As the name Joyce is also commonly a girl's name, Cary implies that Evelyn, as author of this novel, corresponds to the Joyce side of his nature. In fact Thomas Joyce, the pseudonym under which he first chose to write, is the name of the founder of the Joyce family in Ireland. He came from Wales, was of princely birth, and married a daughter of O'Brien, Prince of Thomond, in 1283, before taking her by sea to western Connacht, where their descendants inter-married with Irish families, notably the O'Flahertys, and became 'completely Hibernicised'.[27] Joyce Cary claimed descent from this family, as did the writer James Joyce. The latter wrote to make 'open war' against the Roman Catholic church of his father's family,[28] whereas Cary wrote in opposition to a basic tenet in the Anglican faith that contributed to the Carys' downfall – as *Castle Corner* shows. He wrote also in defence of women; understand-ably therefore, he identified himself, as a writer, with the Joyce part of his blood.

He in fact thought of himself as truly Irish on both sides, as he reveals in a letter of 7 December 1916 to his wife. Insisting that he is as honest with her as with himself, he attributes his tem-peramental 'ups and downs' to his 'Irish blood', and adds: 'The Carys are wayward and the Joyces were strange mountainy men'. Nevertheless, as a Joyce and a Cary, he felt himself to be two different beings, and he has symbolized the fact by the names Evelyn and Harry. Harry recurs in his novels, for characters who reveal his rational and imperialist temperament, while Evelyn recurs for his intuitive self. The meaning 'hazel-nut' for *Evelyn* is appropriate.[29] For, as Yeats tells us, 'The hazel tree was the Irish tree of Life or of Knowledge'.[30] So the power of the hazel to reconcile Cary's divided nature is implied, when Evelyn, in describing how differently he and Harry reacted to a performance of *The Tempest,* mentions someone who made him his 'first pop-gun out of a hazel branch' (*A House of Children*, p. 225). Unless Cary had some such meaning in mind, this remark seems pointless.

Cary states his belief in names as symbols when he says in 'The Meaning of England': 'The name of a country becomes one of the most powerful symbols in the world'. In this late article he again reveals his sense of being a divided man. For 'A man's country is the home of his imagination and men live by their imagination'. But was Ireland or England his country? He writes:

My feeling about England is probably deeper and more conscious than many Englishmen's. For I was born in Ireland to an Anglo-Irish family, long settled there. My earliest memories are of Donegal, its wild hills and the great sea loughs of Foyle and Swilly. I loved the country and the people, spoilers of children. But my heroes were the great men of English history, many of them Anglo-Irishmen like myself; and English history is world history. My imagination played on a world stage. I was engaged for England, I triumphed in her glories and suffered in her defeats and shames.

I was, like my family, sharply critical of the English and often of English policy, but my anger was that of a lover. I could not bear that England should be betrayed by her own children or by party politicians with narrow views and mean aims. I had, that is, a far more definite and romantic idea of England than the average born Englishman because, for my family, she was the mother country and not merely the homeland.

She was for me, as a young man, not only all the riches of English literature and art, but the long history of its free institutions. . . . The British Empire for me was the liberal and liberating power. . . . People think of me as a writer but my years in the African Service, given to that England of my youthful imagination, are richer to my memory than any of my books.[31]

Here the 'Harry' side of Cary's nature might be said to have finally triumphed over Evelyn, with the name owing something to Shakespeare's 'Harry, England and St George'.

For in *Art and Reality* Cary has stressed Shakespeare's supreme influence upon him, from boyhood, and in *A House of Children* he develops the sea symbolism by centring the action on the performance of *The Tempest*. Evelyn says of it, immediately after describing his intuition of goodness in 'Canon P., who loved my mother': 'So bits of the church service remained with me because they were poetry. They gave the feeling of beauty and wisdom joined together in one unity of experience. But no prayer or poem had so powerful an effect as my first great Shakespeare play. When I heard the cry: "All lost, to prayers, to prayers," and the line: "What, must our mouths be cold," I felt death as if I had never heard of it before' (p. 224). Prayer, with acceptance of the mother's death – here through the power of art – is thus shown as this book's main theme, and it is the intuition of grace, through Evelyn, that triumphs.

The boy who wandered like the banished heir in the walled gardens of Castle Cary, became the man who, around the time he wrote 'The Meaning of England', almost bought the property back again, against all the dictates of economics and common sense, so that the Carys might be restored to their former position in Ireland. He would have been restoring the good name of his grandfather, whose names were also his own, and whose tragic death he ascribed to the injustice and dishonour by which this house had been lost to the family, so affecting the whole course of his own life. Cary had Castle Cary in mind when he wrote *Castle Corner,* where the family is drawn from Cary's own. It was also surely in mind when, in later years, he discussed *The Spoils of Poynton,* to exemplify the theme of the tragic destruction of the fine and the good, as used by Henry James. For *Castle Corner,* as it was to have been developed in a trilogy, would have been similarly a story of the destruction of a beautiful house, and so illustrated forcefully the idea on which Cary's treatment of theme and character is chiefly based: 'that people of all ages who are presented with some object . . . some symbol . . . which they haven't been given the means to understand, they want to destroy it'.[32] The various contenders for Castle Corner, particularly James Slatter, seek to destroy the owner, John Chass, whose qualities they admire yet cannot comprehend. By possessing the house they hope to acquire these qualities which, however, will vanish with its owners and creators; so that they will destroy what they seek to possess.

John Chass, with 'his genius in all the arts of life',[33] resembles in all respects Cary's great-uncle Tristram, whom he admired 'as a master in the arts of life'.[34] Like his brother Arthur Lunel, Tristram Cary had lost his Irish property through the Land Acts. He was therefore 'essentially a sad man who, for all his gaiety, his love of entertaining, had little value for life'.[35] His wife Dorothea, whom Cary called Aunt Doll, is clearly pictured in John Chass's wife, Mary Corner, who is similarly of French aristocratic descent, and has borne several children but lost them in infancy.

This aunt and uncle lived in London at 'Cromwell House', which is the title of another late essay. In it Cary explains that, after his mother's death, any time that he was not at school or in Ireland was spent at Cromwell House. He says the Carys, as exiles and refugees from Ireland, 'were still foreigners in England. As a family, we clung together.' The household at Cromwell House was 'deeply foreign to England', and was indeed 'a feudal relic'.[36] Joyce Cary the writer cannot be understood except against this background, his cousin Lionel Stevenson insists. For his whole view of life was shaped by what Stevenson calls 'an individual and baffling phenomenon, little comprehended by the outside world – the mentality of the Anglo-Irish who constituted the "plantation" of Ulster.'[37] Because of their isolation these families became distinct from the larger Anglo-Irish tradition, and they developed strongly marked traits which Stevenson sums up thus: 'Pride in their aristocratic lineage, arrogance arising from dominance over a subject people, confidence in their own opinions, social charm and feckless generosity . . . a heritage that was ominously unsuited for the conditions of the modern world.'

Joyce Cary comes to terms with these traits in his writing. The pride in his aristocratic lineage remained, for the Carys could claim royal ancestry through the Plantagenets back to Charlemagne, and also to King David I of Scotland.[38] But, as he said of his Aunt Doll, who was 'something of a genealogist' and also claimed Plantagenet descent: 'that consciousness of blood did not serve her for pride. It gave her only a closer relation with history, and history for her was the whole troublesome tale of humanity, doomed to insecurity, injustice, and the everlasting revolution of politics.' It was on such terms that Cary came to write novels, as a social historian.[39]

In 'Cromwell House' he writes of Aunt Doll as 'essentially a foreigner' who, 'brought up in France', 'never lost her French accent', and 'commonly talked French' with her brothers and sisters, one of whom, near by, had a household that was 'all French', even to the maid. Her brother Hildebrand made Cromwell House his headquarters, and was also 'an exile and a dreamer'. Cary 'admired Hildebrand immensely', as 'one of the finest, handsomest men I've ever seen'; 'intensely French in mind', and 'French of the old style, to the last degree', with an 'aristocratic poise', and comparable with the society nobles depicted by Proust. Cary's admiration for these relatives, and the constant exposure to their culture, would suffice to explain the French influence apparent in his work. It would be all the stronger because it formed part of that equally foreign, Irish stronghold in the midst of an alien-seeming London.

Aunt Doll championed the Carys, as victims in a world full of injustice, where 'love was for her the only constant, the only dependable thing. Her devotions were passionate. . . . In any trouble, my brother and I flew to her,' says Cary. As the opening paragraph of 'Cromwell House' shows, it was his Irish grandmothers, and above all his French great-aunt, who for Cary replaced his mother, as 'a fortress against all pain'.

3. The Schoolboy

Cary attended a private school in Kent and then Clifton College. *A House of Children* offers the best clues to this aspect of his life also, showing that here he regarded Plato as the major influence. As Evelyn, he writes that their private school was 'rather like a platonic academy', where a boy was trained to be a 'guardian of freedom and justice and peace', believing this to be the 'great destiny' to which an Englishman was born. Such teaching produced a truly religious atmosphere, 'for it was one of real purpose'. This religion was 'livelier, braver, keener than the Church teaching; and much more real' – presumably because it appealed to the boys' desire for glory and goodness in the real world. But 'Of course we heard nothing of the other side of the old Empire: the gold grabbers; the cotton lords of India; and we had no conception, for our masters had none, of a real freedom. Our idea, like theirs, was abstract and legal, or romantic. We had no notion that poverty came into the question and was, with ignorance, the chief enemy of freedom' (p. 34).

As related in *A House of Children,* poverty was something they learned of from their holiday tutor, Freeman, whose name is clearly ironic. Freeman claims that his stories of poverty are funny, because the victims expected someone like himself to 'save' them (p. 44). Cary's point is apparently that help can come only from those with the power to give it, and the will. This was the power that the boys acquired at their 'platonic academy', and at 'that greater world' of the public school, which Evelyn's older cousin Robert is entering at the commencement of this novel.

Through Robert, Cary reveals himself as an older and more composite character than as Harry or Evelyn. For Robert the platonic teaching at the private school has become 'gospel'. This gospel, which Cary describes as 'little more worldly than that of a nurse, who, for her own sake, teaches the purest Christian unselfishness', has persuaded Robert at once that he must become either a missionary or a colonial officer. Thus we recognize the complementary nature of the missionary and colonial officer in Cary's first novel.

The reference to a nurse may be compared with a discarded opening for Cary's early unpublished novel 'Tottenham':

It has been said that the highest moral principles were invented by savage parents to secure their own comfort; and could probably be heard, in a pure form, from the mouth of any father or mother baboon instructing its young. Certainly the purest Christian ethics are preached by nurses, and the more bad tempered and selfish the nurse, the stricter her standards. Little children of seven and eight, who have been left much to nurses, are probably the best people in the world. No one is so quick to forget injustice, so brave in pain and disappointment, so grateful for the smallest kindness, so ready to give and so humble in demands as the child who has lived for years, as defenceless as a bird in a cage, with [unfinished][1]

'Tottenham' grew from 'Whick Macarthur' (p. 16 above), and concerns Johnny Brant, whose story begins on his eighth birthday with a beating demanded by his nurse, followed by the promise that he can attend an expensive private school. At this school John becomes a pet, with the nickname Tottenham, and then a butt, a victim of practical jokes, whose nursery training makes it impossible for him 'to perform a cheeky action',[2] so that he is driven at last to suicide. A link can be established between 'Tottenham' and *A House of Children,* and it seems likely that the early story was inspired by some personal experience – not necessarily Cary's own, or ending in suicide. 'Tottenham' illustrates what he says in *A House of Children*: 'All over the world children suffer their chief discouragements from other children; and this can't be helped. Children live in their own world from which all grown-ups are excluded by the nature of the case' (p. 178). Evelyn recalls that, when he was at his private school, there was 'a reign of terror' under the dictatorship of schoolboy tyrants, who could 'see and know their power, where alone it can be seen, in a change of countenance'. Evelyn himself was for this reason 'always taken by surprise' and was publicly kicked several times; but the kicks did not make him feel an outcast because, he says, 'I had also received a nickname, Whiskey, which I took to be a mark of honour' (pp. 157, 158). Since Whick sounds like Whiskey in shortened form, it seems possible that this nickname, with its Irish spelling, was Cary's for a time. There is certainly a distinct likeness of character between Evelyn and Johnny Brant, whose story similarly shows that the discipline in such a school is platonic with fascist elements,[3] while also showing that a form of platonic love readily develops in such an atmosphere, the actual feelings involved being not unlike those of mistress to lover, or parent to child – for which they become a natural substitute.[4]

'Tottenham' also contributed to *To be a Pilgrim,* where the following epigram leaves no doubt that, for Cary, the Greek ideal inspired the education of England's ruling class: 'Hard-breasted Nan snubbed Socrates. With zeal / Her harder hand moulded the Greek ideal' (p. 203). This ideal, 'called democracy', has probably been implanted by 'some evangelical country nurse', says Tom Wilcher (the book's narrator); it has produced in him, when adult, violent political actions by which he himself is 'often surprised', so that he finds himself dreaming that 'the harmless dignities of old England' are accusing him of 'cruelty and meanness'.

By family tradition, Cary identified himself with these 'dignities' of the Royalist, aristocratic class. His attitude to schools breeding the leaders who are destroying the aristocrats is therefore complex. He clearly shared the feelings of Robert Graves regarding the fascist qualities of Cromwell and his followers, notably Milton – whose influence is explicitly treated in both Cary's trilogies.[5] And all he implies regarding the power of the Nurse in imperialist England is borne out by a recent publication, *The Rise and Fall of the British Nanny.*[6]

Plato's treatment of the nurse, in the *Timaeus,* as the Receptacle of all Becoming, is highly relevant to this theme. For Plato switches also to the analogy of the mother as the receptacle. This relates to Cary's treatment of the nurses' and mothers' roles in his novels, where it underlies his theme of the revolution of the women quite profoundly. Briefly, as in his epigram, his treatment stresses the falsity of Socrates' teaching, of this insistence on women's role as that of passive Receptacle, which ignores the workings of real nature. Employed to shape the Greek ideal by taking the mother's place, the Nanny has damaged the relationship of mother and child, which such women, deprived of motherhood themselves by a false code of society, must envy. They have therefore shaped the children in their care to satisfy their own more truly democratic ideals – thereby snubbing Socrates.[7]

Returning to Robert of *A House of Children,* we learn that he suffers desperately at his public school, as a result of a practical joke (concerning what was expected of a new boy) played on him by another, older cousin, Philip – who was also the perpetrator of the joke played on Harry and Evelyn in the graveyard (p. 20, above). Through Philip, Cary stresses the cruelty of a 'joke', and also the revenge motive, bred from a reaction to unhappiness that contrasts with Johnny Brant's, or his cousins'. He liked to create 'a muddle and fear' in children, feeling compelled, 'by any spectacle of unquestioning faith', to try to break it down. Of such people Cary says: 'Words like truth and justice set up in them, by a natural reaction, an irritation, and they promptly start some ingenious lie or do some small injustice just to show their secret disgust of a world that values truth so little and has no justice at all' (p. 25).

Despite his humiliation by Philip's joke, however, Robert wins respect and honour at rugby, as scrum-half, having played with desperate courage when given the chance to prove himself. Evelyn says that he later understood how Robert 'felt like a man who has achieved greatness by a powerful effort of will', when he became 'a light forward in a light team', and 'lived for a couple of winters in the atmosphere of Sparta before Thermopylae'. His team was regarded as 'a band of heroes'. Moreover, there was true greatness in their school leaders. For the elements of all greatness are 'courage, independence of will, devotion to a cause larger than one's own; a contempt of mean ambition.' Something of Cary's religious theme can be discerned in the words: 'The air about them was charged with their personal magnetism, electrifying my own particles';[8] these youths were like the heroes of all myths who give their lives, for most of them were killed in World War I. All, as described here, were of Cary's supreme all-round type, the poet-philosopher-warrior.[9] Their lives have a beauty denied to someone like Freeman, who could not learn these ideals in the life of his experience. Cary implies that the very character of the Heroic Age is revealed in this community of schoolboys, aged fifteen to eighteen, who 'have been taught only large and fundamental ideas', such as 'the simple large fact, that injustice is a deadly wrong'. Life's realities may later confuse their ideas, 'But this does not mean that they were trivial before' (p. 171).

Thus Cary shows how an education on platonic lines has helped mankind to rise above the juju level still evident in Evelyn at the age of ten. He leaves no doubt that the platonic ideals cause suffering, as when he shows the hurtful effect on Delia, Robert's sister, of the fact that 'Like the Spartans he kept aloof from girls'. But public schools bridge the world of the child and the adult by forcing the individual to form judgements; so Cary implies when he writes in *Power in Men*: 'The true criticism of a modern public school, certainly of the greater schools, is not that they turn out a uniform product but that they cater for so many differences of taste and character among boys that they have no time for sound instruction in first principles.'[10] Unless the words 'modern' and 'greater' are intended to exclude his own schooling, it seems that Cary looked back on his own public school life with general approval, though with regret that there was insufficient instruction in first principles.

He attended Clifton College from 1903 to 1906. The school's strong military tradition would certainly have fostered the spirit of 'Sparta before Thermopylae', and Joyce Cary, slight in build and with poor eyesight, showed there some of the 'desperate courage' that he attributed to his character Robert: he became accepted by his fellows by winning a place in the house football team, and through taking up boxing – at which he had his nose broken. The need to prove himself in this way would suffice to explain why a punch on the nose became, as Enid Starkie says, 'some sort of symbol', suggesting 'an obsession with violence' which seemed 'alien to his personality'.[11] But surely he is insisting that every man must acknowledge the power of the irrational, and admit himself capable of delivering, and taking, a 'punch on the nose', so admitting his 'state of nature' without which he could never achieve a state of grace.[12]

Famous noses, of course, include Socrates' snub nose, the worst feature of his reputedly ugly face, in which the 'Russian Socrates', Tolstoy, resembled him.[13] Tolstoy's nose interested Cary sufficiently for him to note, from Tolstoy's diary: 'Aquiline noses drive me crazy'.[14] But Cary's interest in noses probably owes most to the fact that the Carys were renowned for their aquiline noses – his own being a fine example. His ability to take and give a punch on the nose, as he learnt to do at Clifton, would have symbolized admirably for Cary his own, and his family's, ability, to survive and succeed in a tough and dangerous world, where they believed that they had been unjustly treated.

In speaking of lack of time 'for sound instruction in first principles' at public schools, Cary may well have had in mind his experience when receiving instruction for confirmation. The master preparing him had, as a science master, taught him to cultivate a critical approach. But he presented church teaching dogmatically, giving 'poor answers', as Cary said later, on such fundamental questions, in relation to science, as miracles. As a result, having been confirmed, and still believing himself religious in an orthodox sense, he nevertheless found gradually that he had lost his faith (much as Tolstoy did as he recounted in *A Confession*), from around the age of sixteen. So Cary began to call himself an agnostic – though he claimed later that the word merely dodges the issue.[15]

He saw also that the loss of his faith could not be dissociated from other feelings and events at the time. First, as a new boy, he had felt inadequate at sport, and unhappy. Then, in the spring of 1904, his stepmother, whom he dearly loved, died in circumstances that were very similar to those in which his mother had died. His feelings were such that he left school without permission to go to his father, but never reached him, being waylaid at Paddington station and taken back to Clifton. His letter to his father brought the answer that it was 'another blow' to him, and that at such times in life 'we must not give way no matter how we feel'. How bravely Cary learnt that lesson may be judged from his stoical behaviour in facing his own death. 'Work and play with all your might', his father advised, and so began that 'powerful effort of will' that he attributed to the boy Robert, which made Cary himself accepted as a footballer and boxer.[16] Robert in *A House of Children,* in fact, appears to reveal Cary's feelings at the time of his stepmother's death, just as Evelyn reveals them after the death of his mother. Here, however, the death of Cleeve Corner's mother in *Castle Corner* becomes of interest. It is recorded somewhat callously: 'MRS. FELIX DIED suddenly in '95 of a chill caught spiting a wet field in thin shoes; and Felix came home from Africa in the next month. He was

greatly distressed to find himself so relieved by her disappearance'
(p. 80).

Since Cleeve is the age Cary was when his stepmother died,
Cary appears to be exploring his feelings regarding his own
mother through the later occasion, when his distress was manifest
but crushed by his father. In Cary's memory the two deaths
appear to represent one deepening tragedy – or joke.

To help him recover from his grief he was taken that summer
on a sketching holiday in the Pas de Calais. Here, amongst
artists, he encountered the excited and rebellious spirit prevail-
ing in France at the time in its most persuasive form. He declared
himself an ardent Impressionist. But his writing shows that he
looked back on this conversion as a revolt against his father and
the traditions of his father's family. In *Art and Reality* he links
Impressionism with 'the Lawrence-Woolf school', who revolted
against the previous generation by proclaiming as their theme
that life is 'fundamentally passionate, individual, irrational'.[17] In
A House of Children, Evelyn's father with his eighteenth century
grand manner, overcomes Freeman's surliness: 'The eighteenth
century had overcome the twentieth', and by 'a peculiar expression in his blue eyes', the father has revealed to his son that he
is laughing, 'not at the artist, but at the man.'[18]

This passage, and the events by which Cary was led to study
art, together suggest a personal association with Gulley's account
of becoming an artist. He calls it 'a bad infection':

> I was at about the period when my poor old father was knocked
> out. . . . I was the old school, the old Classic, the old church.
>   . . . But one day I happened to see a Manet. . . . And I saw
> the world again, the world of colour. By Gee and Jay, I said, I
> was dead, and I didn't know it. . . . But of course the old
> classic put up a fight. It was the Church against Darwin, the
> old Lords against the Radicals. And I was the battleground.
> . . . I was so wretched that I hardly noticed . . . even when my
> mother died.[19]

So, perhaps unconsciously, Cary reveals something of his spiritual
confusion around the time of his stepmother's death. But the
complexity of the creative process becomes more apparent when
he explains that Gulley's father is drawn from a painter, met on
this Normandy holiday, whose very world had been shattered

since Darwin taught men to react differently to Reality, and so to the Art by which Reality is understood. This encounter made Cary realize, later, that rebellion against inherited values and tastes is inevitable and always tragic, as much for the old and conservative as for the young whom they too often frustrate. Moreover, it is a tragedy suffered by all mankind, since all men live by values based on strong feelings and attachments, whether or not they express them in works of art. Thus, in *A House of Children*, Cary presents the father as a true artist of life – in the eighteenth century classical style. This character could be modelled on his Uncle Tristram (described above, p. 25) as well as his father. His encounter with the Normandy painter could therefore understandably symbolize for Joyce Cary his own rejection of the kind of world his father's family loved. Cary vividly remembered the painter, in his overgrown garden, with his latest rejected work, weeping and begging him, a youthful stranger, to see its excellence. But Cary, who then thought Impressionism 'the only great and true art', could feel only 'pity and surprise'. Forty years later he believed that the painting would again be appreciated, 'But that man died long ago in misery, and God knows what happened to his wife and children.'[20] As he says in *Art and Reality*: 'The tragedy here is that I could not even understand the tragedy thus offered to me, of a man of sixty, not only ruined financially, but whose whole life and skill had lost its meaning. This tragedy is taking place all the time' (p. 76).

According to an account in *Time*, Cary was encouraged during this holiday by an artist in Étaples, who admired his watercolours: 'I thought, this is a damn good show. I was fed up with school and thought that the life of an artist would be a good life.'[21] With an income of around £300 from the Joyce side of the family, such a life seemed possible. Thus, even at this financial level, it was the Joyce side of his nature that became identified with the rebel and artist, enabling him to go against his father's wishes.

In 1904 Cary returned to Clifton, revived and stimulated by his new-found faith and ready to give that 'punch on the nose' if 'the old classic put up a fight . . . the Church against Darwin, the old Lords against the Radicals'; ready, as his father had urged, to work and play with all his might. He became accepted as something of a sportsman, a painter, and a poet. His contribution to *The Cliftonian*, in the summer that he left Clifton, is a long anonymous poem in blank verse on Adam and Eve, and 'quietly sleeping Nature':

> Here came the lissom sweet-breathed English Eve,
> Care-free, with new-found wonder in her eyes,
>
> . . .
>
> And so he took her by the hand – they passed,
> Two children in the garden of sweet peace.[22]

When Sara, an 'English Eve' to Gulley, says that he thought 'there would be no peace or comfort anywhere till we all went back to live like Adam and Eve in the Garden of Eden',[23] Cary might well have remembered himself as the author of this poem, besides, of course, remembering Blake and other romantics with similar ideas.

4. The Art Student

Leaving school, Cary returned to France as an art student, dividing his time between Paris and Étaples, until Charles Mackie, a Scottish Academician, persuaded him to transfer to Edinburgh. Here he studied art from 1907 until 1909, when he decided to read English at Oxford University, but in fact began reading history and then changed to law[1] – a subject more suited to the family tradition.

Cary's difficulty in choosing a profession was due, he once said, to 'the rootlessness and restlessness of a boy uprooted from the long romantic tradition of a family domain.'[2] His reason for leaving Art School, according to an unpublished essay, was a growing awareness of 'an ignorance which rose up about me, on all sides, like precipices about a mountain track. I seemed to be walking into a blind gulley, with no opening in front. I felt its shadow upon all my work and, so tho[ugh] I still delighted to draw and paint, I had always the sense of one lost.'[3] This account is the best possible clue to the character of Gulley Jimson, whose name may owe something to this 'blind gulley'. For Cary wrote of it while creating Gulley, just after visiting Edinburgh to receive the James Tait Black prize.

The occasion may have revived such feelings and impelled him to speak, when invited to address the students, on the nature of symbolism as he now understood it. The symbol must refer to a reality objective to the mind, he insisted. For 'this universe of discourse, without that root, that reference, in the primitive feelings, and the total objective real, is an escaped balloon, floating in the void, and too often, as I think, filled with very doubtful gas. It is not healthy breathing for artist[s], at the least, and has choked a good many of them.'[4] Thus he warned students against accepting the Symbolism (inseparable from Impressionism) which had almost 'choked' him, while a student in Edinburgh himself.

The city was then gripped by a Celtic revival, or Scottish renaissance. In relation to Cary, this movement is best thought of as part of the movement that grew out of eighteenth century Romanticism; this roused fundamental feelings of race that had been revived once more by late nineteenth century Romanticism, and through it became linked with the Decadents as part of a general reaction against Victorian constraints of every kind. 'I belong to a time of reaction against the Victorians', Cary confessed in *Art and Reality* (p. 83). In Ireland, being involved with demands for Home Rule, the renaissance was part of the movement that actually deprived Cary of his home. The conflict roused in him by this fact is symbolized in *A House of Children,* by his division of himself into Harry the imperialist and Evelyn the artist. He might well have been discussing these ideas in Edinburgh in 1942, for *A House of Children* was the book for which he was receiving the James Tait Black prize. Moreover, in it Freeman is an artist of the nineties, who starts a kind of renaissance in the Ireland of Cary's birth. His name thus has additional symbolic significance, and his treatment in the novel, which anticipates Gulley Jimson, links with what Cary said to the Edinburgh students, against the art world of the Decadents.

The best-known English account of this world, in its literary aspect, is *The Symbolist Movement in Literature,* by Arthur Symons. Louis Cazamian writes that 'English decadentism has no literary programme', and 'The only unity that can be found in the movement is of a psychological order'; but that Symons 'thinks he discovers its focus' in symbolism. 'It is a confused tentative medley of the tendencies which will renovate the literature of the twentieth century', Cazamian judges.[5] By the mid-fifties Cary was saying: 'We don't know yet if the creative art of our time can recreate the symbol we need in so important a department of our real life as that of religion' (*Art and Reality,* p. 60). This view could have developed from reading *The Symbolist Movement;* it is certainly a comment upon the religious symbolism of Yeats and Eliot, who were influenced by it.

Cary was familiar with *The Symbolist Movement* at least by February 1910, when he bought his own copy. His interest in it then is stressed by the fact that he also bought *Sartor Resartus,* to which Symons refers. Quoting Carlyle, Symons argues that men live and work through symbols and that all language is symbolic, so that without symbolism there would be no literature.

'What distinguishes the Symbolism of our day', he says, 'is that it has now become conscious of itself' in a new way, and writers have learnt from Flaubert, whose aim was to make art an 'escape from the burden of reality', and to use the soul as an 'agent of fine literature.' Regarding Decadence, Symons admits that perversity and experiment often accompanied it, 'not only in the direction of style', and he implies that 'conventional vice' and 'the desire to "bewilder the middle-classes" ' are characteristics. In the latter respect, Decadence can be seen to relate to Symon's earlier account of the symbol, as used by the Greeks, for 'every sign, formula or rite by which those initiated in any mystery made themselves secretly known to one another.'[6] For an interest in spiritualism, Rosicrucianism and the like inspired a similar use of symbolic language.

Cary too came to describe all language as symbolic. But he came to respect the symbolism of ordinary men, insisting that a novelist in the English spirit may not take 'a superior condescending attitude towards his fellows'.[7] Above all, quoting Tolstoy, he insisted that art is not an escape from reality. This is the theme of his address on Tolstoy in Edinburgh in 1942, from which *Art and Reality* can be seen to have developed. Thus, Cary appears to have become a symbolist in conscious revolt against the Symbolist movement. But, since he identified Symbolism with Impressionism, and confessed to being a devotee of the latter, it is reasonable to suppose that his revolt stemmed from his previous discipleship. He did confess to 'something Baudelairian' in his nature. He did retain that aim of making the soul an 'agent of fine literature', as well as a strong inclination to secrecy about his sources, symbols, and meanings. The explanation for this is doubtless complex, but it does seem that the fact of secrecy makes the source more significant.

His reticence regarding this Bohemian period of his life is sufficiently explained by his unwillingness to offend his wife, with whom marriage had been most symbolic of reaction against this world (pp. 70–71 below). His reticence about the real implications of his own views on symbolism is explained by what he said about the Normandy painter (p. 35 above). He had come to realize the cruelty of offending deeply-rooted feelings and beliefs, which rarely change, even when people imagine they have. This Cary knew after discovering that he had never lost the faith of his childhood prayer. The whole purpose of his art was to influence people subconsciously, and to be explicit outside this art would have been to defeat his object. In *Seven Types of Ambiguity,* William Empson expresses a similar view[8] – which recalls Eliot's lines about the difficulty of standing 'very much Reality'. In *Art and Reality,* Cary describes his own symbolism with reference to Empson's 'brilliant book' (p. 64). He also devotes much space to the art of reading, and to the full implications of this fact: 'The meaning received is created by the imagination from the symbols, and that imagination must first be educated – as the artist himself was educated – in the use and meaning of a symbolic system' (p. 120). How firmly he adhered to his principles is evident from Enid Starkie's essay on Cary. Though she was his close friend in Oxford, where she taught French literature as an authority on the Symbolists, it seems that she had no idea of his real knowledge of them, much less of his reactionary attitude to them.[9] Of course, if she did, and failed to say so, that supports the other side of the argument: that people only accept and understand what fits into their own picture, and want to destroy any symbol that they do not understand (p. 25 above). These were the truths Cary learnt by the painful process of escaping from the 'blind gulley' into which his life in Edinburgh had almost led him.

His sympathy with the Celtic revival, while a student in Edinburgh, is apparent from his use of a monograph of Celtic inspiration to sign his drawings. Sympathy with the aims of the Scottish renaissance, a return to Nature and simplicity, is evident from the series of poems published in 1908. The fact that he vehemently rejected these poems later, refused to re-read them, and did not even possess a copy of them, signifies how much they had once meant to him. They do in fact closely resemble the poems being written by the young aesthetes of Oxford depicted in *Castle Corner,* who resemble Cary in that he continued to write such verse when he went there. But in *Castle Corner,* as Cleeve, Cary shows himself attending the Oxford of the nineties, much influenced by Oscar Wilde, where he discusses the platonic ideal, studies Baudelaire, and hangs Beardsleys in his room. He describes Cleeve in a synopsis as an 'aesthetic young man from the Oxford of the 90s, so much Wilde as George Moore, but a better scholar than either.'[10] He in fact developed Cleeve from a character named Charles Moore, a somewhat idealized self, who was to have taken up painting while at Oxford.[11]

That George Moore influenced Cary seems likely. For Moore's *Confessions of a Young Man* is marked and annotated in Cary's copy in a way to suggest it, and their backgrounds are somewhat similar. Moore claims to have been the first in England to eulogize the Impressionists, and to have studied art in France after thinking ' "How jolly it would be to be a painter!" ' [12] much as Cary says ' "I thought, this is a damn good show . . . the life of an artist would be a good life" ' (p. 35 above). Moore too was influenced by such French writers as Balzac and Baudelaire. He says 'Flaubert bores me' (as Cary notes), but he continues: 'Happily I have "À Rebours" to read, . . . a page of Huysmans is as a dose of opium . . .'. When Cary wrote of the 'doubtful gas' that is 'not healthy breathing for artists' it was of such comments regarding symbolists that he was surely thinking. Moore's was the first appreciation of Huysmans in English Literature, and his development 'reveals the link that connects aestheticism with the Celtic movement.' [13]

The setting-back in time for Cleeve Corner's story, relates to Cary's only excuse, when condemning his *Verse* as 'real trash': 'in Edinburgh I was moving in a peculiar atmosphere of sentimentalism, a kind of hangover of the greenery-yallery period, or even earlier, late Rossetti.' [14] 'Greenery-yallery' is a quotation from *Patience,* the Gilbert and Sullivan satire on the aesthetic movement, whose members included the Pre-Raphaelites and Oscar Wilde. The word thus expresses Cary's rejection of the verse-writers in Edinburgh connected with that movement. But 'greenery-yallery' also applies appropriately to the movement as it had developed in Edinburgh, where the publication *Evergreen* was described as its *Yellow Book.* [15] The title *Yellow Book* (from *À Rebours*) occurs sufficiently often in Cary's novels to indicate that all associations with it did indeed have a special significance for him.

One of the romantic artists in the movement in Edinburgh in Cary's time was John Duncan, whose work is said to have shown not merely a return to nature and simplicity, but a return to the naive and unconscious, with a hint of Aubrey Beardsley's influence. This is understandable, since Duncan was a friend of Marc-André Raffalovich, who was the patron of Beardsley, and of Father John Gray who, in 1904, had edited a publication of Beardsley's last letters, mainly to Raffalovich. Cary met Gray and Raffalovich at Duncan's studio in Torphicen Street, which was a meeting place for people interested in the arts.[16] When Cary met Raffalovich and Gray they were engaged in building and beautifying St Peter's Church, in Morningside, at Raffalovich's expense for Gray as parish priest. Cary explains:

> I looked upon the whole affair, the church and their attitude, as a kind of aesthetic amusement – which, with them, was perhaps true.
>
> I mention this because I suspect that it was here at the Art School and in this odd encounter with Raffalovich and his friend that I began to uncover a train of thinking and experience which became afterwards important to me. For it was almost entirely through the aesthetic experience that I came to a true faith, that is, a faith which I believe so entirely that nothing has shaken it, or could shake it.
>
> But this process was long and complex. When I decided to abandon the Art School and go to Oxford I was still quite indifferent to religion.[17]

These words are from 'My Religious History', an unpublished essay that Cary wrote when urged to produce a book on religion.[18] To understand the long and complex process that gave him his faith and his theme, therefore, it seems necessary to know more about Raffalovich.

He was a wealthy Jew, who grew up in the atmosphere of his mother's Paris salon, which Symbolists, including Mallarmé, frequented. But she so disliked his ugliness that he settled in London and then Edinburgh. From 1905 his Edinburgh home became a rendezvous for anyone interested in the arts. He wrote poems and articles but is better remembered as writing *Uranisme et unisexualité,* developed from *L'Affaire Oscar Wilde,* published in 1895. He became a Catholic in 1896 and an oblate in 1898, when John Gray became a candidate for Holy Orders. He went to Edinburgh when Gray was appointed there.

They had met in 1892, when Gray was about to publish 'Silverpoints', described as his version of Baudelaire's therapeutic descent into hell. He had contemplated suicide (thus proving himself a true Symbolist in his wish to reject life).[19] He became the most prolific contributor to the *Dial,* a Symbolist review published in Chelsea, which was intended to rival the *Yellow Book.* The *Dial* is a likely inspiration for the *Symbolist* and the

Bankside of *A Fearful Joy,* also (supposedly) published in Chelsea during the nineties.[20]

Cary is likely to have read work by Gray, including contributions to the *Dial,* during his period in Edinburgh, when Gray was highly regarded as a poet and man of culture. He is also likely to have read it while doing the research necessary for the art background of *Castle Corner* during the thirties. He would then have found, amongst Gray's many contributions, his article on Huysmans's *Là-Bas* and *En Route,* exemplifying conversion.[21] Since it was at this time that Cary's own conversion took place, and since *Là-Bas* will be shown to have influenced *The Horse's Mouth,* it seems that, from *Castle Corner* to *The Horse's Mouth,* Cary has depicted the struggle in his own soul between the tradition of his family and that of this world dominated by men like Raffalovich, who formed a living link with the art world of London and Paris, right back to the 1880s. The deaths of Raffalovich and Gray in 1934, fully reported in *The Times,* would have revived Cary's memories, and notes made soon after that date include: 'The hideous man (Raffal) cultivated, adoring beauty, in love with beautiful girl who loves his company and wisdom but loathes even his touch . . . the girl is his religion (cf. Rossetti)'.[22]

These notes are developed in *Castle Corner* where, in introducing Nussbaum, Cary describes Raffalovich, even adding that, because of his ugliness, 'It was said indeed that his mother, still living in France, had refused to see him since his boyhood.' A portrait of Raffalovich's mother, *Marie* by name, hung in his house, but his guests always understood that it must never be discussed. One can only guess how that portrait related to the Mother of Christ.

How Cary thought it related, however, may be guessed from his copy of *The Symbolist Movement.* Here he has noted the sonnet 'Artémis', by Gérard de Nerval, which is based on Gérard's dream, that the goddess explains his malady to him by saying, ' "I am the same as Mary, the same as thy mother, the same also whom, under all forms, thou hast always loved." '[23] Symons traces the beginnings of Symbolism back to Gérard de Nerval's madness, which 'lit up . . . hidden links of distant and divergent things;' and had somewhat the same effect as 'haschisch, opium, and those other drugs by which vision is produced deliberately'; his imagery is that 'known to all dreamers of bought dreams.'[24]

At the close of *Art and Reality* Cary says of the soul that the artist 'must give it – the dream'. He then gives his own dream – of real mother love. Symons continues of Gérard de Nerval: 'we owe to the fortunate accident of madness one of the foundations of what may be called the practical aesthetics of Symbolism.' Since *The Horse's Mouth* is based on Cary's new aesthetics (later expressed in *Art and Reality*) and makes frequent explicit references to Plato, this association readily recalls the key words regarding intuition in the *Phaedrus*: 'Our greatest blessings come to us by way of madness provided the madness is given us by divine gift.'[25] The strong link between this statement and Cary's theme, 'life is a gift', is the chief justification for the emphasis placed on the *Phaedrus* in this study – though the part played by this dialogue, and its image of the soul, as an inspiration for artists, is justification enough.

Cary made notes in his copy of *The Symbolist Movement* while writing the first trilogy. It is therefore illuminating to compare Gérard's dream with Gulley's vision of Sara in *The Horse's Mouth* (p. 229 below). He has rejected the real love of the motherly Sara, but made idealized comments about his dead mother throughout the book.

Thus Cary presents the real, universal tragedy, which 'is taking place all the time', (p. 35 above) as he knew from his own youthful reaction to the tragedy of Raffalovich, as to that of the painter whom he drew as Gulley's father. It is the tragedy of lack of sympathy between real, living people. But the characters he drew from Raffalovich show that he did now comprehend the tragedy: that a man so ugly should love beauty so keenly; and should love it in the person of a beautiful mother who had rejected him, and was therefore idealized by him in Mary the Mother of God.

For Raffalovich is the prototype not only of Nussbaum and Benskin too in *Castle Corner,* but also of Hickson in the first trilogy. This is shown by an addition to the note already quoted (p. 43): 'Still she won't escape back to Raff. i.e. he has additional misery of seeing her broken by misery'. Cary's handwriting here belongs to 1942; so he is clearly describing Hickson and Sara. Regarding Hickson, Sara has the kindness to say: 'A man's face should be for use in battering at the world' (*Herself Surprised,* p. 24). But he was as ugly as Raffalovich, she shows.

Raffalovich's influence on the experience that gave Cary his faith is unmistakable. Yet, when Cary said only 'I suspect' that it began with this encounter, he was possibly thinking of J. K. Huysmans, with whom he associated Raffalovich – as others did also.[26]

Cary reveals Huysmans' significance to him in a typically subtle way in *Art and Reality*: by beginning the book with a reference to Manet, and by quoting *adverse* critcism of the first Impressionist Exhibition (p. 68). He would expect critics of his book to know that Huysmans was the champion of Manet and the 'inventor' of Impressionism, well known for his defence of the artists at this first Exhibition. His annotations in Moore's *Confessions* prove his knowledge of Huysmans (p. 41 above), as do his manuscripts (p. 51 below). But Huysmans was a most controversial, living person, in France, at the very time that Cary became an Impressionist. He was without doubt discussed in the art world of Paris and Étaples, where Cary spent his holidays thereafter, during all his student days. He called this world 'Bohemia', and Étaples the place where all Bohemia met.[27] His friends in Paris included a 'strange and brilliant woman' who greatly resembled, and admired, Oscar Wilde.[28] Wilde's trial had established *À Rebours* as the original 'yellow book', and so as the prime symbol of 'reaction against the Victorians' – the period to which Cary said he belonged. In 1903 Huysmans had published *L'Oblat,* the last of his series of novels, written when he himself had become an oblate. In the same year he proved himself a totally *à rebours* character by republishing *À Rebours,* which he defended in a preface against those who wanted it destroyed, by calling it priming for his Catholic propaganda. In May 1907 he died, after long suffering from mysterious diseases by which he believed he was expiating the sins of others as well as himself. This belief, and the manner of his death, created much publicity, which could not have escaped the art world of Bohemia, which he had been largely responsible for creating.

What Huysmans said, in 1903, in his preface to *À Rebours,* invites comparison with Cary's aims as a novel-writer, which it seems possible to sum up thus: to write a series of novels in reaction against the Symbolists, according to a method of characterization that is comparable with Huysmans', and echoes the very title, *À Rebours,* in Cary's description of it. For he said that a great artist had 'only to imagine his normal impulse in reverse' (p. 10 above), and in *À Rebours* Huysmans, a clerk in the civil service who had studied law 'without much enthusiasm' (as Cary did), imagines himself *à rebours,* as an elegant aristocrat, scion of one of France's oldest families.

In his preface Huysmans explains that *À Rebours* was written in reaction against the Realism and Naturalism of Zola: 'The rest of us . . . were constrained to ask ourselves the question whether Naturalism was not marching up a blind alley and if we were not bound soon to knock up against an impassable wall.'[29] Even if Cary was not, consciously or unconsciously, echoing these words, it is remarkable that he said he felt as if entering a 'blind gulley' amongst Symbolists, and created Gulley who, in *The Horse's Mouth,* says 'I always go up a back alley', and, on this occasion, 'what knocked me down was the east end wall . . . Sent from God'.[30] This is the wall of an old chapel, which will be being demolished as fast as Gulley paints the Creation on it – aided by students who exactly resemble those whom Cary warned against 'doubtful gas' (p. 37 above), immediately before beginning this book. This last scene can be read as a crucifixion (p. 238 below).

Gulley can be seen accepting death, in the very way that Jesus Christ's death has become accepted, as a symbol for the glorification of death, sacrifice, and suffering. For the Symbolists, the suicide pact of Axël expressed their spirit, and John Gray was only one among them who became a Catholic after contemplating suicide (p. 42 above). That Cary wrote against such doctrines is proved by these words from a letter concerning his first novel: 'It seeks to shew that the idea of sacrifice, where removed from that of utility, of service, i.e. pleasing god, becomes pure juju . . . and also self-indulgence'. In this novel, he says, the conversions to the belief 'that to be happy it is only necessary to abandon personal responsibility and give up all to Christ . . . are in fact surrenders, – the escapes of human nature overpowered by the responsibility of judgement, of choosing, into the bosom of a nurse.'[31] Whether Cary had been led to write thus, as a novelist consciously *à rebours* of Huysmans, can here be judged only by assembling a few more scattered facts.

Firstly, in accordance with Cary's belief that men desire change, and relief from boredom, *The Horse's Mouth* depicts taste as one of 'the "created" elements of society.' This intention is illuminated by Huysmans' preface to *À Rebours*: 'There were many things Zola could not understand; in the first place, the craving I felt to open the windows, to escape from surroundings that were stifling me; secondly, the desire that filled me to shake off preconceived ideas, to break the limitations of the novel, to introduce into it art, science, history; in a word not to use this form of literature except as a frame in which to put more serious kinds of work.' This is certainly what Cary tried to do.

In Symons's *The Symbolist Movement,* he read that *À Rebours* had been Huysmans' first sign of escape from a world he found uncomfortable and ridiculous, but that it was into 'an artificial paradise, in which beauty turns to a cruel hallucination and imprisons the soul still more fatally' (p. 139). In his own copy of Symons's book, he noted that *Là-Bas* led to 'The conversion of the Satanist'; he did so at the time he was creating Gulley, whose story begins with his emergence from prison – and whose humour is Falstaffian, and so satanic.[32] When Gulley says he was 'like a chap under witchcraft', at the time that Blake and Plato took him 'forward to black and white drawing',[33] it enriches his meaning to believe that he echoes Cary's thoughts as he concurrently read *Là-Bas,* which is a study of black and white magic, and an attack on what Huysmans calls the black magic of the Rosicrucians.[34] If the closing scenes in this novel and *The Horse's Mouth* are compared, it is difficult not to believe that a comparison is intended. This seems more likely, if the close of *Art and Reality* is compared with the concluding conversation in *Là-Bas,* where it is remarked that positivists and atheists have overset everything but Satanism, and that Satanism is ignored or unknown, because the Devil's greatest feat has been to succeed in getting himself denied.[35]

In *Là-Bas,* Huysmans began his series of novels as thinly disguised autobiography, intended to follow Zola, but 'to trace a parallel pathway in the air', and so create 'a spiritual Naturalism', says Symons. He thus became in his own way a Symbolist, for he was writing 'the history of a soul, a conscience', and in doing so showed that novels are 'capable of competing on their own ground, with poetry, the great "confessions", with philosophy.'[36] This is obviously Cary's aim in writing the books of both trilogies as confessions. Perhaps less obviously it is his aim for the whole series, as his own 'history of a soul, a conscience'.

Moreover, Cary developed an *à rebours* method of characterization within novels, as Huysmans did, drawing on opposite tendencies in himself, as he understood them from the study of other minds, so that these characters are in fact like two sides of one person. The most obvious examples are the family-lawyer Wilcher and the artist Jimson -- who are also *à rebours* characters in themselves, for Wilcher is in fact the platonist and aesthete, and Gulley the family man, however hard he tries to escape it.

One reason for supposing that Cary's interest in Huysmans dated back at least to 1907 – the year when his death made him widely discussed – is that in that year Cary also went to Edinburgh. He would be almost certain to mention Raffalovich to his Bohemian friends, some of whom would certainly know of his books, and so of his relationship to Huysmans.

Symons calls *À Rebours* the 'breviary of the decadence',[37] and the emphasis on homosexuality amongst the decadents owed a great deal to the dreams in it of Huysmans, *The First Decadent*.[38] As Robert Baldick says,[39] the Decadent movement gained impetus only after the publication of *À Rebours,* and the true prototype of the principal character Des Esseintes is Huysmans himself. This is apparent from Huysmans' reply to a questionnaire on homosexuality, which Raffalovich had circulated amongst writers. He had published Huysmans' reply in 1904, the very year in which Cary first encountered the world he would be writing of as 'Bohemia' by 1907. Huysmans' reply includes: 'Your letter and your book bring back to mind some horrifying evenings I once spent in the sodomite world . . . I spent only a few days with these people before it was discovered that I was not a true homosexual – and then I was lucky to get away with my life . . . you really feel like thanking God that you aren't made the same way'. *À Rebours* is a most 'Baudelairian' book, says Baldick; it 'affords evidence of a very real spiritual kinship between the two authors, and shows how well Huysmans understood the terrible sickness of the soul which lies at the root of *Les Fleurs du mal*.'[40]

Cary (with something Baudelairian in his nature)[41] was annotating Enid Starkie's 1942 edition of *Les Fleurs du mal* while writing *The Horse's Mouth,* before going on to write of 'Baudelaire, who teaches me to loathe the flesh', in *The Drunken Sailor,* published in 1947. At this time he had been using this background of Baudelaire for *The Moonlight*;[42] he was also writing of a homosexual artist, Hamper, whose story was cut from *A Fearful Joy* but resumed in 1952, when Cary's own typescript notes include:

HAMPER TRYING TO BE THE ORDINARY man. plays, rides, and chucks the art *which disintegrates without belief in the real god.* . . . HAMPER RAGES AGAINST THE MODERN VULGAR NOTION OF HOMOS the imitations the impossibility of friendship a la the Byron the meanness the cheapness of this civilization, HE IS FIGHTING HIS OWN TENDENCY WHICH HE SCORNS AND DONT BELIEVE IN.[43]

A Fearful Joy still contains a vivid picture of the Symbolist world, with Tabitha a 'living Beardsley'. *À Rebours* of Tabitha, and concurrently with Hamper, Cary created Juno, a character who bears a strong resemblance to Miss Urania, the Circus acrobat in chapter IX of *À Rebours.* This source becomes the more likely if read in connexion with unpublished drafts concerning Boole's relations with prostitutes, developed from that artist in *A Fearful Joy.*[44] Moreover, the chief incident concerned with Boole recalls the most famous incident concerning Schopenhauer, as a mysogynist.[45] To hint at the association in this way would be typical of Cary's technique, the significance being that Huysmans, in his preface to *À Rebours,* admits his devotion to Schopenhauer who, however, 'leaves you, so to say, in the lurch', whereas the Church 'offers remedies.'[46]

These associations become more relevant still when it is remembered that Schopenhauer is the philosopher discussed in *Castle Corner,* and that Raffalovich was a major inspiration for it and the first trilogy. Platonic associations with the role of the Nurse already quoted (pp. 30–31) are echoed in the tentative title of Juno's story, 'The Homely Nurse'; and the account just given justifies the expectation that, if Cary tried to get the whole landscape of existence represented in every single novel, there will be hints at least of platonic or homosexual love in the first trilogy. There are strong hints of it in fact (pp. 218, 227 below).

Following *Là-Bas,* Huysmans wrote a mystical *à rebours* to that novel, *En Route,* to mark the next stage in his conversion back to Catholicism, which he attributed to 'his love for art and his growing hatred of existence.'[47] Léon Bloy persuaded him that suffering was 'the gift of a God . . . so holy that it idealizes or magnifies the most miserable of creatures', and this is a typical expression of his own belief, says Baldick, 'that woman, odious and unclean by nature, cannot be purified or redeemed except through suffering'.[48] *L'Oblat,* closing Huysmans' series, expresses the delights of suffering, symbolically personified in this work as bride, widow, and mother of Christ.

Suffering as the gift of God is the very opposite of 'life is a gift' as Cary understood it. His view of women was equally opposed, being formed from experience that was almost the exact opposite of Huysmans'. Indeed, by repeatedly (but erroneously) stating that his mother died when he was eight years old, he made the parallel closer (as though his subconscious might have intended it). For Huysmans' *father* died when he was eight years old, and the child was offended by his mother's too-hasty marriage. So Huysmans became a mysogynist, and took revenge by banishing the mother from his novels. 'For only in later life, through his devotion to the Mother of Christ, did Huysmans come to know the sense of security and tenderness which was so conspicuously lacking in his childhood and youth', says Baldick.[49]

Thus Huysmans resembled Raffalovich in having a mother who rejected him, and in finding solace in the Mother of Christ. On this point Cary might indeed have been unsure, whether the process by which he re-found his faith began with one or the other. For both revealed to him the true nature of the gift his own mother had given him in his childhood prayer: faith in the family and in 'one universal person' who wished him well. From his self-analysis (p. 17 above), it seems evident that he could readily enter into Huysmans' situation. Guilt or remorse of some kind, even the wish that his mother was still alive but with another man, would be thoughts typical in the mind of such a boy. By writing as warmly as he did, notably in 'Cromwell House', of his own good fortune in knowing security and tenderness, after his mother's death, within an old-fashioned extended family, he was pleading the cause of all unloved children, like Huysmans and Raffalovich.

Both these men, however, embraced Roman Catholicism, and this faith was inevitably associated, for Cary, with the political problems surrounding his Irish disinheritance. This seems a sufficient reason for his reticence regarding Huysmans' influence. He knew how easily people 'turn your meaning into a cliché (p. 4 above), so that in fact 'the Protestant answer to Graham Greene' became the label for him. He would not have wished his religious differences to be enlarged upon as personal political bias. His general secrecy about Symbolists is also a sufficient reason; or the realization that a typical English audience would be unfamiliar with Huysmans, and as a novelist in the English spirit he would not take 'a superior condescending attitude' (p. 39 above).

For it is clear that he would have wished to speak at some length of Huysmans, to judge from an unpublished draft amongst his manuscripts. It was written in 1955, when he was already expressing his religious ideas plainly. He intended it for a French audience, for it has been cut from his article 'Le Roman à thèse'. There his words, 'I hesitate to write about the Catholic novel',[50] suffice to explain why he cut this passage – though it is possible that he cut it because the argument seemed too involved. It concerns his own alternative title for this article, 'Conflict and Contradiction', and he is exemplifying the way a man is 'a highly complex parcel of motives and reactions',[51] who may be likened to a committee composed of a changing membership and chairman. Thus:

> Huysmans' reason was at war with other important members of his committee, with his hatred of society as he saw it, with his fear of life which was probably fear of domination, of treachery; and even with his sympathy, his religious instinct, his love of goodness.
>
> Despair brought this reason to acquiesce in the dogmas of the church, and enabled him to be a Catholic. But had he any true faith, the simple unquestioning faith of Verlaine?
>
> I think he loved goodness, I think he was by nature a man of religion. But whether he took joy in goodness is not at all certain. By the time he had made peace between his reason, his fears, his whims and his prejudices, he was hopelessly damaged; a battlefield so scarred that it was next door to a desert.
>
> Yet he could write, compose; and his work was monumental, permanent. He had found a permanent chairman of committee whose policy, if it did not please all the constituent members, at least satisfied them that there was no other.[52]

By going on to compare Huysmans with Dostoevsky and then with Tolstoy, Cary gives the impression that Huysmans' influence on him had been of comparable significance. His main point about Huysmans is that his creed of beauty was 'merely a dogma and no dogma can convince the soul, only the reason.' By contrast, 'For Verlaine, beauty was the faith of his soul, and Catholicism the creed of a mind which was dominated by that faith'. That beauty was the faith of his own soul, and could be reconciled with the creed he adopted to satisfy his reason, was what Cary came to discover about himself.

The real subject of this article is the contrast between 'contradiction', which leaves the mind divided, and 'conflict', which produces a tension. The conflict springs from powerful feelings, which great writers resolve, if only temporarily, in works of art, which would otherwise lack form. The mainspring of Cary's argument, and a plea that moral values give form to his own novels, is evident when he says (in the published article) that this criterion of moral value was 'true even of Pater, Huysmans, or Wilde. For their aestheticism was a creed, a morality.'[53] These very names would have stood in his mind for the period when his own interests seemed purely aesthetic, and he divided his time between the cities where the influence of these men was actually centred.

It is possible (and could yet be proved true) that during these years a counter-influence entered Cary's life, in the French writer, Roger Martin du Gard. Cary speaks of his novel, *Jean Barois,* in 'My Religious History', as though it revealed the conclusion to the process that began in his meeting with Raffalovich. *Jean Barois* was published in English in 1950, and after that date Cary referred to it several times, as though trying to rouse interest in it, while giving the impression that he had been familiar with it for a long time.

Certainly in 1906, in France, he must have been aware of the dramatic effect on society, when the Dreyfus case ended finally with Dreyfus's innocence established. Cary was acutely aware of anti-Semitism when creating Gulley, whose persecution of Hickson, and of 'Ikey' in the junk shop, points to the kinship he feels with 'Artist Hitler'.[54] Gulley's behaviour probably owes something to the treatment of Jewish boys at Clifton,[55] and Cary had begun plotting a 'Jew story' from the late twenties. Between 1906 and 1910, Martin du Gard was living in the Latin quarter of Paris, collecting material for *Jean Barois,* in which the action hinges on the Dreyfus case. If Cary knew of this, it seems likely that he would have found out what he could about this writer.

Whether then or later, he would have found in Martin du Gard a man with many points of resemblance to himself. Of similar temperament, both published their first works in 1908, at their own expense; Martin du Gard because he feared he might prove to be the unsuccessful writer depicted in his first novel, *Devenir*, and Cary 'to get rid of the desire to publish'. [56] Both studied law 'without much enthusiasm', as did Tolstoy (and also Huysmans), and both made Tolstoy their master. Both faced, as major problems, the conflict between religion and science, the problem of facing death, and above all the problem of Evil: if God is both omnipotent and omnibenevolent, what is the source of suffering and evil?'. [57] Both wrote as social historians, and used historical characters as a basis for characterization, often by a process of dividing or reversing characters, which resembled Huysmans' method, and was called *dédoublement* by Martin du Gard. [58] Both, in their method of work, compiled large dossiers. Both employed irony most subtly. Both believed reason should guide emotions, notably in facing death, as is demonstrated in *Jean Barois* by the character Marc-Elie Luce. By explaining the historical symbolism of his name, Luce reveals that his creator's symbolism is rooted in reality, in a way that contrasts with that of the Symbolists, and in a way that Cary advocated.

The matter of chief interest, however, in the likeness between these two writers, concerns the Alsatian priest, Schertz, in *Jean Barois*. He is drawn from the Abbé Marcel Hébert, who prepared Martin du Gard for confirmation and, in contrast to Cary's mentor at a similar time, gave him helpful answers regarding the conflict between science and religion. His answers are given, through Schertz, in the section of *Jean Barois* entitled 'The Symbolist Compromise'. This is the part of the book to which Cary regularly referred, with approval. It therefore expresses, presumably, a view of symbolism that he accepted.

In 'The Symbolist Compromise', Schertz explains that he has resolved his difficulties, by distinguishing two elements in religion: firstly, 'religious sentiment', amounting to 'a pact with the Divine Being', which includes 'the personal, direct relations existing between God and all whose souls are drawn to Him'; and secondly, a dogmatic element, which 'includes hypotheses made by theologians about God.' Today, only the first of these is appropriate, says Schertz, for the dogma can no longer satisfy human beliefs which, 'like everything else, are subject to the laws of evolution'. Schertz then stresses the 'subjective element' in all belief, and the need for 'mental honesty – which calls what is obviously symbolic by its proper name'. We should apply this principle, he says, 'to each and every statement of fact, when the modern mind cannot admit its credibility'; for by 'truth' we do not mean 'authenticity' but 'moral significance'.[59]

These words accord with the view Cary formed, as can be exemplified from 'The Meaning of England', where he says that the value of the Church lies in the continuity of its traditions, and that any change must therefore come by modifying the individual acceptance and attitude; this has happened, he points out, with the English monarchy, where the old forms have a new function, affirming the Queen's power to be 'symbolic, popular, and ethical.'[60] By distinguishing these two elements in religion, Schertz underlines the difference between the faith of Cary's childhood prayer, and the faith that he lost at school. Like Schertz, he came to recognize the latter as an hypothesis, or 'as if', that every individual understands according to his needs, just as he understands a work of art. By discussing the subjective elements in this way, Schertz also points to Cary's description of art, by which the symbol is created as 'a feeling about a fact.'[61] So, by referring to *Jean Barois,* Cary is expanding what he said about coming to a true faith, through the aesthetic experience that began with meeting Raffalovich.

Darwinism seems the obvious link between Raffalovich and Martin du Gard,[62] and between them and Cary, if Gulley can be taken to be speaking for him, when he identifies Impressionism and Darwinism (p. 34 above). In *Castle Corner* Cary says 'Nussbaum, like all philosophical, free-thinking Frenchmen, believed more profoundly in Darwin even than the Darwinians. For the idea that lurks in Darwin . . . was natural to the French mind before Darwin was born. It appeared in Rousseau' (p. 371). Cary's argument against Rousseau becomes explicit in *Power in Men* (pp. 57–58). But he indicates his viewpoint here through Felix Corner, by adding that he 'used to say, the Frenchmen's economics will be those of nature and providence even longer than the evangelical Americans.' All 'evangelical Americans' in Cary's writing are linked in his mind with Tolstoy, who worshipped Rousseau and was himself revered in America at this time, as well as in France.[63] Martin du Gard, who revered Tolstoy, was a philosophical, free-thinking Frenchman. Unlike Raffalovich, he rejected the Catholic faith. But in *Jean Barois* he has created a scientist who loses his faith because he cannot believe in miracles, yet returns to Catholicism because his heredity and environment have determined that he should. He has created him according to a deterministic, Darwinian creed. But Cary found the character unconvincing, presumably because he had now rejected Darwinism – and believed in freedom.

There is also an apparent link between Raffalovich and Martin du Gard through the latter's character Schertz, and Cary's character Nussbaum, whom he drew from Raffalovich. For he made Nussbaum an Alsatian, as Schertz is. And the name Nussbaum, like Schertz, is German. *Schertz* can be taken to mean 'joke', and Schertz personifies the tragic joke, that Marcel Hébert was dismissed from office in the Church, though Martin du Gard thought him the most truly good man he had known. *Nussbaum* means 'nut tree', and to a writer whose home overlooked the University Parks in Oxford this would mean 'chestnut' – that is, 'joke', appropriately signifying the tragic joke of the ugliness of this aesthete.[64]

In Nussbaum, Cary seems to reveal what he recognized in Raffalovich, by the thirties if not before: that such were the men of real power. In *Castle Corner,* he contrasts them with his family (p. 191 below). But he shows Nussbaum's use of power as highly civilized and rational. For what Nussbaum realized was 'best for everybody' was to preserve what seemed best in world civilization, whether represented by the Corners, or in the world of art. However, he did it all in the way Cary thought Raffalovich 'perhaps' built his church, as a kind of 'aesthetic amusement'. Thus, on an occasion in *Castle Corner,* 'The mayor had risen to propose the toast, "Queen and Empire." Nussbaum . . . did not believe in the Empire any more or less than he believed in God, but he considered that both deserved the support of intelligent men' (p. 371). Here the words *Queen, Empire,* and *God,* are symbolic in the way Cary describes in 'The Meaning of England'. As an intelligent man, Nussbaum finds reasons to support what he does not believe in, and so proves himself an 'ideal Spinoza', who 'found out how to make the best of the world at its worst.' So Cary wrote while creating Hickson, in September 1942, when he noted also, under the heading 'Might is right', Spinoza's likeness to Hobbes and Nietzsche, and his admiration for Machiavelli.[65] These thoughts bear on the war currently being fought, when Cary was planning to re-visit Edinburgh; so the link with

Raffalovich, and Edinburgh in 1907–9, can be traced. It was a world where Darwinism reigned, yet artists of the Scottish renaissance were dedicated to nature and simplicity.

The split that Cary later recognized in Tolstoy's mind had thus been present in his own. His later views are clear in *Art and Reality* where, immediately after stressing the need for a new religious symbol, he discusses the power of the symbols invented by 'poets and dreamers of the romantic age', which have prevailed ever since

> Rousseau created the idea of the noble peasant living the simple life in communion with nature, preferably in a thatched cottage. For thatch . . . is an important part of this symbol for a life of peace in the bosom of nature, . . . And Nature itself, as a word, in this context means, not the indifferent and often cruel enemy of mankind, familiar to us all, but Mother Nature, a loving providence desiring only to make all children happy and good. . . .
>
> What's more, this set of symbols, idealising the simple life of the peasant, with his homespun and his handicrafts, descending through Ruskin to Gandhi, inspired millions in India to revolution, and may yet bring these millions to the real peasant's life, of poverty, squalor and superstition (pp. 61–62).

In *Castle Corner* Cary portrays the 'real peasant's life, of poverty, squalor and superstition', and the efforts of a good, civilized, and real Mary to help them (pp. 177, 192 below).

Cary was 'still quite indifferent to religion' when he abandoned the Art School for Oxford. But there is evidence of an acceptance of his family's values, as in his reply to his father's protestations, regarding this restless son: 'You know I am proud of the family name too, and I know how you have succeeded in pulling it undamaged out of the fire, practically alone and unhelped. Of course I will help you as best I can; I am proud that you confide in me.'[66] The series of poems, *Verse*, had already been published, and signified a desire for understanding and reconciliation in being dedicated to 'Arthur Cary My Father', by the poet here naming himself Arthur Cary.

The poems themselves perfectly illustrate what Cary later contended: that everyone is captive to words as symbols, and as used and admired in the society in which they happen to find themselves. In fairness to Cary, the poems should be judged in the milieu in which they were produced, as his own explanation implies. Who his models were can only be guessed, but the poems are of interest, not only for the reasons already given, but because they show the awakening of his theme, and anticipate the way he came to treat his novels as a series. As in the novels, the Mother symbol dominates, and the Father is propitiated.

Having published these poems, Cary could tell his father: 'So many people – of critical knowledge and some literary standing – advise me to write, since I find I spend most of my time thinking about that kind of work, whatever is going on, and since I seem to be able to labour at it without tiring . . .'.[67] Certainly the poems express genuinely enough his sense of being lost, and the need to come to terms with himself. For Cary's romanticism was rooted in the world of action, which always challenged the romanticism of the artist. Inevitably then, quite apart from any realization that he would not excel as a painter, he was led back to the art of the word, of which he says in *Art and Reality*: 'All the written and spoken arts, since they deal with an historical actuality, are bound to give meaning to human action which is always part, and commonly the greater part, of their theme' (p. 149).

Though he would not have known it in 1908, he found his theme (as he expressed it in *A House of Children*), when in that year he bought *The Memoirs of Robert Cary*. He was the most illustrious of Cary's ancestors, favoured by Essex and Queen Elizabeth I, whose exploits on the Scottish border had inspired Sir Walter Scott, a one-time editor of these memoirs. Thus Cary's enthusiasm for the Celtic renaissance could fuse with a renewed pride in Cary history and the English renaissance; his escapist, literary romanticism could turn, as Yeats's did, to dream of the all-round renaissance man, the poet-philosopher-warrior and supreme type.[68] In this mood he could look forward to Oxford, and agree to read law, which would better fit him for the world of action. The rebel in him, as artist or poet however, turned to his most romantic Celtic ancestor, Thomas Joyce,[69] and by 25 September 1909 (as he told his brother in a letter of that date), he was already writing stories under this pseudonym, expecting to 'play any fool's games I like under it, and have Cary for the drawing-room.'[70]

One story at least by Thomas Joyce had been published by

May 1910. 'Thus Crime is Punished' is an ironic tale of a policeman, a man of small imagination, pursuing a brigand who, having great imagination, persuades the policeman instead to join with him in attacking a poor shepherd. They dress the shepherd in the brigand's clothes and share the ransom money, which the policeman spends in retirement, drinking too much, while the brigand invests his share in a ready-made clothier's shop in a respectable thoroughfare. The shepherd in brigand's clothing has been garroted, having no hope against such witnesses as a policeman and a poor shepherd, reputed 'the only son of his mother'.[71]

Here already is the theme of imagination reconciling freedom with authority, and flouting justice, the shepherd being a paradoxical Christ figure who, in brigand's clothes, implies both good and evil, while the brigand in ready-made shepherd's clothes might be thought to do the same, à rebours.

5. The Law Student

Cary entered Trinity College, Oxford, in October 1909, two months before his twenty-first birthday. Being older than the majority of students, he doubtless felt compelled to make the most of his experience as an art student to explain the difference in age. But as the freedom-loving, rebellious art student he suffered the rebuff of authority, in the person of the philosophy tutor at Trinity College, A. E. Prichard. Cary's encounter with Prichard became as symbolic in his life as his encounters with the Normandy painter, and with Raffalovich. Indeed, his own failure in sympathy as a youth in Normandy, and Prichard's failure in sympathy as an older man in Oxford, can be thought of as reconciled through Cary's aesthetic-religious belief, as he traced it back to an understanding of Raffalovich.

'Sketch for an Idea of Life'[1] and other manuscripts reveal Cary's need to cleanse his soul, as he might have said, of the bitterness of his encounter with Prichard. Finally he did so publicly in 1956, when he was sufficiently well recognized to answer with some authority. He had been invited to contribute to a series of articles by well-known people, describing a turning point in life. Cary called his contribution 'A Slight Case of Demolition'.[2]

As he saw it, Prichard was a Cliftonian who greeted him as a friend and invited him to his home, with some other undergraduates. Cary's ingrained Irish sense of hospitality and eighteenth century good manners prepared him not at all for the possibility that his host might set out to humiliate him, and he was quite incapable, as a guest, of insulting his host.[3] Thus he was at a disadvantage from the start. He conceded Prichard's right, in a professional capacity, to enhance his reputation as a destroyer, demolishing a student's basic assumptions in his first tutorial, to make way for new construction – though often, Cary claims to have heard, he never got far enough in three years to begin building. However, since Cary was not taking philosophy, Prichard chose, 'probably in pure benevolence, and for the logical salvation of my soul', Cary says, to demolish him in front of his friends, leading him on with questions about art, which he as guest assumed were intended to put him at his ease, by allowing him to discourse on a subject that he, alone of the company, had studied for three years, and on which, from one glance at Prichard's own pictures, he judged that his host knew nothing. But Prichard left Cary completely incapable of explaining how he formed his aesthetic judgements (the judgements, we might note, by which, in his own mind at least, Cary had previously demolished the whole foundation on which the Normandy painter had built *his* world). Prichard could not shake his conviction, he claims, that the quality of a picture is something known directly, and equally the conviction that he and his fellow artists had succeeded, in discussions, in comprehending each other's meanings. But when suddenly made aware that there is a form of knowledge to which a mind like Prichard's is completely closed, as something that cannot be learned from books, he had no answer.

He realized later, he says, that he was using the word ' "know" ' in a different sense from Prichard, and relying on quite a different relation with the object. So the demolition ended in his building for himself a satisfying philosophical construction, in answer to that rankling question 'How do you know?' Cary's main point in relating the story is to show that it was through the 'aesthetic' experience that he came to a true faith, for he continues:

> And it did not take me long to see that the judgement of goodness in a man belonged to the same type of knowing. I recognized unselfishness in the same way as I felt beauty; by direct experience of a datum, not mediated by reason or judgment. Thus my faith returned, with all the enormous force of confidence which comes with a personal discovery.

But in 1909 he was demolished: 'very much aggrieved' and even more 'surprised', to find that his friends, who were philosophers, enjoyed his discomfort and, guided by Prichard, judged him 'an innocent, whose ideas were as naïve as his reactions'. This is the surprise of a 'Tottenham' who finds himself suddenly a butt, and an unmistakably keen personal association for *surprise* as a key word in Cary's writing. The occasion casts light on his explanation of the title *Herself Surprised,* which includes the meaning that Sara is surprised into revealing herself to herself, as she appears to others.[4] Cary's reaction can be understood from his characters, Cock Jarvis and Jim Latter, through whom he reveals that side of his nature which invites comparison with Homeric man, for whom 'anything which exposes a man to the contempt or ridicule of his fellows, which causes him to "lose face," is felt as unbearable'.[5] His bitterness is still unmistakable when he says that he 'only once again, at Oxford, raised the question of aesthetic judgement'; and received, from 'The only one who bothered to answer', what amounted to 'analogues' of his own answers to Prichard. But 'The man was a brilliant scholar who took a double first; I didn't dare to accuse him of innocence and naïvety. And I was probably right. He is now an international financier.'

Such remarks reveal the ironic side of Cary's love for Oxford. As Dan Davin puts it: 'sometimes he fretted at the narrowness of Oxford. It was "a hotbed of cold feet", he once said'.[6] That he returned to live in its midst for thirty-seven years, and felt to the end that he had never lived down the reputation established by Prichard, is understandable. He knew, of course, that he could blame himself. His response had been to live up to the role assigned him, of the lightweight dilettante who never opened a book to study, but enjoyed friendship, gaiety, the arts of life. In 'Sketch for an Idea of Life', he stresses that the quality of life offered is the best thing about Oxford, and he justifies his behaviour as part of the lesson he learnt from Prichard. By giving up his whole time to pleasure, he says, he was led later to understand the greatest truth: that happiness involves a knowledge that logic cannot explain. 'For this exultant happiness in which I lived, was I think, the door by which at last I entered the noble mansions of the soul, to which we are all heirs, if we but know of our inheritance and where to seek it. I was, in fact, all this time, and from early childhood, absorbed in an experience, which had gradually become an end. I sought not pleasure but experience.'[7] This conclusion affected his whole theological-political theory.

Nevertheless, the portrait of himself at Oxford, as Cleeve Corner, reveals this happiness as somewhat bewildered. Its nature can be understood from Mister Johnson, whom he was creating, concurrently with Cleeve, to depict man as natural artist, and of whom he noted 'wants help and gets bad help'.[8] This feeling underlies the creation of all Cary's youthful characters. His manuscripts reveal that he greatly regretted those years wasted, from the point of view of scholarship – and that he had the capacity for scholarship, when he chose.

He evidently took little interest in Law, though his studies obviously helped his writing, especially on political matters. He concentrated on poetry, and Blake, whom he discovered for himself, he said later, made the most positive contribution to his Oxford education, introducing him 'into a highly complex universe where what is called the material is entirely dissolved into imaginative construction and states of feeling, where matter, mind and emotion, become simply different aspects of one reality'.[9] As a silent witness to the philosophical discussions of his friends, aided by a little private study of Kant, he had already realized 'that if values, if altruism, have any real existence, they will not fit into a mechanist conception of the world'.[10] But the idea interested merely his mind, not his feelings.

His feelings may already have been affected by Tolstoy's story 'What Men Live By', for his copy of it, in *Twenty Three Tales,* is inscribed 'Trin. Coll.'. His chief book purchases, however, were poetic works, by such writers as Shakespeare, Donne, the English Romantics, Rimbaud, and Yeats. His edition of Blake was the one edited by Ellis, with Yeats's notes, and since he also bought Yeats's *Where There is Nothing,* and collections of old Irish songs and poetry, it seems that his mood was not unlike Yeats's up to this time. For him, as for Yeats, North-west Ireland was equally a dream and a reality. And since he came to write of Freeman as he did (p. 38 above), he might well have dreamt of furthering the Irish renaissance there in his own way.

In February 1910 he bought *The Symbolist Movement in Literature,* partly, perhaps, because of his interest in Yeats. His reading of Rimbaud at that time might have drawn his attention to Symons's comment, that Rimbaud had the mind of a man of action, with above all the will to live.[11] Since the description fits Cary, identifying him still further with the Symbolists, it could even have influenced his decision, after leaving Oxford, to go East, to Montenegro, and then to Africa. But his chief reason for buying Symons's study in 1910 was probably that Oxford students were then beginning to show interest in the Symbolists, through the efforts of Michael Sadler (later known as Michael Sadleir). John Middleton Murry was reading the French Symbolists during Easter 1910, 'because men whom I knew at Oxford appeared to think highly of them'; so he says in *Between Two Worlds*,[12] confessing also that he understood very little of what he read, and was persuaded that he could not hope to do so unless he was familiar with the world from which the writing grew. He arranged therefore to spend the Christmas vacation in Paris with Joyce Cary.

Murry undoubtedly played a major part in Cary's development. When they met, Cary was beginning to discover the confusion of his own split mind, and so laying the foundation for the method of characterization that he developed; that is, of drawing *à rebours* characters from real people in order to understand this split in his own, and the world's, character. This method might be expected to owe something to someone close to Cary in age and experience, and Murry fitted the role in a striking manner. For, as a fellow-student at Oxford said: '. . . his mind was divided; he seemed to look at existence now with the reason, now with the passions, a sort of Pooh-Bah metaphysic . . . ; he did not apparently admit that the claims of emotion and intellect must be worked into some kind of regulative unity.'[13] Murry's split mind is revealed in his study of Dostoevsky, whose split mind came to dominate Cary's writing. It would not be surprising, therefore, if Cary had begun quite early, if only in a vague way, to recognize his other self most readily in Murry.

There were points of comparison in their circumstances – even to their both having a beloved Aunt Doll.[14] Murry's origins were also Irish, but obscure. Cary too had grown up in London's East (or south-east) End; but whereas his father had settled here after the fall of his family's fortunes, and had encouraged Cary's dreams of restoring them (p. 56 above), Murry's father had driven his son intellectually from the earliest age, believing from his own experience that education was the one hope of rising in the world, he himself having had to struggle desperately to educate himself. Thus Murry's intellect was cultivated at the price of his feelings, which suffered, as his young mother's did also, from a certain fear of the father's driving ambition. He was not taught the Christian religion, he records thankfully,[15] thus contrasting with Cary in his gratitude for his first Christian prayer.

But he would have been destined for the Church in former times for, from a Board School, he won a place at Christ's Hospital as a 'Grecian'. The glory of being a Grecian, one of the visible 'lords of the school', can be understood only by an 'old Blue', Murry explains, though it can be recognized in Coleridge's condescension towards Lamb – a mere Deputy Grecian because he stammered – and Lamb's deference towards Coleridge.[16] At Oxford, Murry would doubtless have been delighted to find someone to play Lamb to his Coleridge, especially if he were a true blue in another sense. Murry's conception of a 'Grecian' could well have inspired the many episodes in Cary's novels where he is clearly reminding readers that the true Grecian lived in a harsh world of traders and slave owners, not unlike Africa as Cary came to know it, and very far removed from anything in Murry's experience.

One year Cary's junior, Murry entered Oxford the year before him, with a scholarship, and had already established his Oxford reputation by a brilliant pass in the first-year examinations, when they met. He felt an outsider, however, because of his poor background, and he envied Cary his independent means. Cary, on the other hand, is likely to have developed a sense of guilt, regarding his pedigree as well as his private means, when attacked by Murry's eloquence, for possessing them. Understandably, therefore, he felt a lifelong disgust for Murry, as a 'scamp' and a 'rascal', for borrowing heavily from him and never repaying him, even when he could well afford to do so, and Cary needed money.[17] The many references to debts in both trilogies are coloured by this fact. Regarding his pedigree, Cary must have read with grim amusement, when Murry wrote, in *Between Two Worlds,* that his first experience of living in a great house convinced him that 'I would have become a very convincing member of the aristocracy'.[18] He might even be thought to have granted Murry's wish in the second trilogy, where Jim, of 'the Slapton–Latter dynasty', is unmistakably drawn from Cary, and Chester Nimmo appears to owe much to Murry. For Chester, as Lord Nimmo, wins over the crowd by speaking from the Slapton Arms.[19] In fact, by the time Cary wrote this book, Murry was a gentleman-farmer with a country estate, and Cary was still dreaming in vain of making his family landowners once more in Inishowen.

In treating Murry as a kind of *alter ego,* Cary may have been influenced by Blake's attitude to Milton – of which he became aware at the very time that he met Murry. Even the contrast between his and Murry's role in the Oxford Milton Club is a relevant associated idea. For Cary must have felt as much an outsider academically, since Prichard's 'demolition', as Murry had felt socially. Murry's biographer, F. A. Lea, quotes Cary as saying that Murry was 'brilliant in dialectics'[20] – as Cary might have wished for himself. This very description might even explain why Cary's writing forms a kind of dialectic with Murry's (pp. 100–2 below).

Yet Murry might never have played so vital a part in Cary's life, if his behaviour in connexion with their Paris vacation had not forced Cary to question his own attitude to it. As Murry recalls in *Between Two Worlds,* Cary was 'worldly-wise *and* sweet', when he arrived in Paris some time after him, around 27-29 December 1910. He introduced him to some of his artist friends, including the brilliant woman who so admired Wilde (p. 45 above). He also knew the Left Bank cafés frequented by the *petites femmes.* But he was too late to warn Murry against falling in love with one of them, Marguéritte, a country girl recently arrived in Paris, who had already given up her profession and turned seamstress, in the belief that Murry intended to marry her. According to Murry he would have done so if, like Cary, he had had private means, instead of being totally dependent on scholarships and his career at Oxford. He had landed himself in an impossible position, he was told by Cary (the only person in Oxford who knew about Marguéritte). And 'Cary was right', Lea says.[21] However, Murry returned to Paris during Easter 1911 – borrowing from Cary to do so – and again in that September, but on the last occasion he fled without meeting Marguéritte.

By October he was sharing digs with Cary in Oxford. Gradually he decided 'that the right and proper way to break the spell of Marguéritte was to go to bed with another woman. . . . So I hinted to my friend, who had seen something of the beginning of my affair with Marguéritte, that I was prepared for an "adventure". He kindly undertook the arrangements. I say kindly, with no sense of irony.'[22] *Kind,* as a key word in Cary's writing from around this date, with undertones of the original meaning, 'wellborn', may easily owe something to Murry. In any case, it is probable that Murry's many painful written testimonies of this time, expressing self-pity and self-dramatization, as a means of salvaging his self-esteem, are far less painful than what Cary may

have heard in conversation. Murry claims that he found himself
expected to follow the code of a caste to which he did not belong;
Lea says that his conflict arose because he did *not* feel himself a
'cad', as would have been appropriate to the code of his milieu.[23]
His excuse for deserting Marguéritte had been that he could have
married her only by going to Paris to live, and trying to become a
full-time writer. Ironically, by 1913, he was actually doing this,
but living with Katherine Mansfield, who had quickly persuaded
him, by Easter 1912, soon after their meeting, to do what he
would not do for Marguéritte – leave Oxford, and support himself
by writing. But Katherine Mansfield had private means. If Murry
contributed at all to Chester's character, he seems certainly
recalled in *Prisoner of Grace,* when Chester accuses Nina, ' "You
feel me a cad" ', yet later declares: ' "I always swore I'd get a
lady" ' (p. 272 below).

Immediately on leaving Oxford, Cary began, but abandoned, a
book about the life he had seen in Paris.[24] This is recorded in his
Paris Diary, where it is clear that Marguéritte attracted him very
much also.[25] Other notes show that his plans for novel-writing
then were wholly autobiographical.[26] So it seems that he might
already have tried, in 1912, to use the situation surrounding
Marguéritte. In 1916 Murry used it in *Still Life,* of which Cary
wrote to his wife (on 22 February 1917, from Africa): 'He was a
scamp that fellow. The novel sounds just the sort of thing I would
have expected from him – confused sex relations, neurotic love
affairs – and a great anxiety for originality at all costs. But if he
writes novels – why shouldn't I?? What darling. Except that he
was a much cleverer fellow & gives all his time to it I see no
reason at all.' This reaction was apparently revived in 1935 when,
in *Between Two Worlds,* Murry made what amounted to a confession of Cary's involvement also. But this was around the very
time that Cary's own 'conversion' to his 'true faith' took place.
So he was now ready, inspired by Murry as well as Huysmans, to
write novels as 'great confessions' (p. 47 above). By putting
Sara's confession first, and making it clear in the opening that he
is recalling Marguéritte, he reveals a new understanding of a
woman's plight in the society he and Murry represented, from
opposite classes.

Murry's conversion to Impressionism, or rather post-Impres-
sionism, was an even more overwhelming experience for him, in
1910, it would seem, than Cary's had been in 1904. 'Thanks to

Cary', Lea writes, he had arrived in Paris all prepared to be impressed by it.[27] His most vital encounter, amongst artists, was with John Duncan Fergusson, the Scottish painter, then in his mid-thirties, working in the new, Fauve, post-Impressionist style. Anyone Fergusson respected was, according to him, an artist, by which he meant that they resisted mechanical uniformity, and had *rhythm*. He so greatly impressed Murry that to please him Murry decided that he had to be an artist in Fergusson's sense, and he was inspired to found *Rhythm* as the new *Yellow Book,* with Frederick Goodyear, another Oxford student, as co-editor, and Fergusson as art-editor.

As might be expected Fergusson also influenced Cary, who later formed a theory of art in which all men are artists, and a mechanistic view of the world is false. Not surprisingly, Gulley Jimson is drawn chiefly from Fergusson.[28] One hint of this identity is that Gulley has lived in Glasgow, where Fergusson lived from 1939.[29] Early in that year Fergusson had an exhibition in London, as a result of which he was commissioned to write *Modern Scottish Painting,* which was not published until 1943, because of the war. But if Cary saw Fergusson in 1939 (which is quite probable, since he frequently attended art exhibitions in London, and would be more inclined to do so when he knew the artist) then something of the contents of this book, and everything of Fergusson's humorous, excitable nature, would have been in his mind at the time Gulley was taking shape. There is also time enough for Fergusson's book to have influenced *The Horse's Mouth* directly, and Gulley's dinner at the Beeders comes to mind, when Fergusson describes having dinner with some *'very nice people'* who, like all business men, regarded artists as 'merely inspired idiots unless they can show they have made lots of money'. However, 'Perhaps on account of an extra glass of port I stupidly said, "But where do you put the inventor in all this." One of them turned and looked at me amazed and said, "Oh! those mugs are being born every minute".' Fergusson's comment, that the only person to watch is the clever salesman, is paralleled by Gulley's advice, ' "If you want a good spec, ask the dealers." '[30]

Fergusson's account appears in his last chapter, which is on Calvinism and Art, and expresses views close to Cary's. For Cary said, with reference to *The Horse's Mouth,* that Evangelical people mostly 'don't care twopence about the arts', and support censorship because 'They're just anxious to stop anything they don't happen to like.'[31] Cary had learnt something of Calvinist disapproval while in Edinburgh, where Raffalovich's 'aesthetic amusement' had involved putting his work of art, St Peter's Church, right in the midst of a Scottish community much prejudiced against Catholicism. He had learnt of it also, regarding art, in marriage.[32] Fergusson's remarks on Calvinism and Art would thus have greatly interested him, particularly as they chiefly concern the painting of nudes, which Fergusson himself most enjoyed painting. Indeed, 'La Baignoire', painted in 1907 in his first Paris studio, could well be the original of Gulley's *first Lady in her Bath*.[33] Certainly Fergusson is recalled in Gulley who – almost exactly Fergusson's age – is inspired to paint Sara as 'the everlasting Eve, but all alive-oh . . . the Sara of twenty years ago'. Fergusson's cover design for *Rhythm* is a nude of Eve, offering an apple.

A link between Fergusson and the platonic overtones manifest in the first trilogy is provided by Murry's account of their first conversation. This would surely have amused Cary, and encouraged him to introduce rather fatuous discussions on Plato amongst Oxford students in *Castle Corner* as well as in the trilogy. Plato was evidently Murry's favourite topic, and he was soon giving Fergusson an exposition, in which he was pleased to find Fergusson saw some relevant meaning. He explains: 'Since Plato at Oxford did not appear to *mean* anything to anybody, but to be at best a *corpus vile* for the demonstration of principles of logic, it seemed to me better in general, and more satisfying to me in particular, that he should be made to mean something by F——— in Paris, even though that something might be wrong.'[34] Murry was expounding the relation between Plato's Doctrine of Ideas and his theory of Art – presumably with reference to the *Phaedrus*. It is not surprising, therefore, that Cary's imagination produced a platonic relationship between Gulley and Nosy (p. 226 below).

Indeed, Murry almost invites it, in writing here not only of Fergusson, but of his Oxford tutor Fox, and the farmer Thornhill, all of whom were 'solid and whole', and gave him a sense of security that he otherwise lacked, having 'no stomach for the fight with life': 'That I cleaved to such men is now no wonder to me at all. But the wonder remains that they should have cleaved to me, or been willing that I should cleave to them. . . . I was like the vine which clings . . . I was attaching my weakness and nonentity to their strength and positiveness, in order to live.'[35] This account fits Nosy's relation with Gulley, and also Cary's division of mankind into life givers and life takers (p. 11). It adds a significant association too to the name Cleeve, for the character Cary created in *Castle Corner,* soon after this was published. Being autobiographical, and behaving as badly towards Bridget as Murry did towards Marguéritte, Cleeve virtually acknowledges Cary's guilt in that affair. Finally, Plato might well have become a greater obsession with Cary after Murry returned to share digs with him in October 1911, and 'simply read Plato over and over'.[36]

The first number of *Rhythm* appeared in June 1911, but neither it, nor any subsequent number, contained a contribution by Cary. He would have liked to contribute, and he was certainly capable of contributions, as a writer or artist, quite equal to the general standard. Yet Murry rejected his work, although he accepted Cary's financial help for the venture.[37] That he failed to recognize Cary as the real creative artist, as Murry was not, was ironic, since Murry finally admitted it (p. 298 below).

However, this new *Yellow Book* is filled with ideas relevant to Cary's later writing, about which he may already have been feeling critical. The first editorial is written by Frederick Goodyear, but presumably had Murry's approval. It announces that men have always been homesick for an ideal community, but that the golden age will soon become a reality, because hope has come with the idea of evolution, and futurists have grasped the moral implicit in Hegel and Darwin. Liberty being of two kinds, the artists and philosophers who create free minds will be the true creators of 'the new Thelema', for which the art of the politician is merely obstetric, concerned only with external liberty. If this editorial is compared with Cary's political theory and political trilogy, it seems that both might have been born here. An article by Michael Sadler declares Fauvism to be 'a reaction on the one hand against the lifeless mechanism of Pointillism, on the other against the moribund flickerings of the aesthetic movement'. Impressionists had reached an impasse, he says, notably those allied to literature, who 'followed up the Baudelairism . . . and lost themselves in an orgy of Satanism . . .'. Cary may well have been unsure, then, how to react to such declarations.

The atmosphere in which he moved is captured in the life and letters of E. H. W. Meyerstein, who reveals both how commonly Plato was discussed, and that anti-Semitism was something very real to the minds of such students, so that evidence of both in Cary's writing is to be expected.[38] On 23 October 1911 he wrote:

> Last night I went to a meeting of the Milton Club which is being reformed on modern and post impressionistic lines . . . The leading spirit is one Murry of Brasenose – an earnest brilliant man . . . He was originally a Rossetti enthusiast – but only a year ago the reaction came and he went to live in Paris, – as I understand – like one of the common populace, depriving himself of all comforts and often reduced to starvation diet: he is keen on seeing and bringing others to see the crude pitilessness of life. . . . He is certainly an impressive personality and full of a deep sympathy – [39]

Knowing Murry's own 'crude pitilessness' towards Marguéritte, and his capacity to keep from starvation by borrowing, Cary must already have felt some cynicism regarding his power to impress people in such ways, though there is no doubt that he himself was under Murry's spell for a time. He talked benignly enough of his membership of the Milton Club, when addressing literary societies in later years.[40] But, not being a contributor to *Rhythm,* he may well have attended with mixed feelings. Indeed, he was as much in a 'gulley' in Oxford as he had been in Edinburgh. It is significant therefore that, during that Michaelmas term, in 1911, he was already talking of leaving Oxford without taking his examinations, so that he could devote all his time to writing. Perhaps he wanted to show his friends what he could do. His father, however, persuaded him that he should stay on and take his degree.[41]

The final totally unsettling experience in his life at this time was his relationship with his future wife, whom he had met in Merton Street in 1910.[42] She was Gertrude Ogilvie, youngest of the three sisters of Heneage and Frederick Ogilvie, friends of Cary at Clifton and now at Oxford. Each later received a knighthood for distinction in his field, Sir Heneage in medicine and Sir Frederick in education, his most widely known post being that of Director of the BBC. Their father, William Ogilvie, was a Scot who had prospered in South America; there Gertrude was born, in Valparaiso, on 26 August 1891. Her mother was German, and the family, who now lived at The Glade, Harrow, had been brought up strictly, in the Calvinist faith. Gertrude's proud bearing concealed, judging from her letters, a certain bewilderment caused by an over-directed upbringing. She writes of angry outbursts, followed by remorse, in scenes with her mother, whose life, genuinely devoted to the welfare of others, over whom she nevertheless had great power, clearly filled her daughter with the fondest admiration and equal apprehension, that she could not in honesty follow her in the religious conviction that guided all she did. An equal but opposite conflicting feeling was manifest in her behaviour towards Joyce Cary who, having the reputation of 'bohemianism',[43] with no prospects, had little hope of being accepted as an eligible member of such a family.

From later letters to his wife it seems that Cary knew, almost at once, that this was the woman he wished to marry. A likely reason, outweighing any other considerations, is that she was a woman very like his own mother, whose strict religious upbringing, he knew, would make her an ideal wife.[44] Thus his revolt against tradition suffered its severest blow, for she would have none of him. In a letter of 16 August 1916, he reminds her of her discouragement in 1912 with her forbidding look, which he calls 'AGS' (daggers?): 'The worst AGS you ever looked was at that lunch in 1912 after I had made my hideous proposals to you – and you sat opposite at lunch. It is a good thing we sat side by side this April or I doubt I would ever have dared to repeat the hideous and insinuating suggestions. You are daunting front face, my dear.'

Added to the other unsettling influences and his former refusal to study, this disappointment in love made failure at his examinations inevitable – or rather, his fourth class pass which, in the eyes of Oxford, was rather worse. To understand his bitter regrets, we have only to know how anxious he would be, later, that his own sons should succeed academically; or to read in *Castle Corner* of himself, as Cleeve, whose father fears that he will not 'give the examiners what they want', since he himself, despite his brilliant promise as a philosopher, has taken only a third. Felix reveals Cary's feelings regarding the two people in Oxford who most affected his life: Murry, who took only a second because, like Felix, he was distracted by 'the heat of composition'; and Prichard, the philosopher, who failed to give the fatherly help that Cary believed might have completely altered his career, at that turning-point in his life.

He heard the results in London where, in a room at 10 Store Street, he was struggling to prove himself as a writer. Then, in October, after receiving a telegram from Oxford friends: 'Class 4. Words fail us',[45] he set off for the Balkans, where the Montenegrins were in revolt against the Turks. He followed Heneage Ogilvie, who had gone to get experience in surgery by working with the Red Cross.

6. The Man of Action

Cary's reasons for going to Montenegro cannot be simply assessed. It might be supposed that, having been reading Rimbaud, he was possessed a little by his spirit, and went abroad after quarrelling with his friend. But 'Byronic' is the term that might have occurred to Cary, judging from his later use of the word.[1] 'Byronic' signifies an impulse to glory, stemming from a feeling of suicidal despair, and the need to redeem and vindicate oneself. When Byron went to the aid of the Greeks in their war of independence from the Turks, he was a wealthy and famous writer. Cary was merely a potential writer with a small income, but he went in a somewhat similar spirit – in part. An even more likely influence is Tolstoy who, with other Russian writers, was much discussed in circles where Cary had found himself with Murry. Tolstoy appears in Cary's Paris Diary, and Murry was writing of Tolstoy very soon after.[2] But it is typical of Cary to seek the reality of the experience, instead of merely writing of it.

Without doubt the experience was to be material for writing, as shown by notes for an unfinished novel, 'Mills', written by 1918 – that is, after his marriage. But the notes show Cary assessing the mood that preceded his marriage, and also the development of his theme:

His life a search for god. which he finds in love and only afterwards in self-sacrifice . . . trying to grasp the ideal in art . . . in the Balkans . . . The happy life there. Believes ought to live like a beast Rousseau Tolstoi[3]

This note is elucidated by such later notes as these:

Whats wrong with all the intellectuals is this lack of direct feeling of beauty etc. joys of life. They are not poets. The

73

animal, the poet close together – the sensual joy of the mind
and the body . . . Like an animal like a poet close together. To
live like a poet – valuing *real* things old manners "When God
made men, he was a poet".[4]

'Rousseau Tolstoi', in notes here for 'Mills', show that Cary was
already absorbed with the 'noble peasant' theme.

At some point he must have become aware of a certain likeness
between his background and Tolstoy's. It would then seem totally
in character if, on realizing it, he fostered it, believing that
experience comparable with that of the world's greatest novelist
would provide the best material for his art. Thus, Cary too came
of a long line of provincial nobles – whose semi-feudal rule over
a backward peasantry in Ireland had been ended by movements
inspired to some degree by Tolstoy (Cary's treatment of his own
youth in *A House of Children* seems directly inspired by the early
section of Tolstoy's *Childhood, Boyhood and Youth*); now Cary
too, after reading law, had left the university with an ignominious
record; so he too would turn to soldiering, and would observe a
war, in the hope that he would write a great novel. Since *Castle
Corner* as a trilogy was to have been Cary's *War and Peace,* the
fall of the Carys depicted there clearly relates to Tolstoy's
influence in Ireland. The note quoted above, 'trying to grasp the
ideal in art', which relates Tolstoy to the Balkan experience,
recalls that Cary too made a treatise on art his last complete
work. He did so in the face of death. And it is in the manner
of his death that Cary contrasts with Tolstoy – whose fear of
death appears as a point of specific interest in Cary's notebooks.[5]
He depicts it through Gulley, who owes much to Tolstoy.[6] Facing
death, and life, become the ever-present facts in all his writing,
combined with that other aspect of death, the loss of a loved
one, which he had known since childhood. 'The Firing Line',
heading notes for his first and his last novels,[7] indicates the way
in which facing death dominates the series. The heading clearly
stems from his experience as a man of action.

Cary arrived in Antivari on 20 November 1912, and decided
on the following day to explore the ruined fortress that served
as the arsenal. It blew up, and Cary had his first experience of
what death in battle would be like. The exploit was reported
by journalists, notably Alphonse Courlander of the *Daily Express*
who, describing him as 'the man who was blown up', cast him

in the role of the Irish aristocrat with a chivalric love of adventure.[8] The report set the tone for Cary's own record of his Balkan experience, *Memoir of the Bobotes*. This was not published in Cary's lifetime, and the only extant leaf of his manuscript suggests that it was written directly into the notebook from which it came, this being one of 'a couple of diaries' named in Cary's preface.[9] The tone, as Walter Allen says in a foreword, is that of 'the polite literary essay', the point of view towards the peasantry being 'very much as the primitive, unspoiled men and women of the romantic poets. In a word, Cary's attitude towards the scenes he is witnessing is aesthetic.'[10] This is indeed the Rousseauesque, Tolstoyan attitude to be expected from his career as a student.

Nevertheless, there is evidence of a purpose to see life realistically. Cary is observing a war, in the belief that 'there would be no more wars'.[11] He was right, in the sense that there would be no more wars of this kind, in which the true nature and purpose of men, against a background of Nature, as physical Reality, could be directly observed. He remarks: 'what with the large indifference of hills, skies, sun, moon, and stars to small scuffles (the largest battle is small by comparison), it is by an imaginative effort rather than direct realisation that danger and the possibility of bullets can be understood.'[12] Thus he shows another step in the process by which he came to see death itself as easy, if imagination has not considered the danger, as his had not, when the arsenal blew up.

To avoid being arrested as a spy, he joined the Red Cross, and served throughout the campaign as cook. This fact explains why the cook became a key figure in his novels.[13] His intention may be judged when he writes in the *Memoir*: 'I was cook's mate at Zogaj, and learnt my duty in a stern school' (p. 49). His anecdotes concern Englishmen, whose training in good manners prevails, even though they are living at a basic level. Thus a 'feast' intended for two, who have lived for six weeks on 'sour bread, stinking goat, and cabbage-water', is ungrudgingly shared with unexpected visitors. He observes: 'These seem to be paltry matters for a historical work, but they are after all the most important parts of history, and generally forgotten. No one would have bothered to make history at all but for appetite or, at the lowest, hunger' (p. 51). Thus he saw himself, already, as a social historian.[14]

But in memory at least the sense of adventure dominated, as this account shows: 'I had a certain romantic enthusiasm for the cause of the Montenegrins; in short I was young and eager for any sort of adventure.' 'I saw most of the fighting, and was among the first three over Scutari Bridge, at the surrender of the Turks in 1913. For this campaign I had a little gold medal from the Montenegrin government which I prize very much, though it was earned in what was, for a boy of my age, a holiday.'[15] This campaign was in April 1913, and Cary was back in England by May.

He was naturally eager, on his return, to renew friendships. But he was rebuffed by Murry, in a way that would have increased his disillusionment, not only with Murry, but also with the literary world that Murry was beginning to represent. As he told Dan Davin years later: 'he had called on the Murrys and been told they were not at home, though the house above was loud with the noise of a literary party.'[16]

Cary's next move was even more gallant than the last, and has something in common with Tolstoy's efforts for the betterment of the peasants. He applied to work in Sir Horace Plunkett's land scheme, in Ireland; he would thus have been assisting the very people who had benefited from the Land Acts that ruined families like his own. He had no sooner arrived in Ireland, however, than it was decided to employ specialists, rather than men of Cary's character and background. This experience gives strong personal meaning to Cary's satirical use of the word *expert* throughout his writing.[17] He in fact not only admired the all-round man, and sought to be one, but also made this, the need to be a 'whole man', the theme of his work. The theme owes much to the experience of being unacceptable as an all-round man, which made him observe very keenly how inadequate many 'experts' are. Each disappointment in his career virtually debarred him from specialising in anything else that could have satisfied him, except novel-writing. But when he set out to be an expert in that, he had had a far wider experience than most novelists. He was therefore well equipped to preach this theme – which he believed could be learnt best through the novel.

The Nigerian Colonial Service, to which he now turned, in fact had a tradition, under Sir Frederick (later Lord) Lugard, for which his general experience well fitted him. Moreover, it was a career that would win the approval of his own family, and of the Ogilvies. He took up his appointment as an Assistant District Officer on 29 April 1914, after a brief preparatory training at the Imperial Institute. What Africa immediately taught him was that Nature can be the cruel enemy of mankind, who depend desperately on what reason has contrived, in a world where savages resemble children rather than that noble image of Rousseau's. They too are defenceless in a world that seems mysterious and unjust, and can only mask their fears by an air of resignation. This they wear 'like a magic cloak of the soul . . . as if they said: "With this spread over me I may escape after all." '[18] The symbols of the Romantic poets have a similar function, and are as futile and dangerous, he realized.[19] In *A House of Children,* as Evelyn, he compares his childhood resignation to fears and suffering with that of famine and smallpox victims in Africa. They even laughed at a joke, while 'waiting upon fate with a submission so complete that I had to have some of them spoonfed' (p. 135).

The last quotation contrasts with that from *Memoir of the Bobotes,* where the gentlemanly behaviour of the Englishmen seems artificial by comparison. But this artificiality became essential to Cary's theme: 'that cultures are artificial, constructed.'[20] When he says, 'No one would have bothered to make history at all but for appetite or, at the lowest, hunger', he seems to be deliberately excluding this lower level still, where man is simply at the mercy of Nature. Of course he found long-established cultures in Africa. But land and people were ravaged by climate and disease, and officers of the colonial service like himself had impossibly meagre resources.

Their problems were intensified when World War I broke out, only three months after Cary's arrival in Nigeria, for troops had to be recruited, and fed. Cary was made a second lieutenant, but was not called on for active service himself until April 1915, when an attack on Mora Mountain was planned. With a party of native troops he was required to clear the way for bringing up a large gun. Once more, Cary was observing a war, under conditions vastly different from those on the European battle-front. The nature of his observations are recorded in the first two stories published under his own name. They both take place on this mission with the gun, and centre on Cary himself, as Evelyn Corner. Presumably by design, they concern, respectively, an intuition of freedom and an intuition of grace, and are to be compared with the two instances discussed in the preface to *A House of Children*.

The first story is entitled 'Bush River' (for which the earliest notes appear to have been made in about 1931).[21] The title symbolizes Nature, just as the sea does in *A House of Children*. The following account is a good example of Cary's symbolic method, and vividly conveys what he meant by Freedom. For almost every word carries associations beyond the immediate context, to show that the river represents Nature developing in all its power, which *is* Freedom, and is also in men, but still uncontrolled by any real civilization, or Reason:

> The river was an African river never yet banked up, tamed, dredged, canalised; a river still wild . . . Here it was all in foaming breakers, suddenly cut off by a spear-shaped eddy like pulled brown silk; . . . on the far side, long manila ropes of water which seemed to turn upon themselves as they were dragged under the banks. This savage river not only moved with agile power; it worked. One saw it at work, digging out its own bed, eating at its banks. Every moment some bluff crumbled; stones, bushes fell and vanished.

Here Nature is a living creature, potentially purposive, highly active, and symbolically a force in man's history, where civilizations have vanished because 'some bluff crumbled'. And that is the point of the story.

To this river comes a young officer, Corner, clearly Cary in a retrospectively critical self-portrait. He is therefore a recent Impressionist art student with Symbolist leanings, filled with the jargon of those schools. Since Conrad is to become a named master, *Heart of Darkness* is likely to be somewhere in his mind, together already perhaps with some self-questioning regarding his own real purpose in coming to Africa:

> African rivers fascinated him. Looking at them he understood that old phrase 'the devouring element.' He asked himself how Africa survived against such destruction. At the same time, he thought, how magnificent was the gesture with which Africa abandoned herself to be torn, like a lioness who stretches herself in the sun while her cubs bite at her.

Here then is Nature as the Mother symbol – contrasting with the Romantic thatched cottage, yet, in the imagination of this young 'cub', still female, passive, and willing to be 'devoured'. Though it will clearly endanger the mission and therefore the men he leads, Corner has brought with him a possession with which he is obsessed: a jet black Barbary stallion with 'a crest like the Parthenon chargers', significantly named Satan. The horse thus draws together in its being the pagan elements in Corner's own cultural make-up, from Arabic, Greek, and Hebrew sources.

Corner is startled from his reverie to learn that the expected guide has not come. Having been only nominally leader, he now actually is, and the spirit of Freedom, as Power, begins to possess his imagination, largely as a relief from routine and boredom (boredom being shown in the following quotation as a meaning for Cary's symbolic use of 'wall')[22]:

> 'No guide.' He was startled. And then at once he felt a peculiar sense of anticipation. Not of pleasure, scarcely of excitement. It was as if an opportunity had opened itself before the young man, a gate in the wall of his routine, through which his mind already began to flow. Or rather the force which poured eagerly through this gap was not his at all but that peculiar energy . . . of his passion for Satan, for the wild bush, especially for the wild river. The different streams rushed together at the same gap, and their joined forces were overwhelming. They swept away the whole bank, the whole wall. Young Corner looked severely upon his men and said in a voice of resignation, 'I suppose you want me to give you a lead. Bring Satan, Mamadu.'

The word 'resignation' links the account with that in *A House of Children* where, as 'a magic cloak of the soul', the feeling is ' "With this spread over me I may escape after all." ' Escaping boredom, the conventional Corner '*had* to swim the river. He had a first-class excuse for doing what he had often wanted to do. He told himself that he was not his own master, not in any sense of the word.' Here the word 'master' invites the reader to recognize that Corner has become the hero on his horse, a symbol of man trying to master his *libido*, as Jung would say.[23] Corner's struggle and development are signified by his words to Satan, which begin with his primitive Hausa and end with army-style

English. Again almost every word suggests universal yet everyday associations, including sexual:

> Corner, up to the neck as Satan's hindquarters sank beneath him, . . . found at once that he had no control over the pony. He could only talk to him in Hausa. 'Keep at it, friend – straight ahead.'
>
> And when he spoke, he felt an affection for the little horse, an exultant pride in his courage, so different in quality from anything he had known before that it could not be described. It was more than sympathy, more than the bantering love of a friend; it was a feeling so strong that it seemed to have its own life, full of delight and worship; laughing at Satan and rejoicing in all devotion and courage; the mysterious greatness of the spirit. He wanted to laugh, to call out, like Mamadu. But again, as if constrained by decorum or a sense of what was proper to his responsibilities, he merely looked severe and repeated, this time in English. 'Keep it up, old boy – that's the stuff.'

Corner feels that he too has swum the river, and realizes his folly only at sight of a German helmet ten yards away. In despair he asks himself what drove him, and in terror feels a cold touch – the nose of Satan, who wants a tuft of grass under his leg, and so answers his question. At this moment his men appear, exultant, admiring, and without fear. But 'Corner frowned and walked further away, as if from contagion.' He has been lucky, he knows. Yet he has 'the feeling of one appointed to a special fate, to gratitude.'

The last words suggest that Cary felt appointed to write of this true experience. His horse's mouth symbol can be partly understood from the mouth of Satan, seeking greener grass in the manner here described. Evelyn's relationship to Satan symbolizes Freedom as Cary portrays it through the effect on people of characters like Freeman of *A House of Children*. It is a power we can feel as part of nature, as Evelyn feels it in that novel, when riding the sea, as it were, on the steamer bound for Ireland. In this later experience, that 'compound of fear and glory' finds 'confirmation and development in new intuition': that Freedom must be mastered by reason – yet that civilisation has advanced because this extreme power (*ate* or *menos* to

Homeric man)[24] does take possession of certain people in moments of crisis, appealing to such feelings as love, pride, or greed, and succeeding, as often as not, by luck. Corner's feeling, that he 'had a first-class excuse for doing what he had often wanted to do' is Cary's essential discovery as an observer of men at war, and one he repeatedly illustrated.[25]

The other story from Cary's Cameroons experience illustrates this discovery regarding war in the best sense, by showing how war provides an opportunity for traditional barriers to be broken. The occasion arises because Corner feels sympathy for his men, otherwise destined to sleep in the rain, and arranges for them all to share his tent-fly, lying with their feet to the centre. Corner cannot sleep, and he suddenly realizes that his sergeant, beside him, is also awake. He speaks 'without meditation', 'as if the vivacity of his nerves was glad to find a tongue.' He learns that Sergeant Umaru belongs nowhere, having been born ' "On war" ', meaning with an army on the move. Umaru dismisses friends as ' "no good" '. But after a silence asks:

'In your country, Caftin, among the water, do you keep friends?'

'Of course, plenty.'

The sergeant pondered. At last he exclaimed, 'Plenty. I have friends too – like that.'

Corner is surprised to learn that his sergeant has reflections of his own. He learns his philosophy: that it is good to be lonely; that one should live like a pilgrim, understanding God as ' "our great One" ' – *not* our friend, and therefore not deceiving oneself – as romantic poets do – that storm clouds are ' "grand" '. The story ends:

'God prolong us,' in a growl. He turned on his side. But the young man lay on his back for another hour, and still at the place where his elbow touched Umaru's back he was aware of a certain activity of feeling at work as if by itself; an affectionate concern which did not stop. At least, it was still there when he noticed it some time later. It was laughing, too, by itself, but not at Umaru. It was quite independent, a serene enjoyment.

The story is entitled 'Umaru'.[26] Its ending links it to the quotation on page 61; it seems as though the intuition of mankind's intended happiness, regardless of customary barriers, must have come to Cary in some such moment. As an illustration of an intuition of grace the story speaks for itself. It gives a source for Cary's later claim that, at a certain primitive level, all men can find a common good in morality: in such values as courage, duty, affection, loyalty, self-discipline, truth.[27] Perhaps in some such encounter Cary did come to terms with lost and false friendships at home and, partly in consequence, adopted this pilgrim code, which is also the soldier's code, notably regarding death.[28]

In the attack on Mora mountain, Cary narrowly escaped death when a bullet struck him behind the ear. This time he experienced the physical sensation that he had indeed died. Death itself, he realized from that moment, is easy; he felt ' "only a sort of surprise that such a terrible thing as death should happen so easily and suddenly." '[29] It was facing death, as the relinquishment of life, that became central to his theme.

Though Cary's wound was slight, his nerves were strained, and his health bad, and he returned to England in March 1916, for six months' leave. By 1 June he was married, to Gertrude Ogilvie. Her former diffidence had been broken down by the war-time atmosphere, Cary's own changed circumstances, and by the fact that her brother Frederick, to whom she was particularly close, and who was also home on leave, wounded, from France, pleaded his friend's cause. When Cary returned to Nigeria, in August, it was with the conviction that 'work', from now on, meant writing. Thus, from the first, it was his wife who gave him the encouragement he needed to become a major writer.

His development, during the remainder of his service in Nigeria, is recorded in their daily exchange of letters, broken only by a period of leave in 1918. His letters give a vivid account of 'One Ruler's Burden', the subtitle of an article 'Africa Yesterday', in which, later, he gave some idea of the loneliness and responsibility of government, as he had experienced it, in stark reality, as a serviceman.[30] Quite apart from nationalist and racialist issues, he learned how completely mankind generally depends on the willingness of the few who, for whatever cause, undertake the burden, and inevitable guilt, of government. It is unlikely that he immediately grasped and acted upon the intuitions just described, in those stories of the Cameroons, though the first, at least, relates to actual experiences.[31] What he did come to see clearly was the danger and difficulty of imposing one culture upon another. Two incidents that he recorded in letters, and used in his writing, reveal this strikingly. Again they can be seen to concern goodness, or grace, and freedom.

The first occurred during Cary's absence in England, and he wrote of it in a letter of 13 September 1916. A young Assistant District Officer, Maltby, required to collect taxes from a certain tribe, the Montals, had decided to prove his friendship and trust, by refusing to take a police escort, and forbidding his entire party to carry arms. They were attacked and fifty-nine were killed, including Maltby, whose skull was found in the Montal juju house, wrapped in his burberry. 'Four tribes ate him, and they are all for it', says Cary.[32]

His earliest unpublished novel, 'Daventry', written in Africa, is built around this incident, showing Maltby as Daventry, who is misled by the false code by which he has been brought up, apparently at some private school resembling Cary's own. Thus, his own goodness would have been educated towards becoming a guardian of freedom. But freedom as Cary would now understand it, would have been unknown to his teacher. Daventry is still being encouraged in this code by letters from home, which show how easily people can exert power, even by letters, in order to prove the existence of goodness in the world, so satisfying their own desire for it.[33] Daventry's fiancée and family are shown in this light, but Daventry's goodness proves to be idealistic ignorance and a source of evil, causing the death of his companions, one of whom – the cook – dies with the significant words: ' "For Chris' sake, wa's de good! . . ." ' 'De good' of Christian unselfishness, for such Englishmen, might be said to resemble what is taught by a nurse *for her own sake* (p. 28 above). Already, in writing 'Daventry', therefore, Cary is beginning to see how the word *Christ* is used as a symbol of goodness, for various motives. Daventry has been betrayed by his teachers and by those who gave him authority prematurely. But in so far as he has accepted responsibility for his actions, he is himself the betrayer.

The second incident concerns Cary himself, and is described in a letter of 25 November 1916:

The other day a wire came – By what authority does Lt Cary command H. Coy. Lieut Phillips is the senior officer . . . it looked as if Phillips would supersede me. We should change places – and though you can't understand what all that means, it means a great humiliation for me in the eyes of every native in Nafada & white men too. It would be a sort of public degradation. Because it wouldn't be that Phillips had become a captain over my head. Then I wouldn't mind – the matter could be understood by anyone and I should be in an ordinary simple position. But to change places without changing ranks could never be explained to natives – they would simply think I was purposely degraded by my chiefs and look upon me accordingly with the smallest respect. In fact I should lose all authority whatever – even the authority of a subaltern. . . . After four days of perplexity I got a wire to-day . . . confirming the seniority they had denied. . . . You will think it rather absurd, perhaps vain of me, to want to remain O.C. It is not that I promise you . . . out here it means loss of caste and the position of every white man, sometimes his life, depends on his caste, his prestige. . . . Prestige is important to every white man in Nigeria, so important there are a thousand rules made to support it that are not needed in more civilized places. A white man up here who was known to have broken his word to a black man would be almost an outcast – so too one who showed the white feather to them. But all this does not concern you or interest you greatly . . .

These last lines show that Cary already realized the difficulty of conveying these values, of which Englishmen can read comfortably in studies of the Homeric age, without recognizing that they still exist in themselves, given the circumstances. This letter explains Cary's feelings in creating Harry Jarvis, nicknamed 'Cock' who, in the twenties, became the prototype of all Cary's imperialist characters.[34]

Cary destroyed most of the writing done in Africa, but his letters reveal an increasing criticism of the colonialism to which he had dedicated his life. He had no doubt that the Africans wanted, and benefited from, the impact of European culture, in becoming free from tribalism. But he came to realize that everyone has his own unique idea of goodness, which must be tested in actual circumstances, so that what seems manifestly 'good' in England may not seem so in Africa. For him, the actual circumstances described in his letter of November 1916 would have been complicated in the eyes of those he ruled because, in January 1917, he was returned to civilian rank, as an Assistant District Officer in the Colonial Service. He was then made officer in charge of the most backward area in Nigeria, Borgu, of which he wrote to his wife, on 5 May 1917: 'I shall be lord of some 10,000 square miles, mostly deserted bush, with a large population of lions snakes crocodiles & mosquitoes – the administration is in confusion and the people backward.' In Cary's novels this land became *Daji,* which means 'bush', and this description reveals the irony underlying Jarvis's famous exploit, in becoming 'CONQUEROR OF DAJI'.[35]

For Cary, what was 'good' became increasingly his relationship with his wife. He was driven, more than most men, to reflect on the relationship – by their long parting, by the value of her letters as a link with England, and by hours of solitude, when his mind dwelt on it, not only because of loneliness and sentiment, but also because it was his chief clue to the character of the world, as he had to understand it, if he was ever to become a great writer.

Their first son, Michael, was born in the spring of 1917, and Cary pondered deeply the significance of his change of role. He had been a son who had revolted, and reformed. Now, though he had spent barely two months of marriage with his wife, he was to be – desirably – the responsible father and husband. His feelings are best understood as he set them down in the intimacy of love letters; as when, for example, on 4 September 1916, he wrote that a woman is reborn in new dresses and love letters, according to Balzac. But:

He might have added that a man is reborn by love too – I am your child darling I love to think of the times I lay on your breast as if I really was your child. . . . When I come home I shall have a rival. I am already telling myself I must not be jealous or it will hurt you.

On 14 November he wrote more forcibly:

Last night in bed I made myself unhappy with the inevitability of our loss – we only had 2 months of that first free married life – you and I and no-one else, only the two of us and all our heart for each other, and we shall never have it again. When

I come back, though we shall only have been married in reality two months, we shall be like old married people, with a family and other distractions. It was selfish regret . . . but sometimes I get terribly jealous. I love you so much, you are all I have, and one can't help jealousy . . .

A letter of 15 October 1916 strikes the same note, and also gives a hint that *To be a Pilgrim* and *Prisoner of Grace* are titles bearing some relation to the sentiments expressed here:

I wonder do mothers love their children better than their husbands – I wondered today as I rode along. Perhaps a husband only comes to be a sort of person to be looked for to pay bills – and beyond that rather a nuisance about the house. If I ever find myself in that position I'll run away & go into a monastery. After all I'm a sort of monk already a pilgrim – but my pilgrimage to the Lady of Grace. I shall be a wise man from the East coming to the manger to see the child that Love has given. Dearest what a home coming that will be . . .

That he felt himself a prisoner of grace, compelled by goodness as he now appreciated it, is signified when he says, on 20 August 1916, while still on the voyage out: 'I feel like a Prisoner asking for all these things but then you are my wife and that makes a slight difference, for I love you with all my heart. . . .'

Cary's wife made him a prisoner of grace as a writer, in that he was unwilling to shock her unduly. She writes for example, on 7 September 1916:

. . . don't try & shock people too much – as there must be plenty of things that you say you have seen in life that are just as well not put on paper – Anyhow it is no business of mine to criticize is it? but I would have to tell you honestly if I liked it – and though you mightnt think my opinion mattered one way or the other – I think you would rather I liked what you wrote, wouldnt you?

In the same letter, two days later, she writes that she is reading *The Brothers Karamazov* which she finds 'very interesting', but exasperating, since no character appears to behave normally, and the world would be 'a pretty ghastly place to live in' if it were inhabited by such people. On 9 October, acknowledging this letter, Cary writes:

> I'm afraid my book may shock in places but so does Life shock in places, and I write what I find & see. Its not so bad as Karamazov and has lots of good kind people in it just as there are in life.

These quotations suggest that Cary's symbolism may have developed in part to avoid shocking his wife – simply because he was writing for readers such as she, whom he was trying to persuade to accept his view of life, without offending their susceptibilities (cf. p. 39 above).

The artist-rebel is evident however, in Cary's letter of 21 October 1916: 'I can't help wishing I knew London better and had racketted about in it more – what pictures and scenes for books – I would like to be London's Balzac and make a new Comedie Humaine shewing all sides of life – good bad & indifferent – the finest sort of history as well as interesting novels. I might as well say I would like to be Dante or Shakespeare of course, but there is nothing like trying'. 'The Comedy of Freedom', as Cary's over-all title, may have been born at this point, as further evidence of his French affinities. But his conscious rejection of Decadentism or the Symbolist spirit – perhaps under Tolstoy's influence – seems evident when he writes on 13 November: 'if I want to impress my notions on anyone I mustn't start by offending him and Art for Arts sake is all moonshine.'

The fact that his wife claimed to have loved him for two years before they married, while outwardly, at the time, she still appeared hostile to him – a Bohemian, unacceptable person – suggests that her subconscious responded to this side of his being, just as his traditional self, which had been suffering suppression when they met, responded to the lady in her. Here again a letter is illuminating: on 16 December 1916 Cary wrote of the bachelors in Nigeria, who despise married men: 'because we only have one wife, and she is a lady. You see darling there are plenty of men I know who are afraid of ladies – they have only met one sort of woman for years and years when they go on leave . . . They would run a mile now at the very prospect of meeting a lady'. Such thoughts may bear on Cary's creation of Chester Nimmo, whose determination to 'get a lady' has been linked with Murry

(p. 66 above). For it was in this year, 1916, that Murry's novel, *Still Life,* appeared, and drew from Cary the caustic comment already quoted (p. 66).

In 1916 Murry's study of Dostoevsky was also published, and it seems highly probable that Cary's lifelong absorption with *The Brothers Karamazov,* from this time, when he and his wife discussed it, and his ultimate belief in God as a Person, owe much to this study. For Murry says of Dostoevsky, that he could not believe in Jesus' God because he made Jesus suffer, so that 'God' for him 'could only be the synonym for the love he saw embodied in Jesus'. Dostoevsky wanted Aloysha's faith, says Murry, but 'He knew that belief in God as a person, the faith of religion as we understand religion, was denied him for ever. He asked for no more than a way of life. What must he *do* to be saved? The posing of that terrible problem and the attempt to answer it with something more than barren silence, forms the deep argument of his greatest books.'[36]

Cary's first novel concerns the conflict between Jesus' God, who made him suffer, and that 'synonym' for God that Cary came to see as the true God of the New Testament. The 'deep argument' of Dostoevsky's books is certainly implied by its title, *Aissa Saved.* But the text, backed by his notes, leaves no doubt that Cary is attacking, most vehemently, the sheer egotism of a belief in a personal God, merely from a desire to be 'saved'.[37]

Absorption in reading and writing, in preparation for becoming a novelist, allied to the realization that he was doing a good job as a colonial officer, went far to reconcile Cary to the prospect of years of separation. But his wife became increasingly unhappy, particularly after the birth of her second son, Peter, in December 1918, when the armistice was already making such divided families a rarity. It was no longer fair, or practicable, to live with her parents, and a home without a husband would offer only loneliness. Finally she wrote Cary a letter which he answered, on 30 May 1919, in these terms:

It comes to this – that you do not think I am justified in staying in this Service, and you are prepared to take the risks of my leaving it.

... last night at one time I was very nearly ready to say that I would send in my papers, and risk all our future – ... But I remembered too, later on, that you would learn to like me very much less, as a failure at home – embittered, struggling, and hopeless.

Today I thrashed out the facts more fairly. [Here he talks of his sons, their education, and his infleunce on them.] . . . I hope that both of them will get this from me at least – the tradition of service, and duty – the honourable traditions of their class . . . I will be a better influence as the servant of the Crown in responsibility, than as a struggling author, or clerk at home. . . .

. . . here all the married men except a few are separated from their wives, and the wives I have met . . . are as it were in the Service too. They are proud of it – and bear separation as their husbands stand the climate.

Thus spoke Cary, the imperialist. The potential novelist, clearly fearing failure, defended the viewpoint by reminding his wife of his own previous lack of application, and also of the difficulty for writers, even when recognized, to earn an adequate income.

Cary's decision, that he might after all retire, was made shortly before going on leave in December 1919. He had heard that three stories had been accepted by *The Saturday Evening Post*. Written as pot-boilers, by 'Thomas Joyce' (p. 57 above), they had earned him more money, after a few weeks' leisure-time work, than he received from a year's service as a colonial officer. Then a doctor advised him not to return to the tropics; asthma, from which he had suffered as a child, threatened to become a serious affliction.

The decision was thus made, that he would now set himself to become a professional writer. Number 12 Parks Road, Oxford, was bought as the new family home; and here Cary lived for the rest of his life.

7. The Man of Letters

Though Cary decided to become a man of letters in 1920, it was twelve years before his first novel was published. He himself described these years as a period when he was genuinely educating himself,[1] and he wanted to be sure of his belief before he published. His decision to become a professional writer really hinged on his marriage, which was certainly the chief turning point in his life. Now, like Tolstoy, he settled down to work in the midst of his family and, like him, retired to his room for given hours each day, in the belief that inspiration comes with writing.

Like Tolstoy's Countess, Mrs Cary acted as her husband's amanuensis, until her death in December 1949. In the first novel written after her death critics observed a change of style.[2] Even in the practical matter of assembling the manuscript Cary admitted, 'The truth is that Mrs Cary used to send them off for me and so the thing was properly done. I had no idea it was so difficult'.[3] In the same year, in a lecture, he expressed the belief that we owe Dostoevsky's great works to his wife.[4] That statement regarding Tolstoy would have taken more explaining; but in making it Cary certainly gives the impression that he is admitting his own debt too. He had given this advice in a letter of 4 October 1948 to Graham Ackroyd: 'I know your feeling that family life and an artist's vocation are and must be in conflict but do you know I think the conflict may be a good one. For family life obliges one to keep ones roots in the ground – in the real world of primary feeling.' Here he does admit also something of the struggle.

The fact that Cary himself began a new life at this time gives particular force to his belief, that the end of the war marked a turning point in history.[5] He was bound, by his act, to replace a fixed salary by money earned from his pen. But the effort to produce saleable stories soon conflicted with ideals as a serious writer. A letter of 17 April 1923 includes: 'to tell the truth, in these last three years I have been living on the edge of nervous exhaustion. . . . It is impossible to explain the problems I have had to face because I suppose no one but a writer who had been through the same bewildering phase could understand them. . . . Now I can write of them because I am round the corner. I began to see my way clear in January and now I see it still more clearly'. His feeling, at this point in time, of having to struggle to 'round the corner', lends meaning to his fictional name Corner.[6] It may have become a kind of grim joke, since nine more years passed before he published anything.

To understand Cary's dilemma at all, one must remember the historical situation. The England he remembered seemed literally dead, with so many men he had known killed. He expressed the feeling often in his writing, and this note belongs to his first plans for a trilogy: 'In the war, the heroes were killed, and the rascals came through – the heroes that did come through were damaged. England as a whole was really destroyed'.[7]

His idea is of 'the bourgeois age destroying the aristocratic', which finally found clearest expression in the second trilogy. But both trilogies centre on this period, when strike actions built up to the General Strike of May 1926. Cary served as a docker at this time on Hay's wharf, as he remembered when beginning Gulley's story, 'I was walking by the Thames', but more particularly when writing as Jim Latter in *Not Honour More*. For this novel centres on the General Strike, with Jim serving as a Special Constable, as Cary might well have. Thirty years later he could express the complexity of the situation in a way that satisfied his understanding. At the time he could not reconcile sympathy for the needs of the strikers with fear of revolution provoked by communist agitators.

It is likely that he was shocked, in 1921, by the publication in English of Tolstoy's *A Confession* and *What I Believe*, which Aymler Maude introduced with a warning of its threat to British institutions (p. 7 above). Tolstoy's fables had made Cary feel that he wanted to be a better man (as he wrote to his wife on 16 October 1916). But here was the man behind those fables, with a deeply divided mind. Cary was 'stuck' as a writer for nearly ten years, he said, while seeking the general idea he needed from which to write. But Tolstoy had two answers, and ' "he was awfully muddled in a way: on the one side he believed that Providence ran everything – and that belief impregnates *War and Peace*. . . . On the other side is Tolstoy's terror of death; and also in *Anna Karenina* his ethical judgement, which involves interference with the course of Providence – he's – he's not joined up; but he was such a great artist that he doesn't split up in any of the books. Each of his books belonged to one theory of life." '[8] Since Tolstoy was a Russian liberal, Cary may be assumed to have explained here why the liberal revolution has 'ended in confusion and doubt' (p. 9 above). He shows also that, from 1921, he was seeking an answer to Tolstoy's challenge. He did so, it seems, by analysing his own split mind in terms of Tolstoy's – but also of Dostoevsky's, of which Middleton Murry had written, revealing his own split mind in doing so. Now Murry was proclaiming D. H. Lawrence his messiah. But Murry and Lawrence were 'antipodal' to each other, they later realized.[9] In a complex way, it seems Cary found himself antipodal to both.

Since 1913, Murry had been a leading figure amongst English intellectuals, extolling all things Russian and urging revolution. In that year he had met Lawrence, but their revolutionary ardour had been quenched by the war. They had begun rather to dream of sailing away to an island, ' "where there shall be no money but a sort of communism as far as necessities of life go . . . A community which is established upon the assumption of goodness in the members, instead of the assumption of badness." '[10] Such pacifist escapism, and the assumption of goodness 'instead of' – rather than 'as well as' – badness, is what Cary attacks from his first novel. This aspect of his theme seems to owe much to Murry, whose description of Lawrence as the Jesus of our time would also suffice to explain Cary's treatment of characters similarly. That Lawrence saw himself in this role became clear with the publication of *The Man Who Died*. But his feeling is already unmistakable in a letter of early 1915, when he wrote that since war had begun ' "my soul lay in the tomb . . . and all the time I knew I should have to rise again" '.[11] By 1915 Murry and Lawrence had started a new magazine, *Signature,* for the benefit of the new English society they hoped to shape. There were only two issues, in one of which Murry wished the war away with the words: 'this monstrous thing does not exist.'[12] He then went to the French Riviera with Katherine Mansfield. In April 1916 they went to Cornwall, to form 'a little colony' with the Lawrences.

But Lawrence quarrelled with Murry from his arrival, as he had before.

Lawrence was then writing *Women in Love.* In it he was expressing his disillusionment with the new society that he and Murry had recently planned. He was also rejecting the Bohemian world of Soho, which he had known chiefly through Murry – as Cary had, briefly, in 1911–12. *Women in Love* was a sequel to *The Rainbow,* which had been published in September 1915 and suppressed in November. Cary's admiration for *The Rainbow* is stated in *Art and Reality,* where he writes of this 'brilliant' book: 'The struggle to be read, the hatred which his work excited when it was published at last, embittered Lawrence. And this is the common case of the original artist. He wants not only to express his unique idea of things, but to communicate it. He is, in fact, almost invariably a propagandist, he is convinced that his idea of things is true and important and he wants to convert others, he wants to change the world' (pp. 90–91).

Since Cary also wanted to change the world (as the preface to his first novel makes plain) his use of Lawrence to plead his own cause suggests that this work may have influenced him. He says the description of the Brangwen family expresses Lawrence's 'whole intuition of life as lived finally at the level of fundamental passion and fundamental needs, of an order of life not reducible to logic or rational judgment'.

Perhaps Lawrence helped Cary to find his answer to Prichard, and inspired him to write also of English society in three generations of a family, as in *Castle Corner* and subsequent novels. He probably discerned that in *The Rainbow* Lawrence had broken away from the traditional English novel and adopted poetic methods of narrative comparable to those of the French Symbolists.[13] Lawrence's method of characterization may also have influenced Cary. He drew from recognizable living people, notably Middleton Murry, as in *Women in Love.* It should not be surprising, therefore, to find Cary depicting Murry, and Lawrence too, in his novels.

The ideas that inspired *Women in Love* were certainly a challenge to Cary. They are stated in *Fantasia of the Unconscious,* published in America in May 1921.[14] Cary's method of stating his ideas in essays or treatises, so that his own belief was clear at least to himself, may well owe something to reading such revelations by Tolstoy and Lawrence around this time.

Many of Lawrence's ideas in *Fantasia of the Unconscious* can be recognized in Gulley Jimson, notably the need to live on impulse and reject all education.[15] Lawrence rejects as most 'risky' the motto *'Know thyself'* (which Sara accepts on page one of the first trilogy). He therefore wants all schools closed. '. . . love and benevolence are . . . poison to the giver, and still more to the receiver'; 'The Ideal is *always evil'*, says Lawrence. *'The great mass of humanity should never learn to read and write – never.'* Girls in particular should 'At all cost' be prevented from reading and being self-conscious, and should therefore be kept busy learning 'the domestic arts in their perfection'. Boys should be trained harshly as soldiers, and *'know* that at every moment they are in the shadow of a proud, strong, adult authority . . . training to fight, and preparation for a whole new way of life, a new society'. In this society, 'The secret is, to commit into the hands of the sacred few the responsibility which now lies like torture on the mass. . . . And let the mass be free: free, save for the choice of leaders. Leaders – this is what mankind is craving for.' Since Cary's writing from the beginning shows parallels between fascism, the education at an English public school, and platonic doctrine, his reflections regarding Lawrence's philosophy seem fairly clear: that his 'new society' differs from the old only in rejecting Christ (whom he was to replace). Cary came to see, rather, that freedom implies responsibility in all of us. Moreover, Lawrence's other definition of freedom, as 'the paradisal entry into pure, single being', would probably have struck him as an expression of escapism or self-indulgence.[16] It in fact questions whether Lawrence saw himself as one of the 'sacred few' or one of 'the mass'.

But 'the question of all time', over which 'the battle rages', is whether Man is supreme as 'Lord of life', or 'woman, the great Mother', Lawrence declares in *Fantasia*. Life at present is devoted to 'the great end of Woman, wife and mother', but in truth 'man is responsible to God alone. He may not pause to remember that he has a life to lose, or a wife and children to leave.' These echoes of Milton and the Paradise Lost theme recall Gulley's paintings; and Gulley certainly practises the gospel that Lawrence seems to have taken from Jesus, as reported by Matthew, about leaving his wives and children.[17] Gulley seems to share Lawrence's view, that 'women, when they speak and write, utter not one single word that men have not taught them'; and to agree that man must never teach them. For 'women live for ever by feeling, and men live for ever from an inherent sense of *purpose*', says Lawrence – though, apart from obeying the few leaders in his new society, he never gives any idea what this male purpose could possibly be. Cary was to show that it is 'Woman, wife and mother' who has an inherent sense of purpose. 'It is life we have to live by', Lawrence says, but 'We have made the mistake of turning life inside out', by bringing men and women together according to their 'sympathetic consciousness'. So Lawrence gives his answer to Cary's essential question, and also indicates why Cary noted that he was 'a typical puritan turned inside out' (when creating the character who represents a stage of Gulley's development).[18]

Lawrence says man is of the sun (Gulley's symbol) and woman of the moon (which Cary treats in the book following Gulley's). For Lawrence, the moon is 'the mother of darkness', and 'the begetting of a child is less than the begetting of the man and the woman', in sexual intercourse. In this and all other relations man and woman should 'fight the other out of self-consciousness' by 'the most intense open antagonism'. A man should 'Harry' his wife, who should 'let him have it to his nose'. (The reader will not miss these associations with Cary's symbolism and with the fact that a punch on the nose is 'platonic' for Gulley.) 'We have a vice of love . . . and promiscuous kindness', says Lawrence, in contrast to Cary, for whom kindness is 'the dignity of living'.[19] Lawrence therefore exhorts:

> And so, men, drive your wives, beat them out of their self-consciousness . . . Wives, do the same to your husbands.
> But fight for your life, men. Fight your wife out of her own self-conscious preoccupation with herself. Batter her out of it till she's stunned. . . . Reduce her once more to a naked Eve, and send the apple flying. . . .
> Make her yield once more to the male leadership . . .
> You'll have to fight to make a woman believe in you as a real man, a real pioneer. . . .

Such exhortations fit the picture of 'beating' as what Dostoevsky calls Russia's 'national institution',[20] and go far to explain Gulley's treatment of women. They also suggest why 'The Pioneer' is the title of an early sketch by Cary on women's emancipation.[21]

This association is evident in the fact that Cary wrote *The Moonlight* immediately after *The Horse's Mouth,* to show the true nature of women, and actually linked Lawrence and Tolstoy by name, as complementary theorists to be attacked. They represented for him 'the new feminist' and 'the old conservative'. His treatment is invited by Lawrence in the closing pages of *Fantasia,* where he says *Anna Karenina* exemplifies the hackneyed theme of all modern tragedy: woman and sex as a goal leading to death as the only possible conclusion. On this point, the part played by Lawrence and Tolstoy in the characterization of *The Horse's Mouth* seems closely linked with its attack on the Symbolists, for whom *Axël,* with death as its goal, became a major inspiration. 'Better the woman's goal, sex and death, than some *false* goal of man's', says Lawrence. 'Better Anna Karenina and Vronsky a thousand times than Natasha and that porpoise of a Pierre. . . . Better Vronsky's final statement: "As a soldier I am still some good. As a man I am a ruin" – better than Tolstoi and Tolstoi-ism and that beastly peasant blouse the old man wore.'

Such words sound odd from the miner's son who wanted to sail away to an island when soldiers were needed. He implies that one must be a pacifist in all but sex, when man must prove himself lord and master. In *Anna Karenina* and *The Kreutzer Sonata* Tolstoy says much the same. The difference is that Tolstoy, 'the old conservative', has as his ideal the wife and mother at the heart of the family (as did Frieda's husband, whom she left for Lawrence), whereas Lawrence, 'the new feminist', resembles Vronsky, having said (to Frieda) 'let the family go'. Both views have had great influence on society, and have arisen directly from these men's personal circumstances. Tolstoy wanted his wife (impossibly) to remain for ever his child-bride, a Virgin, the substitute for the Ideal mother he never knew, while peasants and prostitutes satisfied his lust and for that earned his hatred, which was indeed self-hatred yet convinced him that the Magdalen of society was heaven-sent, to preserve the sanctity of the home.[22] Lawrence, on the other hand, wanted a woman not only to replace his mother but also to deny her (as he hoped homosexual love might do more successfully, it seems).[23] But Frieda's rejection of her children, and Lawrence's refusal to recognize her feeling for them, both denied the priority of the mother-child relationship.[24] Lawrence evidently wanted children. But when he realized that he would have none, and that his gospel was sex,

what else was there in his life but sex and death? As a leader,
where was he leading?

Murry evidently had some idea. For the publication of *Fantasia
of the Unconscious* so excited him that he forgot his quarrels with
Lawrence and founded the *Adelphi* specifically to preach its
doctrines. Lawrence arrived in London in the winter of 1923,
wanting to blast and attack everything and, on Murry's refusal,
then proposed that they should form a community in New
Mexico. This was discussed at a supper party early in 1924, to
which Lawrence invited most of his London friends, whom Murry
embarrassed by confessing that he loved Lawrence, but might yet,
like Judas, betray him. The story of the 'last supper' became
common enough gossip for Cary to have heard of it soon after it
took place. It certainly makes it easier to understand what he was
getting at in the story of 'Cock Jarvis', which he began around
1924 (pp. 111 below).

In 1923, the bewilderment he wrote of (p. 91 above) could
well have been due to the realization that he could be profoundly
moved and influenced by writers whose philosophy he rejected.
For later he argued that, because writers influence society quite
as much as politicians, and are generally more skilled with words,
the public should know the man behind the books quite as well
as they expect to know politicians.[25] The experience could explain
why he recognized so profoundly the truth of Tolstoy's theory of
art, as an 'infection' by which a man successfully communicates
a strong feeling to others. Still he ends his lecture on Tolstoy
thus:

> But if Tolstoy, we think, was wrong in his moral theory, he
> does us good service by the courage with which he states
> it. That is one of the greatest services any thinker can
> do, ...
>
> It is because Tolstoy was so completely sincere, so utterly
> scornful, like the aristocrat he was, of popular judgement, that
> he stands before us one of the greatest men and greatest artists
> of the world. His faults were enormous. But he showed them
> to us. He gives us every step in his feeblest argument. And so,
> through him, we know the weakness as well as the powers of
> the human soul, and understand better, by direct experience,
> by the closest sympathy, that world spirit of our time in which
> all of us are at once partakers and creators.

He had chosen to speak, at the first significant opportunity, on the split between Tolstoy's aesthetic and moral theory, so showing that this was the problem of 'the world spirit of our time' with which he was chiefly concerned.[26]

What would have struck him in the twenties, on reading *Fantasia of the Unconscious,* was the vast difference in the way works of art can affect people, as exemplified by Lawrence's reaction to *Anna Karenina.* He would also have recognized that Lawrence was indeed Tolstoy's opposite, and had no illusions about Tolstoy's work for the 'noble peasant'. Yet Lawrence himself was regarded as coming from an equivalent class in England, and this was the class Murry had claimed to campaign for, in Oxford days, presenting himself as their representative.[27] Cary might indeed have felt some responsibility for Murry's career, since his own enthusiasm for 'Bohemia' had prapared Murry for his dramatic conversion in 1910. Murry's skill in literary journalism had been immediately demonstrated in the production of *Rhythm,* and his final power as an editor and critic, over the acceptance or rejection of a writer's work, was something Cary knew all too well from Murry's failure to publish anything by him in *Rhythm.* In 1915 Murry had demonstrated this power again, in his willingness to start a journal to foster Lawrence's revolutionary doctrines, and would do so yet again in 1923. On 7 December 1919 Cary had revealed his keen and distinctly bitter awareness of Murry's role by writing to his wife: 'Do you see that rascal Middleton Murry I dug with at Oxford is Editor of the Athenaeum. But he was a brilliantly clever fellow. I think he might pay me the money he owes me now though.' In January 1921 he wrote to her from Oxford: 'Murry called on me yesterday, he is off to live at Mentone. I believe his wife has consumption, poor thing. He is writing for the Supplement as well as the Athenaeum.'[28]

The underlying feeling of such remarks is that Murry the critic could have helped Cary, as he had helped Lawrence and indeed had been willing to help Eliot.[29] The fact that he failed to acknowledge his financial debt to Cary makes his treatment seem even more of an unkind snub – particularly as he had made a point of excluding Cary from his literary party in 1913 (p. 76 above).

Yet what makes the meeting of January 1921 truly remarkable is that Cary – and presumably Murry – allowed friends to believe that it never occurred.[30] It is therefore a matter of special interest, particularly as the topics Cary mentions are likely to have come up only in a fairly long visit. As it happens, another letter of this date contains the words: 'I will try not to be secretive', so indicating that this was indeed characteristic of Cary. This letter also reveals that, at the very time of Murry's visit, when those long-standing debts could not have failed to enter Cary's mind (if not his conversation), he was being forced into debt to his father-in-law, and this was straining his relations with his wife. For he says of their discussion in London on the matter: 'I did not feel when I came up that you were with me. I gave way, and immediately afterwards you said that you did not understand what all the trouble was about . . . I think you do . . . why dependence is hard for me, and vitally affects my situation. But the matter is now finished, and it is a relief to know that we are secure for this year. I am very grateful to Father . . . I did try to be reasonable, and I surrendered more than he understands.'[31] Cary's reluctance to leave the service, and his wife's acceptance of responsibility for that act here come to mind (p. 88 above). And because Murry's visit would have revived the past for him, a letter of Cary's wife of 18 October 1916 also becomes relevant: 'It is funny the reputation you had for bohemianism isn't it? I am sure you are changed all the same, darling, or else I didn't know you at all before.' At this meeting with Murry he may well have been asking himself just how far and why he had changed. In 1942, when he went to Edinburgh, he made this impression on Professor Dover Wilson (whom he kept up all night, talking): ' "I felt I was as near to the act of creation as I was ever likely to be, with all my ideas about Shakespeare simmering at the time." ' He added: ' "He was incalculable I should think. I don't know how his wife got on." ' In fact, Dover Wilson's wife had 'detested' Cary as 'a very untidy Irishman'.[32] It seems that his Bohemian self was then coming to life, in the act of creating Gulley, narrator of *The Horse's Mouth*. Something similar happened in 1954, when he used four-letter words not normally in his own vocabulary while creating Jim as narrator of *Not Honour More*.[33]

Such scattered evidence of Cary's personality suggests that it was complex, and perpetually adjusting to varied situations which, in these years of trying to become a professional writer, must have been very difficult for him. He and his wife entered fully into the social life of academic friends. But Cary was sometimes teased about what in fact he did, for their friends were all actively involved in university life. If he felt an outsider, still he knew his wife wanted this life, and that Oxford offered the best advantages for his sons, who must now be his first concern.[34] His own solution to their financial problem in 1921 would have been to let their house and rent rooms, but the Ogilvies could not allow that for their daughter. By 22 November 1921 he would be writing of this 'wretched year': 'Thousands would be astonished or contemptuous to know that we fail to live happily on our income'. Still, he had to prove what his wife believed: that he could be a great writer.

What Murry is likely to have brought home to him, during their meeting in January 1921, is the extreme power of writers and critics. Murry was then the most influential English critic, who was promoting Lawrence to become what Cary called the period novelist of our time (as he said Charlotte M. Yonge was of hers). Both were openly planning to destroy English society in a way that Cary strongly opposed. It seems evident that he also opposed T. S. Eliot, for different reasons. But he had been intimate with Murry who, 'brilliant in dialectics', was vividly present to him as a person whenever any of his prolific writings appeared. These concerned subjects that vitally interested Cary, being treated in ways with which he could often sympathize, but emanating from a personality as strongly divided between feeling and intellect as the one with which Murry most identified: Dostoevsky's. Cary was trying to understand his own split mind through the great Russian writers – who had influenced Murry and Lawrence to become confused, antipodal, English revolutionaries. It is not surprising, therefore, that Cary's works can be read as an answer to Murry – and almost a plea to Murry to understand. He certainly remained bitter against Murry for the personal reasons already mentioned,[35] and probably despised himself for doing so. It would be understandable therefore if he strove to shed these feelings by working them into his books, as the following analyses will suggest. He might indeed have hoped that Murry would recognize them and understand. They are more compassionate than cruel – in contrast to Lawrence's (and Huxley's) portrayals of Murry.

Murry's collected essays, *The Evolution of an Intellectual*, had appeared in 1920, and the very title might have inspired Cary to keep Murry in mind when writing of his own evolution, as Murry's opposite. The most obvious example is Cary's story 'A Hero of Our Time', as a comment on Murry's essay of that title. Cary certainly echoed the essay, 'The Honesty of Russia', where Murry says Russian novelists answer the question, 'is life worth living?' by saying that one must live it wholly. Cary went on to discover why the Russians' split minds made living 'wholly' difficult. Murry's fondness for the word 'drunk' was shared by Cary, and also his observations regarding a 'tyranny of names', which he says Plato discovered and was sometimes 'drunk' with.[36] There are many similar hints that Cary reacted to these essays.

Murry's opening essay, 'The Sign-Seekers', is the most significant. Writing it in October 1916, he says that the war has made men aware that 'a religious sense is at work in the world', and that for this reason:

> The writer faces an incalculable future, and he should begin to ask himself whether the inherited armoury will serve his turn. What is this 'novel' and what shall he do with it? Shall he make an advance on Tolstoi and Dostoevsky? Shall he forge some new combination out of the spiritual awareness of the great Russians and the social security of the great Englishmen? . . . In other words, is not the growing spiritual awareness also a premonition of the end of a social order which has been the framework of English literature since the Civil Wars?[37]

These words anticipate what Cary set out to do. The opening of *The Horse's Mouth* possibly gives his most direct answer to Murry, who was not only one of 'The Sign-Seekers' as a literary critic, but also as a superstitious man.[38] Gulley is about to borrow from friends, to whom he already owes more money than they can afford. Then the sun strikes the signboard of the Eagle and Child. 'A sign', Gulley thinks: the barmaid Coker, who is 'in trouble', is the one who will show sympathy. So Cary reveals his mother and child theme and his theme of goodness, which is proved to exist (as Cary knew of Murry) by the way people use it; and he directs Murry, of all readers, to see, as the whole book illustrates, that any 'new combination' for a social order should take this mother-child relationship as its basis.

If such ideas began germinating in 1921, as a result of Murry's influence, it is perhaps not surprising that the last story 'by Thomas Joyce' appeared in 1923, when Cary thought himself 'round the corner' and seeing his way 'more clearly' (p. 91); nor that the story, 'Not Wholly Matrimony', concerns an intellectual woman who almost breaks up a marriage.[39] She talks perpetually to the intellectual wife about Russian literature, and is analysing *The Brothers Karamazov* while writing a novel. Such use of personal reflections and aims (howbeit, *à rebours*) did not satisfy magazine editors, and ceased to satisfy Cary, but the story illustrates how his later work was born.

'The Uncle' is a story of 1921[40] which shows how Cary began digging up his foundations after Murry's visit; it also appears to be the seed from which *Castle Corner* grew. For this uncle is a struggling clerk in England, who fulfils a lifelong dream by visiting his distant relatives, the Dagnalls, of Killyban Castle, Donegal. He finds that the Castle is mortgaged and the family in debt, but that the Squire expects his beautiful daughter Helen to make a successful marriage, if he can borrow £1,000. He borrows – without realizing it is all he has – from the uncle, who lends chiefly because he is sorry that the plain younger daughter, Bridget, is to lose her inheritance to Helen. The loan has been a gentleman's agreement because the Squire's sense of honour would otherwise be offended. But in the end Bridget laughs at the uncle as 'the only Dagnall left', for actually expecting to be repaid. Cary condemned this story on 6 June 1921 as 'a bad yarn'. But as it was written following Murry's visit, refers to debts of honour, and concerns a Bridget and a beautiful Helen, it provides grounds for believing that Cary had Murry in mind when he wrote *Castle Corner* – though by then of course this early cynicism had been overcome by a far wider, more complex vision. 'The Uncle' also introduces plain and pretty sisters, who appear repeatedly in Cary's novels, to illustrate how profoundly the gift of beauty, or lack of it, affects a woman's life.

Cary's intense interest in names is already apparent. In about 1918 he had noted that, by giving characters labels – such as 'Trifle' – for names, the old playwrights cheated people into supposing they understood characters.[41] Nevertheless, Cary's longest-used notebook contains lists and sets of names, which he intended to be suggestive of character, and lists appear in other notebooks.[42]

In about 1922 he was showing his interest in the etymology of names, by creating a Professor of Etymology, who applies this interest to the study of characters. The story Cary began building around this Professor is called 'Ars Amoris', and a note reads: 'enquiring into love (extracts from old book & Mrs A. G. book)'.[43] Though Cary's treatment is light-hearted, this unfinished story points to a serious interest, and suggests that the 'old book' concerned the meaning of names. Reasons for supposing that this may have been Charlotte M. Yonge's book on names have already been given (ch. one, n. 23). What makes Miss Yonge's book most relevant to Cary's theme is that she stresses the historical significance of nomenclature, particularly in connexion with the Reformation. As Cary's writing became, essentially, an exploration into the nature and effects of the Reformation, it would have fitted his scheme perfectly to adopt a symbolism of names, as they relate to the Reformation. Moreover, their etymology produces a symbolism rooted in Reality, which was Cary's aim. This would be a method quite different from Blake's, as Cary says his was (p. 3 above). It belongs to the common imagination and, as Miss Yonge urges readers to remember, it is popular belief, not the fact, that spreads the use of a name. Therefore, though the etymology she gives may be faulty, it has become part of the meaning of the name.

In 1922, the excitement surrounding the publication of *The Waste Land* focussed attention on *The Golden Bough*, to which Eliot refers in his notes. In *Aissa Saved* Cary shows his reaction to *The Waste Land*, and also uses names as if illustrating such truths in *The Golden Bough* as the part played by names in primitive psychology.[44] Cary had first-hand experience of this in Africa, and could not fail to see that his theory about 'A Child's Religion' is upheld by the similarity between a child's and a savage's attitude to names. The habit in modern western society, of regarding names as mere labels, is actually a development of protestantism, and coincides with the loss of religious and family feeling. It probably also reflects our wish to suppress such feelings. The revival of the feelings attached to names is an obvious step, therefore, towards reviving those feelings, and one which Cary is likely to have recognized, as a valuable way of understanding more about our primitive nature. Proof of this intention is the way he shows, in *An American Visitor*, that blindness regarding the significance of names, especially nicknames, actually causes his hero's death (p. 163 below). His last novels stress the power of names in ways that justify the emphasis on name symbolism in this study.[45]

If Cary ever attached symbolic significance to the initials J. C. – as being those of Jesus Christ and Julius Ceasar, and also those under which he himself chose to write – that would suffice to explain why these initials appear significantly in *Castle Corner*, having first appeared in reverse, with equal significance, in 'Cock Jarvis'. The best reason for supposing that Cary intended such symbolic significance will be found in the last novel, where the plot hinges on the coincidence of the initials 'A. R.' (p. 320 below). In common British usage 'A. R.' is the abbreviation for 'Advisory Report',[46] and this seems like Cary's final ironic challenge, to critics in particular, to recognize this symbolism, and also its serious implications.

For he is really pointing to the survival, in modern society, of superstitious belief in omens and prophecies, and to its danger. He illustrates this in *Except the Lord,* where the father's false prediction of the Second Coming turns Chester Nimmo into a communist agitator, having been influenced meanwhile by a dramatization of the famous Victorian murder of Maria Marten (whose name appears also in the first trilogy, but written 'Maria Martin', almost as if Cary hoped the mis-spelling would arrest attention).

Chester Nimmo, whose Irish surname includes the letters MM, will be found to owe much to Middleton Murry, a communist agitator who believed in omens, and was, as a critic, a 'Sign-Seeker'. If, therefore, Cary wove Maria Marten's story into his novels, in the hope that the coincidence of initials would be recognized as a sign, by all his readers, but particularly by Murry, his reasons would not be trivial. The murder story itself, of course, relates to his theme. Regarding the initials, he may have begun as a joke, then given it serious purpose.

Between 1922 and 1925, Cary used the initials 'M. M.' in drafts entitled 'Memoirs of Maurice Moody', whose educational background resembles Cary's. He is 'a citizen of the world' who is seeking his fatherland and eventually discovered to be Irish. Notes include: 'He says does not despair of civilization but thinks it is a long way off. How can we bring it nearer. By being a little less pleased with ourselves. By imagination. By teaching men of what happiness consists . . . of working very hard for other people. . . .'[47] For Cary, such a character would appropriately be

Middleton Murry's opposite, and akin to himself. The name can be taken to mean 'proud sea-warrior', which fits Cary with his love of the sea.[48]

However, the discovery, around 1922, that 'Maurice Moody' is Irish, may well owe something to the publication of *Ulysses*, which could also explain why 'The Uncle' seems associated with Cary's own Homeric novel, *Castle Corner*.[49] James Joyce seems indeed to have been the contemporary writer in English with whom Cary had most in common. Though neither might have been able to prove his descent from the Joyce 'tribe' of Galway, both treated the name Joyce as a kind of omen. By tradition, the characteristic of the Galway Joyces was 'merry' or 'joyous', and James Joyce thought his surname signified that his writing should express 'The holy spirit of joy'.[50] It should not surprise readers, therefore, if Cary treated his initials symbolically. He used the names Evelyn and Harry Corner much as Joyce used the names Stephen Dedalus.

Joyce and Cary were alike in attacking Christian dogma – above all, the glorification of suffering. Both came to see that the very landscape that a man loves – H. C. E. for Joyce – is a symbol of eternity for him. Both recognized, from personal experience, that the mother-child relationship is primary, and the human family the basis of society. Both had to come to terms with the loss of property, which would have made them members of the Irish land-owning class; the role of a father therefore became a chief concern, necessarily replacing the Father image as God or priest. For both, the artist became a kind of priest. Cary's sympathy for Joyce, in the personal circumstances that shaped him, is evident from a lecture. But he reveals a chief point of comparison with himself when he says: 'undoubtedly the deepest tension was that of his conflict with the Church.'[51]

They were alike in their admiration for Tolstoy, but Joyce's technique was less like Tolstoy's than Cary's was. Cary's technique, however, probably owes much to Joyce's, to which he actually directly compared his own – as he did with no other writer. His main point is that all writers feel the limitations of language, if they are 'struggling to express an intuition of life which transcends any possible symbolic form' (*Art and Reality*, p. 152). In *Finnegans Wake*, he continues, James Joyce invented a new language for his purpose, and then found 'he had no public ready trained to understand it. Yet it is beginning to be understood and, in time, will be common reading. For it comes from and goes to universal qualities of men and their occupations.' Here, surely, Cary has expressed an aim and expectation for his own work. He, too, cultivated what he called 'the serious use of the pun', and the 'orchestration' of words, as symbols, to overcome the time-lag involved in reading – where, he says elsewhere: 'Feelings that should be simultaneous in a reader have to be invoked in succession, and therefore become ineffective or false. Joyce's attempt to pack the effect of three or four different symbols into one word often has a brilliant success but, if it should fail, fails disastrously: I mean, it breaks the spell for the reader and jolts him out of pure experience into bewilderment or anxious inquiry.'[52]

This is the essential difference between Cary and James Joyce. It means, however, that readers who are satisfied with the 'spell' Cary casts over them rarely trouble to inquire what more he might be saying. He wanted to avoid being read 'as a kind of crossword puzzle' (p. 3 above). But that is what *Ulysses* and *Finnegans Wake* demand, before they can be appreciated as a totality at all. Gulley Jimson in *The Horse's Mouth* allows Cary to make his similar technique obvious, without breaking the spell. Thus, he calls his would-be biographer a 'biografter' (p. 135), a 'biograbber' (p. 138), and a 'biogrubber' (p. 276). Joyce calls him a 'biografiend', in a context that compares significantly with Cary's theme phrase: 'Life . . . is a wake, livit or krikit'.[53] Cary's symbolism and technique indeed resemble Joyce's in many ways. But it can be appreciated at a subconscious level, or ignored if the reader is unequal to it.

That is, Joyce and Cary as novelists seem to differ chiefly in their attitude to their readers. Where Joyce forces them to try to see the world through his own brilliant mind, Cary forces them to recreate his books according to their own minds and feelings. This fits his role, as a novelist in the Protestant tradition, who is denied a superior, condescending attitude. He said: 'humour belongs essentially to the Protestant sense of life. Wit belongs to authority, to courts, to the system, it is intellectual, logical, formal, sparkling, general in application. Humour belongs to the individual, the character, to the people, to the heart.'[54] Wit in this sense is indeed present in Cary's writing, as it is in Joyce's, but it is clothed in humour, so that it does not intrude upon the feeling of sympathy and compassion for all mankind, which ultimately became his aim. Like Joyce he came to introduce the songs and sayings of ordinary people into his writing and, recognizing 'that the ordinary is the extraordinary', to write of a world where 'The reconciling factor is the imagination, which, working through wit [but also humour], brings opposite ends of the mind together'.[55] Finally, the difference between them is that Cary re-found his faith in God, as Joyce did not.

The publication of *Ulysses* might well have been a chief cause for Cary's bewilderment in 1923. For it would have been likely to revive his own sense of being not only an Irishman, but also a Joyce – as much indeed as he was a Cary. So such questions as matrilineal descent, or the historical accident that made James Joyce a Catholic, and Cary a Protestant, would enter his mind, at the very time that he was facing Tolstoy's (and Lawrence's) challenge to Christianity, as represented in English, patriarchal, Protestant institutions. Thus James Joyce might have indicated the direction that Cary took. With *Ulysses* he would have revealed how much Cary had to learn – yet also what different forms a twentieth century novel might take.

Cary's development through wide reading can be partly traced from annotated books in his library, and from notebooks. He read frequently in the Bodleian, as proved by the Library Entry Books. The earliest relevant surviving Entry Book of the twenties confirms French influence on Cary, his order being for Sainte-Beuve's *Causeries du Lundi*. It also dates his notetaking from it – so illustrating one exact dating method used in this study.[56] Cary probably read books in the library before buying copies.[57] His notes often record a re-reading — certainly those made around 1944 (pp. 240–1 below). In fact, any books published after 1920 that influenced him were probably read by him around the time of their publication. But his studies were always balanced by his direct knowledge and observations – notably of the primitive, as cultivated by artists, as lived out in Africa, and as demonstrated in children.[58] His self-analysis was substantiated by his observation of his sons.

Cary's manuscripts also reveal how his novel-writing developed. 'William' was completed by June 1921,[59] but he apparently destroyed it as now untrue to his intentions. He was already engaged with 'Georgy', for which he took background notes from *Creative Revolution*, such as: 'the movement is throwing up its own intellectuals', and 'the deserts of Tolstoyan pacifism'.[60] The principal male character is Wicklam Tighe, who has 'smashed in greats' but aspires to write. Notes include: 'smiles at idea of killing himself. Not a coward. All I live by is that I can trust myself.'[61] 'Maurice Moody' followed 'Georgy'. A sketch of about 1924 concerns a writer: 'The father was the idealist – preaching love – Tolstoy etc.[62] . . . In this year he began 'Markby', for which a trial dialogue reads:

"But don't you believe in Christ's teaching?"
"You mean love one another and so on. Of course I do. That's good sense. But you can't be a parson on that much."
"Is this a Christian country?"

Robert could not maintain that England was a Christian country, but he declared warmly that if the Liberal party won the elections, it would soon become more so.

This led to some argument on politics, for Brian was a strong conservative; but when Robert asked him how he reconciled his faith with imperialism and war, he reminded him of Christ's saying, 'I came not to bring peace, but a sword'.

"Yet you preach the religion of love."
"If people won't learn to love each other, the worse for them."[63]

This dialogue is a clue to 'Cock Jarvis'. Jarvis first appears as a middle-aged British imperialist defending the institutions, religious and political, threatened by Tolstoyan ideas. As the above dialogue suggests, Cary's difficulty was to discover what tone to adopt. Thus, much of 'Cock Jarvis' rings false, though it is essentially tragic. Jarvis is a man for whom Christianity, as he understands it, proves inadequate; it does not dispel evil or injustice, even in private relations, and he is driven to suicide. At least, Cary intended this. But, as the above note on 'Wicklam Tighe' suggests, he could not reconcile suicide with heroism, and for that reason also he could not complete the book at this time. Jarvis's values are those of Cary's family. But because he was now questioning these values he was uncertain about Jarvis's age and role. He finally resolved this dilemma in *Castle Corner* by making Jarvis a young man in an earlier time, thus showing that his family's values were those already being challenged by the eighteenth century revolutions.

In England the revolutionary who most challenged these institutions in the eighteenth century was William Blake, whom Cary had discovered for himself at Oxford, and whose doctrines Murry was now beginning to preach, linking him with Lawrence who, like Blake, thought his mission was to reinterpret Christ's teaching. Tolstoy's intention was the same, and Murry himself published *The Life of Jesus*, in 1926 – giving it a more explicit title in the American edition: *Jesus, Man of Genius*. All these men were in fact concerned with the Christian attitude to sex, which is centred on the faith that the ideal Mother, the Mother of Jesus, was a Virgin. It is not surprising to find, therefore, recurring in the many versions of 'Cock Jarvis', a situation recognizable as that of the Christ story. This inspiration, notably of Jesus as an illegitimate child, persists throughout Cary's work – most obviously in the second trilogy, where the paternity of Nina's children is made as nebulous as Christ's, and Nina, to both men, seems sometimes a saint, sometimes a Jezebel.[64] The persistent situation in 'Cock Jarvis' is that of an older man who contemplates marrying a much younger woman for the sake of honour as he conceives it, most often because she is pregnant. The young man is generally treated paternally by Jarvis, and is shown to be totally uncomprehending of Jarvis's viewpoint, while Jarvis is shown trying to adjust to the new values developing in the twenties.

In early drafts, *Jarvis* is written *Jervis*, which seems intended to be closer to *Jesus* in spelling, while the initials formed by the nickname 'Cock' reverse those of Jesus Christ, so suggesting an anti-Christ – a name that is actually levelled at Gulley. The occasion is a good example of the slow process of association by which Cary admitted he worked. For this period of 'Cock Jarvis' inspiration is recalled when Gulley says Hickson's efforts to popularize him in 1925 failed because of the General Strike, when his publicity agent was converted, and 'wrote that in his real opinion I was anti-Christ, and one of the chief causes of the decadence of British youth'. He then describes a friend who, painting girls on magazine covers to support his family, 'looks just like St. Lawrence frying over a slow fire' (*The Horse's Mouth*, p. 135). The words hint at Cary's own agony during these years, regarding the temptation to produce popular stories, and also a sense of kinship with Lawrence. In some drafts Jarvis's first name is actually Lawrence;[65] Jimson also appears as the name of the young man responsible for the girl's pregnancy. 'Cock' as a nickname makes Jarvis a universal figure, in whom Cary could well be demonstrating D. H. Lawrence's likely behaviour, if born into

Jarvis's circumstances. Harry and Hal appear as first names for both Jarvis and his young betrayer, each also recognizably Cary's own imperialist self. Since the initials for Cock Jarvis also reverse those of Joyce Cary, they fittingly stand for the imperialist against whom the writer rebelled.

In an early version, Jarvis is the 'conqueror' of Daji.[66] He has been 'a suffragette when even female suffragettes were thought extraordinary', believing women deserve full citizenship, including 'the right to fight'. He seems a platonist in a Spartan sense. In considering the Trinity 'a perfectly absurd and useless' doctrine, he implies a rejection of the trinity of father, mother, and child, which accords with his bachelorhood. He calls Christ his captain, whose most 'common-sense' saying – 'He that saves his life shall lose it' – means 'if you think of keeping alive, you'll never be alive at all'. These words answer Murry's reiterated critical comment (developed in *Aspects of Literature,* 1920): that poetry is concerned with the one real question: 'what shall I do to be saved?'[67] In this version the apparent worship of Stella Ranken persuades Jarvis to propose marriage, before learning that 'she wants a husband pretty badly', having been involved in a scandal as an adulteress. Jarvis wants revenge, swearing, 'What she deserves is to have her nose smashed' to 'spoil her beauty'.

Lawrence advocates nose-smashing and Gulley calls his impulse to punch Sara's nose 'platonic' (p. 95 above). This suggests that Cary had recognized Lawrence as a platonist, and also that platonic ideals foster false sentiments, which readily collapse. This could be Cary's explanation of the confused feelings regarding women confessed to by Murry as an ardent platonist.[68]

Cary's point (which relates to women's emancipation) is apparently that there is no revenge Jarvis can take against this girl. He begins to fear that his old code will no longer work, and this version ends with his acceptance of humiliation; an old man passed over in the service, who can say to a junior, ' "Dear old boy, are you saved?" ', which is the exact opposite of his previous interpretation of Christ's message. He claims to have reached bed-rock, with his 'feet on Christ'. Therefore his famous exploit (repeated in subsequent versions) of apparently walking on the water (crossing a dangerous river by submerged stepping-stones) seems intended to recall Jesus walking on the Sea of Galilee, and to show how miraculous-seeming behaviour becomes attributed to heroes, as gods. The most striking of other Biblical associations

running through these manuscripts concerns Judas and a last
supper (which gains in meaning from Lawrence's 'last supper'
with Murry (p. 97 above).

In a version of about 1928, Jarvis is shown, at the age of forty-
five, infatuated with a girl of eighteen, here named Nancy Collett.
The change of name appears to coincide with Cary's intuition of
grace, her name *Nancy* being derived from *Hannah,* which means
'God has favoured me' – that is 'grace'. Jarvis actually quotes a
poem about her 'exceeding grace'. The girl seems a more sympathetic character as Nancy.[69] But, being of the '1920-25 model',
she is unsure whether she should ridicule or admire Jarvis. (This
is Cary's essential point regarding the twenties: that values were
in conflict, and youth lacked direction, in forming values for
themselves.) Jarvis, clearly 'the old conservative', loves Nancy
with 'the tenderness of a father and the passion of an old rake'.
Then he learns that she is illegitimately pregnant: 'It's a bloody
lie – said Jarvis to himself, trembling; and immediately found
some other voice saying within him "Never mind if it isn't –
if she's in a mess so much the better for you. You can pick her
up. She's yours – and how grateful she'll be" '. This is more or
less Blake's interpretation of Joseph's attitude, and anticipates
Chester's marriage to Nina in the second trilogy. Another scene
of this date shows Jarvis insisting that Nancy's lover must marry
her, with Nancy retorting that hers is not such a 'terrible position',
as he says, and that it is 'humiliating' for a girl to marry a man
who does not love her. She insists that her condition '*is* her fault',
and 'she must do what she can to save the situation'.[70]

This idea of taking responsibility to save a situation contrasts
with that of saving one's soul, as well as with Jarvis's secret
thoughts, just quoted. Since, by 1928, Cary appears already to
have 'The Revolution of the Women' in mind, it is appropriate
here to seek his meaning in that article, where he says it has
resulted in a 'renascence of the family'. The implication is that
women are responding to a dictate of nature, in revolt against the
Western patriarchal system. The young men revolting against this
system, in the name of freedom, are really resisting this pressure
of Nature as fiercely, in their own way, as the Victorians had.
Thus, in a version of 'Cock Jarvis' of about 1930, the young man
(here called Jimson) expresses his contempt for Jarvis's chivalric
marriage with the words: ' "My God, to be caught by that old
trick, the silly old goat. She played it on me but I wasn't having

any. Well, I can wash my hands of her now, that's one good thing." '[71]

Another version shows Nancy urging the young man who, as Thompson, here wants to marry her, that she will do so, if he will concede that Jarvis is a great and noble man. Thompson, however, while agreeing that Jarvis has helped him, says: 'But it's no good being sentimental about him. Especially when you've got this extraordinary notion that he's a sort of demigod.'[72] She then expresses loathing for his refusal to understand anyone finer than himself; Jarvis's help has evoked only hatred in Thompson, and the desire to besmirch his name, as a way of respecting himself (cf. p. 25 above). However, Nancy's offer to marry Thompson to establish Jarvis's honour is as false and fatal as the situation where he offers to save hers. But the girl finds herself unhappy with an old husband, and the young man, visiting them, accuses Jarvis of cruelty towards her. Even if she leaves him, she will feel guilty, solely because he has been kind. Jarvis understands the situation, feels fatherly affection for the young man, and tries to explain his feelings, but he is met by indifference and lack of sympathy. So his pride rebels, and he demands his wife back. She and her young lover say they appreciate Jarvis's goodness and generosity, but Jarvis complains: ' "Giving everything and getting nothing. . . . What do I get out of it?" ' She retorts: ' "But what is there to get?" '[73] This directly comments upon 'life is a gift', as Cary's theme phrase.

If this last version of 'Cock Jarvis' is read with both *An American Visitor* and the second trilogy in mind, it can be seen how both grew from this situation. In the former the man whom Marie is treating as 'a sort of demigod' (having brought about his death) is Bewsher, a man of an old landowning family in Somerset (where the original Castle Cary is situated, and where Cary's father now lived). In the latter, Nina defends Chester Nimmo as a great man, yet shows him to be truly Machiavellian by her use of brackets. Machiavelli was the political writer who most interested Cary,[74] and his influence on English politics from the time of Elizabeth, in relation to men like Jim Latter, gives breadth to Cary's notes regarding the bourgeois age destroying the aristocratic.

The second trilogy shows that the woman best understands the political situation. This accords with Cary's account of Cock Jarvis, given at that date: 'an honest and honourable man who didn't understand what politics was about, that it has to deal all the time with new problems, with an everlasting revolution. And that it hasn't any final answer, any blueprint. . . .'[75] This is of course Cary's polite way of telling his audience that most of them do not know what politics is about, since the majority would be stuck with some acquired blueprint. He hastens to say in this talk that Jarvis is not himself. This is indeed true; Jarvis represents the view of life with which Cary was struggling during these years.

He discovered the truth about politics, it seems, by living and working at home at this time, and recognizing that real government begins with a woman managing her household. As he wrote later in *Power in Man*: 'It is an odd thing that the mothers of families and the mistresses of households, who have daily experience of the real difficulties of government, of the management of human beings, should be commonly the most dogmatic and abstract critics of state government'. His explanation is that such women 'reason unconsciously like anarchists, who, finding love and good will in their own hearts and happiness in their own families, look upon all the evils of life as the invention of the state' (p. 104). This comes close to describing Tolstoy's doctrine. So it seems, from this passage, that 'anarchy', in those terms, was something Cary recognized in his own wife.

8. New Intuition

'There's a War On' became a theme title in Cary's writing around 1926–7. It possibly owed its inspiration to the General Strike. But Cary applied it more widely to the 'war' between generations and cultural ideas. By 1930, when he drafted the letter to Hughes already quoted (p. 46), he said in it that *Aissa Saved* was to be one of several novels in which each of the characters 'is convinced that his culture or philosophy of life is the only true and right one, and these cultures are therefore at war.' But it seems that this plan had just become clear in his mind. For it was around the same date that he had noted:

> The war of cultures.
> In Cocky, the chief point is the destruction of the victim with his diff. ideas by the uncomprehending and cocksure young. Whole trouble is adaptation of old material to this new theme.[1]

The 'old material' had been, rather, an exploration of the Christian code. A note of around 1927 appears to show the transition: 'Christianity with love is a *weapon* and a *stunt*.' Jarvis practises Christian forgiveness and 'it doesn't make any difference'; the younger generation is not even aware of the code, the modern view being 'cool, indifferent'. Yet Jarvis knows he '*must stick to Jesus*'.[2] The last words recall Dostoevsky's claim, that he would follow Jesus even if Jesus were proved wrong. It suggests that here Cary is arriving at his notion of the 'split mind of the west' stemming from liberalism and threatening our civilization.

But in 1926–7 it was the 'war' in Cary's own split mind that had first to be won. In 1919 he had said, when arguing against retirement from the service, that he would be a better father far away in Africa, setting his sons an example of service and duty, rather than 'as a struggling author, or clerk at home' (p. 89 above). He was still in fact 'a struggling author', without having produced a book. But he had fathered his third son, Tristam, in May 1925, and his fourth son, George, would be born in August 1927. His money problems were increasing as the world depression grew nearer. Yet it was in this conflict of family life that he found his theme.

He must have been struck forcibly by the difference between his notions of fatherhood when his first sons were born, and his feelings now, living amidst the practical realities that surround a birth. He had previously expected his wife to face the experience alone, and he might have been realizing that his former view belonged to a totemistic society, as in Africa, when he noted for his first novel: 'The women's war (ab[ou]t their marriage rights) [and elsewhere] It is dangerous for anyone to be present at a childbirth or what in Yanrin is called the women's war.'[3] 'There's a War On', as a theme title, undoubtedly had to include this women's war, which is a fight for life itself and for women's right to share in it, rather than an egotistical battle of ideas, in a war of cultures. The 'women's war', which runs through Cary's novels, illustrates the revolution of the women at this level, which family life forced him to understand.

For the real issue regarding Cary's career, and one affecting all women whose husbands elected to serve God or King in such climates as Africa's, was forced upon his wife at the outset: he had expressed the wish that she would join him in Nigeria. She had replied, on 3 November 1916 – five months before her first son was born: 'When do you want me to go out to Nigeria with you darling – I should be very torn between a husband and child – but I should want to be wherever you needed me – '. As the daughter of a typically religious, Scottish Victorian Liberal family, Mrs Cary has perfectly expressed the cruel dilemma forced upon women like herself.

A similar decision is the key issue in the plot of Cary's first novel, which reveals a religious experience that came to him three years before he completed it, he says in the preface. The experience occurred, that is, around the time his fourth son, George, was born. The baby was delicate and not expected to live. Aissa's sickly baby is saved by the Christian goodness of Hilda Carr. But Hilda and her baby die, because she believes she is needed by her husband – a missioner who preaches the love of an Omnipotent God. In the novel, therefore, Cary reveals his rejection of the creed that might have allowed his own wife and child to die. But he affirms his faith in goodness itself.

Around the time that George was born, Cary considered and solved this problem, according to a notebook entry: 'Is there such a thing as disinterested good on earth. Mothers and children.'[4] His later claim, that unselfish love proves the existence of God, seems to have originated here. At this time he also noted: 'What is the object of life, to do the right and know the good . . . To live richly (Aunt Doll, mother) no comparison of merits because no thought of justice'. In the same notebook he notes 'Importance of prayers . . .'.[5]

These entries seem almost to record the moment when the force of Cary's childhood prayer came home to him, as the most important event in his life. Here his theme 'finds confirmation and development in new intuition', regarding his own parents, his own changed role, and the relation of his wife to their sons and so to him. Above all, the memory of 'Aunt Doll', denied (like Mary Corner) children of her own, convinced him of the power of love to enrich life, with 'no thought of justice'. As a boy he had admired his uncle most, as he confesses in 'Cromwell House'. But he came to see – perhaps at this moment – that it was his small frail aunt who had all the strength and understanding. 'It was life itself she understood.' So that essay ends.

*

The New Year season of 1927–8 brought a great upsurge of work for Cary, according to such diary entries as: 'Start at once. Get the Ass finished and typed first. Then Davent. Then C. J.' 'Ass' clearly refers to *Aissa Saved,* which other diary entries show was near completion, in a first draft, by September 1928. 'Tottenham' is also mentioned with these notes.[6] 'Daventry', that near-complete novel written in Africa, had been judged 'no good' by 30 January, but became incorporated with 'Cock Jarvis' material in *An American Visitor,* where Bewsher is similarly sent out unarmed, killed, and eaten as a juju. Bewsher is also Cock Jarvis, for he is similarly destroyed 'by a young wife of what might be called the 1920–25 model, and her equally cocksure and ruthless young lover.'[7] With his nickname Monkey, Bewsher has also developed recognizably from the story of a 'monkeyfied Jew', (based on Raffalovich) and as such is a Messiah, but not divine. For the nickname stresses the Darwinian humanity of this saviour, and the notebook recording Cary's discovery of distinterested good in mothers and children also shows how he planned to write a life of Christ: 'At end of Daventry. Daventry delirious and sees Christ. At end of Iky – Iky is delirious and sees God . . . Jew Iky or life of Christ shew him born illeg.'

His religious ideas became greatly clarified between 1926 and 1928, through his friendship with John Macmurray, who was then Jowett lecturer in Philosophy, in Oxford. Professor Macmurray writes that they became close friends at that time, and continues: 'I am sure that I shared with him the ideas of which my mind was then full. These were the years in which the guiding principles of my philosophical views, as they were later published, were taking shape. It is quite likely that they had an influence upon Joyce, though he never said so to me, and I should hesitate to claim it.'[8] But *Creative Society*, published in September 1935, is sufficient evidence of this influence, notably regarding the relation between Christianity and communism, particularly if compared with *The African Witch*, published in May 1936. Cary possibly hoped that Macmurray had roused interest in their ideas by his highly successful broadcast talks, which concerned the conflict between science and religion, given under the title 'The Modern Dilemma', in January 1932. These no doubt confirmed Cary's views. But the great advantage was that he had formed them through long, personal conversations.

Something of what they discussed can be learned from Macmurray's published lecture, *Search for Reality in Religion;* in it he says that the quality of his parents' religious life was the most valuable thing they gave him, for it convinced him that religion had its own reality.[9] (This accords with Cary's childhood experience, and his theme 'life is a gift'.) However, when Macmurray studied Paul's epistle to the Romans as the tap root of Christian theology – applying the techniques he had learnt from his study of classics for analysing and comparing the texts, and ignoring the fact that they were the source of doctrine, 'The result was startling', he found; 'these great doctrines of the Christian faith just were not there', and had become attached to the text through what seemed to him to be a misunderstanding. He decided therefore that religion should not be identified with theology or 'with any system of beliefs'. By 1919, after war service, his aim was to eliminate war from human life and to rediscover Christianity, in the belief that the churches 'did not mean what they said; so that what they said, even if it were true, had become irrelevant.'

Speaking in 1965, Macmurray still believes that 'bad faith' stands between the world and the church. But he has always believed in the validity of Christianity, and ' "What is Christianity?" ' has been his basic question. In this he has felt an affinity with Kierkegaard, who wrote of ' "How to become a Christian".' When a conference of churchmen could not answer his question, Macmurray studied modern communism and sex to help his search. Marx persuaded him that idealism is a dangerous illusion, yet he was not convinced that religion is a form of idealism. For the Old Testament is not idealistic, though much Christianity is. He decided therefore that idealism and religion are incompatible, and that Marx's identification of them is a basic error of Marxism. Christianity became idealized when accepted by the Roman Empire, but idealist religion is unreal.

For religion is found in the most primitive communities, Macmurray observes. *'Religion is about community'*. It is centred on work and marriage – that is, communism and sex. Primitive man sees life as cooperation with nature, and dependent on the forces of nature. So religion unifies him with the world, as a personal world; the forces of nature are personal forces, and religious activities are aimed at goodwill for the world. They deal with community between man and nature, of which community between man and man is part. Of the sayings 'Thou shalt love the Lord thy God' and 'Thou shalt love thy neighbour as thyself', the second is like the first, Jesus said. Thus God and man make each other in their own image, and an immature man has an immature concept of the divine. Yet church and state cannot be separated, as they appeal to the same people for support. Indeed a mature religion is universal and monotheistic, based on friendship as a spiritual relationship, and making mankind a single community.

What then is the Christian solution to the problem of the universality of religion, Macmurray asks. To understand Christianity one must begin with the Old Testament, which Christ thought he fulfilled. At the centre of the Hebrew religion is the struggle against dualism, associated with class and kingship. The Hebrews prevented both by instituting the year of Jubilee, and by distinguishing priest and prophet. The prophet might be anyone.

The last sentence points to the symbolic significance of the Jubilee celebration in *Castle Corner,* and invites notice of the fact that Cary toyed with a pseudonym *Maidubi* (in writing early drafts of Sara's story); from Hausa, it can be taken to mean 'Diviner'.[10] *Umaru* in fact seems to combine *Um,* 'yes', with *aruwa,* 'soothsaying', and so to imply prophetic significance. It recalls Lawrence's role as a prophet. Indeed, Macmurray's arguments must have affected Cary's attitude to communism and to Lawrence and Murry in their efforts to found communities. But their problems clearly lay in their attitude to sex and marriage.

Cary formed views that accord with Macmurray's on all points in this summary. He too felt an affinity with Kierkegaard, regarding 'How to become a Christian'. (p. 241 below), and his writing recurrently illustrates that 'what men live by' is often confused dogma which they have never properly examined. How this confusion relates to his new intuition and theme can be judged from the following examples, which also illustrate the way his novels are linked by the theme in key scenes.

Cary certainly studied the epistle to the Romans, where justification by faith is expounded.[11] Paul says it brings the free gift of grace by Jesus Christ, and eternal life as the gift of God. He also says: 'For the woman which hath a husband is bound by the law to her husband so long as he liveth' (vii. 2). In *To be a Pilgrim* Cary hints at a confusion of this passage with Matthew xix. 5, in a scene that most obviously comments upon the split mind of the liberals.

Lucy Wilcher, a woman of the liberal ruling class who believes her own class is dead, has married a 'noble peasant' in the person of the preacher Brown. By his primitive religion he has virtually killed their child, and she has returned home. Her father then faces a dilemma for, as her brother says: ' "Our father had two contradictory views about women: one, that a wife must cleave to her husband at all costs; the other, that a woman, as a living soul, should have all freedom. Many of his generation held the same contradiction; they were Christians as well as Whigs" ' (*To be a Pilgrim,* p. 95). Thus Cary hints at the need to return to the texts, for in Matthew xix. 5–6, Jesus' words are that a man ' "shall cleave to his wife: and they twain shall be one flesh. . . .

What therefore God hath joined together, let no man put asunder." ' He is answering the Pharisees, who ask regarding the law, which holds only for men: ' "Why did Moses then command to give a writing of divorcement, and to put her away?" ' Jesus says Moses allowed it, ' "because of the hardness of your hearts." ' He is opposing his new teaching to Moses' 'command', which had been broken regarding his own mother. For 'Joseph her husband, being a just man, and not willing to make her a publick example, was minded to put her away privily', but was persuaded in a dream, ' "fear not to take unto thee Mary thy wife." ' According to Blake, the spirit of Christianity lies in Joseph's willingness to forgive Mary, who was a harlot.

This is the situation (suggested by Murry and Marguéritte?) that Cary explored in a key episode of *Castle Corner*. Here Cleeve, having become one flesh with Bridget, and soon to father their child, decides to cleave according to the opposite meaning of the word – that is, to sever relations. His uncle has offered him 'the cup of Socrates' in the form of a reasonable way of escaping Jesus' injunction. Thus the name *Cleeve* echoes the word *cleave* in its strange ambiguity, and highlights a conflict between reason and emotion, as understood from the teachings of Plato and Jesus.

These two scenes just described, in *Castle Corner* and *To be a Pilgrim*, concern the same problem. But the Christian solution in the latter contrasts with the former Whig one. For Lucy returns to Brown. As the material of *To be a Pilgrim* was originally for a sequel to *Castle Corner*, the comparison of these scenes is apt. Moreover, as *Castle Corner* developed from Cary's plans to continue the story of 'Cork Jarvis', it seems that here in *Castle Corner* he has told the Christ story, as originally planned for 'Cock Jarvis', but has split the original character into the cousins Cleeve and Cocky. Briefly, Cocky is the Christian, and Cleeve the Whig.

In *To be a Pilgrim*, there is in fact a scene where Socrates' teaching seems intended for comparison with the Christian viewpoint in the scene already described from this novel. The chief point of comparison would concern the gift of eternal life. For Lucy Wilcher's brothers say of their father:

'And look how poor papa clings to life. . . .'
'He does really believe in God – and heaven.'

'But then you would think he would be willing to go to heaven' (p. 75).

In the other scene, their nephew John Wilcher has been reading *The Republic* with his friends. For these boys straight from school are required to fight in World War I. *The Republic* gives a different flavour to the 'cup of Socrates', when it ends (in Jowett's translation, which these boys would have been likely to know): 'Thus shall we live dear to one another and to the gods, both while remaining here and when, like conquerors in the games who go round to gather gifts, we receive our reward. And it shall be well with us both in this life and in the pilgrimage of a thousand years which we have been describing.' Thus the title *To be a Pilgrim* is shown to relate to Plato as well as Bunyan, and readers are reminded that Plato too offered the gift of eternal life in return for self-sacrifice in this world. Cary's own viewpoint is unmistakable, when Tom says the boys' faces have the expression 'of those faces one sees in railway waiting-rooms, at once resigned, impatient, bored and suffering' (p. 245). For 'waiting-room' was Cary's term for any religion that treats this world as a testing-place for another. This fact provides his comment on the key scene of *Prisoner of Grace*.[12] Thus Cary condemned idealism of this kind, just as John Macmurray did and also William James (pp. 128–9 below).

Returning to Matthew xix, where again the reward of ever-lasting life is promised, Cary seems to have recognized too that there are contradictions within the chapter itself (at least in the Authorized Version, which has been used for all quotations in this study). For Jesus' injunction that men should cleave to their wives persuades the disciples that ' "it is not good to marry" ', whereupon Jesus says: ' "All men cannot receive this saying, . . . He that is able to receive it, let him receive it." ' Finally, when Peter says, ' "Behold, we have forsaken all, and followed thee; what shall we have therefore?" ', Jesus promises glory in heaven and everlasting life to ' "every one that hath forsaken houses, or brethren, or sisters, or father, or mother, or wife, or children, or lands, for my name's sake." ' However reconciled by dogma, the injunctions both to cleave and to leave seem strictly contradictory (which could explain why the word 'wife' has been omitted from the list in verse 29 in *The New English Bible*).

What Cary had in mind when letting Tom Wilcher call liberals

'Christians as well as Whigs' thus seems apparent. Like Christ's first followers, such liberals find Jesus' creed regarding marriage too difficult. Moreover, this fact had special relevance to the liberal Tolstoy, who built his moral theories on the fact that he, like most men and women, had 'abandoned the first woman with whom I had connexion', he says, and so gone against Christ's teaching, as he came to interpret it.[13] By this conviction, Tolstoy certainly challenged Murry's and Cary's attitude towards Marguéritte. So the many situations in Cary's novels that can be taken to illustrate or answer Tolstoy's belief in this matter, can be regarded as episodes in the 'book' Cary started to counter Tolstoy's moral theory. He could write it, because he had now resolved the split in his own mind, which had impelled him, too, to put the onus on his wife to 'cleave to her husband at all costs'.

Discussion of Tolstoy was widespread around 1928, the centenary of his birth. Hamlin Garland, for instance, wrote 'The Reformer Tolstoy', and recalled that when he went to Boston as a student in 1884, 'We were nearly all reformers of one kind or another in those days. . . . Mark Twain . . . had put into *A Connecticut Yankee at the Court of King Arthur* valiant side-swings . . . We quoted . . . Tolstoy to reform society. We made use of every available argument his letters offered . . . Now they bring back to me vivid pictures of the "Russian Socrates" . . .'[14] This essay fully explains Tolstoy's influence on evangelical Americans in Cary's novels, in particular on Marie Hasluck (p. 160 below).

By 1928 Cary may already have read 'The Light that Shines in Darkness', which is a dramatization of Tolstoy's quarrels with his wife, over giving away all their property to the peasants. Tolstoy was commanded by 'My conscience, God'. (See p. 331 below.) In Oxford, at this date, similar quarrels were being provoked by Frank Buchman, who also preached an Inner Light doctrine. His God required men to live by Four Absolutes: Absolute Honesty; Absolute Purity; Absolute Unselfishness; Inverted' appear around this time,[16] so indicating that Cary did his friend A. P. Herbert, and he began to plot stories under the heading 'The Buchmanites'.[15]

By 1931, if not before, he had read *The Kreutzer Sonata,* for that is the date inscribed in his copy. Notes headed 'K. S. Inverted' appear around this time,[16] so indicating that Cary did indeed begin a counter book immediately on reading it. He detested Tolstoy's bias, as so unfair to women, he said. All his novels could indeed be called chapters in an 'anti-*Kreutzer Sonata*', and the title fits the trilogies particularly, for both, like Tolstoy's story, end with the murder of the wife. What makes *The Kreutzer Sonata* most relevant to Cary's theme is that Tolstoy has headed it with quotations from Matthew's gospel, including xix. 10, 11, where the disciples decide, regarding a wife, that, if they cannot put her away, 'it is not expedient to marry'. Cary's interest would have been drawn especially to this chapter, because the divorce laws were based on the Churches' interpretation of it. Moreover, A. P. Herbert was the M.P. who succeeded in getting the divorce laws modified, as Cary recalls in his essay on Herbert.[17] Thus the special application of this story to English life would have been readily suggested to him.

Around 1929 he made notes from Freud's *Totem and Taboo*, including: 'F. says really know thyself'.[18] As those notes were found with manuscripts of the first trilogy, which has, on page one of Sara's book, ' "Know thyself", the Chaplain says . . .', there seems no doubt of its direct influence. The facts that Plato uses this saying in the *Phaedrus*, and that Lawrence attacks it (p. 94 above), are both relevant also. For Cary had set out to give the truth about women as a sex, in opposition to all three. Freud has been compared with Plato through the similarity of his concept of *libido* to Plato's of Eros, which is wholly relevant.[19] Indeed, Freud invites comparison with the Greeks by his choice of the term Oedipus complex to describe the son's love for his mother – and jealousy of his father, and the significance of this to Lawrence has been generally noted. The Oedipus complex, shown on page 240 to be central to *The Moonlight*, is central to *Totem and Taboo*, where Freud suggests that mankind, living in 'a state of nature' in small hordes, as described by Darwin, was prevented from promiscuous intercourse by the oldest and strongest male, by whom the sons became expelled from the tribe. Freud presents the following as 'A piece of historic reality':

One day the expelled brothers joined forces, slew and ate the father, and thus put an end to the father horde. . . . The totem feast . . . would be the repetition and commemoration of this memorable, criminal act with which so many things began, social organization, moral restrictions and religion.[20]

In the Christian myth man's original sin is undoubtedly an

offence against God the Father, and if Christ redeems mankind from the weight of original sin by sacrificing his own life, he forces us to the conclusion that this sin was murder . . . The reconciliation with the father is the more thorough because simultaneously with this sacrifice there follows the complete renunciation of woman, for whose sake mankind rebelled against the father. But . . . the son also attains the goal of his wishes against the father. He becomes a god himself beside or rather in place of his father. . . .

. . . At bottom, however, the Christian communion is a new setting aside of the father, a repetition of the crime that must be expiated. We see how well justified is Frazer's dictum that 'the Christian communion has absorbed within itself a sacrament which is doubtless far older than Christianity.'[21]

Freud is quoting from *Eating the God.* He also exemplifies the theory by:

Full fathom five thy father lies
Of his bones are corals made.

These are the only lines (apart from those quoted on p. 25 above) that Evelyn remembers from the performance of *The Tempest,*[22] which dominates, with sea symbolism, *A House of Children.* It seems, therefore, that this novel, like most of Cary's, owes something to *Totem and Taboo.*

Around 1939 he made these notes: 'Catastrophe must arise from separation between girls sentimental and sexual life – the toughness and abstractness of her education. Her hatred of men and fixation on men and her idea of *sexual relations as merely physical and mechanical. Her separation of them.* This arises from Freud and all the rest. Such relations are possible – but *the idea* must be of kindness even with a prostitute.' This novel was to show women 'enslaved in a scheme which *they accept* but which does not suit them'; it was to show 'the fierce prejudice against women's freedom', typified in 'a man like Cecil', who is 'religious –. a retired M.P.' and 'really frightened'.[23] The title was to be 'The Forgotten Women', which certainly springs to mind, after reading *Totem and Taboo,* as appropriate for a book presenting women as active, purposive beings, in revolt against a scheme that 'does not suit them'.

'A State of Nature' might be equally appropriate, and in fact Cary considered it, while writing *The Moonlight,* as an over-all title for what became the second trilogy. 'A State of Nature' had been advertised as the title by 1947.[24] It draws attention to points in the trilogy directly related to *Totem and Taboo,* such as the problem of incest, stated in *Prisoner of Grace,*[25] and fear of demons surviving in the attitude to the dead, evident in *Except the Lord.* In *The Moonlight,* Robin Sant outlines Tolstoy's theory in *The Kreutzer Sonata,* and Amanda reflects: ' "Yes, one ought to know more about primitive psychology. I did read Frazer on the Old Testament, but I've rather forgotten the general line" ' (p. 93). Cary's novels in fact illustrate that the central problem of the 'state of nature' which still survives in modern society is the killing of the father, mother, or child. He, like Kierkegaard, recognized the key to Old Testament faith in Abraham's realization that he should not kill Isaac.[26] Abraham is the God of Preedy in the last novel, who kills his child, and he appears to be the God of Harry Carr in the first, who does the same – cf. also p. 119 above.

Cary's notes on *Totem and Taboo* include this summary of a case, in which Freud explains how a fear or desire represents the opposite in the unconscious: 'A wants the child away in order to have wife. Later when he loves child, he almost kills it. The wish has remained, but in other circumstances.'[27] This note links with Cary's explanation that the primitive imagination combines opposite ideas in the same emotion. Since he said also that family life roots one 'in the real world of primary feeling', and admitted from the first his fear of jealousy of his sons, it is not hard to see how his imagination would have worked on this case, in order to understand the primitive feelings beneath his key title 'There's a War On'.

Around 1929, Cary was making notes under the title 'The Horse's Mouth'. The paper and handwriting for some of these notes match those of the notes on *Totem and Taboo.*[28] And the dominant symbol of the first trilogy gives its title to the last book: *The Horse's Mouth.* Cary says of it:

Gulley Jimson in his book is accepting the aesthetic God. (I didn't put any metaphysics in there directly; it's full of metaphysics indirectly.) When he says this is pure horsemeat, you see, the horse's mouth is the mouth of God, the voice of God

as known to an artist. Why should a man . . . behave just like
any religious maniac in pursuit of a certain kind of composition
. . . ? It doesn't belong to the mechanical world. It belongs
to a very mysterious world in which God, the God of beauty,
dominates his soul, his character, and his life.[29]

Since he says also that he himself came to a true faith through
the aesthetic experience, and since his manuscripts leave ample
evidence of his own struggle to achieve a certain kind of composition, notably with regard to this symbol of 'the horse's
mouth', it is reasonable to suppose that this description of Gulley
applies equally to Cary.

His early notes on 'the horse's mouth' include:

Conscience is simply subconscious + nurture etc. . . .
Inner light defeatist fears the battle.[30]
Must have inner light. H.M which says always give – give, but
also *suffer*. She is worried and *fearful*. ? Whether idea of
propitiation lies behind self-sacrifice and ascetic religion –
mortifying the flesh.[31]
Central idea of story is H.M. that inner light is inf. comp.
speaking.[32]
Must have shorter simpler story . . . with the necessary theme
clear i.e. horses mouth – trying to escape from the conscience
which tells to give up self . . . [next on another fol.]
Hor. mouth below the conscience
? if it could be the laws of sympathy, justice –
but these compete with greed etc. [next on another fol.]
The horses mouth.
The girl impelled by kindness, by sympathy which is of god?[33]

These notes reveal Cary's search for the meaning of his own
symbol. The suggestion here offered is that they show how he
came to imagine his symbol as having two sides, arising from
man's divided nature: one is rooted in the family and society
and ultimately tribal; the other expresses the creative spirit,
'which is of god?' The former appears more Freudian, and the
latter Jungian, so that notes seem to reveal the growing influence
of Jung rather than Freud, notably with regard to the *libido*. An
essay of this date on psychology supports the suggestion,[34] as does

Cary's treatment of symbolism in both *An American Visitor* and *The African Witch*.[35]

Cary's inspiration for 'the horse's mouth' as a symbol seems likely to come from Freud and Jung. In fact, Freud's theory in *Totem and Taboo* is based on a case-history that concerns a horse's mouth, and illuminates Cary's findings in every respect. It is the case of 'Little Hans' (that is, 'Little John'), who loved but feared his father, because he feared his father's attitude to his own love for his mother. John transferred his ambivalent emotions to horses, especially one wearing a black muzzle on its mouth, for the horse's mouth then reminded him of his father's mouth, with its black moustache. But when his fears became modified, John identified with the horse, and then John bit his father. Relating this case-history to others, and actually acknowledging his debt to James Frazer (as Cary did also), Freud concluded that all societies are based on this family relationship, and all begin with a system of totemism, in which the animal is regarded as the primal father. The ties of totemism become stronger than family ties, which are matrilineal. Moreover, taboos, says Freud, are still alive in our midst, being recognizable in Kant's Categorical Imperative,[36] while conscience derives from the oldest form of taboo. His argument, he says, can be treated allegorically as man's higher nature overcoming the animal nature, though for him it has historical reality.

Cary's self-analysis at this time found expression in a Freudian treatment of Whick Macarthur, who developed into John Brant, whose story ('Tottenham') became linked with Sadie Brant's in 'The Horse's Mouth'. Sadie became Marie in *An American Visitor,* and John Brant's story was resumed in 1939, to produce Brander in *Charley is my Darling*, and John Wilcher in *To be a Pilgrim*. What links the characters is their relation to 'The Horse's Mouth' as a symbol of the totems and taboos of society. The name *Brant* carries the meaning 'branded'. For the first trilogy, Cary's notes include the saying, 'Don't look a gift horse in the mouth' – or 'teeth', as he usually wrote – to signify popular awareness of the symbol. Meanwhile, he was using his own juju horse in *A House of Children* and *To be a Pilgrim,* and he later described this horse in his essay 'A Child's Religion', to support his belief that everyone's religion begins at the level of his stone-age ancestors. This view accords with Freud's in *Totem and Taboo*.[37]

The horse's mouth as a Jungian symbol differs, as already suggested by Satan in 'Bush River' (p. 80 above). It is the natural instrument for eating and self-satisfaction, which can be transformed by art into an instrument of speech and song. Here the many talking horses of mythology may come to mind. The idea accords with that of the *libido* gradually transforming itself, and Judy Coote conveys it in *The African Witch,* by saying: ' "I hate nature" ' but ' "I love what poets have made of [it]" ' (pp. 158–9).

Indeed, from Cary's notes on both Jung and Whitehead, it is not hard to see how he identified the *libido* as the creative principle in Jung with the principle of creativity in Whitehead, to form his own belief in the creative imagination.[38]

Yet the horse's mouth in Plato's symbol of the soul was probably the most powerful influence on Cary's symbol. Plato imagined the human soul as a charioteer driving a good and bad horse, and controlling them because he 'pulls back the bit from between the teeth of the riotous horse, thereby drenching his jaws and railing tongue with blood'.[39] This treatment of the irrational, identified by Plato also with the woman (in the *Timaeus*) is what Cary's writing attacks. Still, if Cary's symbol of the world soul is a horse, he has Plato's authority in the *Phaedrus* where, having spoken of the winged horses of the gods, Socrates says: 'without having either seen or formed any adequate conception of a god, we picture him to ourselves as an immortal animal'.[40]

All such sources of ideas are brought together by William James in *The Varieties of Religious Experience,* to shape what he calls a science of religions, and it is to this book that Cary directed readers for an understanding of his work. Around 1930 he made annotations, with page references, as follows. '513 Subconscious', where James says the subconscious continuation of our conscious life preserves a contact with 'science' which the theologian lacks, yet vindicates a religious man's belief that he is moved by an external power, since invasions from the subconscious do take on objective appearances. '518 Constitution of world' refers to James's belief that 'The world interpreted religiously' must have 'a natural constitution different at some point from that which a materialistic world would have.' He says 'only transcendentalist metaphysicians' think you make Nature more divine, 'by simply calling it the expression of absolute spirit.' This links with '522 Faults of idealism', which refers to James's condemnation of Transcendental idealism, which he calls the 'blind corner into which Christian thought has worked itself.' '526 Poly-theism' relates to James's personal rejection of an after life, and his conviction that 'a final philosophy of religion will have to consider the pluralistic hypothesis more seriously'. The last note might explain why Cary came to quote the philosophy of Samuel Alexander, in *Power in Men*.[41]

This survey may have conveyed to the reader something of the inspirational pressure experienced by Cary during the years it took him to complete his first novel. During this time, 'Cock Jarvis', as his dominant symbol, gave way to 'The Horse's Mouth'. Reducing the argument to its simplest terms, it might be said that Cary recognized the totemism still operative in imperialist ideals, and equally in any causes inspired by the brotherhood of man. The women's revolution, asserting the priority of family ties, would thus be a revolution against totemism.

His political ideas around 1930 are stated in an unpublished essay, 'The Pattern of a Free Man', which gives the background for the discussion on natural education in chapter IX of *An American Visitor*. It is inspired by a talk Cary heard at the Dragon School, Oxford, which his older sons attended. The speaker had argued that children should be allowed to develop on their own lines, and the discussion surrounding his talk impelled Cary to note: 'if this nonsense can be swallowed by very intelligent people what security is there for the truth.'[42] Cary's main point is that human education cannot be 'natural', like that of 'a wild flower', because even the physical hazards of growing up require care and guidance from someone in authority. This means, however, that a child, and finally each human society, is an artificial creation, a work of art created according to the ideas of some authority. Thus: 'a boy of natural cleverness, . . . can be as easily turned into a great criminal as a great judge or churchman; . . . of preponderant sensibility can as easily become a great saint as a great artist or philosopher; . . . either can more easily still grow into what is called the average man, a capable clerk or an honest vestryman.'[43] Here in its very essence is Cary's intuition of freedom, recognized as eternally posing this central problem: 'How is the necessity for authority in education to be reconciled with the freedom of the individual.'[44]

Cary stated the case, and his answer, most fully later in *Power in Men.* But it is already evident that he differs in his idea of freedom from those who see it as an escape from responsibility, and an 'absence of restraint', as old liberals maintained.[45] For him it is rather the power to shape one's own life, according to potentialities. Here a passage amongst Cary's manuscripts is particularly relevant, because it appears to have been copied by someone else, a younger person who is most likely to have been one of his sons. It is headed 'Fate' which, so the passage runs, '*does* control a person's life; but only partially. . . . A little man cannot win the high jump . . . And yet, some of the greatest men have been small. It all depends on how the little man takes life. Does he choose to say "I'm no good for anything," or face up to it, and say "Fate has given me life, the greatest gift of all, so I must take advantage of it while I have it'.[46] Here is an early clue to Cary's reconciliation of authority and freedom, by grace as a gift.

'Write a little book on religion for everybody – call it t[he] intelligent person's guide to religion.'[47] This note of about 1931 indicates that Cary had a religious treatise in mind as a background to his entire novel series. An incomplete draft of this date may be part of this proposed book. It certainly clarifies his religious ideas. In it he says that a religion is by definition 'a binding, that is, a gathering together of people for a purpose. It is therefore political. All religions containing more than two adherents are political.'[48] From Cary's subsequent writing, this can be taken to mean that what draws two people together in marriage is their religion, which immediately becomes political when they produce a child. The relationship of father, mother, child thus becomes the true basis of the human soul, as Jung implies.[49]

In this early essay Cary argues that the origin of all religions is the propitiation of a personal god, but that any evidence of a personal God has been based on the intuitions of saints and mystics, which may prove to be nothing more than 'a condition of morbid nervous excitement in themselves', according to modern psychology. There are innumerable personal, propitiatory religions. They tend to become ethical, however. In doing so they become more alike, in devotion to one god of truth, beauty and goodness. Whitehead has called this God the 'valuation of the world', but such a definition does not satisfy human feelings. For, though a religion need not have a god, it does need a ritual and an object of personal devotion. He writes: 'Christ combined both these qualities in one, for Christianity, with great value. But even if the divine side of Christ be given up, as doctrine, he remains as an object of devotion; perhaps even more efficacious than he was before, as god.'

This draft-essay leaves no doubt that Cary did not regard Jesus Christ as God. His view of Christianity is summed up in these notes:

> Christianity / Christs message of love good very good – it *creates* the keenest happiness and also serves internationalism (politically good) But his godship bad because of theological implications and complications. The idea of god derived from Christianity very bad – i.e. the cruel legal god.
> The idea of world as waiting or testing place bad.
> Most of his political statements (goods in common) etc bad because impoverishing life and spiritual life.
> Property is the body of a political spirit.[50]

At the end of his life Cary looked back on these formative years in his essay 'My Religious History'. In it he says that 'somewhere in the twenties' he discovered that even according to orthodox theology God's power is limited; Aquinas lists nine things God cannot do. Thus words like 'Almighty', 'All-powerful', to which Cary had been accustomed from childhood, are used deceitfully. What of God's Omnibenevolence? On this point, to judge from his notebooks, Cary learned most from psychology and anthropology, and found his ideas clarified by an article that he read soon after its publication in October 1927. The article, by Leon Roth, entitled 'The Goodness of God',[51] considers the relationship between religion and morality: how do we know that God is good, since the fact is not implicit in His divinity? Religious experience falls into two parts: one rational, which is moralizing; the other non-rational, which is awesome and numinous. These two parts supply the terms of the propositions Goodness and God. Anthropology teaches that the most constant factor in religion is awe of the numinous, or mana, as a mysterious energy or force 'altogether distinct from physical power, which acts in all kinds of ways for good and evil'. Goodness is a value formed from 'an original and distinct intuition', experienced within ourselves. The personal experience of these two intuitions, one religious and the other moral, are facts having absolute validity for the person concerned, and can no more be denied than colour can be denied by a colour-blind man. But the problem, says Roth, is that there is no third intuition that the numinous is good, which is the basis of holy and ethical religion. Such a religion is not based on intuition but on inference, following a long process of rationalization that goes beyond the merely moral, and introduces the idea of an ideal, impartial observer in any quarrel. The voice of conscience is in fact the opinion of an impartial third party, which becomes an ideal centre in relation to which all particular points of view disappear. It is God who can alone be the impartial observer. This argument does not prove God's existence, but His relation to goodness. God is not impartial because He is good, but good because He is impartial, and to ask how God becomes impartial is to ask how god becomes God. Religion is the moralizing of the numinous, by which the 'numen' becomes a 'nomen', and the awesome power becomes a Universal Father.

The reader will recognize that the two intuitions Cary describes from his own childhood, in the preface to *A House of Children* (p. 18 above), accord perfectly with Roth's argument. *Aissa Saved* can be understood in terms of the split between such intuitions of power and goodness in minds like Tolstoy's, and the way the split is reconciled in Western society can be understood from the manner in which their pupils emulate the Carrs (p. 152 below). Mrs Carr becomes the Christ-like figure sacrificed to Carr's Omnipotent God. For, though all intuitions have validity for the person concerned, the danger remains of making the false inference described by Roth, according to the animistic impulse to omnipotence that remains typical of all children, as of primitive men. From the first to last, the preachers in Cary's novels cause tragedy by persuading people to believe in the God whom they regard as all-good and all-powerful, but who, in the last analysis, can only be a construct of their own minds. 'There's a War On', therefore, implies the battle between rival intuitions of power and of goodness, as well as the rivalry between power and goodness in the individual.

But where Roth assumes that by 'good' one means 'just' or 'impartial', Cary reveals that for him 'good' primarily describes an aesthetic experience. For he has noted beside Roth's words: 'Goodness used ambiguously. There is direct experience of a personal delight which is supremely good – but not "just" or "impartial" '. This comment elucidates 'My Religious History',

where he says he does not know when he first had an intuition
of the unique quality in aesthetic experience:

> that the emotion or feeling of beauty is something that has no
> rational explanation, and cannot be referred to anything else.
> What's more, that everything can be the object of the emotion.
> That is to say, it is an aspect of the whole world as con-
> templated in its essence and without regard to ethical, or what
> I then called religious value.
>
> Here was an emotion, a feeling, grounded in colour, form,
> sound, texture, which was highly personal, instinctive and
> innate. And it was part of universal nature, it was a fact as
> much as any other fact examined by pure scientists. . . .
>
> Moreover, this powerful and universal experience of beauty
> had no material use, it did not feed the hungry or discover
> facts. It was purely sensational, personal and delightful. . . .
>
> And I did not merely perceive the extraordinary nature of
> this truth as I had perceived the arguments of Kant on the
> autonomy of the will, I felt it and reacted to it. That is to
> say, it had the force of a conversion.

Then Cary refers to *The Varieties of Religious Experience,* saying
that in personalities like his own, conversion takes place 'by a
gradual exploration of a new and larger realm of experience in
which former intuitions which had seemed in conflict are
discovered to be part of one whole.' Cary's annotation on Roth's
article certainly marks a stage in this exploration.[52]
Between 1941 and 1944 he had been reflecting on the experience
while creating Gulley, and had written of it in the unpublished
'Sketch'. He could not date the stages of the development, but
'sometime let us say in the thirties, I perceived that experience
itself was my only question', he writes. So he came to think of
all experience as 'a personal experience'. Already accustomed to
the idea of goodness as something imparted by an object, and felt,
he now saw that colour was a feeling, and so must also belong
to a personality; that this personality 'must pervade, in some kind
or other, all nature'. Unwilling to believe in 'so strange and
enormous a being', he adopted a view close to Whitehead's,
'although in a more Platonic and simple form', with particular
feelings partaking of eternal types. He regarded the physical
world as 'the necessary machinery of this experience, the body

of this soul', which as Nature is 'literally the nature of the being of the universe', in so far as it can be measured. Because the word 'being' implies having a certain nature or character, he came to think of activity and character as the two essential aspects of 'being', which he described as 'activity' of a certain 'character', or characteristic activity. Because this character of being determines the activity according to fixed laws, it seemed to be mechanistic, and to leave no room for freedom. Yet Cary clung to his intuition of freedom, despite the reasoning that denied it, and he continued to search for an answer.

Until one day, when I was walking in the Parks . . . it struck me with force that it is impossible in fact in [in = to] conceive of personality in the terms which I had used, as a diffuse psychological character. . . . I perceived that by a personal experience one means something quite different from a psychological experience, one means something in short that happens not to the mind but to the self. When I had said before that the experience of colour was a personal experience I had failed to comprehend my own meaning which was simply that colour could only be felt by a self, and communicated by a self. So [?instantly], as it were, in the middle of the parks, I stood in the presence of god, not indeed the god of religion and theology, but a god so close and present, since he spoke to me through my very eyes, that I felt in a very true sense, my being as part of his being. . . . It was as obvious to me as the earth and the sky that all experience took place in the self, in the person of the universe, [an]d could not take place in any other way.[53]

This is the experience Cary was remembering when he returned to Edinburgh and spoke on symbolism in 1942 (p. 37 above). For in a notebook of that date, entitled 'Horse's Mouth / Aesthetic', he wrote: 'The forms, the colours, the fundamental aesthetic qualities are *given*. / They come from the *Horse's Mouth*.'[54] This was the aesthetic god who, for Cary as for Gulley, 'dominates his soul, his character, and his life' (p. 126 above). And if, as he said, he traced the experience back to his meeting with Raffalovich, he realized that it was this god of beauty who reconciled power and goodness in Raffalovich also.

At the same time, since *A House of Children* had brought him to Edinburgh, he would remember that in it he had written of Canon Potter, whose very voice and look had given him 'the experience of compassionate love; a true intuition of goodness in its own spirit' (p. 20 above).

So, when he finally published 'A Slight Case of Demolition', as an explicit answer to Prichard, the title probably had its usual ambiguity for him; he was convinced that Prichard was demolished. He could write that he knew beauty because he felt it, 'by direct experience of a datum'. And he could say more: 'that the judgement of goodness in a man belongs to the same type of knowing. I recognized unselfishness in the same way as I felt beauty'. For everything can be the object of the feeling for beauty. It is by this feeling that a man is made whole.

Cary's final message in *Art and Reality* thus becomes clear. 'For beauty is not only a feeling, it is also a relation', he writes. It is the relation between the intuition of freedom, by which man knows himself an individual, and the intuition of grace, by which, chiefly through his fellowmen, he knows God. Beauty is the relation between man and God.

PART II

EXPRESSION OF
THE THEME

9. The Novels as a Series

Cary outlined his plans for a novel series in 1930 in a rough draft that includes the following:

> This war of cultures . . . is now being intensified every year by the rapid organisation of the nations. Up to now only Germany, America, Russia, the English public school, the Jesuits etc. have deliberately set about this work of construction which has been carelessly and inefficiently performed by every parent and educator since before the self-invention of man. But soon the inefficient and with them the laissez faire school of the pseudo-Freudians, Russel[1] etc., will not be tolerated any longer. . . .
>
> I meant at one time to call this series of books of which several are in construction 'There's a War On', as a general title . . . since they all deal with this theme of war between incompatible ideals, between equal rights, and cuckoo values in the same nest.[1]

Cary obviously wrote his novels for the 'intelligent person' to whom his book on religion would also have been addressed (p. 130 above). Faced with events that were already making World War II inevitable, and with such doctrines as Buchmanism and 'natural education' at home (pp. 122, 129 above), Cary evidently wanted 'every parent and educator' especially, to 'dig up his foundations', as he himself had done, to discover what, if necessary, he should be defending, or constructing.

A letter drafted for his publisher, Gollancz, in September 1936, is more explicit:

> The history of the last century and especially the last 30 years interests me because I think I see in it a turning point or

watershed in all history. Roughly speaking, ancient history stopped with the war and modern history is now making a start which cannot be a false start even if it leads to nothing. Ancient history I call that which was founded upon the notion of supernatural providence. This notion can be traced not only in its religions but its sciences; in Adam Smith and Darwin as well as Jonathan Edmunden. It informed Gladstonian liberalism as well as the peculiar people.

This basic faith, as old at least as humanity, is now being replaced by the notion of man's responsibility for his own fate. The Faith is replaced by the plan.

It is true of course that the plan, whatever it is, involves judgement of value and therefore an ethical creed, which, not recognised by its possessor or rather its possessed, as a religious faith, is implicit in all the plans of its dictators. But the interesting part to me is that the creeds, whether communist, socialist or fascist, all turn upon man's responsibility for man. This in its present force of application is the new thing in history; a turning point.

Such a new thing of politics raises enormous questions. What is a right use of power, and why? Why should the faith of a Lenin be preferred to that of a Hitler? I want to deal in my books with this period in which real people, struggling with their problems of life, according to the ideas of their own time, are involved also in the sudden collapse or change of their ideas; and faced with these large questions to which most of them can't find an answer, except in the language of these very ideas whose disappearance raised the question.[2]

Cary, it seems, had a plan himself, but saw language as his chief problem, because all words are coloured by the beliefs that shaped them. One way of escaping this tyranny of words was James Joyce's, which Cary employed to a limited extent (p. 106 above). Another was the use of ordinary words in contexts that prompted the reader to question them. That has been illustrated with regard to the word 'cleave', with the name Cleeve echoing that meaning, as if it were symbolic (p. 120 above).

A symbolism of proper names is accepted for the modern poet who, 'deprived of sacred names, has in his use of proper names in poetry to lean very hard on latent suggestiveness'; so writes G. S. Fraser of Eliot, with special reference to 'Gerontion', where names suggest 'a plot, a background of information about the characters named which the poem does not, in fact, give, but merely leaves teasingly to the reader's imagination.'[3] This seems true too of Cary, and also Lawrence. *Women in Love*, says Moore, has a mythological framework; 'Loerke' suggests 'Loki' in Scandinavian mythology; 'Gudrun' recalls Siegried's wife, and 'Gerald is the old Teutonic word for spear-bearer, warrior.'[4] Cary's use is similar, but built into a system that links the novels together. Indeed, when he wrote to Schorer, he possibly hoped for special insight into his method which, in its use of language as a clue to form and theme, accords fully with Schorer's theories in 'Fiction and the "Matrix of Analogy" '.[5]

The meaning of names given by Charlotte M. Yonge provides a symbolism rooted in reality, readily recognizable by all readers, and above all in accord with this belief, which Cary stressed in *Power in Men*: 'Not merely the action of a great genius, but of every one of us, has effect upon the course of events. As we realize our ideas in concrete action, we make history' (p. 237). Christening a child is just such an event, as Cary reminds us,[6] and the most frequent, universal, given name is John – the name that chiefly links Cary's novels.

John means 'Jehovah has favoured' (Withycombe). Thus it perfectly expresses Cary's theme of injustice, and mankind's deep-rooted knowledge, despite any dogmas to the contrary, that a just God does not rule human affairs. The name also supports Cary's view that the basis of all religions is propitiation, in so far as the name expresses a wish. 'Little John', whose love for his mother chiefly inspired Freud's theories (p. 127 above), may well have inspired Cary, who created John Brant of 'Tottenham' around the time he read of 'Little John'. John Brant, in name and character, conveys the tragic irony of Cary's theme, especially if the meaning 'the Lord's grace' (Yonge) is remembered. For, by grace of temperament, John becomes a favourite and then a butt; a victim of his own grace and innocence, and equally of the jealousy and spite of others who, as Cary consistently illustrated, want to destroy anyone who possesses, or symbolizes, qualities they do not themselves have or understand. Every character named John in Cary's novels depicts a variation on this theme. The name Hannah, by its derivatives, does the same, and 'grace', attributed to Nancy in 'Cock Jarvis', suggests that even here Cary had this symbolic use in mind (p. 111 above). Grace is the name of the only prefect to show kindness to the small boys in 'Tottenham', and the headmaster feels 'disgraced' that a boy in his care should be driven to suicide. Cary rejected this novel, possibly because it makes his point too obvious. It is therefore a good clue to the series.

'Life is a birthday present' appears in a note of about 1924.[7] As an early expression of 'Life is a gift', it is also expressed in 'Tottenham', where John's tragic life is shaped by events on his eighth birthday. Names and sayings associated with 'life is a gift' appear in every novel, in contexts that reveal the chief inspiration of that book, and show its place in the series. It contrasts with 'Life is a battle', which directly expresses 'There's a War On', as a name for the series. The two sayings perfectly express Cary's intuitions of grace and freedom. His view of such sayings is clear in *To be a Pilgrim*, where he says of Amy and Sara: 'They had the penetration of innocence which can see the force of a platitude. Amy's "got to die sometime" has been on the lips of every private soldier since the first army went into battle. For her it was still profound' (p. 339). He in fact wrote in a personal letter, on 16 November 1948, to Graham Akroyd: 'Life is a battle and what has often sustained me under defeat or check is simply the old soldier's refusal to be beaten by fate.' At that date the battle was chiefly for his wife's life.

The saying 'It's a Gift' appeared in Cary's notebooks,[8] around the very time, in 1938, that W. C. Fields' classic film comedy, *It's a Gift*, was being re-shown in Oxford.[9] In his novels, Cary gives this form of his theme phrase an ironic meaning comparable with Fields'. Moreover, around this time, he began creating the characters Freeman and Gulley Jimson who, like Fields, tell 'funny stories' that always show them in a humiliating light, and their cynicism is due to a similar background. Even Fields' bulbous nose, the result of his father's cruel beatings, could have inspired Cary to use 'a punch on the nose' as a symbol of man in a state of nature. Whether or not Cary was influenced by Fields, consciously or unconsciously, it is certainly the nature of his art to incorporate such popular wisdom – as it was James Joyce's.

However, by this time Cary had come to recognize life as a gift from God as 'the person of the universe'. As he said in 1954, when prepared to speak openly of religion: 'I am obliged to believe in God as a person. . . . It is by His grace that we know beauty and love, . . . Without that belief I could not make sense of the world and I could not write.'[10] He himself probably had this faith, as well as his plan, by September 1936, when he wrote that man now realizes he is responsible for his own fate (p. 140 above). The notes that reflect his new-found faith appear to be those like 'Elation of creators', 'Elation of creativity', which accompany the idea: *Creative imagination the life. A man must have feeling of its worthiness'.[11] By the words 'creative imagina- tion' he could avoid the word 'God'. That he sought to do so, prior to 1954, is evident from this reply (of September 1949) when asked why he never wrote of God: 'I avoid the word with its narrow implications. But all my books are about Final reality, that is God. There is nothing else.'[12] When he did begin to use the word 'God', he qualified it with such remarks as 'I don't suppose any church would accept me' – which appears in the interview just quoted.

Cary's novel series is indeed concerned throughout with Final reality in the widest possible terms. But most readers have sensed a change between *Mister Johnson*, and the preceding novels, and seem right to do so, for Johnson's story grew out of the notes just discussed. From this time there is in Cary himself a new feeling of life's worthiness – drawn from the experience that was for him a conversion.

In 'The Revolution of the Women', which has resulted in 'the renascence of the family', he says: 'Such a phenomenon, altogether apart from its affirmation of faith, is exciting to the social historian because it raises the question what is behind history, . . . What is the mysterious power which, itself unseen and unsuspected, sets in motion these vast complex movements in society?' The 'mysterious power' was for him, without doubt, the creative imagination, with which he, as an artist, co-operated, in pursuing this theme.

As a social historian, he explained his novels thus: 'I take out of history what I want for my theme but then my theme is already related . . . to a general view of things, of what things have happened'. His themes grow, he continues, from this 'real history' – which would indeed be all-inclusive. But each book stresses a significant point. Thus, 'why this change in history?' is the question in *A Fearful Joy,* where his answer is that men 'need novelty to revive their lives.'[13]

His driving impulse was to resolve what he called, as the title of an unpublished essay, 'The Split Mind of the West'. It was written concurrently with his last novel, and gives the central theme of them all: that God is not Omnipotent, and depends on man's co-operation. A man becomes 'whole' by realizing that he is a free, reasoning, individual, in order to serve God, whose grace he knows and shares, through sensibility. Man's great temptation is to use, or deny, natural goodness – which is God's spirit, re-born in every child – in order to satisfy selfish ends (cf. p. 199 below). This essay contains a key statement to all Cary's novels, regarding the battle between scientists and churchmen. Neither can be proved wrong, he says. But the consequences of their claims drive men to reject them. Thus to regard men as machine-like is to make human feelings meaningless and unreal; and to admit the possibility of sympathy, in one unselfish action, is to deny the mechanistic theory. Similarly, to believe in a benevolent God capable of miracles is to believe that God would not allow innocent children to suffer; but to admit that 'every day some child dies in agony' is then to say that 'God does immediate and unjustified evil'. To argue that God allows such evil for a greater good is a fatal objection, for: 'this argument contradicts a fundamental tenet of Christianity, that every individual soul, not excepting a small child's, has a right to individual respect. To allow a child to die for some greater good is to treat that child as a means rather than an end. And that is not only a crime, it is a betrayal of Christ.'[14]

Here Cary is answering 'Pro and Contra' in *The Brothers Karamazov*. The novel series can indeed be read as an answer to this work, even more obviously than to *The Kreutzer Sonata*. But both their great Russian authors reveal dramatically the problem underlying the liberal crisis; that, at this turning-point in time, men like themselves have intuited that man is responsible for man, but cannot reconcile this intuition with belief in an Omnipotent God. For the latter is explained thus, says Cary: 'Mankind has always felt the unique quality of its own powers, and postulated a father or absolute god to explain them' (*Power in Men*, p. 45). In a patriarchal society, therefore, men are likely to find it difficult to concede freedom to women and children, unless they can find a new conception of God.

Several circumstances contributed to making 'Pro and Contra' dominate Cary's novel series. Chief was perhaps the fact that Middleton Murry identified with Ivan Karamazov, so that Cary could feel the situation intensely as concerning 'real people in a real world', which was his aim as a writer. Moreover, Murry's communist and pacifist activities during the thirties sufficed in themselves to concern someone like Cary. Conversely, of course, absorption with 'Pro and Contra' could in itself have led him to treat Murry as a kind of *alter ego,* regarding it. An inspiration to do so came in 1930, when a monograph entitled *The Grand Inquisitor* appeared, with an introduction by D. H. Lawrence. In it, Lawrence recalls how, in 1913, Murry called this story the clue to Dostoevsky.[15] Lawrence had then thought it 'rubbish', he says. But he now finds it a devastating answer to Christ, as 'inadequate'. The Inquisitor is Ivan himself, says Lawrence: 'the thinking mind of the human being in rebellion, . . . He is also, of course, Dostoevsky himself, in his thoughtful, as apart from his passional and inspirational self.'

By this time, 1930, Murry and Lawrence had found themselves 'antipodal' to each other – as Murry was to show the next year in *Son of Woman,* having felt the need to 'betray' Lawrence. Lawrence had died in 1930, and his books *Apocalypse* and *The Man Who Died* were then published. Public attention at this time on Lawrence and his writing, and particularly on his ideas regarding *The Grand Inquisitor,* might well have influenced Cary to buy a copy of *The Brothers Karamazov;* it was printed in 1930, and became a constant reference book until, as notes show, he wrote his last novel as a conscious answer to it. This novel gains greatly in meaning if Hooper the journalist and Preedy the preacher are recognized as respectively what Lawrence calls Dostoevsky's 'thoughtful' and 'passional' self – but equally as Murry and Lawrence.

That is, Cary's last novel brings his series full circle. For his first three novels also gain in meaning if read as a triptych, each in turn concerned with the three powers that Dostoevsky says hold captive the human conscience: miracle, mystery, and authority. This inspiration would have greatly complicated but enriched Cary's notes on the conscience inspired by Tolstoy and Freud, and surrounding 'the horse's mouth' (p. 126 above). It might also have been coloured by Lawrence's comments on *The Grand Inquisitor.*

Above all, Lawrence again reveals his contempt for the mass of humanity, who find freedom an impossible burden, he says, and prefer to bow down to an elect few. They want miracle, and find it in seed-time and the grain, which makes earthly bread, if received from the great Giver, seem heavenly; they want mystery, and 'The sight of a true lord, . . . is one of the real mysteries.' Finally, says Lawrence, they want authority, as ' "that which men bow down to" '. These three descriptions are exactly illustrated in Cary's first three novels. In the second, he even introduces Christian science, which Lawrence says satisfies modern man as a mystery. In any case, in 1930, Cary would surely have been roused to answer these words by Lawrence: 'Russia destroyed the Tsar to have Lenin and the present mechanical despotism, Italy has the rationalised despotism of Mussolini, and England is longing for a despot.'

The words 'captive' and 'free' appear for plotting and character-drawing in Cary's notebooks from the early thirties until the final novel which, as an attempt to 'rewrite' Dostoevsky's novel (p. 305 below), he entitled *The Captive and the Free*. It seems evident therefore that the Inquisitor's use of these words was his chief inspiration. This seems even more likely because he began a long poem about Christ in the early thirties, and Christ is said for example to have given 'Power which is freedom and they made him a captive'.[16] The poem had the tentative title: 'Hymn to the two-faced Angel: Freedom and Death',[17] which accords with the Inquisitor's account of Christ and Satan.

This poem developed into *The Drunken Sailor*, described on the jacket as 'a kind of Flying Dutchman', whose crew includes Dostoevsky and Tolstoy, and many other writers. The title of the earlier poem perhaps merged into the symbol of 'the horse's mouth', with its two sides, which could have far wider application. The later poem itself better fitted his inspiration for a world of 'men learning from men and teaching men' (*Power in Men*, p. 237).

For Cary the novelist, writing poetry satisfied his sensibility, just as writing treatises satisfied his reason. Any excess of feeling or fact, which had perhaps tended to overload his first novels, was thus drained away from the remainder of the series.

From the first, however, the chief clue to the novels can be discovered in the concluding words of his conversation with Lord David Cecil, regarding Form.

Cary: . . . the form enters into everything; and that's why I think the approach to a book, the time when you're thinking

and feeling it over, is so terribly important, and that's why I
think it's an advantage to me that my books grow so slowly . . .
    Cecil: Would you agree that the crucial moment of creation
in literature is when you first see the whole form for that
matter?
    Cary: Yes – you see how it fits together, how the form can
be embodied, and . . . it comes over to you in that form. . . .
It comes over to you and moves you.

In the following pages, therefore, the theme will be sought in
the form. The form begins with single words, as symbols, which
are built into phrases, sentences, paragraphs, chapters but, 'like
the movement of a symphony, do not have a complete significance
until the whole work is known. . . . the separate forms do not
possess their whole content until the work is complete. That's
why I call the book a total symbol' (*Art and Reality*, p. 103).
    Cary's final total symbol is the whole series, his whole view of
life. Understandably, therefore, certain words, as basic symbols,
recur. Besides names, and those words already discussed (p. 11
above) the word 'coat' should be mentioned. With all its easily
recognizable associations, it is Cary's key symbol in every novel,
for some aspect of authority. *Art and Reality* contains his final
comment upon it, when he writes: 'any wife knows the difficulty
of removing her husband from an old coat' (p. 73). *The Horse's
Mouth* contains the most sinister example, when Gulley sets fire
to the coat of a pushing young man with the comment,
'Vengeance is mine, saith the Lord. . . . But why should you
know' (p. 131). Quoting Dostoevsky's final creed thus, Cary might
be thought to have addressed Murry.
    Murry's last subject for literary criticism was Jonathan Swift,
whom he regarded as the 'antipodes' of himself.[18] But Cary
resembles Swift in many ways. He can be thought of as the kind
of man Swift might have become, had he left the church and
found happiness in marriage. While creating Gulley, Cary noted
in his copy of *The Symbolist Movement*: 'Fundamental laughter
of Swift, Rabelais', which the author of *Axël* described as a
revenge of beauty upon ugliness, Symons says. Cary seems in
fact to have directed such laughter against what could be called
the ugliness of *Axël* and the *À Rebours* view of life. And because
Swift's style was his ideal, it becomes reasonable to suppose that
he also adopted Swift's manner of attacking his enemies, as in

Gulliver's Travels. This may well be the best approach to Cary's symbolism. Then the coat as a symbol of religious authority in *A Tale of a Tub* becomes an obvious precedent for Cary's use of the coat as a symbol.

As already suggested when comparing him with James Joyce (p. 106), Cary's laughter is generally compassionate. But his writing is always likely to express irony. Enid Starkie says: 'he had a rich fund of comedy and fun, an eye for a ridiculous and humorous situation, and a delightful irony – that was the most Irish thing about him. This was sometimes of the *humour noir* variety, and, on his death-bed, he joked with the irony of a Scarron. I loved his irony'.[19] She also says, 'I never heard him say anything catty or nasty about anyone'.[20] He could of course shed any such feelings in his books, especially if they were veiled in symbolism.

His symbolism differs from Blake's. But in saying so (p. 3 above) Cary clearly wanted to draw attention to some resemblances. These apparently concern traditional symbols and ideas shaping our society. For the following interpretations are totally justified by Blake's preface to *Milton,* where he defends the Bible against the 'Perverted Writings of Homer & Ovid, of Plato & Cicero', and declares that 'Shakespeare & Milton were both curb'd by the general malady & infection from the silly Greek & Latin slaves of the Sword.' He continues: 'we have Hirelings in the Camp, the Court & the University, . . . We do not want either Greek or Roman Models if we are but just & true to our own Imaginations, those Worlds of Eternity in which we shall live for ever in JESUS OUR LORD.' For Blake, Jesus was the Imagination, and 'the giver of every Mental Gift' (*Jerusalem* f. 77). This inspiration must clearly colour all Cary's thoughts regarding the creative imagination, and his theme phrase 'Life is a gift'.

'Life tragic to the soul; to mind a joke' probably best describes Cary himself, as well as Gulley Jimson (p. 238 below) – that is, if all the ambiguities of his theme phrase are appreciated. His greatest strength is in character creation. But this can be fully appreciated only if it is remembered that he is really portraying the living character of one ever-changing world, which each of us knows only subjectively, yet is perpetually influenced by in incomprehensible ways (p. 5 above). For in Cary's view we are truly individuals – and in this sense free – only in our reasoning minds; whereas it is by feelings only that we know ourselves part of this one living world.[21] So, anyone we identify as an individual is really 'a highly complex parcel of motives and reactions' (p. 51 above).

This explains the complexity of Cary's plotting, which increased as he matured. It explains also the form of the following analyses where, (for the later novels especially) it has seemed best to interpret his theme by recounting the plot.

For his theme, as his whole view of life, is essentially the character of the world, which we know only through our reactions to such 'individuals' in action. His characters are indeed real people, like ourselves. That is, they have been shaped by characters of the past, and are being influenced by characters and events in the present. Thus Gulley is being influenced by William Blake, whose relevance to our time can be judged from the events of his story. This method is indeed the opposite of allegory, which Cary said he detested. But this means that his characters are also symbols. They build up, by individual actions, into a total symbol of the character of the world, just as the very words that describe them do. His major women characters in later novels can be understood from this note: 'Idea, the childish soul of the world, loving, curious fearful – in prison to the [?beguiled] rulers'.[22] But the idea casts light on the whole series.

Cary's series of novels reveals the re-making of his own soul, from the time he began to 'dig up his foundations'. His characters are all in some sense aspects of himself, but also in some sense aspects of the whole – as is true of all of us. Since a novel 'means what it feels'[23] each novel can be said to reveal what it felt like to be Cary, at the particular time in world history in which it was written. The novels as a series, then, symbolize 'that world spirit of our time in which all of us are at once partakers and creators.'[24]

10. African Triptych

Aissa Saved

An American Visitor

The African Witch

Aissa Saved

'April is the cruellest month', according to Eliot's opening in *The Waste Land*. So Cary might have hoped that critics would recognize a real Waste Land, when he described drought-ridden Yanrin, where, in April, 'villages were full of half-starved people . . . who expected to die in the most miserable fashion if the rains did not fall and the crops did not grow' (p. 30). Eliot had admitted his debt to *The Golden Bough*, 'which has influenced our generation profoundly'; so Cary could hope that his audience was prepared to read a book that supplemented that profound influence with his real experience. The tone of Eliot's poem is set by his epigraph, in which the Sibyl at Cumae, hanging in a cage (or bottle), declares, 'I wish to die'. But Aissa, whose name introduces Cary's novel, has been 'famous for her noise and liveliness' (p. 46), as a prostitute in the local beer-house, before becoming what the pagans call a 'Christian witch' (p. 58), and her fellow-Christians call 'the priestess of Jesus' (p. 173).

Aissa's name suggests that she personifies 'the childish soul of the world' (p. 149 above), in a form expressive of 'life is a gift'. For the name derives from a verb meaning 'to be alive'.[1] It is a corruption of A'isha, which is the name of the Prophet's wife, and Aissa can be seen also to mean Jesus, since *Ai* in Hausa means 'verily', and Isa from the Arabic means Jesus. *Aisa,* moreover, is synonymous with *moira*, in the oldest form of Hellenic speech;[2] aptly, therefore, it points to the way in which Aissa's Christian misson teacher, Harry Carr, is saved from shame and

150

dishonour, through the death of his wife Hilda, which the death of Aissa helps us to understand. And since this code of honour in European society owes much to the *Iliad*, the irrational *aisa* in Agamemnon comes to mind, as the chief instrument of the plot. This concerns his quarrel with Achilles, who had tried to avoid serving with the Greek forces in Troy by disguising himself as a girl. One name he used was *Aissa*, here meaning 'fleet', for Achilles has inherited fleetness of foot from his mother, Thetis, supposedly a goddess. Aissa in Cary's novel 'could run as fast and stay as long as a man' (p. 60). By her fleetness of foot, while carrying her baby to save their lives, she wins the reputation of being a witch who could turn herself into a bitch.

So Cary reminds readers of the way divine or magical powers become attached to real people, in societies comparable with those in Africa. Because of Homeric poetic genius, the *Iliad* became required reading for European youths like himself. But he might well have been asking whether this is any wiser than giving the Bible to savages – of which he complains in his preface. Achilles' refusal to surrender the captive Trojan wife Briseis to replace Agamemnon's captive, Chryseis, is scarcely an example to implant fine family feelings in British youth (and could well have accounted for his own attitude to Marguéritte, in a quarrel not wholly unlike Homer's epic).

The name Aissa certainly serves to suggest that 'whole landscape of existence' that Cary strove to present in his novels. But the numbering of chapters in the novel points to the Bible as the dominant symbol – as indeed Cary's preface invites readers to see. For chapter 39 breaks the chronology to report Hilda's death, and the outcome of the riots that she helped to cause. It also reveals the court judgement on the riots, which is given by MacEwen ('son of John'). He is said to have acted as 'a tactful friend', rather than as a 'go-getter expert'. As this chapter follows immediately after Aissa sees her vision of Jesus, at her first communion, it can be taken to symbolize the true Christian message, dividing the New Testament from the Old Testament – in which there are 39 books. This chapter also symbolizes the fact that Christ believed he fulfilled the Old Testament (p. 118 above). Lawrence's *Apocalypse* (published in 1931) revealed how far the attitudes of 'uneducated people', in a Pentecost Chapel, are based on *The Revelation of St John the Divine,* in their feelings of spite that the poor shall inherit the earth. This is how Cary depicts the riots, which are judged in this chapter. He ends it by foretelling the arrival of rival missions: 'the Original Apocalypse at Ketemfe, who preach the full Bible and the end of the world in five years, and the Mennonites at Yanrin.' By contrast, the message of his final chapter can be seen to make of Cary's own book his Revelation, through Aissa. As such, 'it comes over to you, and moves you' (p. 147 above).

Aissa's story centres on her intuition that her sickly baby, Abba, should not be destroyed as a witch.[3] Her mother love is recognized as 'a natural thing', 'common to cats, bitches, and hyenas' (p. 46). Nevertheless, her people, the Kolua, are 'surprised', and judge her uncustomary objection stupid and ridiculous. So Aissa, once a favourite, becomes a 'butt', particularly for children, 'who knew that she was funny because their elders laughed at her' (p. 47). Weak and starving, she is being pelted by children when rescued by Ojo and taken to the mission, where she and Abba are soon restored to health. So kindness, as the essence of Christianity, is demonstrated.

Aissa becomes to Hilda what Ojo is to Harry: the favourite pupil. These pupils fully understand their teachers' feelings, by direct intuition (p. 18). Thus, 'the scavenger carrying his buckets to the latrine frowned like a pontif (or like Carr) and stared before him with the rapt gaze of a saint or a Mrs. Carr' (p. 14). However, as converts, they are inevitably at the level of Christians in New Testament times, in their beliefs. For Cary explains in the preface that converts 'start, so to speak, several hundred years behind the old believers', for whom literal beliefs have become 'metaphors or symbols'. But the Church 'can't change the form of expression without offending simple people'. Harry and Hilda seem to be themselves somewhat simple, representing a sect called, descriptively, 'the Winkworth Memorial Mission', which has built a chapel and hospital on a site previously condemned by the colonial service doctor, because of its proximity to mosquito-ridden swamps. Cary explains this in his opening paragraph. The site, a 'high mud bank', had been chosen by Bradgate, the assistant resident, a 'sportsman' with 'an eye for views'.

So Cary leaves little doubt that Carr and Bradgate represent opposite sides of himself, in a novel revealing the discovery that some of his foundations were mud. The name *Carr,* differing by one letter only from Cary, is old Norse for 'marsh, wet ground' – whereas *Cary* means 'pleasant stream', from the Keltic name for the Somerset river where Cary's Norman ancestors settled. Thus the very names seem to question his purpose, in being in Africa. The name Harry, for Carr, comments on the missionary zeal of British Empire builders, besides questioning Harry Carr's wisdom, as a father and 'home-ruler' in that sense, in being there. *Hilda,* meaning 'battle maid', is well-chosen for Cary's first European protagonist in his 'women's war'.

Harry, in a cynical judgement, calls Hilda 'anti-ratonal', with 'no brain to understand', and with the typical religious woman's answer to criticism: 'What she felt to be right was God's will.' Indeed, 'Why had he married? How right the Catholics were to save their priests from that folly' (p. 25). The novel fulfils that near death-wish. But Carr's other, emotional, self is soon after, in a 'miraculous' moment, 'converted' to singing with her, and all their pupils, the hymn, 'a favourite at the mission':

'Yet He found me, I beheld Him
Bleeding on the accursed tree.'

Carr had been trusting his own intelligence, he reflects. Yet, ' "Trust God," he had told them; "take no thought for the morrow" '. So now, 'With what gratitude for her love and sympathy, for all God's goodness', he can hold hands with Hilda and sing, ' "None of self and all of Thee." ' They set off to take the Christian message to Kolu, where the pagans are holding a festival, to propitiate the local goddess, Oke. Carr finds himself praying there – in rivalry, the Kolua think, to prove his God superior to theirs, regarding the most primitive notion of miracle: rain-making. But Carr's Christians cause the riots.

Thus Cary comments upon the confused notions by which Rousseau, through Tolstoy, has caused revolution in the world, of which this African district is a microcosm. He may indeed be foretelling that Africa will become a chief world problem, and a target for communism. For Carr's behaviour depicts Tolstoy's split mind, as becomes unmistakable from the part played in the riots by Ojo (p. 156 below). It is Ojo (in his 'white uniform coat') who starts singing the hymn that converts Carr to go to Kolu; and it is really because Aissa wants to find Abba's father, Gajere, that the Christians, including Hilda, have started out for Kolu, without telling Harry, in the first place. It seems, therefore, that Ojo and Aissa, as their favourite pupils, know, and enact, the irrational, subconscious selves of Harry and Hilda. They personify the other self of each, just as the Muslim boy, Ali, does for Bradgate. 'He even copied Bradgate's voice' (p. 93), and Bradgate 'liked in Ali what he liked in his own sons' (p. 118).

The book actually began with Ali, says Cary in the preface. He is drawn from a clerk in Cary's administration, who had been trained in the Government school, and had learnt the lesson of devotion to duty so zealously that he had almost died for it. Ali does die, trying desperately to do it with the heroism he has been taught to admire. He is killed by Shangoedi, who had previously kissed his feet as a saviour and ' "friend of Jesus" ' (p. 89). Now in a position of advantage, she enjoys breaking down his proud, honourable bearing, and making him die in agony – as did Jesus, whom Ali, a devout Muslim, cannot bring himself to call a god.

In describing Ali's death, Cary depicts the two sides of his horse's mouth (or animal mouth) symbol, at its simplest level. It is in the way that he closes his mouth, which he knows to be 'one of his ugliest features', that Ali betrays his desire to die honourably. But 'Shangoedi, knife in hand, crouched over him, straddling his legs, grinning with joy, open-mouthed as if for a good meal' (p. 193). Finally, she and 'the mob, intoxicated by the long draught of cruelty, tore his body to pieces and even broke up his bones as if to make them also suffer. Many put pieces of flesh into their neck-bags for charms or philtres. For Ali had been a mallam. He could read and write and therefore he had magical powers.'

However, Cary was diverted from his study of honour and ethics by his religious experience of 1927–8 (pp. 115–16 above). By explaining this in the preface, he directs attention to the death of Aissa, and so of Hilda and also of Ishe. Each of these mothers dies with her son, in a way Cary clearly wants readers to compare. And the names point the way, for Ishe has the same derivation as Aissa, but Aissa echoes the name Isa, and so symbolizes the dilemma of this character, divided between two conflicting faiths.

Cary recounts Ishe's fate first, vividly. Her son Numi is selected by Oke's priestess, Moshalo, whom Oke has told in a dream 'that no rain would fall until the people gave her a virgin girl or boy' (p. 31). The headman of Kolu, Musa, warns Moshalo that, because Ishe's husband is a Christian, she will complain to the 'judge', Bradgate. But Moshalo retorts 'contemptuously: "What do you know about it? The mother has to give the child. It must

be a gift. So we need the woman too" ' (p. 37). So Cary introduces his theme phrase in a key situation. He not only shows the
danger of importing the religion of one country into another; he
stresses the pagan acceptance of the mother as the giver of life,
in contrast to her situation in a Christian, patriarchal society.
Ishe herself would not have been killed, except that her com-
plaint would bring punishment to her tribe. Yet her realization
that human sacrifice is wrong is something the English have
taught her. Her agreement to sacrifice Numi is achieved by
making her 'drunk', in every sense of the word, until, prompted
by religious arts, of dance and drum-beating, she finally sighs,
' "I give all – I give Numi." ' At this she is rushed to Oke's
sacred mound, pressed to her knees, secured with a rope 'in the
posture of adoration and sacrifice' and, the moment Numi is
thrust into her arms, his head is struck off so that the blood falls
on Oke's sacred mound. His death is a sacrifice, but Ishe, 'thrown
into the river', has been murdered in the eyes of her people who,
feeling guilty, 'hated the white man for it' (p. 124).

Aissa is next shown, near death, having struggled, with
immense suffering, to return to her child – and to Gajere, whom
she had married at Kolu. She has reached Ojo's compound, which
is the real religious centre for the African converts. In the midst
of Ojo's prophesying, Aissa is found to be lying against 'the juju
stool' (p. 134). Sara, a matron respected because she can read
and moreover has 'the authority of goodness', undertakes to
convey God's message to Aissa: ' "He put Gajere and Abba in
hell." ' (They are actually alive.) Aissa would now have died,
except that Hilda consoled her by recounting her own suffering
the previous year, when her baby died. Then she had felt com-
forted by remembering how Jesus had suffered, and felt it wicked
to have 'opposed God's will who had permitted her baby to
die. . . . "so that I had never been so happy before" ' (p. 147).
Aissa is revived, and Hilda 'did not need to thank God in words for
the miracle of his goodness . . . It had been revealed to her once
more what was the meaning of the grace of God" '. Exhausted
after her night's ministering, she hears 'the crowing cocks', and
begins reflecting upon her happy life with Carr, who 'was certainly
far from well', and should not be 'worrying her to go home when
he knew that he needed her' (pp. 149–50). She is in fact pregnant
again, and Carr wants her to return to England. But his Omnipotent God, who 'permitted' their first child to die from fever

(doubtless due to the mosquito-ridden swamps), had been merely testing their faith, Hilda would be justified in thinking. In any case, her religion told her to 'cleave to her husband at all costs' (p. 122 above).

Aissa now accepts the role of a saint, like Hilda. But at her first communion she sees Jesus in a vision telling her to fight for him at Kolu – where she will find Abba and Gajere. Carr, 'with a wise smile', decides Aissa's state is 'like sleep-walking'. But Hilda stays absent from her bedside for long enough to allow Ojo and others to carry her, shoulder high, as their saviour, to begin the riots. It seems that Hilda's subconscious wants a united family for Aissa, as she does for herself.

The next brief chapter, 39, records the court findings on the riots described in the remaining chapters. MacEwen 'exonerated everybody', and many think he 'had been affected by the sudden death, in painful circumstances, of Carr's wife, which occurred on the day before the enquiry opened.' The death of Hilda and her child, presumably in childbirth, is as much a sacrifice to Carr's god as Ishe's was to Oke. But, by the very contrast in the way he tells of it, Cary stresses the way in which Europeans cover up such signs of their still primitive beliefs. By the break in the chronology, however, the reader senses that Hilda's suffering can be understood by what is now told of Aissa.

Surrounded by hymn-singing Christians, Aissa is inspired by their 'magic words' to attack the 'giant devil', in the form of Oke's priest Owule, in a mask. As she strikes off the head, she expects the devil 'to tear her flesh'. Instead, she finds Abba and Gajere restored to her. By her proven powers, she is now expected to bring about the miracle of rain. She replies: ' "Yes, I give you de rain, I give you de Kingdom of Heaven" ' (p. 181). Clearly this, for her, is the trinity of father, mother, child. By contrast, Ojo is immediately shown proclaiming the Kingdom of Heaven, in an unmistakable parody of Tolstoy's moral theory, which would abolish property, money, marriage, liquor, judges, law, books, and all men except Christians (p. 182).

From now on, 'it is said in Yanrin that the Christians are the only reliable rain-makers' (p. 195), and the pagans, deprived of Owule, demand that the Christians produce it, or be killed. Ojo decides that Jesus objects to Gajere as Aissa's husband; so Gajere is killed. Aissa then mutilates herself, to satisfy Jesus. But the crowds insist that she must sacrifice Abba; 'a score of exasperated experts' insist that 'Aissa wanted to give Abba', and they try to kill the protesting Ojo. Suddenly, ' "It is juju," he shrieked', and 'The miracle of his resurrection' almost deters them. But Aissa is now in an ecstasy of drunken surrender, singing:

> 'All de tings I lak de mos
> I sacrifice dem to His blood.'

Kneeling to kiss her wounds, Ojo is 'Astonished by the violence and suddenness of his conversion', and kneels singing beside her. So Aissa gives Abba just as Ishe gave Numi, except that his blood falls short of the cross, and the crowd become angry that Aissa is not co-operating, and the sacrifice might fail.

At this point defenders of Oke's faith are reported to be riding towards them. With Ojo and Aissa now useless, the crowd find another saviour who, having spun the cross, leads where it points, across an 'unfathomable' river made passable by the drought. They give thanks to God, but forget Aissa and Ojo. The horseman who kills Ojo is called *Ajala,* which means 'decree, day of death', and so recalls the apocalyptic horseman, Death. But he fears Aissa as a witch; so she is dragged to an ants' nest to die. Here, unmindful of 'soldier ants born and bred for self-sacrifice', Aissa believes Jesus is taking her to Gajere and Abba in heaven. In a vision she sees 'the spirit like a goat with white horns', with Abba on its back, surrounded by angels. She fears Abba may cry and 'disgrace himself', but to her delight he smiles gravely at her, and she laughs: ' "Oh, you rascal." . . . She was helpless with laughter.'

So the book ends, recalling the helpless laughter of famine victims whom Cary had spoon-fed in Africa (p. 77). The smallpox, from which they suffered, is in fact called *Yan rani,* 'dry season sickness', which gives the name Yanrin to this Waste Land. Aissa's death, however, defies the Grand Inquisitor's claim, that men seek happiness in a 'harmonious ant-heap'.[4] They seek it in family love, which their imagination will idealize, if the reality is denied them.[5]

Cary could scarcely have conceived a stronger attack on the doctrine of suffering, as a gift of God, to women especially. As his first novel, *Aissa Saved* justifies the belief that Cary's series is above all *à rebours* of Huysman's where, by Cary's definition, suffering is indeed 'pure juju' and 'self-indulgence' (p. 46 above).

An indulgence in suffering is also evident in Dostoevsky, Murry, and Lawrence, so that an attack on them in this respect can be assumed also. But above all, he establishes in this novel what he means by miracle, grace, and conversion, and his message, despite the violence, is positive. Laughter is established too, as man's unique gift, to overcome bitterness, or pain. The theme of responsibility also runs through the novel, in others besides Ali, as a manifestation of real government in ordinary people. Tanawe, a child who braves the lonely bush to carry a message, demonstrates the wisdom of teaching responsibility young. This is the idea of sacrifice as utility, service, and 'pleasing god', which Cary was in fact preaching.

His symbolic method has been illustrated, as unobtrusive, but widely suggestive. Of this novel he said: 'You cannot get the whole spectacle of life into a single book', as though he had indeed tried to do so; and also: 'A book means what it feels'.[6] The feeling is, surely, that Christians should understand how and why the Bible is the source of their faith. The escape by the river, for example, recalls the sea, through which God allowed the Israelites to pass – after killing the firstborn, which the Passover commemorates. The spirit, as a goat, with Abba upon it, suggests the triumph of family life over imperialism – Daniel viii, 21, having shown Alexander, the first Western imperialist, as a goat. (*Castle Corner,* p. 167, illustrates Christian absorption with Daniel, as a prophetic book.) However, if this is Cary's book of Revelation, the symbol may be more appropriately contrasted with the whore of Babylon, seated on a beast, about whom ministers like Harry Carr thundered. For Abba is the son of a whore, whom Carr tried to convert into a saint. 'MYSTERY . . . THE MOTHER OF HARLOTS AND ABOMINATIONS OF THE EARTH' (Revelation xvii, 5) certainly links Cary's first novel appropriately with his second – if he was also illustrating the second power that holds captive the human conscience.

An American Visitor
Marie Hasluck, the 'visitor' of this book, is drawn, according to the preface, from a 'young anarchist mother – with a mind completely closed to any need of authority – which trusted *absolutely* to providence in the narrowest sense'; she had told Cary that in America ' "we believe that children should get their own ideas of right and wrong" . . . without guidance' from parents. By the

words 'absolutely' and 'guidance', Cary hints at the doctrines of
Frank Buchman, an American visitor to Oxford whose ideas
certainly contributed to this novel.[7] Cary was also influenced by
an American visitor to India, Miss K. Mayo, whose book, Mother
India, was published in 1927. Reviewing this book, Wyndham
Lewis had condemned her irresponsible judgements, which had
'sent up an appreciable distance the international tension and
fever',[8] and he had imagined how easily the picture might be
reversed: 'if an indian lady journalist, for instance, hurried to
America . . . she could very easily draw an equally untruthful
picture. . . . The indian lady visitor to the United States, let us
suppose, has arrived'.[9] An American Visitor, in a discarded opening, reads, as a question asked by the Resident: 'Was she the
same old journalist looking for a Mother India stunt, or a genuine
anthropologist (that's what she calls herself) or a regular
Bolshie?'[10] Lewis had reprinted his review in Paleface: the
Philosophy of the 'Melting-Pot', of which Cary had written to his
wife, on 7 August 1929: 'It deals with the theme of the supposed
"Inferiority complex["] of the white races, and also with the philosophies of Behaviourism etc. – the anti-mind philosophies which
contribute to that inferiority complex.' This comment shows the
appropriateness of 'The Horse's Mouth' as a title for this book
(p. 126 above). But the meaning of that would have been even
more lost on readers than the title Cary actually chose; at least
three reviewers criticized it as, for example, 'absurd and misleading'.[11]

'The original American visitor' (of Cary's preface), and also
Paleface, apparently influenced Cary's essay, 'The Pattern of a
Free Man' (p. 129 above), on which chapter IX of this novel
draws. In Paleface Lewis stresses the shock to early, self-righteous,
puritan emigrants to America, to find themselves slaughtering
Indians and enslaving negroes, and accounts for American
evangelism partly by a guilt complex. He also attacks Lawrence
and the school of 'dark demons', and opposes to 'the "mystical"
"dark" race of the romantic-White imagination . . . the "daimon"
of Socrates, this White Demon we have inherited'. With this
White Demon the White Race may be saved, he suggests, adding
that a more practical use should be made of 'White laughter',
since 'It is a little over-christian to be this perpetual "dignified"
butt! '[12]

Prichard had taught Cary the power of Socratic laughter,

though his temptation to use it is generally offset by his sympathy (without which 'there is no revelation' – *Art and Reality*, p. 133). Cottee in this novel does reveal the degree to which he agreed with Lewis. The force of his attack can be appreciated, however, only if it is realized that it was drained off, as it were, by writing 'Arabella', a wild satire in which the heroine, personifying England, ends up with Hoopey, drawn from Bertrand Russell, amidst the ruins of New York, following its devastation in a war between Russia and America, for world supremacy. It contains an unmistakable attack on Buchman, whose victims include Sadie Gotham – who developed from Sadie Brant, from whom Marie Hasluck developed. That 'Arabella' had been prophetic, and was now timely, in Cary's view, is shown by the fact that he wanted to publish it in 1956.[13] It is perhaps a necessary chapter, to make the series complete.

In *An American Visitor*, chapter IX, Cottee counters Marie's beliefs in the noble savage and natural education, by comparing her with 'real primitive protestants', Doukhobors, and Hussites. Thus, having already said that England has the protestant strain, he invites readers to recall fourteenth-century Oxford, where John Wycliff – the sort of 'spellbinder' who fascinated Cary – really started the Reformation, by questioning papal authority and so inspiring Huss, whose followers practised Biblical communism and then formed terrorist armies as Warriors of God. By naming the Hussites with the Doukhobors, Cary implies a parallel with Russian communism. For the Doukhobors were Russian pacifists, who emigrated to Canada, with the aid of Tolstoy and English Quakers; they have embarrassed Canadian authorities ever since, notably those calling themselves 'Sons of Freedom' who, as Cottee says (likening Marie to them), ' "even protest against clothes" '. Cary read of the Doukhobors in *Resurrection,* which he bought in 1928 – Tolstoy's centenary.

In Marie, Cary has typified the many Europeans whose forbears went to America, inspired by the ideas of freedom that Tolstoy both revealed and fostered, especially in America, and above all Boston. Hamlin Garland's account of Mark Twain's reforming zeal, as an example (p. 122 above), suffices to explain why Marie, at the end of her book, is said always to think of the Englishman Gore as 'King Arthur at the court of Mark Twain'. The fact that Garland writes from New York as 'The most pagan city in the world', certainly explains why Marie is both Tolstoyan and pagan, as Cary conceived her; it reveals a view of Tolstoy's influence, that is, which Cary's treatment of Marie follows. Marie's quarrel with Cottee might fittingly be described as between a reformer inspired by the 'Russian Socrates', and someone possessed by the 'White Demon' of the Greek Socrates. (That Socrates inspired Cary – but differently – is clear from the note, concerning the character of Bewsher, 'As Socrates said virtue is knowledge. . . '.)[14] Cottee calls Marie 'the real Boston mystic' (p. 150), relating this disposition at once to her latest faith, Christian Science. Thus 'Mystery', in a form that Lawrence said would satisfy modern man (p. 146 above), becomes a key to this novel.

The title, *An American Visitor,* seems intended to include anyone from the New World who becomes a kind of pilgrim in reverse. This description certainly fits Eliot, who might also be called a Boston mystic; and as he apparently influenced Cary's first novel, which was once part of the massive material that became the second and third, Eliot was probably in Cary's mind here also. Indeed, he is a classic example of the rebel who turns authority, having converted disciples to a view of life he has now rejected, at least in that form. Regarding *The Waste Land,* Cary seems to have sensed, from the first, what the TLS reviewer discovered, after publication of the full text: 'that the most influential English poem of our time was impelled by a hatred and fear (oh yes, that much we have learnt – hatred, and therefore fear) of woman as a sexual partner. It could be the occasion for a quite momentous clearing of our minds of cant. Unfortunately this will not happen. . .' .[15] It would indeed be appropriate if Cary had created Marie as a rebel against the influence of this other American visitor. For, by 1928, Eliot had declared his view to be anglo-catholic in religion and royalist in politics, as well as classicist in literature. As such he was wholly acceptable to authority as arbiter of English taste, and as critic, editor, and publisher, had unrivalled power in the world of letters – to which Cary aspired. With Murry as the leader of the opposite, unorthodox camp, these men could scarcely have failed to enter Cary's mind, in depicting the 'war' between authority and freedom.

Both Eliot and Murry gained power through Oxford's support, as indeed Wyclif had done – and as Buchman was doing during the writing of this novel, actually calling his movement 'The Oxford Group'.[16] This character of Oxford, as a 'hotbed' of world movements – but also cold feet (p. 61 above) – is what underlies the question asked in the novel: ' "Where do these politicals get their pacifism from. Is it Oxford, or where?" ' (p. 181). The answer, in the voice of a character but essentially Cary's own, adds up to saying that everyone, from childhood, accepts the ideas of an inspired leader, until another changes what is, in an ultimate sense ' "Just a fashion" '. The change will come more quickly, however, if the fashion conflicts with the fundamental character of the world.

Cary expected his readers to grasp his clues about the far-reaching significance of his book, as is shown by the draft of a letter.[17] It raises urgent questions about the policy and develop-ment of the Empire, he says, and contains much that is apposite to Roosevelt's New Deal of March 1933. (The novel appeared in August.) This 'Deal' seems likely to have struck Cary much as it would surely have struck Lawrence: as a perfect example of man-kind's eagerness to accept earthly bread from the great Giver. Miracle and mystery 'merge', says Lawrence; with authority, they are for him all aspects of the power that impels men to bow to the elect. But 'The sight of a true lord, a noble, a nature-hero puts the sun into the heart of the ordinary man, . . . This is one of the real mysteries.'[18]

Mystery in these terms is exactly what Cary has depicted in Bewsher, who is symbolized throughout by the sun, from his first appearance, with a leap from a boat on the sunlit water, that makes Marie exclaim: ' "Wasn't that just beautiful?" ' (p. 38). She immediately recognized a 'true lord'; loves and marries him. But he represents British imperialism which, by upbringing, she hates and wants destroyed. So this 'horse's mouth' of 'subcon-scious + nurture' (p. 126) triumphs over the truth of her new intuition; so, as she admits herself, she kills him, though the manner is complex. The novel is in fact shaped with the Mystery of Death and Resurrection as its dominant symbol. This, and Cary's struggle to shape it, is shown by the note: 'The weak spot is where you get this old young god – atavistic – study in'.[19] His approach accords with an article he read, around 1927: 'The Drama of Death and Resurrection', stating that mystery religions surrounded personages *one and all,* members of ruling families, or closely associated with gods'.[20]

Bewsher is drawn partly from older men he admired in the service. But he represents the Carys, and the Empire as they served it. The book is dedicated to Cary's father, who now lived in Somerset, near Castle Cary, where the family first settled. Bewsher's people come from Somerset and, as his widow, Marie inherits 'a pretty good income' (p. 234). Her name 'Has luck' describes her. She will clearly marry Gore, the young officer whose nickname, Stork, may hint that he, not Bewsher, is to be the father of her child; she is seven months pregnant when the book ends.'[21] Bewsher and Gore are both 'Feudal anachronisms' (p. 235), and so fulfil the idea of death and resurrection in relation to Cary himself; that is, as a product of Oxford in the twenties, Cary might have resembled Gore, about whom the question regarding pacifism is asked. By his pacifist sympathies Gore ensures the death of Bewsher, who is, in all but name, Cock Jarvis, destroyed by two young lovers. The likeliest reason for changing the name would be to accord with the new symbolic form.

Eustace means 'happy in harvest', and just before his death he wakes from sleep, 'his hair sticking out in tufts like a cornfield after a storm', while members of his favourite tribe, the Birri, approach 'across two cornfields', to kill him (p. 225). *Eustace* thus indicates that he is the corn god. Asleep he had looked like an 'old soldier', so recalling the Roman soldier who became St Eustacius, patron saint of huntsmen – for Bewsher with his Birri has been 'the hunter, the meat-giver' (p. 74). *Bew* is a surname that is a nickname 'descriptive of the ancestor's face, figure temper, morals, tastes, clothes, and the rest'; it means 'handsome, beautiful', in Old French; *Shere* means ' "bright" (? from a stream)';[22] so this name is a perfect substitute for *Cary*. With the demeanour of a 'sporting bishop' (p. 49), the legs of a jockey and a parsonical voice, he apparently depicts 'horse' and 'mouth' in controlled harmony.

Monkey, however, is his nickname, which even Marie adopts, though she is an anthropologist, and speaks the Birri language well. She must know, therefore, that its use is inciting the Birri to kill and eat Monkey as their juju; for *Birri* means 'monkey', and is their totem animal. They are not allowed to eat monkey, the reader learns (p. 161), from Bewsher's first would-be assassin, nicknamed Fish (for reasons giving insight into nicknames, p. 64). Here Fish is being persuaded to break totem taboos by Henry, a criminal who has ' "a kind of right to be helped back to Birri" ' (p. 24), Marie decides – because the British have expelled him. At the end he 'is doing a splendid trade in condemned tinned meats' etc. (p 233). So the name *Henry* symbolizes the new imperialism.

Marie's character is complex indeed, but the key to it is the key to all philosophies, including Plato's: 'I Want to be Happy', expressed in her case by the song so entitled, and popular from 1924, when composed in New York. 'What Marie Wanted' was a considered title for her book.[23] When Allday calls her Bolshy, Cottee observes: 'that if Allday was an Amurcan girl brought up on Freud and the fourteen points mixed in with Valentino and turned loose in a wilderness of notion salesmen and ward politicians, he'd be Bolshy. But the fact was that the poor bitch didn't know what she was or what she wanted. That was the trouble' (p. 28). Freud's doctrines are manifest in Marie to the point of caricature. Thus, the book opens with her having given Henry her hat, 'bright green felt shaped like a pudding basin', and her 'green silk stockings' to Musa to darn – odoriferous objects being fetichistic substitutes, according to Cary's Freudian source book.[24] Since they call her 'Mam', and the English, jokingly, 'Mah-rie', then 'MYSTERY . . . THE MOTHER OF HARLOTS' is established as the theme for her from the start.

Women's dilemma, when faced with 'new feminist' theories of the twenties, is summed up in Marie's characteristically cynical rendering of 'life is a gift'. With reference to Cottee and Bewsher, she reflects: 'Probably all Englishmen made illicit love in the same way. The difference was in the man behind the gun – and the end was the same everywhere. If you gave them what they wanted they went off without a thank you, and if you did not, they went even more quickly; that is, unless you were a platinum blonde or had a hundred thousand dollars' (p. 114). Marie has quarrelled on this issue with Cottee, as Musa reports (p. 15); and ' "Marie wants children. She told me so" ', says Cottee (p. 77), so revealing that he knows, but rejects, what she wants. Bewsher gives it to her, but the word 'gun', as used above, proves her undoing. It indicates that a 'new feminist' like Lawrence, who presents his idea of an ancient priestess in *The Man Who Died*, is indeed a romantic, whose idea of the primitive merely suits his imaginings. For finally, Marie recalls the goddess Ma, whose male worshippers castrated themselves in her honour, as Frazer explains.[25]

Cary contrives the scene with great subtlety, leading up to it with mythological and religious associations, including Christian, too numerous to mention here. Marie's behaviour is partly accounted for by sunstroke. She is also testing the truth of Dobson's sermon shortly before, that a man who faces his enemies unarmed will be protected by an Omnipotent God of love. That her own god is pagan is clear from her thought: 'it's God's sun' (p. 223). But the sun symbolizes both god and devil, says Jung.[26] And Cary could be consciously illustrating Lawrence's last words in his *Apocalypse*: 'Start with the sun, and the rest will slowly, slowly happen.' For Marie does just this, and so kills Bewsher.

Cary seems obviously too to be illustrating Tolstoy's split mind, regarding *Anna Karenina*. For he frequently recalled how this novel grew from Tolstoy's observation of his embroidered dressing-gown, which suggested to him the great difference between men's and women's work, and the tragedy that Anna cut herself off from the world of women. *An American Visitor* begins with Musa darning Marie's stockings, and prompting her to ask: ' "Where did you learn to do woman's work?" ' (p. 20). His scissors have fallen as he sews, presumably forming a cross, and making this scene anticipate what becomes woman's work for Marie. Instead of fetching Bewsher his gun, she hides it 'among her clean linen' (p. 227), and he, instead, snatches up 'Mrs Dobson's steel-covered scissor-case', which therefore resembles a dagger. Thus armed by the missioner's wife, yet castrated, according to Marie's use of the word 'gun', he risks facing the Birri, hoping that the sun glinting on the steel will deceive them. They are led by his favourite, Obai, whom he addresses, ' "Is it you, my friend?" ', so signifying his relation to both Julius Caesar and Jesus Christ, towards Brutus and Judas, and so to Cock Jarvis (p. 104 above). But his last words are ' "bloody rascals" ', and his amused thought is: ' "the joke is on you" '. So his death recalls, yet contrasts with, the death of Aissa.

The mounds where the blood of Numi and Abba was spilled are recalled in the very last scene. This mound, at which Marie kneels, is 'covered with strange looking bush flowers', under which is a 'chop box' containing Bewsher's remains: 'Bewsher's smashed and mummified head, . . . and a bagful of his finger joints. The other bones were probably Birri and one femur was certainly goat' (p. 233). So the goat of imperialism and totemism in Aissa's novel is buried, and the father, in place of the mother and child, is the victim. The level of religious belief is indicated by the words with which Marie ends the novel: ' "where Monkey is, the ground feels kind of different." ' Gore, looking like King Arthur, is in attendance on the pregnant Marie, and so is Cottee, who is moved to realize, incredulously, that this is the nature of epic tragedy. 'This ugly little woman a tragic queen, Monkey Bewsher a hero, it was absurd.'

Cary's aim, and his problem in achieving it, is shown by this note: 'In A.V. better if Bewsher's death brought abt. by fanatic who *always has believed like that* – this avoids complicated psychology.'[27] This fanatic is Doll Dans, whose 'religion at least had nothing to do with facts. It was her passion, her life, and she did not ask whether God was to be trusted. She gave without condition or bargain. Probably she would like to die for Him, whatever He was, as people died for kings they had never seen and creeds they could not understand' (p. 226). So, in Doll's presence, 'Marie accepted her responsibility', and hid the gun. Doll's God is in part jealousy, and in her relationship to Marie Cary has practised *dédoublement*. For they are related, and very alike, yet Marie's 'play of expression' makes people think her pretty, while Doll, 'tight-lipped and austere', is plain (p. 110). In an early version, 'The American Visitors', they are pretty and plain sisters, Sadie and Dorothy Brant. The nickname Doll, associated with prettiness, is cruel; since it is short for *Dorothy*, meaning 'gift of God', it conveys her God's nature. *Sadie* is the USA pet-form of Sara, and by it Cary hints at sadism as a natural feeling, which Marie actually betrays, by the 'thrill' she feels, when she 'confidently expected to see Bewsher's entrails tumbled out' (p. 72). This is when they first meet, and her presence immediately threatens his life.

By changing her name to Marie, Cary fittingly chose the name used by Tolstoy for the character representing his wife, in 'The Light that Shines in Darkness' (p. 122 above). Like Tolstoy, Marie is prompted by the inner light – or 'horse's mouth', and her story is indeed *The Kreutzer Sonata* inverted. 'Rebellion' (Withycombe) and 'bitter' (Yonge) are both appropriate suggested meanings for her name, as Marie, while the symbolism Cary builds around her justifies the belief that he was using inspiration from Jung who, in *Psychology of the Unconscious,* connects *mare* for horse, with *mar* meaning to die; *mara,* the dead or death, and Latin *mare* for sea, which makes 'Ave Maris stella' a hymn to Mary.[28] Indeed, this work by Jung illuminates the novel at almost every point, but most obviously when he interprets modern folk psychology in terms of the phantasies of a modern American girl, which concern memories of a minister discussing 'Chaos, Cosmos, and don d'amour', which Jung says meant that she was facing the common human problem, ' "How am I to be creative?" ' to which Nature answers ' "Through the child" '.[29] As in the case Jung recounts, Marie's story begins with a night journey by water. During this she tells Obai: ' "Those who have children know how keen is that happiness, and in Birri every woman can have a husband and a child. But the white priests, the Christians say – " ' (p. 34); so she condemns a religion 'which spoils the happiness of this life in order to make people ready for another which doesn't exist'. How fully Cary agreed with her he would show plainly in *Power in Men* (p. 159; cf. p. 115 above).

Thus Cary seems finally sympathetic to Marie, though her lesson is learnt at such a price. It is dramatically symbolized in Chapter IX, when Marie dons Bewsher's 'old-fashioned British jacket, to ' "feel what it's like to be British and Imperial" ', and Cottee observes: ' "Take care then that you don't feel like playing hanky panky with boundaries" '. Marie's own coat is equally symbolic: 'a brown garment with a fur collar' (p. 99). The final message of this novel is that belief in the noble savage acknowledges 'the good man, as an ultimate fact',[30] and it is goodness in oneself, as in Marie, that recognizes it. The essential point, however, is that goodness must be educated, for evil is also real. Belief in *absolute* love and goodness denies the evil in oneself, and belief in absolute pacifism expresses a death wish, which is often suicidal. The traditional symbol of death is the sunset, and the action of the novel is contained between the sunsets at which Marie gazes (p. 20), and in which Bewsher actually dies (p. 223 ff.). But this death-wish is by no means confined to Marie. For one note reads: 'General subject suicide of the Empire – the destruction of the ruling and imperial class by the libertarians'.[31] Bewsher depicts Cary's ideal, dedicated, ruling class figure, and also, it seems, the eponymous hero of his epic poem, *The Drunken Sailor*; for so Bewsher is actually described (p. 69). On the jacket of the book containing the poem, Cary describes him thus: 'the mysterious implacable spirit in the soul of the world, which drives humanity still to seek understanding and power, more life, that is more richness of experience, in spite of every kind of misery and confusion.'

The African Witch

Bewsher is recalled in the district officer *Sangster,*[32] and Cary actually invites readers to link this novel with the previous two, by comparing Sangster with 'Bewsher of Gwanki' and 'Bradgate in Yanrin', as symbols of British authority (p. 237). He even names 'the redoubtable Cock Jarvis' as though the reader should be familiar with him, and so reveals that parts of that novel are here included.[33] However, in this last book of a triptych of 'The Horse's Mouth' material, Cary is also answering Lawrence's idea of authority, as 'that which men bow down to'. He answers unmistakably, with stunning and contrasting realism, in the person of Elizabeth Aladai. She, at the close, forces her husband, Akande Tom, to bow down so low that he resembles, finally, 'a black jelly, protoplasm'. Here she clearly resembles Nature herself, warning the human race of their fate if they fail to recognize the true character of the world. For Tom has dared to swagger in European clothes, and defy her.

To see Elizabeth as The Witch of the book's title, as most readers seem to have done, is surely to miss Cary's point, however. For she grew, as a *dédoublement,* from Elizabeth Hargreaves (the aunt of Charles Moore – p. 40 above), who was to be an English matriarch defending her way of life against those in revolt against the Victorians – as Cary had been. This English counterpart is described as a 'Gulliver amongst the Lilliputs'; a 'woman who lived with God – on into the ages which did not understand her'.[34] The name Elizabeth fittingly means 'oath of god'. Elizabeth Aladai, too, is defending an ancient religious tradition again alien forces.

It is as priestess of her ancient *ju-ju*[35] that Elizabeth Aladai condemns Osi as a witch. Osi is a beautiful young wife who has disrupted family life, by causing jealousy. She forms a *dédoublement* in the book with the beautiful English girl, Dryas Honeywood; that is, Osi fills a role exactly comparable with Aissa's in Cary's first novel, in relation to Hilda Carr; she reveals the subconscious self of the pretty English girl. The riots, in this African district of Rimi, can all be traced back to the false values personified in this English visitor, Dryas. Dryas is in fact the English counterpart of Marie Hasluck. She represents what the English regard as an ideal product of a girls' school. But what the hero, Jock Rackham, discovers about her too late is this: ' "No foundations, that's the trouble. She'll never break, never go to bits. But she might sink bodily into the mud." . . . "Yes, that's what it floats on, all that sentimental sixth-form culture. Slush, a crocodile swamp" ' (p. 267). Thus the swamp as a dominant symbol in this novel develops from the previous two.[36] Though the manner of her death is glossed over in the same way as Hilda's death, it seems highly likely that Dryas, like Osi, dies in the crocodile swamp. Thus the book's title would refer to Dryas with a subtlety similar to that of *An American Visitor,* regarding Marie.

Dryas seems in fact to fulfil what was plotted for Dorothy Brant regarding Louis Aladai: 'at end her conscience rouses her and she goes to him'.[37] For in Dryas Cary depicts the guilt of the white races (described by Wyndham Lewis) following a realization of racial prejudice which is based chiefly on fear. Cary himself had shown that an Englishman's life in Africa depended on seeming to be superior (p. 84 above). As he shows in this novel, it is much easier to treat as equals in England, the chosen few amongst Africans who are given a place at Oxford University, for example, as Louis Aladai, Elizabeth's brother, has been. That an Oxford graduate's sister can be head of the *ju-ju* is thus a vital point.

Louis is the other self of Jock Rackham, who is an Irishman, and one of many whose lives have been 'twisted by the war' (p. 16), so that, though 'a scholar of his public school', who 'would probably have taken a Cambridge Blue in 1917' (p. 206), he has missed the university education that Aladai has been favoured with. But Rackham's latent jealousy is roused still further when he sees Judy Coote behaving towards Aladai exactly as she had behaved towards him at Oxford – where she had been a don and Aladai her student. For Rackham is engaged to Judy, who is to be contrasted with Dryas, and compared with Doll Dans, as another visitor to Africa. Judy is, to all appearances, very plain. But Rackham, who has had 'plenty of love affairs' and is now thought to be 'inoculated against marriage', has actually discovered, after having her company thrust upon him, that the intelligent, highly educated Judy is a woman he wants to marry. She has even come to seem beautiful to him. So Cary challenges still further the current view of women.

'The Horse's Mouth' is more obviously an appropriate alternative title to this novel than to the previous two. For it opens with a race meeting in the district of Rimi, where Louis Aladai and his relative, a mulatto revivalist minister called the Rev. Selah

Coker, venture into the enclosure that the whites regard as their preserve. ' "I do hate people like that – they're so frightfully pushing, that kind of black men" ', says Dryas. Rackham has 'turned white with anger' (p. 17), which expresses his underlying prejudice ironically. Judy saves the situation by showing her genuine pleasure in meeting Aladai, and by steering him and Coker towards the town, which she asks him to show her.

Jock is dressed as a jockey (so recalling Bewsher, p. 163 above). He is about to race on a 'man-killer' horse called the Kraken, which has 'a habit of whirling round until he had unseated his rider'. Jock mounts and masters the horse, as he rears, jerking the reins 'out of the brute's teeth' (p. 43), and he wins the race – so thrilling Dryas, who exclaims excitedly, ' "I thought you would be killed" ' (cf. Marie, p. 166 above). They then play tennis, and a bond is struck between them, because Dryas gives satisfying expression to Jock's feelings; though 'His objection was deeper. He did not examine it' (p. 45). At this very time, which is sunset, Aladai is in Rimi town with Judy; he is riding a horse that exactly resembles the Kraken and, as it rears, 'The cruel native curb cut into the jaw of the lunatic beast' (p. 54). Riding it, Aladai is almost killed by a spearman. But he is saved by a prayer book in the pocket of his coat, which his Christian aunts have sewn into it as – in their eyes – a charm. The spear has penetrated to 'Page 163' which, in many pocket-size prayer books, gives the Gospel for the Thursday before Easter, when Jesus is mocked, and 'arrayed in a gorgeous robe', after refusing to perform a miracle, as Herod has hoped he will. But Aladai misses the truth of this sign, and his coat becomes for him his *ju-ju* coat, which he believes will bring him luck in his contest to become ruler of Rimi.

Cary's point clearly is that, at the very moment that Dryas begins to fill the role of 'The African Witch', in relation to Rackham, his other self, Aladai, similarly sinks to a *ju-ju* level. As the rider on horseback, each has symbolized mankind's struggle to master his *libido,* by literally controlling 'the horse's mouth'. That the nature of the struggle concerns an imperialist and nationalist notion of authority is shown by a third depiction of a man on a rearing horse, this time in the form of the ancient Emir, whom Aladai hopes to replace, and who is scarcely visible, beneath his robes, in a ceremony that is necessary to confirm his authority. For he is actually tied to this horse which 'fighting with his bit . . . reared at every third pace, catching on his chest the foam that slavered from his mouth. Then . . . stood straight up, its lower jaw wrenched back, its forehooves in the air' (pp. 72–73). ' "Oh, the poor little thing!" ' is Dryas's comment upon the Emir – and so upon the notion of rulership that her presence challenges.

At the obvious level, 'Who shall rule the state?' is the theme of this book, and it is perfectly symbolized by Cary's chosen name for the region under dispute: Rimi. For *rimi* in Hausa means 'a rearing horse', besides being the name of the sacred silk-cotton tree, a symbol of peace. Thus it perfectly recalls the legend symbolizing War and Peace, in the contest between Poseidon and Athena for rulership of Athens, when the tree of peace is accepted, rather than the horse of war. In this book the contest is finally between what Dryas and Elizabeth Aladai stand for. Dryas starts bloody riots, and is herself killed, because she represents, and so fosters, prejudiced nationalist notions, in Aladai as well as the British. Elizabeth, on the other hand, starts a 'women's war' by cutting twigs from a tree, and nicking the leaves, thereby conveying messages to every village in Rimi within twelve hours. 'The women's war began the next morning, so peaceably that nobody noticed it' (p. 234). The women reduce the Resident Burwash to a humiliating defeat by forming a laughing, mocking human barrier on a bridge. Their war song includes:

> 'Be careful, judge, of women, they are strong.
> Out of a woman and into a woman:
> The world is a woman, big judge,
> Bringing forth all things, all men' (p. 240).

Meanwhile Elizabeth enacts the women's war, by going into the bush to give birth (cf. p. 115 above). For 'In Rimi, a mother is left alone to bear her child, in case the child should be a witch' (p. 275). By the time this is accomplished, the other women have made Burwash ready to hold counsel. The meeting is arranged by Judy, who has by now lost Rackham in her women's war with Dryas.

The way Dryas personifies the theme of the novel has been revealed by the way Rackham has delivered Cary's theme phrase, while doing gymnastics with her: ' "A good figure is the gift of God" – with an intonation which left her in doubt whether he was paying a compliment or not' (p. 124). Rackham escapes her influence because 'the horse's mouth' as 'conscience' and 'inferiority complex' actually impels her to go to Aladai – who expresses the theme phrase by reflecting: 'It was good to give one's life' (p. 292). As he says it, he is looking at the mummified head of the missioner, Schlemm. It has been brought to the crocodile swamp close to his mission, where Coker is now converting souls to the belief that they will go to heaven pure, if they are eaten by the crocodile immediately after conversion. Schlemm's mission is at Kifi, which means Fish. It was to Kifi that Marie had come, to see Bewsher's life threatened by a Birri boy, whose nickname 'Fish' referred to his big fish mouth. The ship had borne them to Kifi, which awaited them 'like a kind of dark bluish mouth in the forest' (*An American Visitor,* p. 44). Thus in both novels, Kifi is the mouth of Nature and spells death. For, in *The African Witch,* Judy and Dryas have set off by boat to the mission there, with Aladai and a zealous mission supporter, Mrs Vowls. But again the sun has proved to be the devil God, by affecting Mrs Vowls with sunstroke. Judy returns with her, overland to Rimi, leaving Dryas to return by river with Aladai. It is because she has been alone with Aladai that Dryas causes the riots. For on their return he is thrown into the river by Rackham. This is the key scene. Rackham's act seems due to racial prejudice, but sexual jealousy is obviously present.

In the early notes, Aladai's name was spelt 'Aladé'. Aladé is the singular form of Aladai, which means 'pigs'. It thus links with the Death and Resurrection theme in the second novel, the pig being traditionally sacrificed to the moon and to Osiris. By changing the name Aladé to the plural form, Cary possibly had in mind the fact that, in this third novel, several people become sacrificial victims to their false faiths: Aladai, Schlemm, Dryas and Osi. The manner of Rackham's escape from the prison of a mud hut is highly symbolic, in ways the reader will readily recognize:

> He picked a hole in a two-foot mud wall with his knife, which was fitted with a leather borer, and jumped down the bank of the crocodile swamp. According to his own tale, he landed on the *ju-ju* crocodile's back, and got such a fright that he jumped twenty feet into the air again and landed on the other side. But this is an Irish story. He tells it in English clubs, when he has leisure from his training-stable on the Berkshire downs. But he

has little leisure, as he is already doing very well. He doesn't run horses for himself, and he doesn't bet (p. 298).

Rackham loses Judy, however. She too almost dies, during her efforts to stop the riots. But 'her brain was always alive, as if it carried on a private existence' (p. 299); this presumably illustrates Cary's ideas of the creative imagination at work. For she is assisted by Captain Rubin, the first character in whom Cary realized the 'elation of creators' by which such people become general favourites. Judy's key chapter is number 33 (perhaps intentionally symbolic of true Christianity, this being traditionally Christ's age at his death). The hour is around sunset – again symbolic of death and life. 'The police were already putting out the club chairs under the kuka tree', while Rubin fetched Judy from the hospital for her first outing. On the road they are met by 'a tall negro' whose now crumpled clothes indicate that he is Akande Tom, Elizabeth's husband. Aladai before his death told Tom to find Judy, an enemy of *ju-ju,* who would teach him to read. So Judy is inspired, and so revived, to plan schools for Africans. ' "But *not* mission schools. . . ." ' Moreover, ' "an out of work intelligentsia is a *frightful* danger and nuisance, and it would be *awfully* wrong to take them from their farms." ' So she urges officialdom to adapt ideas which are clearly Cary's own – as his treatise *The Case for African Freedom* makes clear. Judy becomes a true spellbinder, in her enthusiasm. Indeed, in manner of speech, she has been described, throughout the book, as here, with the Resident: she 'fluted at him'. Earlier she has explained of her surname *Coote,* ' "In English it's a kind of bird" ' (p. 144). *Judy* means 'praise' (Yonge). Thus she personifies the notion of the mouth transformed by art (p. 128 above). In this sense she might be called a white witch. For, in her efforts to persuade: 'She smiled her most charming smile; she was going to bewitch the doctor.'

In the next and final chapter, by contrast, Akande Tom is 'bewitched' by Elizabeth Aladai, in being reduced to 'protoplasm' at her feet. Having 'kicked away his face', she 'smiled at the crowd' (p. 308), but nobody dared to smile back. 'They dared not even meet the look of a person so terrible in power.' This ending contrasts with the power of laughter in the previous novels, and answers, horrifyingly, anyone like Lawrence believing in Dark Demons. Cary's message however is Judy Coote's: education is mankind's only hope. That he was also answering Murry with his communist propaganda, might also be assumed, when he reports Judy's answer, to the argument that her efforts will spread communism. 'Communism would be more dangerous if the people did not know anything. They could still hear propaganda. And what would happen when they got richer, and bought wireless sets capable of hearing Moscow?'

The way World War I had 'twisted' Rackham is shown by the way he masters the Kraken, which has German blood. That war had fostered narrow nationalism and racial prejudice, and the rising tide of nationalism, in 1935, was again doing the same.

11. 'The *Castle Corner* monument'

By this description, in his preface to *The African Witch*, Cary suggests that this work was for him more of a commemoration than a novel. It recorded his family history, and also the failure of his hopes, to produce his greatest trilogy. In it he had dug up his own foundations most frankly; the work remains a monument to their burial.

His message is summed up in the very last words, spoken by Sukey, the Castle cook, ' "Me feet, the Judases." ' It depicts, that is, the many false faiths that create the nonsense of world politics. This novel was, in fact, to do for politics what Tolstoy had done for war. 'Shew political novel of ideas parallel with the private, cf. War & Peace'.[1] Thus Cary continued the theme of *The African Witch,* with Tolstoy's masterpiece in mind. As already suggested, he was also inspired by the *Iliad,* traditionally thought to reveal 'life is a battle', in contrast to 'life is a journey' in the *Odyssey,* which James Joyce's novel had shown to be acceptable as a dominant novel form.

As the story of a virtual ten-year siege of the Castle, for love of a beautiful Helen, the parallel with the *Iliad* seems obvious. Once this form is recognized, the vastness of the novel disappears. It is divided into ten parts, each covering a period within this decade of the 1890s, and viewing history from it, according to the technique of the *Iliad.* The number ten itself recurs throughout the novel, as part of Cary's attack on faith in a mathematical universe. Ten has dominated Western thought, since Pythagoras declared it to be the divine number, and the Ten Commandments have strengthened popular belief.

Cary's inspiration, to write thus of his family history, may well owe its immediate inspiration to Vincent Sheean, whose study, *In Search of History,* covering the decade following World War I, appeared in 1935; Cary made notes from it.[2] Sheean's book ends:

'The decade in which I had pursued such a conclusion through the outer storms had ended, and I was on my way back to a civilization that could never again be so sure of itself, never again so blind.' He advocates 'the long view', as the only possible view of history, particularly regarding the problem of Palestine, caused by Zionist demands for a promised land. Events in *Castle Corner* hint at a parallel between Zionism in the 1890s and the demands for Corner land in Ireland. This inspiration would explain why Cary switched to Ireland in 1936, from the English story on which he had been working (intending to use it in the sequel). *Between Two Worlds* might also have inspired Cary at this time, to treat the Marguéritte story in terms of the family code that Murry questioned.

Sheean may have clarified Cary's view, that the twenties marked a turning point in all history, when mankind in general found themselves no longer believing in a supernatural providence. This novel dwells on the decade at the turn of the century, by which the later turning point is best understood. By the 1890s, 'The master faith of the age' was that 'some power in nature itself, a scientific providence discovered and proved by Darwin, had ordained progress by universal war' (pp. 160–61). 'The imperialist god of Darwin' had become supreme in all forms of thought, assuming, for example, 'the white man's right to Christianize the world'. It was as though the individual human imagination, escaping through Darwin from belief in a God that intervened in human affairs, felt free to create whatever world suited it. Even though the old religious symbolism remained, it was being regarded differently. In Cary's terminology, the creative imagination itself was freed. Above all, it began to assert the rights of women and children in a society hitherto suited to men's idea of themselves.[3] Cary's theme and vision demanded as vast a stage and cast as the *Iliad*, or *War and Peace*. The following is a guide to the ten parts of the novel.

I. April 1890; Cleeve Corner is aged eleven – entering his second decade. He is at family prayers, and the jar he breaks, through dreaming curiosity, symbolizes the way Corner rule will be broken. His grandfather, old John Corner, prays in the belief that 'God was Father of creation, the King was father of his people, and he, John, was father of his tenants, both English and Irish, especially the Irish here at Castle Corner. He found them helpless and foolish children.' A women's war against such notions is declared by Mrs Foy, beating a drum. John is evicting her family, and his comment ' "The women – what do they know about it" ' shows John's incomprehension. For Bridget Foy now fetches Mary Corner, who stops the eviction; at the Castle Bridget is introduced to Cleeve, as her 'cousin', since her uncle Dan Egan is directly descended, too, from John Corner's great grandfather. But Dan's one-roomed hut at Ballycorner – not Castle Corner – would have to accommodate nine evicted Foys.

John, 'God favours him', has appropriately been the given name of the eldest son inheriting the Castle. Therefore *Felix*, for the eldest, has broken that tradition, and perhaps prompted Old John to leave the Castle to John Chass. Felix persuades John Chass to invest in an African trading company, with himself as agent.

II. In October 1891, Felix, a brilliant Oxford graduate, sets off, by dugout through forests, up the muddy Mosi river, feeling 'a Napoleon of commerce'. He believes that 'the scene itself is not an active partner in the relationship' (p. 55), so showing himself a true platonist in his view of nature, as passive. But he is told ' "It gets you" ', and indeed finds himself buying an African mistress, Dinah, as a washerwoman – to save her from being sacrificed. Thus imperialists, finding their code unequal to new primitive situations, have influenced its breakdown in Europe. There Bridget is comparable with Dinah, as shown when her brother Manus reads: ' "Saint Bridget, having given herself to God, built a cell for herself" ' (p. 57). 'Life is a gift' thus expressed is what Bridget Foy rebels against. She has not been taught to read. But Manus 'was the glory of the Foys in Dan's house. He was the one who had the best of the food and the only pair of boots on Sunday.' He is expected to save the Foys from misery by becoming a priest.

Mrs Foy's declaration of war, on John Corner's idea of God, is followed by an actual attack on the Castle, just before the departure for America of Con Foy, who had sworn revenge on the Corners regarding the eviction. John Chass, with typical luck, returns home to prevent the Castle being wrecked. But Bridget has stolen a locket, and risks hell fire to keep it, so deceiving Father MacFee and satisfying herself that God is not Omnipotent. She then undermines faith in Manus, who becomes a political agitator instead of a priest. It is Power itself he has worshipped, Cary implies. Meanwhile Theodore Benskin, filled with a new sense of power from wealth accrued in Africa, has been pressing to buy Castle Corner, and also Corner property in Devonshire. And an heir has been born to John Chass and Mary Corner – named John, but called Shon.

III. In spring 1895 Felix returns to Castle Corner, following his wife's death, and is treated as 'a Napoleon of commerce'. He explains that slavery seems ' "The natural thing" ' when established, and recalls *Totem and Taboo* by continuing: ' "You might even call it an idea of nature like the family and the tribe, one of the earliest social ideas. Ants keep slaves. Every tribe of baboons is in subjection to old man baboon, and it must have been the same with men until some busybody said it was a scandal. Then of course they all saw it!" ' (pp. 84–85). ' "You think so?" ' asks MacEwen, clearly questioning Western civilization. MacEwen speaks for Cary, as did MacEwen in *Aissa Saved* (p. 151 above). He counters, ' "all politics are religious" ', when Felix declares ' "All religions are political." '

By recalling Blake's dictum in this context, Cary seems certainly to be reminding readers of Murry's current political activities, for which his slogan, adapted from Blake, was: 'Religion is Politics and Politics is Brotherhood'. For his pacifist activities he was being denounced as a Judas on one side and hailed as a Messiah on the other,[4] and this fact also anticipates the second trilogy, which has many links with this novel.

Murry and 'The New Thelema' have apparently contributed to Felix, whose 'idea of the golden age was simply a universal Oxford' (pp. 86–87; cf. p. 69 above). His degeneration in Africa illustrates the likely response of such romantics to such a challenge.

By now Africa challenges the Castle in the person of Benskin, renting near-by Knockeen Hall for a shooting holiday. John Chass refuses to sell the Castle, but borrows from Benskin, though knowing him a 'real schemer'. Benskin is accompanied by Helen Pynsant, 'a new species in Annish'. Harry Jarvis, on leave from his regiment, falls in love with Helen's daughter, Stella. But Helen captures the imagination of both Bridget and Cleeve, and Bridget gets work as kitchenmaid at the Castle, as if a purpose begins to form immediately in her subconscious.

IV. Con Foy, with his wife Kitty, returns from America to give Annishmen new ideas of acquiring Corner land. For ' "What happened to the English when they tried to grab the States?" ' (p. 132). Kitty, developing tuberculosis, is nevertheless allowed to return to the Castle as nurse to Shon, on whom she dotes. Mary's belief in an Omnipotent God of Love calms her fears.

Bridget is now chamber maid, and meets Cleeve in his bedroom. On holiday, he encourages her to flirt with gifts and suggestions of her becoming an actress. But the seduction is all part of one occasion, when John Chass, as magistrate, entertains a crowd at the Castle. Benskin admires a portrait of the first John Corner as 'A man of the imperialist spirit', and rouses Cleeve's imagination with talk of the imagination of men like Rhodes, whom he calls an imperialist and a Home Ruler (pp. 146, 147).

This conversation prepares the reader for what follows; it shows how John Chass is a home ruler of the Castle. He has abandoned prayers and church-going, but faith in the number ten persists. Thus he accepts a wager that he can cover the treacherous road from the Castle to Dunvil in ten minutes or less each way. He will win ten pounds for every minute under the ten, and lose ten for every minute over. ' "D'ye want him to kill himself?" ' Slatter shouts, so betraying the secret hope of this local business man, another contender for the Castle – as the name *James*, meaning 'supplanter', implies. (Being derived from *Jacob*, whose 'hand took hold on Esau's heel' (Genesis xxv, 26), the name reminds readers that John Chass, as favourite, has re-enacted Jacob's triumph over Esau, and is himself a supplanter.) Slatter has actually bet that John Chass ' "wouldn't drive the little devil for leader" ' (p. 150), his reference being to Dapple, a rearing, spirited gelding, whom John Chass is to drive with Grey Lady in his tandem cart. Dressed in his box coat, he almost succeeds. But, returning through the Castle gate, Dapple bolts, and jumps the low wall, and Grey Lady, pulled against the wall, falls, so that the cart turns over, and John Chass falls in the mud. Nevertheless, as he walks down the drive, 'there was the dignity which is supposed to belong only to conquerors. It was not less dignity because John Chass was laughing at himself' (p. 156).

Thus John Chass and the manner and future of his rule of

Castle Corner are revealed. Being 'a classical driver' (p. 155), John Chass is intended also, surely, to recall Plato's symbol of the soul, with reason driving a good and bad horse. For, during this race, Cleeve and Bridget are performing the sex act that will finally overthrow Corner rule of the Castle – symbolized by the cart – because of Bridget's ambition for their son. Cleeve has promised to take Bridget to London and marry her; he has also encouraged her to emulate Helen Pynsant, whom he so 'greatly admired'. But he now longs to escape to London, alone, to see the real Helen. It seems that this pagan Helen, as the symbol of the new age, is challenging a society based on a Christianity derived largely from Plato. Perhaps Helen of Troy challenged a Greek patriarchal society similarly, in Cary's 'long view'.

V. This spirit of the age strikes a different response in Cleeve's other self, Jarvis. He is visiting Felix, now ensconced on the Niger in an abandoned slave ship, the *Maria Fry* – whose owners have apparently been Quakers. These traders' slave-women and their children have been banished below deck, as Felix dines Jarvis above, in colonial-service style. Captain Pooley, 'in command of the nearest troops', converses on current theories regarding the millennium and sums them up with the magic formula: ' "How was an ordinary chap like me to guess that everything depended on the ten toes of the prophet Daniel?" ' (p. 167). His name suggests that today he might bet on the pools, and his statement implies that 'ten' becomes magical to any child who discovers it has ten toes as well as ten fingers. Pooley ' "couldn't make any sense of religion" ' without this guide.

Unfortunately this cultured gathering is unexpectedly joined by Hatto, a deserter-turned-trader, who expects to return to his family in England in two years, with a fortune. He inspires Jarvis to venture over the Niger to Laka, guided by Jingler, who is described thus:

> [He] was a famous character on the Mosi, where he visited the various stations, begging for beads and tobaco, singing rude songs, and dancing obscene dances. He also acted as pimp, . . . In fact, as Felix knew he was a recognized poet of the middle Niger valley, known to every tribe for hundreds of miles, and passing safely among them even in wartime. They gave him passage, just as in the old days all the warring tribes of Greece

or Ireland gave safe conduct to the wandering poets who brought them amusements and carried their fame (p. 169).

Thus Cary suggests the parallel that should be drawn by classicists and Celtic revivalists. Jarvis would feel less impressive, if he realized how the Laka chief's words differ from Jingler's translation. But he produces a map by which he is accepted as an African expert at home, and John Chass talks with pride about him, and the British Empire, so rousing Irish nationalist pride.

It is now 1897, Queen Victoria's Diamond Jubilee, and John Chass, inspired by Jarvis, plans a grand celebration. Cleeve, by contrast, is dreaming of Helen Pynsant's London world, and is 'sick of Bridget'. However, on entering the Castle dining-room, he is greeted by a loud hiss, from 'The blue yard-cat, whose life ambition it was to establish herself in the house' (p. 181). This 'blue Peter' is clearly Bridget's talisman, warning him. Nevertheless, the moment Bridget is absent from the Castle, Cleeve departs for London, and calls at once on Helen Pynsant. He gains entrance by encountering her aged husband, a hero of the Indian Mutiny and Crimea, who knew Cleeve's grandfather. He finds Helen holding court to young men, whom Benskin is said to support in extravagances, along with Helen, aided by 'his friend and partner, Nussbaum' here mentioned for the first time (introduced above, p. 43).

Cleeve now meets Helen's lover Cobden Chorley, an aesthetic youth already at Oxford, who immediately quotes Plato and is then shown making love most gauchely to Helen, being 'a highly innocent person . . . capable of anything' (p. 200). Helen's appearance afterwards, Benskin recognizes, is 'of a cat that has just had a meal of fish'. So female cat symbolism is repeated with variations; Cobden's character in the book would fit Cary's idea of Murry. When his sister Lucy invites Cleeve to stay at their home, Bellavista, Cleeve escapes from his hotel without paying the bill – presumably demonstrating how he has been infected by his new-found faith. Copies of the *Yellow Book* and *Foundations of Belief* on his bed-table at Bellavista suggest someone 'between two worlds'.

Meanwhile, in Ireland, Shon is ill on Jubilee day. But his nurse leaves him and, going outside, he is petted by Kitty and others as ' "a princely beauty" '. A mountain man's voice 'made a joy and marvel of conquest', in describing how the Corners 'stole all Annish', and all eyes stare at Shon 'as if each man was striving to comprehend within himself a quality, a power, and a beauty' (p. 209). But 'It was the mountain men who burnt alive the Corner children in the rebellion of 1641'; so Shon's grace makes him too a victim, of those who destroy what they cannot understand. Shon dies bravely of fever – leaving John Chass without an heir. His death could be attributed to Jarvis's African exploits.

Cleeve returns to the funeral, and Bridget's undeniable pregnancy. He insists that he is bound in honour to marry her, but John Chass offers 'the cup of Socrates' in the form of escape to Oxford, while he arranges a good dowry for Bridget, in order to win her a Catholic husband. He chooses Rifty, the groom who, as he bargains with John Chass, 'struck Dapple on the nose to save his left ear from its teeth' (p. 220); assuming that Dapple represents Cleeve (p. 180 above), this action skilfully combines Cary's symbols of a punch on the nose and the horse's mouth. Father MacFee has wanted Bridget 'to feel disgrace' in Annish instead of emigrating to America.

Cary has created a situation that any reader would find hard to judge, and his own viewpoint is uncertain. Neither Father MacFee nor John Chass was willing to abide by Christ's teaching in Matthew xix, as Tolstoy would have pointed out (p. 122 above). So Cary would probably have said, as John Macmurray did, that what the churches have to say has become irrelevant (p. 118 above). By indicating that Bridget is likely to become another Helen Pynsant, whose background is equally obscure, and who attracts Cleeve so strongly, he implies that Cleeve should have married her. This would certainly have resolved the political and social aspects of Catholic and Protestant antagonism. Moreover, he was to show, in the sequel, that Cleeve preferred his son by Bridget to children by Stella, whom he wins from Jarvis. Helen was scarcely a good choice for a grandmother.

VI. Cleeve escapes to Bellavista as 'an earthy paradise', where this prosperous, evangelical, liberal family engages hourly in good works, much as the Ogilvies evidently did. The minister, Porfit, anticipates Chester, in preaching against landlords and aspiring to marry Lucy.

On his first day at Oxford, Cleeve is handed a dirty envelope, with news of his son's birth. His name, *Finian,* meaning 'fair offspring' (Yonge), accords with Bridget's description: *'he is beutiful boy'* (p. 232). But that world is far removed from Oxford, where Cleeve becomes an unpopular aesthete, under Cobden's tutelage.

VII. In Jubilee year Jarvis in Africa has won distinction for intercepting slave raiders, while his uncle Felix has married his slave, Dinah, and now marries Bandy, her daughter by another man. He lives in 'dirt and idleness'. Yet he is 'greatly surprised' when reproached by Hatto for ' "goin' native" ', for 'He was simply living his life as it came to him' (p. 245). 'The scene itself' has certainly proved 'an active partner', as he had not at first anticipated. Bandy is already pregnant when he marries her, as is not permitted in Laka, and when Felix excuses her, he is condemned by Laka chiefs as a corrupting influence. Thus English Liberals see their gospel message questioned. The very name, Felix, invites such questioning.

By the end of 1898, however, the real danger to Laka civilization is from Daji slave raiders, as Felix warns. But Laka religion forbids any preparation for war during the festival of the yam planting; so, even when the Emir is known to be on the march, the chiefs dare not offend the spirit of fertility, who requires 'the sacrifice of ten young virgins to the yam spirit, ten to the fish spirit and ten young men in full strength to the palm trees' (p. 249). Besides stressing 'ten' as significant, as in Europe, Cary invites a comparison with Christian 'juju' faith in suffering; he shows how the real suffering of a victim, nailed through his feet to a tree, is not felt at all by priests and worshippers intent only on personal salvation. The raiders strike in the midst of the festival, and only the mothers with children show resistance. The chief's wife, Hama, dies defending her son, Azai, aged ten, under a Rimi tree; and Azai's life is saved, by drinking milk from the breast of Bandy, who flees here with her baby. The Rimi tree has been made sacred for them by the blood of Hama, and under it, feeling secure, 'In three days Bandy had formed a household which was in miniature the household of a Laka native' (p. 266). Civilization depends on women, apparently.

VIII. ' "The hour is dark" ' introduces this section as words from a sermon by Porfit. They are chosen to suit the mood of the Liberal Party, who then 'seemed hopelessly beaten'. Bandy, in the part before and in the part to follow, is shown to have no time for such self-pity. By contrast the Liberals are preoccupied with self-advancement. Porfit gains strength from a portrait of Gladstone; then goes to New Grange. Here Helen, now a widow, is holding a skating party, and Nussbaum recognizes the scene as 'a perfect Breughel'. He has spent most of the previous night with Helen, but now he has observed her with Cobden, 'and his small, screwed up eyes were full of such pain that Benskin, even in his own preoccupation, noticed it' (p. 275). Nussbaum's superbly cultivated taste would make him more acutely aware than most people of the degree to which his ugliness repelled Helen. Now he declares that it would be 'quite natural' for her to love a good-looking boy, seventeen years younger than herself. For the boy it could be ' "A religious profession, then. Helen could be a cult." ' For ' "A faith must have its martyrs – even the aesthetic faith" '.

So Nussbaum gives the key to the book, directly revealing the faith that Cary traced back to Raffalovich (p. 42 above). It is as if, being forced to detach himself from his own ugliness, and having wealth to compensate, Nussbaum is more capable than most people of a long world view. He sees the tragic joke of it all, as his name implies, if taken to mean 'chestnut' (p. 55 above). But Nussbaum cannot even enjoy smiling, because he then looks even more ugly.

Benskin is working to get Liberal Imperialists into Parliament, but Cary writes of Nussbaum:

> He understood Benskin's idea. He, too, had known Rhodes, to whom the Empire with its system of decentralized local governments was the nucleus of a world state. But to Nussbaum, with his Continental mind, this Rhodes imperialism was a dream. He was sceptical of all ideas of security; of lasting peace. He did not think of the world in the first place as a complex of powers, but of cultures, in which he savoured each, the French, the German, the English for its special flavour, not only in art but in all its character (p. 276).

Here Cary hints that his own long view is Continental rather than merely English. That it stretches back in this book to Troy seems evident, when Nussbaum says: ' "Helen could become a cult." ' Immediately the parallel of Troy with Castle Corner seems unmisakable. Ilius built Ilion, as Corner built Castle Corner. Each is an outpost of an imperialist civilization trying to sustain itself by unique trading opportunities. Cleeve, the aesthete, resembles Paris, and introduces the cult of Helen through Bridget. Jarvis is a Hector. But Troy fell, Rome grew, and colonized Britain. So John Chass has 'the handsome features of a classical Roman. His eyes were dark blue. His whiskers and hair, of a true auburn.' He belongs to the class who have, by tradition, ruled, but 'enjoyed life so much that he detested any interrupton of that enjoyment, above all, bad feeling. . . . He loved people, sport, good company and probably he loved Castle Corner too, without noticing it; as a man loves an old coat, and does not know his love until the coat falls to pieces' (pp. 12–13). Here the coat reveals the problem of all authority: that defending it conflicts with the individual purpose for which it was sought, unless the individual has a higher political or religious purpose. And these had been lost by John Chass – a true Liberal.

Helen's cult of beauty and enjoyment is symbolized by her skating party. Here Cleeve is skating for the first time, and his antics create 'natural joy' and 'general delight'. Even Nussbaum, 'forgetting himself, opening his mouth like a cavern', expresses this power for happiness emerging from the mouth of nature. But Cobden Chorley's father is talking to him about the need for a missioner among Kaffir miners, and now Nussbaum's face has 'that indescribable expression of the Continental freethinker, faced by an evangelical; a look in which boredom, contempt, and the consideration which distorts the faces of asylum visitors into a kind of fearful politeness, mixed and contradicted each other' (p. 278). At this moment the laughter surrounding Helen continues, but 'Benskin, however, did not laugh because he knew without turning round that they were no longer laughing at Cleeve. The laughter had a different sound.' They are laughing at Porfit, who supposedly preaches the faith that Chorley wants for Kaffir miners. But only Benskin can sympathize with 'an aspiring man', and his sympathy brings the realization that Benskin's own origins are obscure. No one else apparently cares to reflect on his own origins. Thus the two kinds of laughter, of joy and of spite, reveal the two sides of the horse's mouth – and the true weakness of Liberalism.

Porfit, however, knows the Liberal recipe for success is to 'get a lady' (cf. p. 66 above). He is thus deaf to laughter, while:

'his eyes were fixed on Lucy.' Working on her natural sympathy and a conscience shaped to feel guilt towards the oppressed, he cannot fail, though Lucy's antipathy to him as a husband is evident. Meanwhile a women's war is in progress, with Stella weaning Cleeve's affections from Lucy to herself. Benskin also shows his power, against men like Lucy's father, whose religion denounces a 'randlord' like himself, yet whose politics want him as a business partner. He challenges Helen, who now depends on his wealth for her extravagances. When he takes off to stay with James Slatter in Ireland, accompanied by Stella, Helen decides she had better join them.

Slatter's story has accompanied the main tale throughout. If Castle Corner is Ilion, Slatter fills the role of Agamemnon, who was also a would-be supplanter, and sought power as the ruler of a great house. Slatter is 'amongst the richest men in the county' as a result of 'buying up the estates of landlords ruined by the boycotts and rent strikes of the land wars' (p. 29). A widower with two daughters, whom he despises with a true Greek contempt for women, he wants the Castle for his nephew Philip Feenix, whose intelligence and good looks convince Slatter that he is a distant Corner relative.

Philip is the son of the Castle rector. The father, 'who had lost his pretty young wife in the first year of marriage, who himself had been buried alive in Annish for thirty years, spoke eloquently about the triumph over suffering' (p. 39). This background, giving Philip a mother who must have seemed as remote to him as a goddess, suffices to cast Philip as Achilles – whose foster father was Phoenix. Philip, in Greek, means 'lover of horses', and *Feenix* almost reproduces *fenix*, as the form of phoenix used before 1100 A.D., for the mythical bird. By spelling it *Feenix*, Cary not only ensures the correct pronunciation, but also links Father McFee with Feenix, whose similar faith in an Omnipotent God contributes to the death of Shon,[5] and also loses Feenix his own son. Though Feenix resists Slatter's demands to let him adopt Philip, he loses Philip because, from giving Philip the education Feenix cannot afford, Slatter goes on to indulge him, so that he ends up a mere drunkard. But first he has been torn between his two fathers, and has left Feenix when convinced that the Omnipotent God he preaches is false. He becomes a political anarchist, with Manus, for the same reason, so showing what Cary thought was the chief Irish problem, shared by both sides. That

D. H. Lawrence adopted the Phoenix as his personal symbol would of course be wholly relevant. As Achilles, who used the name Aissa when disguised as a girl, Philip seems indeed to represent, as Aissa did, the childish soul of the world, and life itself (see pp. 193, 242 below).

Philip is already living at Carnmore (Slatter's home), and acting as his agent, when Benskin, Helen, and Stella arrive to stay. Having previously stayed at Knockeen, for the shooting, Benskin can here be seen as joining the enemy camp besieging the Castle. The presence of Helen and Stella changes Philip, temporarily, from the slatternly ways into which he has sunk. They bring new life to Annish generally – a renewed sense of beauty.

Cocky, on leave, proposes to Stella, but does so on a tour of the Castle, while showing her 'the dead cellar', where three Corner children were murdered. Having mentioned that ' "John Felix, the elder . . . had seventeen children to make sure of the line" ', he asks whether Stella believes in big families, which he thinks 'the natural thing'. Stella does not know, but Helen has no doubts. Having just agreed to marry Benskin, but have no children, she ensures that Stella and Cocky do not marry at once, as they have agreed to do, to the delight of John Chass and Mary Corner.

Helen's argument with Mary is the pagan against the Christian, taking Mary's to be the latter, in its 'early Victorian' form: ' "There is no secure happiness anywhere, except in love, in giving." ' Helen Pynsant would have asked, ' "Why should anyone be asked to make sacrifices? You say, for civilization, for the next generation. But why should I trouble about something that doesn't even exist?" ' (p. 308). Both women speak from a 'very strong' position, remarks Cary, who has in fact answered Helen in *Power in Men* as well as in this book. He says that a state must stand for values worth preserving.[6] Mary's values clearly are, and Cary believes in them, yet thinks women carry an unequal burden. John Chass is understandably embarrassed by the argument, but when Mary leaves the room, Helen's charms persuade him that Stella must ' "get her season" '.

Stella could clearly have saved Philip, whose complete decline is marked by the drinking bout following news of her engagement to Jarvis. He finds himself shaking hands with a stick, addressing it ' "Phillyfilly, phillyfill, hallophilly" ', as if, this 'lover of horses', is fit only to love a 'filly'. Now 'He suspected that the whole world was having a joke at his expense. . . . The stream of ragged clouds, . . . were all making mouths at him. They had no faces but their black mouths full of broken teeth twisted every instant into grins of painful malice. They were like the grins of prisoners or unhappy wretches whose laughter is full of spite, because they don't want to laugh at anything or anybody, because they have been made to laugh by their own grotesque misery' (pp. 312–13).

Here Cary has presented the horse of pure male energy, as described by Lawrence, reduced by the horse's mouth of nature in a way Lawrence never attempted.

IX. Jarvis returns to Africa unmarried, and is posted to Pooley's company in Laka, which is now reduced to a 'mud hole' (p. 317). Pooley, consulting his *Christian Intelligencer,* decides that the antichrist is Louis Napoleon, whose name works out to 666. Directed thus by Revelation xiii, 18, he decides the world will end in six months. The world that ends is the Corners' world, and Jarvis is the Napoleon.[7]

First comes Cary's direct answer to the argument between Mary and Helen, however. Of the Laka people, he says: 'Bandy and the other mothers with young broods alone were active and purposeful; . . . they could not despair because they had no more thought for themselves than the leopards and hyaenas, which with their own young to feed, hunted beside them through the forest' (p. 323).

Cary's general title 'There's a War On' is here shown at the stage following 'The women's war' as childbirth. It is more fundamental than 'life is a battle', as depicted in the *Iliad,* which is directly suggested now by Jarvis as 'conqueror of Daji'. His exploit is in fact made possible by Jingler, already likened to the poets of Greek epic.

It is as if Jarvis's intense feelings for Stella, in which he saw her above all as a mother, are forced into an unreal, idealized image, to find expression in an act of superhuman energy, in service to a mother country for which he is prepared to die as a lover – particularly if he can impress Stella. Cary's two references to the creative imagination in *Power in Men* are explained by Jarvis's act.[8] Moreover: 'His feat was as much beyond head-quarters' reach of idea as Cezanne's pictures in that same year were beyond that of the Salon jury. Both were original and simple acts of imagination' (pp. 324–5). Here Cary's identification of Impressionism and Darwinism is explained. Jarvis is described as an 'instinctive idealist', inspiring his men with the power of a demon, so that, though near death, 'The demon, for his own ends, had resurrected them' (p. 327). He should indeed have felt as Evelyn did in 'Bush River' (p. 80 above). Yet 'His brain was a calculating machine, planning, arranging, with the foresight and refinement of an insect' (p. 329). Thus Cary depicts the effect of mechanized warfare. But the battle consists almost entirely (yet appropriately for Cary), of the Emir falling off his horse. Entering Daji, 'Jarvis, the conqueror, and the conquering army, had to wait for five minutes; and at last, since the women would not clear the road, to take another one (p. 333). As a campaign in the women's war, this recalls *The African Witch* (p. 171 above).

It contrasts with the women's war being waged by Helen in England. She has now married Benskin, who expects her to be 'a wife of the true breed at the head of his table worthy of her responsibility; children to carry on his name' (p. 337). She has no intention of filling this role, and will thwart him. On the other hand, Benskin, as a new style of imperialist, will use Jarvis's exploit to further his own ends in ways that will ultimately work against Jarvis and the Corners. By getting Jarvis's exploit glorified in newspapers, he influences John Chass to take 'imperial views' when presiding as a magistrate; so the editor of the *Annish Gazette* predicts (as indeed happens) that this 'Saxon imperialist' will be defeated in the Council election by the grocer Joseph Giveen. Padsy Foy expects Giveen to divide up the Castle grounds, for ' "It's Egan ground" ', and ' "Didn't he promise to divide up the land?" ' (p. 348). Sukey is called upon to prophesy, by throwing herring 'melts' at the wall (as Cary had seen done in Inishowen), and the scene suggests the writing on the wall in Daniel, from which Pooley accepts predictions (p. 180 above).

Joe Giveen seems intended to hint at Joseph Chamberlain, whom Felix compares later to ' "Bismarck, in his career of nationalist wars" ' (p. 363). By having Felix apologize 'for bringing in anything so foolish as present politics', Cary draws the reader's attention to Joseph Chamberlain's politics at that time, and Neville Chamberlain's at the time of writing. At each time the Jews were central to 'present politics'. In the 1890s, Zionism was encouraged by British imperialist ideals (for a land route to India), and by the success of comparable demands in Ireland for their promised land. Events in *Castle Corner* point to the way the World Zionist Organization was formed, to declare its policy, at a World Congress in August 1897, of making a Zionist state in Palestine. The founder of this Zionist Organization was Theodore Herzl who, by his name and aims, would explain why Theodore Benskin is a home ruler and imperialist. Moreover, he developed from Cary's early 'monkeyfied Jew', who had the politics of Benjamin Disraeli and the philosophy of Benedict de Spinoza.[9] Since Zionism, for British imperialists, owed much to Disraeli's imperialism, and since Spinoza, too, dreamed of making Palestine a Jewish homeland, the name 'Theodore Bens' kin' (?) seems highly descriptive of this character. Theodore means 'god's gift'. By introducing Pooley into the novel, Cary reminds us that Zionism succeeded chiefly by winning the support of such people in England, predicting the millenium by studying the Bible, and the books of Daniel and Revelation in particular, aided by such literature as the *Christian Intelligencer*.

This interpretation accords with Cary's aims of getting 'a whole view of life' into his novels; of showing that we all contribute to shaping history; and of showing the need to study history in order to understand ourselves in our present situation which, in 1938, concerned a war fought chiefly in the Jewish cause. It was a war which concerned all that Cary held dear. For his sons would be called on to fight in it.

X. This final part covers the months from September 1899 to the end of 1900, so completing the form of the novel as a ten-year period. It centres on the outbreak of war in South Africa in October 1899, when the Liberals had to face the problem that has always proved their political failure, in Cary's eyes. It reflects the split mind of the Liberal Tolstoy, regarding pacifism;[10] Felix states the case plainly thus: ' "And the reason our Liberal friends are in such a muddle is that they're always obsessed by this idea of a moral providence – it messed up their economics and it always messes them up in a war. Liberal democracy collapses in the presence of violence because it has never faced the problem of force" ' (p. 376). Cary illustrates his point chiefly through the evangelist Chorley, and his minister Porfit, who both gain power through pro-Boer, pacifist propaganda.

Benskin, supporting the war, rouses enthusiasm by staging the welcome for Jarvis; then arranges for workers to wreck Porfit's pro-Boer meeting. Porfit has tricked Cleeve into appearing as Oxford's pacifist representative, and when he is injured in the fighting, Stella turns against the war, and so against Jarvis.

Meanwhile, the African investment market becomes a war for profiteers, directed chiefly by Benskin and Nussbaum. Cary writes: 'Nussbaum did not think of himself as a speculator. He had inherited a fortune and his chief pleasure was the enjoyment of it. He regarded money as a squire regards his land; as the necessary foundation of his existence but not its first interest.' By involvement in this world of international loan capital, into which Felix has led him, John Chass finds himself bankrupt. He then realizes the difference between Nussbaum and his father, as men of power. Old John, a true squire 'laying out two thousand pounds on the drainage of Knockeen bog, had spoken of the money as an investment for his grandchildren' (p. 387). But Nussbaum's is a different, strange kind of power. 'It seemed to be power over values; John Chass had thought himself to be gambling, but he saw now that the transaction was not like a bet; it was more like a battle in which the defeated enemy could expect no quarter.' Reflecting thus (on the theme of the *Iliad*) as he walks through London, John Chass observes: ' "But they don't look like a lot of blaggards. They're more like church-wardens." ' He realizes the truth that 'all politics are religious'.

His future is now in the hands of Benskin and Nussbaum. By liquidating the Mosi companies, Benskin will get Castle Corner. But Nussbaum wants a merger. The decision to merge, which saves the Corners, is made by tossing a penny. Nussbaum smiled, 'forgetting in his relief the enormous size of his mouth. "Yes, it is the best for everybody." He suddenly looked fierce again, drawing his lips together' (p. 408). Again, the mouth reveals the feelings of nature; Nussbaum's nickname is 'the frog' (p. 275). Benskin's willingness not to press for Castle Corner follows his latest skirmish with Helen, when he 'felt like a commander brought to a decisive battle on ground of which all the maps have proved wrong' (p. 404).

'This was the beginning of the castle's time of splendour' (p. 409), when 'The African gold fountain' made even old Dan

Egan richer. Bridget now has the run of Castle Corner as a maid, and almost succeeds in killing Sukey's ward Theresa, by making it seem that the child has upset an urn of scalding water over herself. Theresa does not die, but her blinded eye makes her shunned by Sukey and her kin as a 'starer who gave bad luck' and here 'is much feared' – so showing that juju exists in Ireland, as in Africa. Finian will now get Sukey's money. But Mary Corner takes care of Theresa, who lives in Mary's own quarters. Theresa's father Con had cursed Mary, on the day of the eviction. His curse could be shown to have achieved Shon's death. But now Mary has rescued Con's child and, 'with her training', feels tenderness and sympathy. She 'felt no grievance against a world in which there were children to love' (p. 413). Cary thus presents his message, that mankind's natural power to love must be educated by understanding. Then this power can do something to counter selfish creeds based on glory and salvation. The happiest time in Mary's day is telling stories to Theresa, whose favourite story concerns 'the cat's clever triumph over the world' (p. 412). This cat, ' "cleverer even than blue Peter", who "is always trying to get into the drawing room" ', ends up living in a ' "magnificent castle" ' which, in Theresa's imagination, resembles Mary's shabby room and garden, while the word 'magnificent' means 'secure, peaceful and safe'.

At this point, Mary receives a message that ' "Mr Philly is for doing murder up there at Carnmore." ' So the magnificent male world of Philly ('lover of horses') threatens this female, cat's world – as the Greeks threatened the world of Trojan women.

By now Philip has produced an heir for Slatter, in August 1899. Slatter has 'thanked God ten times a day for the boy', and begun at once to plan his education 'as a gentleman fit to inherit an estate' (p. 409). James Slatter clearly still expects to claim the Castle. The child is named *James John,* which suggests a threat, a truce, or a reconciliation. John Chass is godfather. The mother is Slatter's daughter Coo, whose desire for a child has driven her to propose marriage to Philip, as the only available male, even though she and her sister are convinced he is mad. Her proposal rouses his wrath, and his reply is ' "Don't ye think I might kill ye?" ' (p. 378). On their wedding night, he threatens to kill her. Slatter has denied him drink, and to save her own life Coo steals brandy from the dining room of their cheap hotel. Slowly 'from the drunken, excited cells, the stimulated blood, rose up the passion and the optimism of nature itself, the peacock's vanity, the monkey's curiosity, and sentimental tenderness, the energy and life of the fungus under a cellar which splits the pavement to reach the light and air' (p. 390). So Philip regains self-confidence, and sufficient 'good natured condescension', to climb into bed. The women's war now, for Coo, is to procure drink, without Slatter's knowledge, to keep Philip amiable. She succeeds until the day of their son's christening, which is the day just described, when Mary's storytelling is interrupted.

The christening party is over, but Philip has mixed his drinks. He now decides 'to shoot Coo at least and perhaps everybody in the house' (p. 414). But he wastes one cartridge by chasing the nurse and firing at her, so giving Coo time to barricade herself in. Having only one cartridge left, and being thwarted by Coo, he shoots himself, feeling 'greatly surprised', 'that he, Philip Feenix, had performed this bold, this terrible deed' (p. 416). So Cary dismisses the heroics of suicide, and indicates that a wrath like that of Achilles is suffered by many a wife like Coo, whose husband cannot realize the dreams suggested to him by epic and romance.

Briseis and Chryseis were probably not unlike Maddy and Coo, he implies. (Cf. Cottee, for whom Marie as a tragic queen seemed absurd, p. 166 above.)

The 'clever cat' of Mary's tale, who resembles Bridget's talisman, 'blue Peter', clearly predicts Bridget's ownership of Castle Corner. That this is a prediction to which Biblical predictions are comparable is evident when the Protestant man-servant Grogan settles down 'to count the silver and to read his Bible' which, 'marking the end of the day and so a day nearer to the glorious resurrection into eternal joy, were, with the tea, the chief pleasures of his life' (p. 417). His chief delight is in reading Revelation.

According to Bridget's faith 'her career was too wonderful for luck; it was the working of a fate, a secret power'. She would be ready to thank God, the Blessed Virgin, or St Bridget.

But for Cary, the secret power is undoubtedly the creative imagination, in which all mankind shares, above all someone like Bridget, whose own powerful imagination has caused her to act, throughout the book, on her direct intuitions. Because Bridget is uneducated, and moreover unjustly treated even in her own family, she points the way in which the creative imagination of the world may eventually act. That is, societies will collapse if they fail to recognize the true character of the real world, in which a Bridget and her Finian deserve their rightful place.

Through Felix Corner, Cary has revealed his own philosophical viewpoint, and also his bitterness regarding his failure as a student at Oxford. His points are clearly made in this final part, when Felix returns to England, in September 1899, feeling far less concerned about a bankruptcy petition than about a letter from Cleeve, who has found the pamphlet his father published, at his own expense, while an Oxford undergraduate. Felix had expected it to revolutionize the world. But it had succeeded only in ruining his career. For, 'owing to the excitement of composition, Felix had taken a third-class degree' (p. 28). His inclination is to tell Cleeve ' "to give the examiners what they want" ' (p. 359). But he fears that this cynical attitude will 'prevent Cleeve from obtaining any real good from philosophy'.

His pamphlet had concerned Schopenhauer and Darwin, to prove that *a bare will to live is impossible'*. This accords with Cary's theory: 'that there is a purpose in nature *which is always trying to emerge' (Power in Men,* p. 261). Cleeve takes up the argument eagerly with such points as, ' "Plato saw that education was the secret" ' (p. 361); Aquinas ' "doesn't prove that his first cause is a moral agent" ' (p. 362); and ' "all living things want – to be happy" ' (p. 363). Felix concedes: ' "Nature can enjoy pain, or any other kind of nervous stimulation, anything, I suppose, except boredom or frustration." ' Cleeve agrees, and insists that nature has invented within itself the raw material of happiness: ' "Rich material – why is there colour, scent, music in the world, or sex, for the matter of that – except for happiness. Sex is an extraordinary idea when you think of it. . . . And why did nature invent it except for enjoyment, all kinds of enjoyment?" ' Here Felix interjects with a reference to ethics, and Cary's point is clear; that mankind must be educated to enjoy nature according to a code that allows others equal enjoyment. He states it in *Power in Men* as 'the greatest liberty for the greatest number'.

It becomes obvious why Cary considered 'They want to be Happy' as an over-all title for this trilogy. He made the note in July 1936, when the song, 'I want to be Happy', was being revived at the London Hippodrome. It seems therefore that it also revived this source for Cary's theme in his mind.[11] His main point regarding Felix is apparently that his academic failure had driven him to reject his true faith, founded on an original intuition. His reasoning mind remained active, but totally divided from his feelings. This divided self is dramatically depicted by Felix who, in England, is the sage revered for his Liberal views, but, in Africa is a physically degenerate creature ruled almost literally by Nature – in the person of Dinah.

He writes of John Chass as an idealized member of his own family who, with Mary, rules in Castle Corner as well as a man could rule. His names suggest a balance between an artistic or religious temperament, and that which makes a Charlemagne. They are repeated so often throughout the book that their initials especially must eventually strike the reader as significant. Since John Chass can be said to combine the ideals of Jesus Christ and Julius Ceasar, it seems reasonable to suppose that Cary intended these associations. In so far as John Chass is Joyce Cary's ideal, the initials are appropriately recognized as his also.

How Cary accounted for John Chass's persistent 'luck' is not clear. But it is certain that he now believed in the mysterious power of the creative imagination. This 'luck' therefore might be due rather to John Chass's particular form of genius, in which intuition, imagination and reason were in total accord. They would therefore provide an ideal medium for that purpose in nature which is *always trying to emerge'*, and must clearly do so through the creative imagination of individuals. 'God favours him' might therefore rightly apply to someone like John Chass. Bridget's career, by contrast, indicates that the creative imagination is a-moral, unless educated by reason to know justice.

This interpretation accords with *Power in Men,* by which Cary hoped to make his own viewpoint plain. What the novel illustrates, above all else, is the multiplicity and complexity of motives that rule human affairs; above all, the tragedy of false faiths, and the need to escape from those of the past which make it so difficult to shape the future differently. Yet we cannot be free unless we understand *how* we are captive. The need to be aware of this captivity, as a total experience, therefore fully justifies the form of this novel, which is indeed its meaning. The other novels can most easily be understood from it. In it Cary even explains a 'punch on the nose'; it is an expression of 'pathological rage', for which 'words of equivalent violence to the nerves' are a substitute. His explanation concerns Stella, whose hatred of the Boer war is 'like the protest of her womanhood against the interruption of its calm leisurely purpose'. Her words thus strike a blow in the women's war. Yet they attack Jarvis, whom Stella loves: ' "You think I'm a fool, but it's you who are the fool to have anything to do with this war" ' (pp. 396, 397).

12. Three Novels of Boyhood

Mister Johnson

Charley is My Darling

A House of Children

Mister Johnson

Having summed up the message of his four novels in *Power in Men*, Cary relaxed with the simple tale of *Mister Johnson*, which became his most popular, and in fact tellingly sums up his theme, regarding European marriage.

Johnson is a boy of seventeen, with no tribal connexions, whose name signifies his desire to become a true son of John Bull, with the dignified title of Mister. His story concerns his longing to make a true English wife of the girl Bamu who, however, prefers her tribal customs. His tragedy results from his inability to make the required payments for her, and the key point of his story is reached when her brothers take Bamu and her child back to her family – immediately after Johnson has exclaimed that she is his 'gift from God' (p. 182). The Old English meaning of *gift* is in fact 'payment for a wife'.

Johnson can be understood from *Castle Corner*. For he is man as natural artist, with a temperament exactly similar to that of John Chass. But, born in totally different circumstances, he resembles Jingler. His songs are those that might have been sung by Jingler, or (as mentioned here) by 'an Elizabethan or an Irishman' (p. 136). By these songs, Johnson leads the men who actually build the road, of which Harry Rudbeck dreams. Rudbeck is the District Officer, whom Johnson, his clerk, idolizes.

Johnson builds the road to the beat of drums, ' "*To call his army for the war*" ' (p. 136), while the Rimi tree in his path declares:

197

I am Rimi the king of the trees, . . .
My war horse is the strong earth, he prances through the sky,

to which the road-men reply, as they wield their axes in the name of imperialism, or trade,

Put your hands on the ground
Put your face in the dust (p. 157).

Thus Cary continues earlier symbolism, even naming Johnson's apparent friend *Ajali,* to point to the fact that it is chiefly Ajali who destroys Johnson (cf. p. 157 above). By intuition, Johnson has in fact sensed that money is juggled by the English officials to achieve anything like this road, and he is aware of corruption in Arab officialdom. By fate, therefore, he is really a scapegoat, which he becomes through his temperament as a popular artist. He is akin to Gollup, the English sergeant-turned-storekeeper, whose artistic temperament indicates that he is the precursor of Gulley Jimson; Cary's first name for *Gollup* was in fact *Gulley.*[1] Every Sunday, having eulogized his wife in England as ' "The angel in the 'ouse" ' (p. 128), Gollup beats his African mistress Matumbi, presumably with something of Gulley's sense of duty, or guilt, when beating Sara. Gollup is merely lucky that he has not murdered Matumbi, or Johnson, before Johnson murders him – incited by Ajali, but really by accident. Johnson escapes to Bamu, but she betrays him to Rudbeck.

Johnson's last songs repeat Cary's theme, that religion and politics, as we know them, are largely what men's imaginations have built, as substitutes for a happy family life.[2] Johnson sings of that life, which he has missed, in terms of the world as his father, the sky his mother, the night his wife; and his feelings find reality in Rudbeck, whose 'goodness' makes Johnson call on the world to admit 'that there is no god like his god . . . "my frien' Mister Rudbeck – de bigges' heart in de worl' ".' As he utters these words Rudbeck aims his gun at Johnson, 'blows his brains out', and is 'surprised at himself', yet 'feels a peculiar relief and escape' (p. 225).

His 'surprise', anticipating *Herself Surprised,* shows that he realizes what he has done, by complying with Johnson's dying wish, to shoot him instead of having him hanged. For Rudbeck has thus taken upon himself the guilt of a murderer, and Johnson recalls Ishe, who forced a sense of guilt upon her people (p. 155 above). By his action, however, Rudbeck has escaped from, and is no longer captive to, conscience, as a power telling him that Authority, a mere abstract word, is to blame. We are all guilty, and all responsible, is the final message of this book.

Johnson can be understood from the play that Cary wrote at this time entitled 'The King is Dead, Long Live the King'. In it the chief character, Isa, is clearly intended to be another Christ, and Isa preaches that politics involve religion which, when based on the principles of justice, truth, love and beauty 'is simply God's spirit speaking in us all.'[3] This message is apparently taken from the First Epistle of John: 'Hereby know we that we dwell in him, and he in us, because he hath given us of his Spirit' (1 John iv. 13). Spinoza used these words as an epigraph for his *Tractatus Theologico-Politicus,* which influenced Cary's writing of *Power in Men* at this time (even to the numbering of paragraphs).

It seems, therefore, that Spinoza's epigraph from John inspired Cary's epigraph for *Mister Johnson* – the only novel for which he wrote one. It is addressed *'To* MUSA', and reads: *' "Remembered goodness is a benediction" '*. Musa is presumably the clerk described in Cary's preface, who had worked all night, unasked, copying a report, because he had not wanted Cary to 'catch trouble'. Here Cary writes of the general warm-heartedness of Africans, and it is this feeling of grace received, that the book conveys. Johnson is a son of St John, rather than John Bull.

Charley is My Darling

A feeling of benediction carries over into this novel, where Charley, like Johnson, 'is lost in the world, wants help and gets bad help'.[4] Johnson had resembled John Chass Corner, in having qualities that made him a son of St John. Charles has qualities rather, that Cary had transferred from Charles Moore to John Chass; those that had made a Charlemagne, and could make a Hitler.

That Charley Brown, aged fifteen, is a born leader and ruler of men, is conveyed in the opening pages, which describe how he and some other evacuee children from London have arrived safely in Devon, in September 1939, chiefly through Charley's organization. When war was declared Cary was on holiday in Sherford, near Kingsbridge – the Twyport of this novel. By January 1940 the novel was finished, an urgent tract for the time, regarding children like Charley. Cary had intended him to be a character in his novel of childhood, in Ireland. But he now divided the book, so that this one would appear quickly. As his preface shows, he is arguing that all children are by nature delinquents. When war makes adults behave as delinquents do, children are even less able to form a general idea of proper behaviour, he implies.

His message is conveyed in the key scene, where these Cockney children, after an escapade in which they have wrecked a stolen car, are walking in the darkness through the fields. They anticipate their punishments by recalling past beatings; and they seek the general idea, by which their parents, who whip them to save them from hell, are called 'strict'; whereas Germans, who ' "wip Jews to death in Germany" ' (p. 100) are called cruel and wicked, and must be fought – so totally disrupting these children's lives. From comparing beatings, and their personal scars, they consider their futures, and the need ' "to learn how to do things" '. Ginger would like to be in a band, but ' "you have to be awfully good for a good band. It's a gift" ', he says. ' "You get born with a gift. You get born with money and everything" ' (p. 106).

Cary's theme phrase appears nowhere more poignantly than here, in these children's realization of life's injustice, and their desire to sustain the sympathy they have discovered in each other as a 'gang' rather than a 'band', which gains a glorious connotation from 'we band of brothers', whereby Shakespeare had inspired generations to go to war.

The form of this novel seems to be derived from Blake's lines in section 27 of *Jerusalem*, headed 'To the Jews'. Here Blake presents a vision of God akin to Cary's, in the person of the Giant Albion, which unites all men in 'The Religion of Jesus'. It is a fitting inspiration, since the current war chiefly concerned the Jews, and since Blake, a London boy, might well have been Charley, had he been living at that hour. Cary gives his clue in the events of the story, which recall these lines of *Jerusalem*:

> The Jew's-harp-house & the Green Man
> The Ponds where Boys to bathe delight,
>   The fields of Cows by Willan's farm,
> Shine in Jerusalem's pleasant sight.

Charley's story is briefly that, on his arrival from London, he has to live down the humiliation of having his head shaved and being nicknamed 'Lousy'. This drives him to such feats as letting out the bull at Wicken's farm – a truly symbolic creature to this town boy – and being almost drowned in the pond near the Green Man,[5] by the deliberate malice of the boy Mort – whose name spells death, just as the name Ajali did for Johnson. Mort jumps on Charley's fingers clutching the bridge, as he calls ' "Go on, you baastard, drown. I'll freeze you" ' (p. 193). And his behaviour is enjoyed and supported by Charley's supposed friends, while it is ignored by adult onlookers. That Mort personifies the universal death-wish against the hero is evident, and Charley is saved only by the love and help of the village girl Liz. She is plain, and considered 'barmy' because fever has left her deaf. Having rescued Charley from drowning, and slept with him to comfort and revive him, she becomes pregnant. This, of all Charley's unlawful acts, is considered to be the most wicked by everyone in authority – people who would think it no crime at all in anyone a year or two older. Before they go their separate ways, under police escort, to unknown destinations, Charley and Liz are told that they will never meet again. It seems indeed likely that Charley could become another Hitler. Yet, he remembers the week he spent in hiding with Liz as ' "bess time I ever ad" '. And the rare comment that Cary allows himself, as author, makes the message of this book, too, a positive one. Here perhaps, is Cary's truest expression of his intuition of grace:

> what he means is that in that week he has made the discovery which transforms the world, that kindness is the dignity of living, which transforms the most grotesque gesture, the ugliest face into the expression of eternal beauty (p. 316).

A House of Children

> This was our feeling as children. We sought glory, but not our own exclusively; we wanted to be part of a glorious experience; . . . a member of the grown-up world, which was all-glorious (pp. 206–7).

These words reveal Cary's intuition of freedom in an ideal form. With the last words quoted from Charley's book, they probably express most truly the gifts of feeling that he would have wished each generation to pass on to the next. They express his gratitude, and only gratitude seems possible in this book, following the tale of injustice suffered by Charley and Liz – even though – or perhaps because – the events centre on the death of Cary's mother. Such injustice as he had known, he implies, is nothing beside the sufferings and cruelty that surround us. Ivan Karamazov's account of deliberate human cruelty clearly influenced Charley's story directly (ch. 7, n. 20 above). Understandably, therefore, this was the time for Cary to rid himself of any feelings of self-pity.[6]

In *A House of Children* he has explored his childhood memories, as if to discover, from his own experience, the true nature of the soul. The Giant Albion of *Jerusalem* contains scenes of London, dear to Blake, from which Cary has given tragic form to *Charley is my Darling*. The sea, as it lived in Cary's senses, from his earliest memories of Inishowen, symbolizes the world soul as he discovered it in himself; so the sea gives this book its dominant, all-embracing form. Reverting again to the name Annish, he writes:

> There is no more beautiful view in the world than that great lough, seventy square miles of salt water, from the mountains of Annish. . . . my memories are full of enormous skies, as bright as water, in which clouds sailed bigger than any others; . . . They seemed to follow a curving surface of air concentric with the curve of the Atlantic which I could see bending down on either hand, a bow, which, even as a child of three or four, I knew to be the actual shape of the earth. . . .
>
> In Annish we lived in a world which we realised as a floating planet, and in a beauty which we had been taught to appreciate, as greatly as small children are capable of enjoying spectacle (pp. 18–19).

Thus Cary stresses his good fortune, that his earliest memories were of a world of glorious beauty, which he had been taught to feel and understand.

The action of the novel, however, concerns the tenth year of his life, when he had to adjust to the death of his mother. The sea as the symbol of the mother and of the unconscious can be explained by the beginning of life in the womb; the women's song in *The African Witch* indeed anticipates the symbolism of the world as the mother in this novel. But as the all-embracing sea it encourages the children to be venturesome – just as any mother, human or animal, must encourage her young. Thus, if they sailed out into the Atlantic, they would seem like a 'Mother Carey's chicken', Cary writes, as a clue, on his opening page. His intuition throughout is of the need to give children a confident understanding of the meaning of freedom; above all, to realize that all children, beginning at the level of their stone-age ancestors, need careful guidance to adjust to a particular society. Their power to love must be educated, or a power to hate will triumph.

In *A House of Children* Cary discovers in himself the sacredness of the family as the structure of society (p. 21 above). Any weakening of the trinity of the child's relationship to its father and mother, for whatever cause, must therefore be a blow to the child's very being, to which he must adjust. The birth of a brother, the death of a parent, as exemplified in this novel, are common experiences, from which jealousy or fear may develop as the chief characteristics of the grown man. Cary writes: 'For the average man or woman of forty, however successful, has been so battered and crippled by various accidents that he has gradually been restricted to a small compass of enterprise. Above all, he is perplexed. He has found out numerous holes and inconsistencies in his plan of life and yet he has no time to begin the vast work of making a new one' (p.66). Here Cary recalls the message of his earlier novels, as he would later explain it in a preface to the first, where he says he had hoped the book would help readers to re-draw their maps, in the way he had done.

By the *dédoublement* of Harry and Evelyn, Cary has illustrated the struggle in his own soul to adjust to experience, and to the expectations of his family. In his cousin Kathy, at ten, his subconscious self, Evelyn, found a substitute for his mother, and they pledged to marry (p. 62). Yet of this trinity he writes: 'Harry had begun to form ideas of government, the world and so on; very simple ideas, but coherent and rational; whereas Kathy and I were still like savages, who understand so little of the forces surrounding them that they cannot even imagine a means of controlling them' (p. 149). Here surely is the soul being shaped by a platonic education, in a society which has been dominated by the symbol of the soul in the *Phaedrus,* at least since the Renaissance.

He depicts the situation amusingly when the boys attend a Christmas party. The chief effect of a term at a private school has been to give Harry 'a passion for encyclopaedias and dictionaries' (p. 58). On arriving at the party, therefore, he goes straight to a bookshelf, takes down a dictionary, and enjoys the party, because he spends almost the entire time in reading it. On the way home he asks Evelyn 'to notice the frosforescence of the lough', and he speaks with 'the voice of a mystic contemplating wonders.' Thus Harry represents the Cary who accepted authority as Reason in the form of such books. Evelyn by contrast, when deserted by Harry on their arrival at the party, feels 'such painful shyness that I did not know where to look' (p. 58). He is rescued by Kathy, who shows him the steps of the dance in progress. On any other occasion Evelyn would have resented dancing with Kathy, he explains.

> It was the fashion to resent everything Kathy did or said to us, to say that she was bossy and selfish. In fact, she was a sensible child, who was always getting us out of trouble, . . . I don't know when this fashion to snub Kathy began. . . . Perhaps like small animals, our instinct was to pursue only the female who ran away from us, and Kathy, in showing us her affection, was breaking some rule of nature, as cruel and stupid as most of her sexual arrangements. . . .
> . . . She looked at us often with blank wonder, asking herself no doubt what crime she had committed, and how she could discover it and make up for it without offending us further. We, feeling her perplexity on such occasions, always looked still more calm and indifferent (pp. 60–61).

This account suggests that the view of life by which the boys were being educated was inadequate. It is during the dance that Evelyn falls in love with Kathy and proposes marriage. In his manner of telling Cary is possibly recognizing that his cousin Helen took the pledge he made, at ten, to marry her, more seriously than he did. Certainly he goes on to stress Evelyn's naive, impressionable, irresponsible nature, as in his wild escapade with 'Red Cheeks', whom he calls 'My leader' (p. 72). Regarding this escapade 'Pinto' Freeman expresses a view that is close to Cary's own, that in such circumstances a child is exhibiting the spirit of ' "every original genius' " who ' "wants to *change* the situation –" and he began to talk about creating a better world and so on, making the girls laugh, and obviously amusing himself' (p. 77).

Regarding Freeman himself, however, Cary's point seems to be that he has no real sense of purpose as an artist; he may also be saying that the public nowadays expect artists to amuse, rather than instruct them, for this was certainly the problem Cary faced. His abandoned title for this novel is 'Teach Me to Live',[7] which recalls the prayer in Tolstoy's *Childhood, Boyhood, & Youth.*[8]

He had already begun his attack on the symbolists in *Castle Corner,* and continues it here, when Pinto chooses to think that Evelyn has been spying on a maid undressing: 'His idea, of course, was the common one, among the young men of the nineties, not only the decadent, but the patriots and the supermen, that all restraint upon living natural impulse is evil, and that ugliness and unhappiness arise only from restraint; in fact, the anarchist views which now seem so old-fashioned and even childish' (p. 78). His final judgement of Pinto is this:

I read now about the men of the nineties, their bohemianism and disillusionment, and their figures seem romantic. In Pinto, as I realised long afterwards, I knew one of those men, or at least one of the provincials who were affected by the same movement of the time spirit; but he did not seem romantic to us. He was either a shabby, depressed little man in a bad suit, or a lively and amusing companion; or sometimes, when he was dealing with plays or poetry or music, masterful and positive, as little romantic as any of the local magistrates, laying down the law (p. 184).

Yet, in directing the play, Pinto 'obtained an extraordinary power over all his people', who suffered his bullying 'because they felt he was in earnest about something important' (pp. 217, 218). In fact, for Pinto, 'the rehearsal and production of any serious play was like a religious act, and that was why, I suppose, he had such an extraordinary hold over his amateur performers. People without strong opinions and definite standards are always liable to fall under the sway of one who has both, especially if he sets them above his own advantage. They can't help feeling, even while they laugh at his earnestness, that he has some private source of inspiration which entitles him to a certain respect; that to go against him may be slightly wicked' (pp. 226–7). Thus Cary has explained the common basis of art and religion, and also the power of any spellbinder. But his main point regarding Pinto is that his standards are those of the nineties. His actions are all selfish and dishonest. His nickname, *Pinto,* would appropriately refer to the meaning 'piebald horse'; for the children, however, it would be more likely to refer to his reliance on alcohol to sustain him: 'We used to laugh at each other when he went for his drink' (p. 10). Pinto betrays everyone's hopes of him – in instructing the children, in staging a Shakespeare festival – because he has no sense of responsibility. Moreover, he betrays their family's trust by running off with Delia, the boys' older cousin.

Delia is presented as a true life giver, as when the children 'all wanted to touch her, as if to feel the source of our new confidence and happiness' (pp. 46–47). She hopes to be a concert pianist, but her brother and uncles tease her for 'affecting the genius' (p. 122). At this time Pinto argues that to tease anyone studying an art is ' "the meanest thing" ', because it spoils their confidence. Yet it is Pinto himself who finally discourages Delia and, when reproached by her mother, the boy's Aunt Hersey, 'He answered that he had told the truth; Delia's playing was not real playing at all. There was nothing in it. She had nothing to say in music' (p. 156). As a result Delia gives up the piano. It almost seems that Pinto has in this way deliberately won for himself the slave that Delia becomes, for Evelyn writes: 'We were astonished to see how humbly Delia accepted his angry abuse, often unjust, and how patiently she worked for him' (p. 217). Pinto is in fact the age of Aunt Hersey, whom people have expected him to marry, and his behaviour certainly hurts and insults her. Yet Evelyn's father pays his debts, while Pinto, in Paris, meets 'an American lady who might produce a play for him', and Delia becomes 'a regular French housekeeper, visiting the markets every morning at the earliest hour' (pp. 236–7).

Cary's picture is indeed of people of integrity betrayed by an unscrupulous self-seeker, who nevertheless brings them to life, while also challenging their code. The feeling of change belonging to this *fin de siècle* period is also stressed, and that too affects Delia. Pinto's 'funny stories' of hardhip bring a sense of uneasiness even to Evelyn regarding society as he knows it, and they apparently give Delia some sense of guilt. But it is Kathy who gives us the truth: ' "Aunty says that he was a genius and Deely thought someone ought to take care of him. Is he a genius, Harry? Robert says he's only a minor poet. What is a minor poet? . . . they think poor Deely has spoilt her whole life" ' (p. 231).

Cary's theme includes: 'How far are people to be exploited or used to support the work of art, the genius.'[9]

Evelyn and Harry have always recognized their Aunt Hersey as 'a slave' to her brother; they also recognize in her a 'finished grace', which is 'a natural sympathy with men which had been increased by education and strenthened by art' (pp. 82, 83). But this very charm in Aunt Hersey 'laid her open to exploitation by any man' for, according to the code of her society a woman was 'someone put into the world to look after a man, and a house, and children'. So Cary indicates why a man like Pinto seeks a wife in this class.

As Cary's intuitive self, Evelyn is shown as having absorbed these impressions which he now, as writer, shapes into this book. It is he who stores memories of his Corner (Cary) aunts, whom circumstances had forced to earn their living, and so to question this role for women from a different standpoint. It is at the very time that Evelyn is being initiated into the masculine world of the 'sportsman' that he also discovers himself to be a poet, or writer. It is as if Cary is saying that the two worlds had been necessary to him, as the author of his theme.

He expects to be recognized as a sportsman because he is now ten years old, and Harry has been included in a shooting party at that age. But he fears that 'what I imagined the proper rules of life . . . might not apply to me personally'. All children suffer from such fears, he continues, and recalls the broken wooden horse which had served him, when younger 'as a reassurance that some things did continue to be themselves' (p. 196). Thus he stresses the need for a child's natural sense of justice to be fostered, and rightly directed, if the world of his physical existence is to make sense to him. Evelyn is included in the shooting party, but in his excitement he has forgotten to eat, and he faints. His father then tactfully excuses him by suggesting that he has been composing another poem, like one he has already shown to his friends, who then all agree that Evelyn will some day be a great poet whom they will be proud to know.

Again Cary stresses the value of encouragement to children. Moreover: 'The two glories were open to me: that of a sportsman and that of a poet.' Riding home in the ass cart, he boasts of these glories to Oweny, the poor gardener's boy who drives it:

> 'Do you think,' I asked him, 'a man can be a poet and nothing else?'
> 'Aye, it could be as good as anything else and better than some,' with another howl.
> 'It's a good thing to be a poet, isn't it? But you have to be born a poet. It's a gift.'
> 'Ah, there's a tinker comes to Dunvil every Easter has it. But it's a poor tale he tells. All the real poets is dead this thousand years. Haoooooo.' (pp. 209–10).

As in the previous novels, this expression of the theme phrase can be taken as the clue to the book. First, then, would be Cary's belief that everyone is 'born a poet'; we are poets by nature. Yet to be 'a poet and nothing else' will be 'a good thing' presumably, only if the poet has something worth saying and can afford to wait to be heard. Cary then describes an ass cart in a long passage that begins: 'Nothing travels more slowly than an ass cart, and it cannot be hurried; so that the ass traveller, like an invalid or a prisoner, is committed to a special kind of existence.' He concludes: 'Ass cart travelling is pure life in the present', and at this point tells how he and Oweny are joined by Anketel, Kathy's small brother. For Anketel, 'All human sympathies had come upon him at once,' in a concern for Oweny. He has been 'struck by Oweny's poverty', and so 'Some natural sense of justice' has stirred in Evelyn. Yet he has then accepted his aunt's explanation, 'that Oweny was not fit for better work because he could not read or write'. 'I could understand that limitation, and I did not ask why Oweny suffered from it. I, like most children, accepted the world as I found it. It was very gradually that I came to have any doubts at all about the excellence of its arrangements.' Yet Anketel, by his sympathy 'seemed so completely changed in nature, as if he had grown a new mind and a new heart' (pp. 212–13). Soon after this, Cary would describe himself as a man who had dug up his foundations in order to 'found a new life and a new mind' (p. 9 above). From these clues, it seems that Cary is here presenting a symbol of the soul that for him replaces the platonic symbol. The ass cart certainly recalls *The Golden Ass* of Apuleius, which concerns the making of a soul, and contains the story of Psyche. Moreover, the name Anketel comes from the Norse word *âss*, which signifies 'god' or 'divinity', combined with *ketel*, which is of doubtful origin, but can be related to the word cart.[10] Certainly, if the cart symbolizes the Castle in the scene suggesting Plato's symbol in *Castle Corner*, the ass cart here carries a very different message: of truth from childish intuition, rather than from reason, and with amity between the favoured and unfavoured members of society, rather than the brutal treatment of the irrational horse. It also incorporates amity between fathers and sons. Indeed, Cary actually attributes to Anketel some sayings of his own son Tristram, which he noted in 1930;[11] it is therefore possible that he was then actually influenced by similar sympathies in Tristram. In the novel, however, this episode shows the effect on Evelyn, of feeling sure of his father's love, despite his mother's death. That would obviously be the most significant aspect of such a symbol, for him. 'The experience of compassionate love' was 'something new about the world', which Evelyn intuited when the Canon visited their school; this suggests that such education of feelings was lacking in their schooling. Evelyn's slowness in recognizing real injustice to Oweny would thus be explained. His sense of injustice was indeed concerned solely with himself.

The need to reconcile the sportsman and poet in ourselves is the final thought of the novel. Though Evelyn is writing an epic, it seems flat and lifeless beside the excitement of trying to dive, as his father does. This description too, can be taken to symbolize the boy's desire for reunion with the mother, as the sea. He comments: 'Yet the quality of our living experience could be translated only into the experience of poetry which people would not read.' Here he certainly challenges readers to recognize such poetic meanings in Cary's writing.

The three novels of boyhood all carry the same message, in different ways. All three concern boys of similar temperament though of vastly different circumstances. The gift called genius is not uncommon, Cary seems to say. But it is easily stifled and moreover requires experience and understanding of life, before it can produce anything of value. In *A House of Children* he draws attention explicitly to the way in which he had been influenced by Shakespeare and the Bible, and shaped by a classical education, in schools actually organized according to Greek heroic and philosophical ideals. He could thus be said to have prepared the reader for the interpretations that follow.

13. The First Trilogy

Herself Surprised
To be a Pilgrim
The Horse's Mouth

Castle Corner had been as little understood as the previous novels, chiefly, it seems, because readers did not recognize the form. Cary therefore devised the form of a triple confession, which may owe something to the confessional tone and bias of *Between Two Worlds*. It may also appropriately depict the *Phaedrus* symbol of the soul, with 'The horse's mouth' of the 'irrational', much-beaten Sara, giving her testimony first – beginning 'Know thyself'. This accords with Cary's belief in intuition as direct knowledge of truth, and his already frequent use of the word 'surprise', to indicate an intuition, makes it fit the title of Sara's book perfectly. He had intended the three books to present the same events from different points of view. This suggests that they are testimonies at a trial, and the prospect of being sentenced to prison dominates all three characters. Yet 'The Horse's Mouth' is the dominant symbol. If this is taken to represent what has been called 'The Inherited Conglomerate',[1] of beliefs by which men live, then the trilogy gains greatly in meaning. Cary's readers become judge and jury, in a trial of the worth of our society, which is dominated by this platonic symbolism; these three characters, fairly representing the charioteer and his two horses, are the chief witnesses, but themselves on trial.

While writing *Mister Johnson* Cary had begun a woman's confession, which makes his view of Sara clear. He actually headed it 'For W.O. [Women Only] by Maidubi A. L. C.'; the meaning 'Diviner' for *Maidubi* accords with Cary's treatment hitherto of The Revelation of St John the Divine. This woman's confession reads: 'He [Dick the son] is like my poor darling husband, he hates anything unpleasant. His whole life is really a series of careful arrangements to avoid shocks or disappointments. That is not his fault. It is his fathers and mine. But Sara's [the daughter's] unhappiness is entirely my fault because I have never trusted myself to tell what a fraud the life of a woman is, in this modern world'.[2]

As is usual with Cary, the clue to Sara's book is on the first page. The judge has complained, before sending her to prison: ' "She may be ill-educated, as the defence has urged, but she is certainly intelligent. I am forced to conclude that she is another unhappy example of that laxity and contempt for all religious principle and social obligation which threatens to undermine the whole fabric of our civilization." ' The crime is of course society's own: that anyone of Sara's intelligence should be ill-educated. She is typical of English women, forced at the risk of being beaten to fit into a social system 'that does not suit them' (p. 124 above).

The name Sara seems to convey Cary's reaction to the Symbolists (besides deliberately recalling the Biblical Sara). For Sara is the heroine of *Axël,* which Symons calls a Symbolist drama of the soul in conflict with the 'modesty' of Nature, and disdainfully rejecting life itself. He calls this Sara 'the haughtiest woman in literature' who, as a woman, desires life and finds it in Axël, but 'Pride, and the woman's devotion to the man, aid her to take the last cold step with Axël, in that transcendental giving up of life at the moment when life becomes ideal'; she does so in response to Axël's boast, ' "Live? Our servants will do that for us." '[3] Sara Monday, treated by all as a servant, is doing just that. She is both modest and proud. Indeed Gulley says, 'Sara was an empress. It was a glory to have that woman, and to beat her' (*The Horse's Mouth*, pp. 252–3). His impulse to kill her could thus stem from his own Symbolist spirit, against which he is fighting, but which provokes him to attack her very capacity to 'Live'. By nature however Sara is a mother; so the Bible, which above all else has shaped our society, readily brings to mind Sarah 'the mother of nations', whose name, meaning 'princess', was chosen by God for this universal mother.[4] Sara in fact thinks 'If I had my deserts I should ride a King's coach' (p. 161), and *Herself Surprised* hinges on her thought: 'a cat may look at a king' (p. 23).

This king is the Jewish millionaire Hickson, who grew from

'the Jew story' based on Raffalovich.[5] In 1937, when Sara's book is supposedly written, anti-Semitism was already making the war inevitable. Therefore the name *Hickson,* derived from *Isaacson,*[6] is keenly ironic, since *Isaac* means 'God may laugh', because the Biblical Sarah laughed at the birth of this child of promise. (Sara twice describes Hickson as like a child.)[7] That Cary intends this derivation seems evident, from the name above the junk shop that Gulley regularly tries to rob: 'Isaacson and Waller'. The names suggest Hickson and also Gulley, whose eternal ambition to paint on walls makes him end his book by thanking God for them. But 'Ikey' is the name he gives to the succession of lessees whom this junk shop ruins – and Gulley laughs at the prospect of cheating them. His telephoning of Hickson, which he recounts so amusingly, is really a mild form of Jew-baiting, to which his sense of kinship with 'Artist Hitler' points.[8]

Cary's view of Nazism seems to have been coloured by an article, 'Kierkegaard and the "Existential" Philosophy', which includes: 'until we have faced these "existential" religious categories . . . we shall not know how to speak to that in the German spirit of which Nazism is a perversion'.[9] His notes from this article include:

K's central tenet: *No external standard of truth & morality* above individual decision (But what is an individual? J.C.) . . . He then turns on to the world & makes decision in which his whole self is involved. Choosing himself as freedom./ *Cannot be justified by appeal to universal.* Jaspers as against Nazi Heidegger interprets this as call to realize one's absolute freedom (but this is anarchism & back to tyranny) . . . Freedom is 'this was right & so I did it' (he may break the ethical which is a *matter of codes* (e.g. my objection to Kant categorical) . . . K. says real triumph of Abraham's faith was in accepting inspiration that he ought not to sacrifice Isaac.[10]

It seems likely that these notes influenced *The Horse's Mouth,* where Gulley is fighting a fundamental despair, where the sacrifice of Isaac is a main point, and where Nazism is debated.

Cary's three narrators are all very convincing yet misleading witnesses in this trial of our society. Sara's unwillingness to speak ill of anyone is the typical mother's habit of lying to children to encourage them. She is a true mother to Robert Brown, Wilcher's nephew, and to Tom Jimson, Gulley's illegitimate son (by Sara's best friend Rozzie, though she does not know it until the end of Gulley's book). It is actually to raise money for the schooling of this gifted boy[11] that Sara steals from Wilcher.

'The horse's mouth' applies to Sara thus, as notes show: 'My mother would not let me complain if my older sister had the best of everything, she would say How would it be if you'd never been born at all. Don't you forget that, and don't look a gift horse in the teeth. Life is a gift and you're lucky only to be alive.'[12] It is only by a kind of push from Nature on both sides that she finds herself married to Matt Monday, an Oxford graduate who is nevertheless a doormat to his mother, to whom Sara is cook. When Sara finds herself in Paris with him, looking dubiously at her big Paris hat, she differs from Marguéritte, whose small hat was preferred by Murry, the Oxford gentleman who did not marry her. Marguéritte's 'gay brown eyes' also attracted Murry, and Sara says 'my eyes were nothing but brown'.[13] That Sara's story is rooted in Marguéritte's seems even more obvious when, having got a husband, and Hickson's patronage, Sara is in fact acceptable at Oxford, and describes her enjoyment of life there much as Cary did himself (pp. 35–36). She has three daughters, and one son *Matthew,* whose name means 'gift of Jehovah'. Matt, which describes her husband's temperament, should not blind the reader to the clear evidence that Matthew is Hickson's child. Sara's reaction to the baby's sudden death is to think 'God strikes when you least expect and His wrath is terrible' (p. 33). Her religion is clearly at the propitiatory level and her penance is to wear coarse linen and 'take no pleasure' in sex. But Matt prevails, and her next child is Nancy, 'a kind baby from birth . . . So God struck the balance for the child'.

Nancy is a child of grace, as signified by her name. Gulley Jimson's wife in this novel has the name Nina, also derived from Hannah. As it was at this time that Cary began a dossier for his archetypal Hannah,[14] the fact that these names show the significance of the characters seems proof that Cary intends them to do so. Of Nina Jimson Sara writes; 'He made her a slave' and 'even beat her' (p. 46) so revealing that Nina's grace is the acceptance of suffering. Sara decides, 'that if Jimson was not her religion, he was most of it, and perhaps the beatings were part of it too' (p. 58). But she is horrified that Gulley beats Nina, and it is her refusal to accept this right in him that is the chief quarrel between them.

Hickson has introduced Gulley to Sara, no doubt to get a portrait of her. But Gulley makes him jealous; so Hickson poisons Matt's mind against her, thus ending his own intimacy with her. But the fact that Sara brought life and happiness to Hickson, and through him to Matt and Gulley, is surely a key point of her story.

She is surprised that the clever Hickson finds wisdom in her view of life – which is based on Charlotte M. Yonge and the country sayings of her 'good mother', such as ' "life was a gift that Solomons miss; and none so plain but the sun will kiss" ' (p. 26).

As the clue to the story, this has many associations. The most obvious is the one Cary has already shown in two novels: that the kiss of the sun can be disastrous (pp. 165, 172 above). Moreover, he makes the sun the symbol of the elect, and it will be Gulley's symbol, so that the saying foretells that Jimson (a son of *James*)[15] will supplant Hickson. The word 'Solomons' is accepted by Hickson with reference to himself, and Sara explains that he 'did often complain to me of his sad life'. He could in fact be Benskin, who expected his wife Helen 'to use his son as a weapon' (*Castle Corner*, p. 405). Finally 'Solomons' almost certainly relates to Tolstoy's *A Confession* (chapter VI), where he attributes the words of the Preacher in Ecclesiastes to Solomon. Tolstoy quotes the many references to what is done 'under the sun' to prove the stupidity of life if there is no life after death, and to explain his own melancholy, prior to his conversion. William James's analysis of Tolstoy, with reference to this passage, makes it the more likely that Cary has it in mind.[16] If he is proposing to rival the great confessions (p. 47 above), then it is appropriate to draw attention to this famous confession by Tolstoy, whose *Kreutzer Sonata* he is answering. Sara's confession indeed directly answers Tolstoy's.

Sara's tragedy is that at thirty-nine she is widowed, unwanted by her daughters because uneducated, and abandoned by Hickson through his jealousy of Gulley. Gulley misleads her into thinking he will marry her, and in fact acquires in her a model, a mistress, and a housekeeper who actually spends her own money on him. When Gulley leaves her, she goes to work for the bachelor lawyer, Wilcher, whose reputation among servants is that he is a miserly millionaire, whose sexual aberrations would have sent him to court long before, but for his social position. Sara decides 'that if a gentleman like Mr. Wilcher, who was so strict about church-going, went so far with the girls that it came to the police, then he could not help it and ought to be pitied, or, if mad, locked up, or married' (p. 142).

Wilcher too recognizes good nature in Sara, who finds herself doing for him 'four women's work, for less than the wages of one' (p. 160). That she finds ways of cheating him on occasions is scarcely surprising. He, too, misleads her into believing that he wants to marry her, though he merely wants to save himself the discomfort of going out to Julie, his mistress (who ends in an asylum). Sara reports Wilcher's statement 'that life was truly a battle, a terrible battle' (p. 191). Thus he echoes John Chass's discovery that 'life is a battle', where ' "the blaggards" ' look ' "more like church-wardens" ' (p. 191 above). Wilcher is a church warden.

It seems evident, to judge from Cary's treatment of Arabella (p. 160 above) that Sara is intended to represent England, on trial as a nation amidst world politics of 1937. The plot of her story derives partly from 'He Must Die Again', which Cary began in 1940. It criticizes current pacifism, and attacks the 'rottenness' of Dostoevsky's view of Christianity.[17] Therefore the title of Sara's book may well owe something to the chapter in *The Brothers Karamazov* where these words occur: ' "I wonder at myself" '. ' "You have revealed me to myself. You have seen through me and explained me to myself!" ' The chapter is entitled 'A Lady of Little Faith', and it concerns a character who claims to be ' " a hired servant." ' She seems like Sara's opposite – yet the Sara whom Gulley depicts.[18]

The three narrators of the trilogy can best be judged from the one occasion when all three are together. Sara tells of it in her chapter 65. Gulley has appeared at Wilcher's London home, after an absence of three years, expecting her to return to him, and she writes: 'I dreaded it and yet I knew he had only to say the word. For cruel as he was, he had yet a hold on me. I don't know how it is but when you've lived with a man, and cooked and cleaned for him and nursed him and been through troubles with him, he gets into your blood, whoever he is, and you can't get him out. Besides, there was no doubt Gulley was the most of a man I ever knew. For he carried his own burden, which was a heavy one; and even if he was cruel, it was only when driven mad' (pp. 166-7). She then unwisely hints that Gulley wants her to return to him only because he is ' "stuck" ', at which 'bang, his arm came out . . . like a snake striking. And so hard the blood flew over his own face' (p. 168). Then Wilcher returns, Sara rushes past him to bathe her face, and learns only afterwards, from the butler, that, 'bloody as he was', Gulley shook hands with the amiable Wilcher, who talked art, asked Gulley to stay, and even accompanied him down the road 'talking all the way'. It is from this time that Wilcher makes the advances by which Sara becomes his mistress.

Gulley describes the scene in chapter 28 of *The Horse's Mouth*. He describes Wilcher as a 'Boorjwar', 'a regular Boorjwarrior', so identifying him with the evangelical Liberals who gained power during the Boer war when, as shown in *Castle Corner*, 'the bourgeois age destroying the aristocratic' gained its greatest victory. Also likening Wilcher to 'demons, afreets and poltergeists', he reveals that he agreed Wilcher could have Sara as his mistress, if he paid Gulley 'twenty-two and six' a week. But Sara from this time also pays Gulley weekly instalments 'whether to keep him in some comfort and please my conscience, or only to keep him away and please my flesh, I never could tell' (*Herself Surprised*, p. 169). It is when Wilcher learns of Sara's payments, and the fact that she has been visiting Gulley and his family, that he has her charged for 'pawning some old trinkets which I had forgotten' (*To be a Pilgrim*, p. 9). By this time, however, he is being charged himself, by a girl he has molested in the park, and has decided to marry Sara, to escape from his own nature. He is prevented by the woman whom Sara calls her 'chief enemy' (p. 151). She is Mrs Loftus Wilcher, his heir's wife, who proves that Sarah is a thief to prevent her getting Wilcher's money; and she has Wilcher pronounced insane to save him from prison. He is put in the charge of Ann, a doctor, who is the daughter of his brother Edward.

To be a Pilgrim continues the story, as Wilcher's diary or confession, until September 1938. As a practised lawyer, he can be expected to make out a better case for himself than Sara for herself. Nevertheless, it does seem that Wilcher has experienced a conversion, from the time he asked Sara to marry him.

Ann takes him to his neglected country house, Tolbrook, because she expects Robert, son of Wilcher's sister Lucy, to come there. The real pilgrims of the book are perhaps Ann and Robert, who have never been given a real home by their parents, but succeed, during this year, in marrying and making a productive farm of the property. Their child is named John, chiefly through Tom Wilcher's contriving. Tom has revived family prayers, and is moved to read of John the Baptist, whose father has been struck dumb by an angel until he agrees that, though custom requires the child to be named Zacharias, after its father, it shall instead be John. Reading this, Tom says, 'the words took hold of me and carried me into grace' (p. 127). So John becomes the baby's name. In this scene mother and nurse attend the child while outside is heard 'the sudden clank of the horse's chains'. Cary's intentions regarding the horse, as male energy, and the name John as signifying grace, seem here undeniable.

Tom is moved, it seems, by memories of his nephew John — whose character can be traced back, through an abortive novel 'Tod',[19] to Johnny Brant. This is the character who went to World War I as a platonic pilgrim, his face resembling those seen in 'railway waiting rooms'.[20] He is met on his return by his mother and Tom, at the railway station, and exclaims: ' "I never thought I'd see this again. Very nice. Very nice indeed. It's a gift" ' (p. 258). Here again is the clue to the book. John's grace of temperament tempts Tom to deny him the university education he expects, though Tom knows John to be a 'scholar in the very spirit' (p. 284); and to take John into his firm, in order to enjoy the company of this 'beloved boy'. Since it is John who urges Tom to publish his book concerning 'the positive power of evil', and John's girl-friend who calls Tom 'Uncle Lucifer' (p. 273), shortly before Tom says 'And with John, I was on the closest terms of intimacy' (p. 275), there seems little doubt that Tom is responsible for John's degeneration. When John is finally 'run over by a car in Bond Street' (p. 287), his death symbolizes the total failure of Tom, as a member of the Liberal ruling class. John has been the 'good horse' of Plato's symbol. But Tom has made a poor charioteer. He talks of saving John from 'that Delilah' (p. 285), with reference to the good-time girl of the twenties, Gladys. But Gladys says of Tom's mistress, ' "I'm not like that old soak, Julie – I'd be ashamed" ' (p. 288).

At Oxford in 1887 Tom became 'a dandy', modelled on his older brother Edward, who had been one of 'that group of rich young men who were scholars and dandies . . . who pursued actresses and carried a Homer in their pockets' (p. 71). Of his own career Tom writes: 'I remember very well that I discussed with several Oxford friends the question – ought one to keep a mistress? Our argument was that in all the great civilizations, in Greece, Rome, Italy, France, mistresses played an important. part' (p. 70). At Edward's suggestion he contrived to 'knock into' their 'between-maid' (p. 76), and has been molesting servants ever since; he has kept Julie (won from Edward), as his mistress, in the belief that this conduct contributes to England's greatness, as marriage will not. Intended for the Church, he has instead become a lawyer, so gaining control of the family property. Though his chief problem has been to pay Edward's debts, he is rich. Yet he neglects both town and country houses, and has set fire to the town house just before leaving it (in Sara's book). Now he is at the country house, Tolbrook, and by re-living his childhood there, gains grace.

He recalls their fondness, as children, for playing at funerals and preaching, ' "as the heir of Wycliffe and Cromwell and Stiggins" ' (p. 28). Their father's strict rules resulted in frequent beatings, which set up a strong sexual bond between him and his daughter Lucy. She in turn gained a hold over Tom and 'made me murderous with her devil', Tom says (p. 27). In the closing pages his character becomes wholly comprehensible. In a childhood game, Lucy had once locked him in a linen basket, and the feeling had then grown upon him, when nobody answered his cries, that the family had planned to get rid of him by letting him die there: 'in that basket more than sixty years ago I suffered a torture so extreme, so fearful that it twists my heart now. . . . And through the child, it is a pain for all childhood, so easily hurt, so helpless. . . . What surprises me is not that I screamed in the basket, but that I did not die there, that my childish heart and brain could stand such shocks of agony without bursting' (pp. 333–4). Tom believes he would have died, except that their doctor acceded to his wish to sleep with his mother. 'I took my father's place in the big bed. . . . I was in paradise. And yet I knew, even then, that kind as she was, my mother suffered me with difficulty in her bed; and that she had never cared greatly for my plain face, my awkward ways, my spectacled eyes. I got on her nerves, as they say. It was by mere contact, I suppose, that I regained, on my mother's breast, the power to live'. So, perhaps through his sympathetic understanding of

Raffalovich, whose mother found him too ugly to love, Cary
gives us sympathetic understanding of Wilcher's attitude towards
women, and towards his family. But there are hints of other
associations in Cary's mind. Being saved from dying by sleeping
with the mother recalls a similar situation in *Sons and Lovers*,[21]
and Lawrence certainly contributes to Wilcher.[22] Another strong
hint is of Tolstoy, who describes similar feelings when locked
in a box room, and in desiring sex first with a maid.[23] Thus
Cary's characters reveal, simultaneously, how the world's and the
reader's own characters and values are shaped.

Lucy has married Brown, the leader of the Benjamites
(suggestive of the Buchmanites), because she thinks ' "that her
own class is finished" ', says Edward. Brown rules as 'God
commands' (p. 88) and, apparently having in mind Abraham,
Sarah and Hagar,[24] commands Lucy, while pregnant, to sleep
on the floor, so that their child is born dead (as perhaps he
actually wants), while he sleeps with Ella, Lucy being forced to
' "serve Ella as a handmaiden" '. But then God reveals to Lucy
that he did not command this; and Brown ' "could not tell
whether it was God who had commanded him to put me away,
or the devil, who had made him lust after Ella" ' (p. 88). So Cary
stresses the reality of the devil, but dismisses the inner light of
such sects. Since the name *Lucy* means 'light', it appropriately
comments on that fact. He also suggests that she saw the light,
in believing her own class finished. For she does bear a child to
Brown, and he, Robert, becomes the hope of the Wilchers. But
Lucy has also discovered the truth about the noble peasant
Brown and his followers. So, when dying, she begs: ' "Tommy,
promise me, keep Robert away from them . . . they don't
understand children . . . and make a gentleman of him . . . with
a proper education . . . you'll find I've left enough money."
And then putting up her arms, "Promise me, Tom, quickly.
There's no time – quickly, Tom" ' (p. 298).

But Tom does not promise, and so gets his final revenge on
her. For, as Sara tells us, he denies Robert the education the boy
desperately wants himself, and even, apparently, the money Lucy
left for him, for Tom keeps him looking 'like a charity boy.'
Robert is 'expecting wonders from Oxford, not only enjoyments,
but discoveries, about the way the world really worked and what
he should do to help it on.' But Tom decides 'Oxford might spoil
him. For as Mrs Loftus had said, it was full of socialists and

playboys, a disgrace to their class' (*Herself Surprised,* pp. 177, 178). Mrs Loftus is Blanche Wilcher, Sara's 'chief enemy' (p. 217 above). But Tom has 'always admired and respected her' (*To be a Pilgrim,* p. 132). We know from Sara however that Blanche's sister, Clary, would have married Loftus Wilcher, if Blanche had not won him from her while she was nursing a sick aunt. This skirmish, in a women's war, leads Clary to declare:

> 'It's a man's world and so it will be until we have polygamy, like the Africans, and we can all live at peace in our own families and just send for a good husband when we need him. Then I could borrow my flower among men for a day or two.'
> 'Perhaps it would be enough,' I said.
> 'Of course it would,' she said, 'I know I'd be tired of him in the house. But that's no consolation as you ought to know if you've ever been in love' (*Herself Surprised,* p. 187).

She thus echoes Cary in *Power in Men,*[25] and there seems no doubt that Tom's approval of Blanche would damn him in Cary eyes.

Denied Oxford, Robert has proved himself in an Estate Agency, so successfully that he dreams of making Tolbrook a real manor again. Tom has agreed, yet at Blanche's urging has let Tolbrook, and Robert in disgust has gone to Canada and 'worked his own way up to a farm' (*Herself Surprised,* p. 181). When introducing Robert in his book, however, Tom quotes Blanche as saying Robert 'would like to get hold of Tolbrook', and adds: 'he has brought back nothing from his ten years farming in Canada and South America. He lost his inheritance in bad speculations, and he has not stayed long enough in any job to save a new capital sum' (p. 18). This seems scarcely a fair statement of the facts.

Without doubt the linen basket in which Tom was locked by Lucy is a key to the novel, perfectly symbolizing the way natural feelings of love and charity can be stifled by a misguided and unlucky upbringing. In fact, 'Baskett' was previously the surname of this family.[26] Now, significantly, the basket in which Tom almost died is 'better than new, cleaned and polished and oiled by the faithful, busy hands of Sara, whom my faithlessness attempted to murder' (p. 333).

Near the end of his narrative, Wilcher has indeed tried to

murder Sara. He escapes from Tolbrook to Lewisham where she is now living with a young man, who says ' "Mrs Jimson is my business, like any decent chap's" ' (p. 312). As Tom interrupts this account of his own threatening behaviour with a reference to Hitler, it seems that Sara again symbolizes England, whose politicians are behaving as madly as Tom is at this moment. But Sara diplomatically settles Tom before her fire, having ensured that Robert will come to fetch him back to Tolbrook. On realizing that she has tricked him, and does not wish to marry him, Tom rushes at Sara, and 'meant to hit her on the nose' (p. 322). As he confesses, his impulse is murderous. He is indeed Gulley *à rebours*. At the same time, both men represent the spirit that threatens to destroy England, as Sara. This meaning is clear when Wilcher finally talks of England as 'the pilgrim and scapegoat of the world' (p. 342), having written of Sara: 'Only to hear Sara's step in the passage was a reminder of the truth, which was the tap-root of her own faith, that we were travellers in the world, enjoined to live "like men upon a journey" ' (p. 320).

It is in this sense that Cary himself accepted the pilgrim faith, which is also the soldier's faith, as the story of 'Umaru' implies, and as he shows here by linking Sara with Amy, wife to Tom's soldier-brother Bill: 'countrywomen both. They didn't submit themselves to any belief. They used it. They made it. They had the courage of the simple, which is not to be surprised' (p. 339). Following Sara's book and Cary's use of the word 'surprise', this statement possibly indicates how limited Tom's viewpoint really is.

Yet, having returned to Tolbrook to die, he does appear to refind his faith here. He finds it in the very landscape, as Cary did in *A House of Children* and, whereas for Evelyn the sea dominated, for Tom it is the trees. 'In the religious history of the Aryan race in Europe the worship of trees has played an important part', writes Frazer.[27] So Tom writes:

All the trees were dear to me, dearer than my own life, and perhaps my soul's good. But specially the great lime. I had always known it. Its delicate branches against the winter sky, its thin quivering leaves in summer, had stood before my bedroom window and the nursery windows on the same floor, for all my life. . . .

> Only to stand beneath the lime was such a delight to me
> that often I turned aside to avoid that strong feeling. . . .
> Within that burning tree I felt God's presence. And there I
> bathed in an essence of eternity. My very consciousness was
> dissolved in sensation, and I stood less entranced than myself
> the trance; the experience of that moment and that place, in
> the living spirit (pp. 220–1).

Tree symbolism for Cary is as significant as it was for either
Forster or Lawrence. His treatment of the landscape as a Being
recalls Blake and also Joyce.

It does seem that Cary intends a parallel in *To be a Pilgrim*
with Joyce's *Ulysses*. The supposition is strengthened by the fact
that this book grew from material for the sequel to *Castle Corner*.
Thus 'life is a battle' in that book is appropriately followed by
'life is a journey', (which is what Tom learns, from Sara in
particular) in this book. Critics have compared Sara to Moll
Flanders, but Cary strongly denied Defoe's influence.[28] On the
other hand, it seems likely that Molly Bloom owes something
to Moll.[29] And where *Ulysses* ends with Molly Bloom's 'Yes',
so *To be a Pilgrim* ends with ' "Yes" '. But it is spoken by Ann
Wilcher. The effect is to suggest a totally different attitude to
women, in Joyce and Cary, and that seems Cary's deliberate
intention.

Tom is now facing death without fear, and that for him is a
triumph. But he accuses Ann of taking life too seriously:

> 'Don't you think it is rather serious?'
> 'My dear child, you're not thirty yet. You have forty, forty-
> five years in front of you.'
> 'Yes.'

England's triumph or defeat, in World War II, will depend a
good deal on the spirit of its women, Cary seems to say.

The Horse's Mouth appeared in August 1944, when defeat in
World War II had been definitely averted, and people were ready
for such a book, to make them laugh.[30] The feeling it conveys
is one of exuberance, emanating also from Cary's realization that
he was definitely accepted as a major novelist – with the added
'joke' that the 'crickets' (as Gulley calls them), gave little evidence
of knowing what the books were really about. Recognition in

Edinburgh had been followed, in 1943, by the invitation to travel to Africa as script writer for a film showing the good work of the Empire. Thus Cary the writer had proved that he could serve his country more effectively than the serviceman who had retired twenty-three years before. On the voyage to Africa he shared a cabin with the camera-man Desmond Dickinson, a real dyed-in-the-wool Cockney, according to Thorold Dickinson, who was directing the enterprise.[31] So Cary lived with the true Cockney humour and vitality that the book unmistakably exudes. This is the spirit in which the blitz of London was withstood, the book clearly says. Yet the characters, like Plant, are earnest people, forming self-education societies, and holding meetings in their cellars, as Plant does in the key chapter (15): ' "it's generally on Ruskin, or Plato or Owen or Marx" ' (p. 28), their popularity being in that order – and Cary calls Ruskin 'a modern Platonic'.[32] Here Gulley says:

> Spinoza is one of the most popular London philosophers, especially in the East End, and round the Isle of Dogs, but he is not so strong in Greenbank, which belongs more to the upper river cultural sphere. In Greenbank they drink in Plato and Ruskin with the Oxford bath water. Postie has always been a Platonist and a Dark Blue. Bert Swope was a passionate Dark Blue. On the Boat Race day of 1930, Swope tore the favours off two Cambridge men from Poplar and threw them into the river. He would have been a leading Platonist if he had ever heard of Plato. But about 1933 or 1936, Plantie who had read all the philosophers, began to take a special interest in Spinoza. Anarchists who love God always fall for Spinoza because he tells them that God doesn't love them. This is just what they need. A poke in the eye. To a real anarchist, a poke in the eye is better than a bunch of flowers. It makes him see stars (p. 87).

Thus Cary presents his theological-political thesis, in a form calculated to 'get under the skin of this pachyderm' of a complacent world.[33] The humour is his weapon, to point out how desperately England is looking to the privileged few, above all at Oxford, to provide better leaders than men like Wilcher, but also a new form, or symbol, of Reality. A symbol like Plato's, which denies real freedom, will no longer work, he implies.

Spinoza was the philosopher to whom Cary always returned.[34] But in a general way Gulley speaks for Cary when he says that he turned from Spinoza to Blake, who 'led me back to Plato, because he didn't like him, and the pair of them took me forward to black and white drawing and formal composition' (pp. 86–87). In other words, Cary composed a form of reality that satisfied him, and equally created this book in particular, with Huysmans' treatment of black and white magic in *Là-Bas* as a special inspiration.[35]

Huysmans, Dostoevsky, and other advocates of sufferng as a gift of God are answered in Gulley's life history, which must be vital to the novel because Cary risked artistic failure to write it. For it does not accord with Gulley's history in Sara's book (p. 69), where he is the son of a doctor, whose money has been gambled away on horses by an older brother; moreover, his son Tom, who was still at school in 1937 has, by 1939, in Gulley's book, not only won a scholarship to Oxford, but also graduated, so that now ' "Tommy is a scholar and a gentleman, and he's gone to China in a bank, so he needn't know me any more" ' (pp. 35, 44). Even Sara's and Gulley's propensity to lying cannot account for such conflicting statements, which can only be justified by Cary's new conception of Gulley. It seems indeed that his visit to Edinburgh, at a critical point in the war, gave him an overwhelming urge to come to terms with himself, firstly as the art student who might never have escaped from the gulley in which he then found himself; and secondly as the progeny of an exiled, former ruling class family, who might, like Gulley, still be living in London's East End if, for example, he had been the child of someone like Delia in *A House of Children*. For she is clearly the inspiration for Gulley's mother, and Freeman's London background is like Gulley's. Like Bridget's story also, Gulley's life history challenges the patriarchal and patrilineal family. For here the child of a woman who has married beneath her has been lost to the family.

Cary's conversations with Professor Dover Wilson in 1942 would suffice to explain how such thoughts would carry him back to Falstaff in Eastcheap. There, the original Harry of Cary's imperialist self says he has been 'violently carried away from grace' by 'that villainous abominable misleader of youth, Falstaff, that old white-bearded Satan' (I Henry IV, II.iv). This thought links with Cary's note that *Là-Bas* concerned 'The conversion of

the Satanist'. For Wilcher in *To be a Pilgrim* has already filled
that description, and Gulley is Wilcher *à rebours*. Gulley is a
man who would belong to the ruling class, but for a change of
fortune. In this his situation resembles Falstaff's, and
Shakespeare's interest in such unwanted members of the ruling
class would readily have arrested Cary's interest. In his copy of
Dover Wilson's book on Falstaff Cary noted: 'Hal's conversion
from the vanity of forgetting his royal hereditary duty'.[36] He has
even created Gulley as a misleader of youth, most obviously in
the pub scene of chapter 42, but more subtly through Harry
Barbon, whom Gulley nicknames 'Nosy', so that even the names
invite comparison with an aristocratic Harry.

Gulley tells the story as though he has discouraged Nosy, but
he becomes increasingly dependent on him. By chapter 32 Gulley
has commandeered the wealthy Beeders' flat, and is using Nosy's
post office savings to buy liquor. When the Beeders unexpectedly
return, and call the police, Nosy escapes with Gulley, who shows
he has much experience of such situations. By chapter 33, 'waiting for another bus to take us anywhere', and fortifying himself
with whisky, he begins denouncing 'Governments and the People
and the World' so dangerously that he himself believes he has
brought on the stroke he has always feared – and of which he
finally dies, as if this death is itself symbolic of his state of mind
towards the world. His argument against the government of
Chamberlain, with passengers on the bus, becomes equally
symbolic. It ends when their tickets will not take them any
further, and they are left in the middle of a forest, while the bus
goes off 'like the flaming world.' They are alone in the dark, in
the rain. The account now takes on unmistakable echoes of the
Phaedrus, where Phaedrus invites Socrates to find 'a bed' with
him under a 'towering plane-tree' (229) and Socrates praises him
as 'a most admirable guide' for finding 'this abundant grass, with
its gentle slope just made for the head to fall back on luxuriously'
(230). Phaedrus observes that Socrates is 'just like a stranger
who is being shown the beauties of the place, and not like a
native of the country; the consequence this of your never leaving
the city either to cross the frontier, or even, I do believe, for so
much as a walk outside the walls.' Socrates replies, 'I am so fond
of learning. Now trees, you know, and fields cannot teach me
anything, but men in the city can.' Wilcher, a city man who
worships fields and trees in the country, is thus recalled (p.

222 above), and Gulley might have Socrates in mind when he writes:

> 'You don't know how I suffered in London, neither did I,' I said. For the country was a bit of a surprise to me. It always is. And I hadn't seen a real wild tree for twelve years. I couldn't take my eyes off 'em, bulging out into the moon as solid as whales. By God, I thought, no one has seen a tree till this moment. . . .

> Thou knowest, I said, that the ancient trees seen by their eyes, have fruit
> And knowest thou that trees and fruits flourish upon the earth
> To gratify senses unknown
> In places yet unvisited by the voyager.

> That is, until the voyager arrives. With the eye of imagination
> And sees the strange thing. And throws a loop of creation around it.
> 'What we want is a place between the roots where leaves have drifted,' I said.
>   . . .
> I spread out Sir William's overcoat and curled it round us.
> And put the mac on top, and we slept like birds (p. 222).

This treatment of stolen coats of authority (one a mac, meaning son) can be read as a judgement on the Socrates whom Athens condemned, since the quotation from Blake's *Visions of the Daughters of Albion* invites sexual associations. Gulley's study of Blake at this time no doubt fosters his denunciation of government and Sara has told us: 'He thought all the badness and misery in the world came from governments, and that there would be no peace or comfort anywhere till we all went back to live like Adam and Eve in the Garden of Eden' (*Herself Surprised*, p. 97). Here his kinship with Tolstoy as well as Blake is obvious.

Murry's religion and politics were essentially Blake's;[37] so, in view of Murry's current public activities, it would not be surprising if Cary were symbolizing this influence through

Gulley's relationship with Nosy. In creating Nosy, he noted: '?M.M. Serious, grave, quiet, longnosed, looking wise, and suddenly producing romantic nonsense';[38] the initials, the description, and the fact that Barbon is an East End boy studying for a scholarship to Oxford, all point to Murry. The name 'Harry' and the nickname 'Nosy', suggest that Cary is treating him as a would-be imperialist by nature, with aristocratic ambitions (cf. p. 64 above). *Barbon* in French means 'greybeard, dotard fogy'. That Cary intends this meaning, and has Murry in mind, is suggested in *Herself Surprised.* For there 'Greybeard' is Sara's nickname for an art-critic and dealer, who says to her: ' "I have to go to Paris today and I couldn't repeat the offer, because I shall spend the money over there" ' (p. 123). As Cary called himself Carré in France (and probably derived his fictional name 'Corner' from this word) he would appropriately have chosen a French name for Murry. This interpretation continues to be pertinent, when Gulley finally declares: ' "You'll never be any bloody good as an artist, Nosy, you were born for the Church or big business. Faith rather than works. You ought to be a rising Ford or an early Christian" ' (p. 265).

This identifies Nosy with Gulley's opposite, Wilcher and, because both these characters depict Tolstoy's split mind, it incorporates a comment on Tolstoy's chapter IX of *What I Believe,* entitled 'Faith and Works'. So Cary invites us to see that Jimson, a son of James, strives to create works, but has no faith, and contrasts with Mister Johnson who had 'the true light' as the foundation of faith.[39] Addressed to Nosy, Gulley's comment concerns Nosy's faith in his pictures as ' "great" ', and his latest picture, the Creation (which is not yet painted), as ' "the greatest of them all" '. This picture is to be painted on the wall of a derelict chapel at the very time it is being demolished. Nosy's objection has been; ' "B-but you *must* wait – till we've propped up the roof" ' (p. 265). This can be taken to express Murry's belated realization of the danger of his revolutionary doctrines.

The picture of the Creation has, as its focal point, a whale with its face on the back of its head. When Nosy objects, Gulley insists: ' "Stick it on like a mask on the side of a gasometer. If you don't, that whale will be a corpse, it won't have reality" ' (p. 271).

These words recall Cary's in 1942, to the students in Edinburgh, regarding artists choked by 'doubtful gas' because their art is not rooted in the 'objective real' (p. 37 above). For Gulley decides that his whale needs Hitler's blue eyes, after hearing his student assistants say that Hitler is a ' "boss" ' whose ' "blue eyes got the girls," ' and ' "he gives 'em ideas." ' Gulley says Hitler's eyes will match the sky, but a 'real' reason, surely, is that his own mother 'fell in love with papa's blue eyes' (p. 57), which must have made him too 'a boss', for 'Her vision was, perfect service' (pp. 57-58). This suggests that Gulley hits Sara because she refuses to give him 'perfect service'. When he returns to his wall, climbing the ladders, and swinging out on a platform to paint, he is crying. For on the pub radio he has heard a police notice that Sara Monday is now dead, but has first given an account of her murderer. Her murderer is Gulley, who hit her on the head while breaking into her trunk (because he wanted an old sketch from which to fake an 'early Jimson', and so get some money). His haste to paint the Creation is in fact due to his fear of being caught for Sara's murder. Now she appears to him in a vision, reminding him that he had ' "a gift for enjoying himself" ', and urges:

'Come, dearie, give it up. Listen to your Sara. Didn't I give you comfort and peace often and often when you were fit to be tied with worrying about your greens and your blues and the rest of your nonsense? Yes, even though you did hit me on the nose, weren't you glad to come into my arms after, yes, with the very blood on your pyjamas, and think you were back with your mother again.' 'There you go, Sall, you old blue-mange, you've thrown away your stays at last and taken the whole world to your bosom.' 'Well, I go on asking myself, why can't people be happy, poor dears?' . . . 'And you don't really want me?' 'Not just now, my dear.' 'And aren't you sorry I'm dead?' 'Well, look at me, my dear, boo-hoo, . . . But after all, we mustn't get too upset, must we? It's the way things are.' 'Oh dear, oh dear, I ought to know what life is.' 'Yes,' I said, putting another touch on the old 'un's nose, to give it more elevation. 'Practically A MATTER OF LIFE AND DEATH, you might say, or thereabouts' (pp. 291-2).

By that touch to the nose Gulley rejects the true intuition he might have got from Sara's real motherly love, because he prefers ' "the way things are" '. What he paints, however, seems an escape from the reality of 'the way things are'. This seems Cary's intention, if Gulley's vision is compared with Gérard de Nerval's (p. 43 above).

By morning he learns that Sara has saved him, having given the wrong description. 'I began to laugh. I was surprised. But I thought, just like Sara. To diddle a man with her last breath' (p. 293). So he even misjudges her forgiveness. When demolition of the chapel starts, Gulley says they will not touch the essential structure. But his platform wobbles,

> And just then the whale smiled. Her eyes grew bigger and brighter and she bent slowly forward as if she wanted to kiss me. . . .
> And all at once the smile broke in half, the eyes crumpled, and the whole wall fell slowly away from my brush; . . . when the dust began to clear I saw through the cloud about ten thousand angels in caps, helmets, bowlers and even one top hat, sitting on walls, dustbins, gutters, roofs, window sills and other people's cabbages, laughing. That's funny, I thought, they've all seen the same joke. God bless them. It must be a work of eternity, a chestnut, a horse-laugh.
> Then I perceived that they were laughing at me (p. 295).

The kiss of the whale (or Hobbes's *Leviathan*)[40] recalls the kiss of Judas. The smile that echoes in the crowd's horse-laugh recalls, yet contracts with, the laughter of Nussbaum (p. 191 above); for by that 'chestnut' John Chass was saved. The scene depicts Cary's theme, by illustrating from Blake's *Visions of the Daughter of Albion*:

> 'Does not the great mouth laugh at a gift, & the narrow eyelids mock
> 'At the labour that is above payment? And wilt thou take the ape
> 'For thy counsellor, or the dog for a schoolmaster to thy children?

The book ends with Gulley warning Nosy against a sense of justice, ' "I once had a sense of justice myself, when I was very young. I resented seeing my mother scrub the floor while her worsers went to take the air in Heaven-sent bonnets and shining two-horse chariots that were a glory to the Lord. Works of passion and imagination. Even when I was a young man older than you, I didn't like being kicked up the gutter by cod-eyed money-changers warm from the banquets of reason, the wine of the masters, and the arms of beauty, that hoor of paradise. I was a bit inclined to think it a raw deal" ' (pp. 296-7). Gulley's sense of injustice is thus purely personal and, by likening a woman's beauty to the 'hoor of paradise', he betrays an attitude to women similar to Tolstoy's in *The Kreutzer Sonata*. His impulse to hit and finally murder Sara is thus explained, while the hint from Revelation also links this with Cary's earlier books, and with his plans to write as a Diviner (p. 211 above). Sara, for Gulley, is Sara 'THE MOTHER OF HARLOTS' rather than the mother of nations. His last words are to a nun, caring for him in the ambulance. She makes him want to laugh because, though he is seriously ill, he says: ' "Not so seriously as you're well. How don't you enjoy life, mother." '

Gulley must be one of the most complex characters in literature. J. D. Fergusson provided the primary inspiration (p. 67 above). But Gulley also includes something of all the artists who have chiefly shaped our century, in Cary's understanding, and he is probably best understood from Cary's belief, that we have been led from Blake, who denounced Rousseau, to Tolstoy who worshipped him, and to a turning point in history, when the split minds of Tolstoy, and also Dostoevsky, reveal our dilemma most acutely. Cary's notes on Tolstoy, and his lecture on the split between Tolstoy's views on art and morals,[41] leave no doubt that Gulley is best understood from him. Like Tolstoy, Gulley idolizes a dead mother, but hates women. Yet his religion, Sara discovers, is ' "to be all serene" '. This echoes Cary's early women's confession, and also his note from Tolstoy's diary: 'avoid everything that upsets one' – of which Cary notes: 'a great escapist'.[42] Tolstoy's need to reconcile his feelings with those desirable in a husband and father can all be recognized in Gulley, whose soliloquy on the respective merits of Sara and Rozzie reproduces imaginatively Tolstoy's impulse to escape from his wife to the peasants. That Sara takes responsibility for Gulley's child by Rozzie, adds to the whole picture of a society that has to take responsibility for the actions of a Gulley. The note quoted regarding Delia comes to mind (p. 207 above).

Yet, as *Power in Men* makes clear, any society depends on the creative power of its artists: 'It is absurd to say, "Blake ought to have enjoyed special immunity from the law because he was a genius," but it is good sense to say, "Blake, because he was a genius, should have had every help from the state to realize his extraordinary powers, for the state's own good." Genius is entitled to a special liberty, to special education, to special help and opportunity.'[43] Gulley is studying Blake, whose ideas are therefore influencing his Tolstoyan temperament. The tone of his book is strongly reminiscent of Dostoevsky's in such works as *Letters from the Underworld*, to which Gulley's great respect for walls may indeed be indebted.[44] *The Dream of a Ridiculous Man* hints at the form of Gulley's book, which can only represent the thoughts of a dying man. For, having fallen and suffered a stroke in September 1939, he has been dead long enough for a 'Life and Works of Gulley Jimson' to be already published in 1940.[45] 'He must Die Again', as the book Cary actually began in 1940, as an answer to Dostoevskian Christianity, suggests by its title that *The Man Who Died*, by D. H. Lawrence, was also in Cary's mind, as a similar but false attempt to solve the world's problems. Notes certainly make it clear that both Wilcher and Jimson owe much to Lawrence, as 'a typical puritan turned inside out'.

Cary's chosen title, *The Horse's Mouth,* can be understood immediately from 'the great mouth' of Blake's poem, and the spiteful laughter that emerges from it. But the same 'State of Nature' made Plato envisage the human soul as in part like an irrational horse that must be controlled by brute force; so Plato the puritan dominates Western society, and is largely responsible for its treatment of women, Cary implies.[46] Relating Plato's view to Freud's, he had the picture of the individual soul composed of the father, mother, child relationship, in which the child's natural love for its mother is destroyed by the father's jealousy and the child's consequent fear and rivalry – symbolized in Little John by his attitude to a horse's mouth. But Cary's own intuition (closer to Jung's) was of an impulse in nature to create beauty through the power to love in every human being. This is the horse's mouth that is constantly surprising Gulley with intuitions. Unfortunately, he has never formed the clear picture of Reality that Cary thought necessary before an artist can produce anything of value.

His problem seems to be that he has never escaped from the 'blind gulley' in which Cary found himself as an art student.

Gulley's own account (chapter 13) is that he began in 1899 painting water colours in the classical style; was then converted to impressionism (around the same time as Cary) and, after about four years, had mastered the technique sufficiently to sell his paintings and make money. But because impressionism 'hasn't any idea in it', he grew tired of it, and gave up painting for arguing and drinking. Then Blake inspired the idea of 'the new Classic', but Gulley could not depict the world he now lived in: 'a new world with a new formal character'. He 'drank more than ever', and was 'like a chap under witchcraft', because 'The job is to get hold of the form you need. And nothing is so coy'. In 1937, he had had a 'Nice little wife, two kids,' and a 'Half-finished picture, eight by twelve, The Living God. . . . All you could want' (p. 14). From this description, it seems that Gulley did have here the form he needed. But he (as well as Sara) had been sent to prison in that year, apparently also charged by Wilcher and, when he emerged, all had vanished. What had been lacking, then, had been a responsible father.

This picture is a link with *Herself Surprised*, where Sara tells us that Gulley's idea was 'of God, like a glass man, with the people running about in His veins and nerves and some of them fighting and giving Him a pain in His stomach' (p. 206). This description suggests that Gulley was trying to depict the intuition that Cary himself had of God around this time. By allowing Sara to make it sound comic, Cary perhaps intended to show the limitations of pictorial art, and the reasons for Gulley's discontent. Regarding Gulley while painting it, Sara ' "had never known him more content" '; he had never struck Lizzie, with whom he was living, though she did no housework, and left Gulley to do it. (He, in turn, allowed Sara to come on her days off to do it.)

Sara writes: 'She was a queer girl, a lady by her rights and as pretty as a supplement, though gypsy in her colour, but as helpless as a sheep' (p. 208). She has been an artist, and thinks Gulley 'the genius of the world.' She might well be Lawrence's goddess in *The Man Who Died*. That she is by right a lady, and well educated, apparently explains why Gulley never beats her. This links with the fact that, like Lawrence and Tolstoy, Gulley has never escaped his mother's influence. She had been 'a belle of the season' before marrying his father, who in this book is described to recall the Normandy painter whom Cary met in the

Pas de Calais, whose paintings had gone out of fashion. After his death they have lived with an uncle, who beat Gulley so violently that his mother would make him pray not to hate him – then console him by telling him stories from a picture book, while she nursed him in her lap. This suggests why Gulley's ideas for pictures are escapist, like those of the Symbolists; his idolization of his mother is similar.

Cary's usual clue, on the first page of the book, bears out this interpretation. The sun strikes the new signboard of The Eagle and Child pub, and Gulley thinks this a sign that the barmaid Coker will lend him money, because people in trouble are the most sympathetic; Coker is in trouble because she got pregnant by Willie, a young man who had promised to marry her, but has deserted her for a 'Blondie'. By announcing his theme thus, Cary might indeed be answering Murry's essay 'The Sign-Seekers' (p. 101 above) – saying, in effect: This is the world that artists must face. For Coker's pregnancy loses her her job, and the only help she gets is from her mother, who beats her furiously while giving it. But she is able to commandeer the boat-shed that Gulley has been using for a home and studio, because by this time Gulley is spending another six months in prison – for robbing Hickson. She has paid the back rent, and made the shed clean and homely, and also waterproof, by mending the roof with Gulley's current masterpiece, the Fall. Insisting that the picture was worth five thousand pounds, Gulley calls Coker's mother a ' "spiteful old devil" ':

> 'Don't you call mother names. She's had a hard time and don't you forget it.'
> 'What's that got to do with my picture?'
> 'What's the good of pictures to poor mum. Pictures never did anything for her. Pictures never gave her what she'd a right to expect, did they?'
> 'What about my rights, Coker?'
> 'You don't need any rights. You're a man. But you won't be, if mother catches you here again' (p. 167).

That this is a key scene is evident from Cary's first chapter, later published as *The Old Strife at Plant's*. Mother Coker resembles the old woman, whom Gulley encounters at one of Plant's meetings. Plant's speaker is an evangelical American, talking about the universal power of love, revelation, and grace, while the old strife tells her life story as a true battle for survival, so giving an unconscious commentary on the talk, while Gulley throughout composes versions of a picture, intuitively, on the label of a beer bottle, and while Blake's 'The Crystal Cabinet' runs through his head. What the old strife reveals is the war against mothers, when they become useless and difficult. When this happened, she and her husband had kept her mother in bed for sixteen years – taking away her clothes, so that she could not escape. (*The Horse's Mouth*, p. 248, shows Gulley similarly imprisoned, by Coker.) The old strife fears that her daughter will do the same, if she stops charring and goes to live with her.

This of course explains Sara's dilemma. The intuition comes to Gulley through recollecting the famous murder case of Maria Marten, and drawing her murdered body in the mud. His intuition seems to be that mankind is naturally cruel. In *The Horse's Mouth*, it seems that his murder of Sara follows this association of ideas. For, just before he murders her, she says of his painting of her, that he has given her too long a chin: ' "you've made me look like the villian in Maria Martin" '[47] [sic]. At the close of the discarded chapter, having seen the old strife on to a bus, Gulley belatedly realizes that here is his true inspiration. But it eludes him in a vision of a young maiden, escaping as his 'pink'. He has been given the intuition, but he has not used it as God intended, is apparently Cary's point.

Cary discarded this chapter as upsetting the balance of the book, but in modified form it is chapter 15, with Sara as the old strife. The meeting ends with the singing of Blake's *Jerusalem*, and Sara's comment, that she loves the song because of the tune, ' "and whatever you say about Jews, they're good family people" ' (p. 84). Its theme is continued in the key chapter 42, already quoted, where the spirit of the dying Sara is revealed by the white cat Snow. As Sara's death is announced, Gulley leaves the pub, and then he says: 'something like a fiery comet whizzed past my left ear and I saw old Snow land in the light in front of me: all four feet at once. And then with one spring, in every joyful lovely muscle, ascend into Heaven; or the garden wall' (p. 288). So the spirit of Sara escapes the garden of Eden, as Gulley, like Milton, imagined it. For Gulley's idea of education for a girl is 'Milton and cooking; so she might go into service and see some of the inside world'.[48] In this scene, Gulley describes Coker, now barmaid at the Feathers, as 'almost a woman. No one knows how she knows what she does know. But it's definitely horse meat' (p. 288). She has immediately sensed that Gulley has murdered Sara, and turned off the wireless, in case a description is given of him, as murderer. Thus 'horsemeat' is intuitive knowledge. She is 'Queen of the Feathers. Because of the basket. But one girl's error is another's glory' (p. 281). The word 'basket' refers to her child, named John, and it recalls the basket theme of *To be a Pilgrim*. The words following 'basket' anticipate the theme in the next two novels.[49]

Gulley's own problem, he realizes, is this: 'THE OLD HORSE DOESN'T SPEAK ONLY HORSE. And I can't speak only Greenbank' (p. 50). What he lacks is the education that Cary argues Blake should have had, and his sense of injustice stems chiefly from this. In an introduction for the novel Cary wrote:

> William Blake . . . understood the workings of this free spirit, creative and restless, in a world full of injustice, of conflict . . . To live in such a world as Gulley tells himself, one must have a soldiers virtues, faith, courage, and endurance . . . One must say, life is a gift. I did nothing to deserve it. Any happiness it has offered to me is clear profit . . . Gulley is not altogether successful in taking his own advice . . . And even while he is telling himself not to be resentful, he is full of anger . . .[50]

Here Cary shows his own acceptance of Blake, for whom Imagination was the greatest gift of God (p. 148 above).

But in the novel he shows Gulley resisting this philosophy, which is attributed to Spinoza (by the cobbler, Plant):

> "What he said was, 'Life is a gift, and what right have we to complain that we weren't given it different.' No, he never complained against good or bad luck. . . ." (p. 87)

In the *Tractatus Theologico-Politicus,* Spinoza describes reason as 'the greatest of gifts and a light from on high', leading man to faith by love of justice and charity, which is the spirit of God. He might thus be assumed to have said 'Life is a gift'. Blake, however, denounced reason as Negation. Thus, in admiring Blake and rejecting Spinoza, Gulley is accepting the imagination and rejecting reason. But when Hickson, his patron, dies, Gulley feels 'as lonely as a man who loses half his family in a shipwreck' (p. 247). And Hickson developed from 'an ideal Spinoza'. Moreover, for Cary, reason *is* the gift by which man becomes an individual and on which all progress depends.[51] The problem Cary saw in Spinoza was that his philosophy remains divided, and denies freedom, because he begins with reason, which has already divided, by analysis, what imagination previously united as one, in a symbol.

So, in the relationship of Gulley and Hickson, Cary has illustrated the interdependence of imagination and reason, and this is the main message of the novel. Gulley ends it by quoting as 'real horse meat', Blake's 'Go love, without the help of anything on earth', and Gulley himself is based chiefly on Tolstoy, who attempted to destroy the idol of imperial glory by believing in love as absolute ruler. But he brought anarchy to Russia instead of democracy, Cary declares, because he should have trusted 'love working in liberty by reason'.[52] In England Murry's prophet of revolution had been Lawrence, trying to replace Christ's gospel of love by one of hate, and it is his spirit that Gulley is also fighting.

The degree to which Cary says the irrational rules even our greatest geniuses, like Tolstoy, is clearly depicted in Gulley (cf. p. 6 above). He tells of the sufferings of his mother and above all his beloved sister Jenny, clearly expecting the reader's sympathy. But Jenny suffers far less from her husband Ranken than Sara does from Gulley. That Cary intends us to compare them is evident from his use of his key words 'teeth' (of The Horse's Mouth) and 'gift'. Thus Gulley resents the fact that when he gives Jenny fifteen pounds to buy herself new teeth (echoes of *The Waste Land*) she gives the money to her husband Ranken, an inventor whom she loves, and calls it a 'gift from God' (p. 159), because given with Gulley's true love for her. Yet he appears not to see that Sara's gifts are given to him in the same spirit. He tells Sara's story as a joke – so well that indeed we laugh at her sufferings. Tolstoy's theory of art as an infection is thus exemplified, and Gulley's artistic powers, at least as a storyteller, confirmed. Jenny's story parallels the story of Tom's sister Lucy, who chooses suffering masochistically – as Sara says Gulley's first wife Nina chose it (p. 214 above). The name Jenny, too, means grace. Jenny Ranken commits suicide (p. 282).

That Gulley himself is captive to this old Christian notion of grace as suffering is evident from his death, which he has apparently chosen as a form of suicide, or crucifixion. For, when he finds the wall, he has thought: 'It's a catch. It's the old devil again. . . . But my legs kept on trembling and my heart went on beating. Jesus Christ, I thought, suppose it was true. Suppose it's meant for me. Oh for a drink.'[53] There seems here an intentionally shocking hint of Jesus Christ's prayer, before his crucifixion: 'O my Father, if this cup may not pass away from me, except I drink it, thy will be done' (Matt. xxvi.42). The meaning of the name Gulley fits Cary's theme. It is 'divine relic', from Danish, says Yonge, adding that it was then lengthened into Gulliver, and used by Swift. The name thus perfectly accords with Cary's aim of achieving Swiftian satire, especially if it is taken to include associations with the word Gull – to which Sara shortens the name.

Gulley is clearly also a bad witness in this trial of English society, for he is captive to an intuition he has not truly understood. He is destroyed by *The Horse's Mouth* of society and, as the thoughts of a dying man, his book can be considered as an equivalent to Christ's words: 'forgive them, for they know not what they do' (Luke xxiii.34). This suggests that the book may be Cary's final expression of his long poem: 'Hymn to the two-faced Angel: Freedom and Death' (p. 146 above). But Gulley is probably better understood by the lines of verse Tom Wilcher found, written just before his death by his brother Edward. He has been given all the advantages that Gulley has lacked, but has followed the false faith of the aesthetes, amongst whom he had been a leader at Oxford. Cary may have intended these verses to link Edward, for comparison, with Gulley, and to prepare the reader for Gulley's book. They include:

Life tragic to the soul; to mind a joke
Now tragi-comic, gives its cruellest stroke.

. . .

Not time destroys the old but creeping spite
For all they fought for, in a bungled fight.
For fame along the street, June's summer gush
Choking the sun with gilt, the leaves with plush,
For triumphs lost which won would still be mean –
They die of laughing at their might have been (*To be a Pilgrim*, p. 282).

14. The Women's War

The Moonlight

A Fearful Joy

The Moonlight

That Cary was primarily answering Tolstoy and Lawrence in *The Horse's Mouth* is immediately confirmed by *The Moonlight*. Here both are named in the text, as major influences on the twenties, above all on the views held of, and by, women at that time. His prefatory essay denounces them both, and shortly afterwards, in 'The Revolution of the Women', he made his viewpoint even clearer. He says that women of the twenties, in spite of the theorists, discovered that 'love is not all selfishness or appetite, and children needed it'. So came a 'renascence of the family'.

Cary has already illustrated this 'renascence' in Ann of *To be a Pilgrim,* who is writing a book on her father Edward, but finds he had a 'small' view. So when Tom argues that Edward's ideas were so advanced that he talked of abolishing marriage, she replies: ' "Yes, that's what I mean. That's how they used to think. I shall have to look up the early communists, too" ' (p. 283).

Tolstoy, as an early communist, had attacked marriage in *The Kreutzer Sonata,* and of this book Cary writes, in his preface to *The Moonlight*:

> Tolstoy's bias was so detestable to me that I began at once to write a counterbook, which was to be called (as answer to *The Kreutzer) The Moonlight*. It was to be the exact reverse of *The Kreutzer*. An old woman in a railway carriage (instead of Tolstoy's old man) was to tell how she had murdered her sister for preventing her daughter's marriage. And in the course of the story, she would give the true case for women as a sex, the real dilemma of a girl who is held by nature in so firm a grip;

239

to whom, as it were, nature says, 'You are so necessary to me in my creation of society, that I shall mark you for my own You shall be set apart like a dynastic clan. You shall have the privilege of the blood and also its pain. If you try to escape into triviality and decadence, you shall be condemned to frustration, for you were born to deal, generation after generation, with great issues, the primal issues of creation, love and birth, the first education. But you shall suffer also, like a dynastic house, the burden of inescapable duty, the constriction of power. And so I seal you with my mark (p. 10).

This passage explains Cary's treatment of women throughout his novel series. In his preface he also indicates that this book compares with the previous one, by showing how fashions in ethics change, just as they do in art. But underlying fashion, he argues, is the eternal character of being itself, with values from which the standards of any generation can be finally judged. By these standards, 'the Victorian's answer to the eternal problem of sex will always have greatness and dignity'. For it recognized woman's 'responsibility as wife, as mother', and also that 'the family is a fundamental character of civilization, not a construction, but from nature itself' (as Cary states in *A House of Children,* p. 21 above). The modern woman has 'a sense of responsibility and integrity which, in this completely different situation, has value and distinction possibly greater than the other' – that of her grandmother. Her mother, however, suffered from the confusion of her times, he implies, and this confusion can be understood from Tolstoy. Because women excited his lust, he condemned them and the sexual attraction by which marriages are made. Yet he believed in the family, and the mother's place at the heart of it. Therefore, by the twenties, women were being expected to choose, either to marry and have a family, or to have freedom which, for 'The new feminist', meant freedom from all family ties – as was then being accepted in Russia.

Cary's plans for a 'K. S. Inverted' (p. 122 above), influenced *An American Visitor,* to which *The Moonlight* can be obviously compared. For Amanda in the latter is of Marie's generation, and an anthropologist, and Cary's notes for *The Moonlight* show him returning to anthropological studies. For example: 'Oedipus complex does not apply to matrilineal family. . . . In all the world, mother child relation important. But pregnancy . . . is regarded as a burden *and a nuisance* in Christian Aryan society. . . . In Europe, in *poor* families, father a tyrant and often a brute. In Melanesia, father has no rights except of affection [an]d so is seldom a tyrant. Father-right a source of family conflict.'[1] 'Father-right' dominates *Castle Corner,* where a connexion is shown between a women's war in Africa and Europe. Clary, in *Herself Surprised,* is shown to have formed ideas from the 'woman's war' in Africa (p. 221 above). World War II intensified the women's war.

For the denial of freedom to women became more obviously outrageous, when women were actively defending Britain, in the name of freedom, against Nazism. Nazi philosophers, Plato and Hobbes, are named together, as state absolutists, in *Power in Men* (p. 38). Such thoughts dominate Cary's first trilogy. It is coloured also by his study of Kierkegaard: 'Kierkegaard and the "Existential" Philosophy' in relation to Nazism (p. 213 above).

By August 1944 he was making a close study of Kierkegaard, and emphasized the following note with marginal strokes suggesting strong agreement:

Truth lies in subjectivity – the truth that God exists is given to YOU – is only valid for YOU.[2]

He was particularly interested in Kierkegaard's relationship with Regina, his betrothed. Cary notes: 'He runs away. His pride is broken because he has lost his honour. He takes comfort in Job, who ignores his friends and the world. What he needs is *reintegration of his personality*'.[3]

Kierkegaard now seems to take precedence over other aesthetes, in Cary's treatment of aesthetic experience as the basis of religion. He particularly influenced *The Moonlight*.

The main plot of *The Moonlight,* as it concerns three sisters, can be found in drafts of the early thirties which grew out of the 'Jew story', and were tentatively entitled 'The Captives' and 'Captive and Free'.[4] The 'first version' of *The Moonlight,* of which Cary speaks in the preface, is probably 'The Forgotten Women' which, by its title, seems equally indebted to Freud's *Totem and Taboo*. Notes already quoted show its relevance to his theme (pp. 124 above). His treatment of women in the first trilogy led him, in 1942, to begin the dossier labelled 'Hannah' where 'Captive and Free' is the theme title, and where the origins of his main women characters, in his remaining novels, can all be discovered (p. 214 above).

On completing *The Horse's Mouth* Cary returned to 'Captive and Free', pasting the following to the cover of the 'Hannah' dossier:

> The secret nation as title of whole book. Captives and the free. Clannishness as against man. divisions in itself. attitude towards government (as man) make it *do* something Suffragette sabotage (like a woman who 'turns nasty')
> Captive and Free. Captive of sex, but free with its *special power* of love and the creation of character
> . . .
> Captive and free. applies to special position of women. Study of women's character – in *different* generations. . . .
> As background. 1. change of *idea* of women's position. Shown operating in women's minds . . . Women as non-combatants. Hannah appalled by the waste of life after war. on account of absence of feeling. . . .[5]

With these thoughts in mind, Cary returned from *The Horse's Mouth* as published, to 'The Horse's Mouth' as originally conceived around 1930. A story of about 1928, 'The Church and the Toadstools',[6] provides the clue to the main character Ella Venn, of whom it is said:

> 'She's like a force of nature – they say mushrooms will lift a cathedral if they're put to it.'
> 'I suppose they have to if they're going to live.'
> 'The force of life might almost be measured in foot pounds' (p. 128).

Cary had written something similar of Philip Feenix (pp. 192–3 above), and also noted that Hitler was 'the suppressed artist. the fungus that lifts the pavement'.[7] Ella, then, reveals a similar power of life in women.

The form of the novel is the music of The Moonlight Sonata, which Ella plays at the beginning and the end. The 'romantic and passionate' feeling that she expresses by her playing is what makes it Cary's answer to *The Kreutzer Sonata* of Tolstoy.

'Miss Ella Venn, aged seventy four, . . . saw her niece Amanda in the arms of a young farmer called Harry Dawbarn, . . . She was tearful with joy.' So the novel begins, slowly unfolding the truth that Amanda, aged thirty-two, and born in April 1906, is in fact Ella's illegitimate daughter. Ella's family had disapproved of the father, and forced Ella to act the part of aunt to Amanda, who had been brought up as the daughter of Ella's older sister, Bessie. Bessie in youth has been a life-giver: ' "She brought life to everything and everybody" ' (p. 44). But she has been compelled to marry Professor James Groom, a scientist more than twenty years older than herself, whom she instinctively detests but learns to suffer, and so becomes a life-giver by bearing him, masochistically, nine children. The marriage is arranged by the eldest of the three sisters, Rose, who loves Groom herself, and has been engaged to him. But when their mother dies she has been required to run the house and care for their father, who decides she is indispensable. So, for love of Groom, Rose persuades Bessie to marry him, and the marriage becomes a 'crucifixion' for Rose, while Bessie, 'being prepared to suffer, was pleased to take humiliation to her breast and press in the thorns' (p. 51). So Cary develops the horse's mouth of his early notes (p. 126 above), and Groom, whose manners in youth were those of a 'colt' (p. 38), expresses in name and action everything in Cary's horse symbolism associated with a state of nature. Groom is a true Darwinian, and Rose has accepted this master faith of the age wholeheartedly, in a spirit of evangelical dedication. She is totally unselfish in achieving what she believes to be right. Because society denies her any experience of sex, sex remains throughout her life a 'mystery . . . so gross to her imagination, and for that very reason so sacred to her creed' (p. 49). All she knows of marriage is in the church service, so she declares: ' "What God Himself ordained could never be horrible." ' Moreover, in this Darwinian world, 'Professor' signifies the worth of a man, especially if he is a scientist. The name James, for Groom, signifies that the scientist has supplanted the artist (a Gulley) as leader of society. But Ella is the real artist of this book. Rose is dying when it opens, yet still controlling the family; she now wants Amanda to marry a Professor, aged sixty. Ella fears she will prevent Amanda's happiness, as she did her own and, in a state of nervous excitement bordering on insanity, she thwarts her in this – and perhaps takes a final revenge.

Cary's main point, however, is that Rose, Bessie, and Ella are all victims of their society. They have been brought up strictly in the early Victorian creed, which for Cary had dignity and value in its view of women. Their father has rejected the creed, but ensures that his daughters have it firmly instilled at an early age, so that conscience, or the categorical imperative – the horse's mouth – will make them feel guilty if they ever transgress it. So Venn obtains complete earthly grace for himself by promising heavenly grace to his daughters. Helen Pynsant had done the same, with Stella.[8] Indeed, as this novel developed from the same material as *Castle Corner,* there are many points of comparison between the two. Essentially, both are the story of a house, which is to be lost to its owners because the values for which it stood are attacked. In *The Moonlight* the attack comes from Ella, who, as a 'force of nature' reveals the nature of that force, by express-ing Cary's theme phrase thus: ' "So much happiness in the world – and simply – given to us" ' (p. 55). She says it as she pats the old sheep dog, tied to a hurdle, whose bark and expression say: ' "Look what they've done to me: put me out, taken my sheep from me." ' Ella's feelings resemble this dog's.

Her grandfather, son of a farmer-brewer, built Florence Villa in 1832. The date and Cary's account of him signify that he gained political and social status and power from the Parlia-mentary Reform Bill of that year, when he made a wedding trip to Italy. This 'British Italian' house is clearly an architectural disaster, with a roof 'wont to leak' (p. 53). Its foundations are not mentioned, but the name *Venn* is the southern form of *Fenn,* meaning 'marsh', and so serves Cary's purpose (cf. p. 152 above). Venn is appropriate as a commonplace name in Devon, but equally for suggesting the theme of this novel of women, by recalling Venus, goddess of grace and love. Ella's father, John, is a liberal business man, with a double first degree, and 'proud to be enlightened', so that he is 'an authority on the Italian primitives', and has entertained at Florence Villa, 'all the celebrities whom he could catch' (p. 37). John Venn is described as 'rich, spoilt, successful in every way, even in luck', and 'a man who hated discomfort'. His wife, equally selfish but with less chance of satisfaction, 'understood completely this charming, selfish, sensitive husband, whose hypocrisies were so carelessly assumed that they sat on him like an additional grace' (p. 35). If this John is compared with John Chass, then 'grace', as Venn understood it, will be seen in contrast to the grace that made

John Chass a fitting husband for Mary Corner. The one advantage of John Venn's selfishness is that he avoids beating his
daughters. But they worship him, as their chief deity, with even
greater ardour than they otherwise might. The problem is that
his 'enlightened' ideas are intended to serve his own ends, not
theirs.

Ella, the 'most gifted' and romantic daughter, had fallen in
love at eighteen with Geoffrey Tew. He, 'a rising poet, had been
captured for the week-end by her father' (p. 69). He recites
passionate verses, and discourses on art for art's sake, but Ella
loves him because he is young and alone. Rose however condemns him, chiefly for having no prospects. At this time her
family responsibilities include saving her father from a public
scandal with a married woman. Now dying herself, she reminds
Ella:

'Your Geoffrey died in an asylum, after writing some of the
most disgusting poems in the language, and he deserved to die.
God punished him for his hideous life with a hideous disease.'
'No, no,' Ella cried. 'He was driven to it – by me – by you'
(p. 102).

So these sisters represent opposite viewpoints, the one formed
from rigid authority, the other from feeling. Ella reflects: 'How
wretched Geoffrey made me, but oh! would I have been without
a single moment of what he gave me, even the pain? That is what
Rose can't understand. No, she speaks of love, of Christian
marriage. But in her heart she is jealous of all lovers. Because
she lost her own fulfilment, she wants to deny it to others. And
there is nothing to be done' (p. 103). Ella knows that it is cruel
to condemn Rose, in this war between them.

At thirty-eight, Ella is courted by Ernest Cranage. He is a
demonstrator at the Groom Academy (now out of date), who
has been one of many men with whom Bessie flirts – in safety,
as Groom's wife. Ella (with the same credulity as Bridget and
Sara – and Marguéritte) believes Cranage when he says his wife
has just died, so that they can be married and sail to South
America. Then he confesses that he has lied to her. So she finds
herself pregnant, and living meanly in Liverpool, until Rose
finds her, decides that Ernest's plan had been ' "to get money
out of the family" ' (p. 157); gives him money and, a month

after the baby's birth, sees that he does leave for South America. His letter from Buenos Aires still moves Ella, after thirty-two years:

> . . . *My own mother sacrificed herself to give me what educa-*
> *tion I had. And with you for a few months I lived in that*
> *heaven for which I must thank not only your true soul, but the*
> *sister who brought you up.* . . .
> *Perhaps it is even necessary that her ideals of life should*
> *bring into the world cruelty as well as happiness, purity*
> *and chastity for some women, prostitution and disease for*
> *others.*[9] . . .
> *. . . Bessie . . . gave me back my life, even if it was life with-*
> *out hope. For it was you alone who gave me hope, who did*
> *not merely pity me but entered into my life and lent it your*
> *energy. You alone, simply by the power of imagination, com-*
> *prehended what I had suffered – the grind of poverty and*
> *squalor, on body and soul* (p. 160).

These quotations seem intended to show the special quality of these women.

Ella almost died when Ernest disappeared, but clung to her child, naming her Amanda (fit to be loved). She became strong in purpose, and even resisted Rose and Bessie. But Rose sent for Papa, who argued that it was dangerous to break a convention, and ' "stupid and selfish" ' to keep her child because she loved her, so making the child suffer the stigma of illegitimacy.

' "Dear, darling Papa," said Ella, as she remembered that homily . . . "And he had come straight from Mrs Wilmot in Paris" ' (p. 191). Thus the god of total selfishness and hypocrisy prevails.

Amanda is brought up as the youngest child of James Groom, whose wife dies at fifty-eight, 'quite worn out', when Amanda is twelve. Bessie has married him because she has been taught to believe in a God who expects women to suffer; so she suffers James as her 'great man', though he is an atheist. As the victims of this split between religion and science, their children are merely selfish and unfeeling; they find it too much trouble to visit Bessie, when she is dying. When Rose has urged ' "She gives you nothing but love" ', their retort has been, ' "That's what she's for, isn't it?" ' (p. 292). The attitude to motherhood by the twenties became derision, Cary thus suggests. Yet Bessie wielded great power. Amanda looking back, reflects: ' "But really it's so stupid, so dangerous. There's no sense in it, that people should have power just because they have suffered" ' (p. 206).

Here she surely speaks for Cary, who has revealed a source for his ideas through Bessie's brilliant son William; he has become ' "dreadfully unhappy about the lie in his soul" ' (p. 205). This is Murry's phrase, in an essay that fully illuminates Cary's use of it, both here and in the second trilogy.[10] Cary's final comments comes in the last novel, in Preedy's sermon (p. 323 below). Here William is said to be unhappy because he wants religion, which shocks his father; he wants it during wartime, and Bessie ' "suffered dreadfully for William" '. The idea that he fears suffering and is strengthened by Bessie, accords fully with Murry's use of the phrase.

Ella realizes that in fact Bessie, driven into this marriage, had 'created James for herself – yes, and for the world too. It was Bessie who made Brent Square a kind of palace where people would go up the steps with quite a special expression – I've seen them taking off their hats four steps from the door. They felt they were approaching a kind of holy of holies of science, where the great James Groom reigned in glory with Queen Bessie' (p. 101). As Queen Bess, she was thus the spirit of England, in April 1906, the year of Amanda's birth.

Amanda is presented as a brilliant intellectual, who treats any feelings she has as matters of mild scientific interest. At Oxford during the twenties D. H. Lawrence had become a 'craze', as she recalls when visited by a cousin who was at Oxford with her, Robin Sant. He enters her life again in this year 1938, the point in time from which the story is told.

Ella's story emerges slowly with tragic vividness, conveying simultaneously the reason for her intense neurosis. She has been born with all her father's gifts of looks, intelligence, and sensitivity. But she has been taught nothing, except how to play the piano, and pray. Her power to love, concentrated finally and totally on the birth of her child, when she is forty-two, has been declared stupid and selfish by the only god she really knows: her father. For the sake of the family name, she has been required to sacrifice and hide her own passionate feelings, and watch her child brought up to be totally unfeeling, towards her also. Ella is incapable of any responsibility, yet acts with a kind of spontaneous cunning, which her guilt complex promptly forces her to confess. Thus, she cannot bring herself to kill Rose. But when she is buying the pills, prescribed for Rose's heart trouble, she also buys some that have proved too strong for Rose. Then, when required to administer the dose, she hands Rose the strong pills, in the box. Rose immediately guesses her intention, realizes how completely her own sacrifices and devotion to the family have won her hatred rather than love and so, later and alone, takes the final responsibility of swallowing three of the strong pills, and dies. Then Ella, unable to bear either responsibility or guilt, feels bound to make a confession. And this woman's confession, dismissed condescendingly as a complex in a mad old lady, is really a confession by nature itself, for an age in which she had been abused.

Ella wants above all to feel herself a mother to Amanda. The idea of the soul as a trinity of father, mother, and child is conveyed in the scene where Ella shows Amanda a photograph of her father, and also his only letter to Ella, which together give Amanda a basis for understanding her own nature. Ella has been driving Amanda to understand Nature in the person of Harry Dawbarn. But then Robin Sant, the intellectual, appears. He has separated from his wife, and argues from *The Kreutzer Sonata* that Tolstoy's statements regarding sex, and God, are irrefutable – yet suggests sex and even marriage as a way of life.

Amanda feels no natural inclination for sex or motherhood. But from her realization of Ella's tragedy she decides, according to a somewhat scientific analysis, that the manifestations of this power in herself should be satisfied. Robin is shocked when she insists that they must take no precautions if they have sexual relations, so she turns to the earthy Harry Dawbarn, and the country girls' manner of getting husbands.

The ditch at Pinmouth Fair contrasts with the romantic Moonlight Sonata, as a dominant symbol – also mentioned on the first page. The fertility festivals in Cary's African novels come to mind as comparable, when the cider and dancing at the Fair send couples to the ditch, where individuals become indistinguishable. Amanda goes, fully aware of Ella's hopes. ' "One would think you wanted me to fall" ' (p. 200). This can be read as a comment on Gulley's picture of the Fall, which Mother Coker cut up to keep the rain off her daughter and grandson (p. 234 above). Ella concedes that the country girls get pregnant ' "to bring some of these country boys to the point" ' (p. 201). So the Fair becomes like a religious festival. Described in chapter 25, it is dominated by horse symbolism: the 'horsy peak' cap worn by Harry; the woman Amanda pities, with her large family, married to a 'Horseman'; and the horses of the merry-go-round. Amanda has found Harry 'one of the Kings of the Fair . . . permitted to do what was forbidden to ordinary persons; to risk his life, to ride the horses sideways . . . She thought, "Poor Harry! So this is his glory," and at the same time her whole body seemed to rejoice in the expertness and courage, even in that arrogance' (p. 215). So Amanda recognizes the noble peasant, and finally, in the ditch, that, as Harry says, the sex act is ' "nothing to mind." ' For ' "What is serious is what comes after. . . . A woman's life, a real woman with husband and children – that is really serious, terribly, terribly serious. You can't get over it, never." ' Thus Amanda develops Ann's thought, when she says ' "Yes" ', at the close of *To be a Pilgrim*.

For Harry, however, getting married has to be fitted in with farm work. Amanda becomes less of a catch because Ella, over-eager, provides him in advance with his own farm. Moreover, Nelly Raft, the previous year, had failed to ' "nail you with a baby" ', as Amanda observes to Harry, quoting the common notion of fatherhood as a crucifixion. He retorts, ' "Ah, and everyone knows it. They'd laugh at me if I'd let myself be cot by that old trick." '[11] But now he has a farm, Mother Raft will 'nail' Harry. So Amanda, already pregnant, concedes Nelly's prior claim – in this women's war.

She has already reflected, too: ' "Perhaps I've put myself in the wrong not only with convention but with nature, too. After all, the natural unit is not mother and child, but the family. Papa, a settled regular papa, is a necessary part of the arrangement, even among monkeys and birds. And perhaps he is necessary even to the mother's feelings" ' (p. 226). Robin Sant can intel-lectualize on such matters and, learning that Amanda has chosen to become pregnant to Harry, comments: ' "you're lucky, you girls. You're born to be caught and racketeered – it's in your blood – and when you're caught you have to fight for your lives and so your lives are worth something. Now if I'd had the luck to catch galloping consumption I might have been a poet, but if I went deliberately and caught it, I'd only be a lunatic or a masochist" ' (p. 265). He concluded that ' "women always manage to make a

religion,"' and Amanda should enjoy '"being damned uncomfortable around a family farm. That's real primitive religion,
women's religion, the oldest in the world. You're starting at the
bottom again. And Harry Dawbarn will be your household
priest."' But Nellie has Harry and, through Ella's contriving,
Robin has returned to his wife. So Amanda is left, to form the
incomplete family of mother and child. The book ends with
her wearily facing her desk, and the scientific work from which
she will have to support her child. She has the sense of 'existing
in a feeling that seemed not her own, since it was without will
or desire. And this feeling was one of pity and emptiness; not
self-pity, but a universal pity as for all the loss, the frustration,
the waste, in the world, and the emptiness was the shell of this
pity. . . . It was merely a vast still grief.' Then, putting her hand
to her thickening waist, she asks the question that all Cary's
novels are intended to answer: '"But do miracles happen? It
will be interesting to see."'

Meanwhile Ella has taken an overdose of pills. But first she has
ensured that Florence Villa and its contents are all sold. Her
actions take on an unmistakable symbolic meaning, as loads of
'Victoriana' are collected in the Villa. She and Amanda are
'alone in a place which was neither home nor store; in which
everything was growing dirtier and more senseless, more squalid,
every day; in which history itself seemed to be bleeding slowly
to death' (p. 204). On their last night together there, before
Ella's suicide (to be contrasted with Philip's in *Castle Corner*),
they are seated on an old sofa 'specially made' for Ella's grandmother; 'The horse-hair stuffing was curling out from large tears
in the cover';[12] ' "Thank God for a breeze," said Amanda. The
leaves of a horse chestnut, to be seen through the open window
in front, by the attic light, were shaken suddenly with a loud
metallic rattle' (p. 305). It is as if the spirit of the tree answers
her. They step outside, where 'all distances were uncertain. There
was, indeed, no horizon. The only clearly defined object was the
chestnut tree with its enormous structure of leaves, picked out
sharply by the attic light and resembling one of those centre
pieces of Victorian silver work, enlarged a hundred times.' Ella
says:

'I suppose they will cut that tree down – it darkens the
dining-room. Grandpapa planted it for the Great Exhibition.'

'Yes, it's too big – it's due to it to come down, as Harry would say.'

'Poor Harry!'

Cary's symbolism becomes unmistakable, and this horse chest-nut tree links Ella's life story with Gulley's, as 'a chestnut, a horse laugh', and with Nussbaum's in *Castle Corner*.[13] But it is a laugh 'from the other side' of the horse's mouth, and so links directly with the next novel.

A Fearful Joy

'Its a Gift. Then I laughed. I had to laugh. It made me laugh, the other side of the mouth.'[14] This note is headed '(March 1947) Captive and Free (or State of Nature)'. It concerns Hannah, but develops into the story of Tabitha Baskett, whose first name reveals her true puritan origin; being derived from the charit-able disciple raised by St Peter, *Tabitha* became endeared to the Puritans, and 'a generic term for an old maid, or a black and grey cat', says Yonge. The need to escape this stigma lends mean-ing to Cary's use of cat symbolism, for women. *Baskett* was his first name for the Wilchers (p. 221 above), but Tabitha escapes from the implications of both names.

From his 'Captive and Free' material, concerning Hannah, Cary had concurrently developed the story of Juno (nicknamed Poddy) who was captive to her beauty, in contrast to Hannah, who was plain. It was around 1947, too, that Cary noted: 'Idea, the childish soul of the world, loving, curious fearful – in prison to the [? beguiled] rulers'.[15] This casts light on the earlier novels but now Cary uses it more deliberately. His problem is whether the character so depicted should be pretty or plain, rich or poor. He solves it in *A Fearful Joy* by making Tabitha ordinary in every way. Paragraph one introduces her as a baby, with danger-ous curiosity, egotism, greed, shouts of rage, and a 'power of uproarious laughter at nothing at all'. This power seems intended to represent our age. For she is poor and plain, but becomes rich because adopted, according to Decadent tastes, as 'a living Beardsley. "Quite beautiful –"'

Tabitha begins to laugh, but seeing in Sturge's eyes a sad reproachful look, she grows serious again. And when she des-cribes this scene to Manklow, he says with mild disgust, 'It's what I said, didn't I? You're the new style – well, take my tip and make your hay quick, before some of those artists think up another funny one' (p. 56).

Such laughter, from 'the horse's mouth', dominates the novel from the first to the last page. It recalls *The Brothers Karamazov* – as may well be Cary's intention. Cary's likeliest inspiration is the conversation in *The Brothers Karamazov*, where the father questions Ivan and Aloysha, on the existence of God and immortality, and decides that Ivan's denial of both is probably right:

'Who is laughing at mankind, Ivan?'
'It must be the devil,' said Ivan, smiling.
'And the devil? Does he exist?'
'No, there's no devil either' (p. 135).

Laughter comes from 'The Horse's Mouth' – which is the mouth of the devil and god – from within mankind, says Cary. Tabitha's power is basically the helpless laughter that Cary observed in children and Africans (p. 77 above), and it is the power that chiefly helps her to survive. Her character and life story seem intended as the very antithesis of Ella's, and through Tabitha Cary gives a picture of our age, showing how freedom works. It is an age where the effect of Darwinism has gradually spread through society. People generally have recognized that the old God of the Christian churches is dead. This has left the majority with mean standards, and bored. Others have felt their creative energy released. But if their only purpose becomes personal power and self indulgence they are virtually worshipping the devil. Yet the devil can help us to rediscover God. This seems to explain Dick Bonser in Tabitha's life, and Hitler in our age, as Cary treats them both in this book. It is told in the present tense, to give the feeling that life drives us eternally to act, with little time for reflection. The 'fearful joy' of the title is essentially the power to love and create happiness.

There are at least three possible sources for this title. Cary may have believed it came to him independently; it is more likely that he hoped all three would awaken associations in readers' minds. The most relevant, since he acknowledged Hardy to be a master, is at the close of chapter XXIII in *Far From The*

Madding Crowd, where it is said of Bathsheba, a heroine not unlike Tabitha: 'To have brought all this about her ears was terrible; but after a while the situation was not without a fearful joy. The facility with which even the most timid women sometimes acquire a relish for the dreadful when that is amalgamated with a little triumph, is marvellous.' Again Fanny Burney's *Evelina*, at the close of her book: 'This morning, with fearful joy, and trembling gratitude, she united herself for ever with the object of her dearest, her eternal affection!' Finally, Cary had no doubt read, in Gray's 'Ode on a Distant Prospect of Eton College' which Blake illustrated: [16]

> Some bold adventurers disdain
> The limits of their little reign,
> And unknown regions dare descry.
> Still as they run they look behind,
> They hear a voice in every wind,
> And snatch a fearful joy.

In any case, all three quotations accord with the feeling that is essentially Cary's: that life offers happiness, but not as part of nature – for 'I can't imagine that bees and ants *are* happy' he said in various ways.[17] We are not, in fact, 'born of joy and mirth'. Joy is rather something men create but, if they are wise, they live in the fearful knowledge that this joy may at any time be lost to them.

Tabitha's mother, like Ella's, dies when she is young, and her father dies when she is fourteen, and he over sixty. He is an old-fashioned doctor in Frood Green, where his failing practice is saved by his son Harry. But Harry 'killed his father' (p. 10). He did so by marrying a determined woman, Edith, who forced the old man from his home, which 'finished him off in six months'. Such 'killing' is typical of 'A State of Nature', in Cary's novels. A Harry Dawbarn reduced women to a 'last ditch' level. But Tabitha revolts against the mean standards of a Harry Baskett.

Her father has shown 'no great kindness to his plain daughter'. But just before he dies, he buys Tabitha a bicycle:

'Harry and his madam don't believe in bicycles for young misses. Most dangerous and improper. So now go and learn to ride, and if you break your nose or anything more serious, they can blame Papa. It won't worry me after next week.'

And by this single act of imagination, or what to Harry and Edith seemed a piece of wanton spite, he secured Tabitha's affection, which he did not want, so entirely, that for the first time in her life she prayed with real ardour, imploring, therefore, a real god to give the old man life (p. 11).

This bicycle seems almost symbolic of Tabitha, as the soul of this new machine age, in which aeroplanes will eventually prove as decisive to her happiness. It symbolizes a woman's power for self-propulsion, given the courage. But above all it awakened her power to love, and her belief in a real god – or the power of a father to give love. Her life is a true pilgrim's progress, beginning in revolt against Frood Green, and ending in 'her own orthodoxy'.[18]

She is attracted to Dick Bonser because, at the moment when he first appears, she is reflecting restlessly ' "if only something would happen! " ' (p. 13). His surname, suggesting 'bouncing' and 'bounder', is accurately descriptive, as Tabitha immediately recognizes.[19] But when Edith calls him 'common', and Harry 'dangerous', her curiosity is roused. Like Ella, she is deceived by a romantic tale into eloping. Tabitha's realistic self is doubtful, but 'Her whole body is filled with laughter which is not so much incredulous as astonished' (p. 18). *Herself Surprised* as a title comes to mind, but 'elation' describes Tabitha's feeling, whereas Sara was more concerned with moral judgements. Tabitha 'feels no remorse whatever. There is no room for it in the density of her other sensations' (p. 20).

Bonser has in fact pursued her only because he believes she is to receive one thousand pounds a year income; he makes her feel guilty that this is untrue. He fails to marry her, and life with him becomes a succession of dishonest adventures with Tabitha persuading herself that she may reform him. When he says he has 'a real regular job', it proves to be for her to play the piano in a café. It has been arranged by Bonser's friend Manklow, whose careers as school teacher and journalist have both ended. in scandal, but have convinced him that in this 'rotten age', mass education offers golden opportunities. Sturge, who is ' "Rotten with money" ', promenades at this seaside resort, attended by young writers and painters of impressionist landscapes. His *Symbolist* magazine is ' "a bit of dirt wrapped up in hand-made paper" ', says Manklow. ' "It's the biggest open-ing in the century; there's been nothing like it since before the French Revolution" ' (p. 47). Tabitha becomes Sturge's mistress because Bonser, like Dawbarn, refuses to be ' "nailed with this baby – " ' (p. 49). She is surprised that he does not want their baby, and even more surprised when he punches her in the face, and disappears.

Tabitha decides immediately to kill herself and, rushing through the streets, is knocked down by a cab horse. The horse's mouth now appears in Tabitha's own laughter, 'dissolving her will, her anger', at sight of herself in a mirror of the draper's shop to which she is taken. The cabby drives her home, where Manklow reveals 'new elation', and she finds herself amused but not cynical. Back at her job at the café, 'The warmth of that big laugh is no longer a pervasive luxury, it is a more con-centrated heat in her breast. . . . she is impatient, she is full of that restless sensation which is life looking for a purpose' (p. 53). Manklow introduces her to Sturge, who says Tabithas ' "great gift" ' for music makes him feel ' "born again" '. For ' "Life is experience, it is personal in its very essence, it is feeling, it is the true joy which arises from the sensation – " ' (pp. 55–56). Tabitha's natural response to such talk is to laugh, which is indeed joy from the sensation. But she is silenced by her own 'life looking for a purpose', which responds to 'life is experience', as offered by Sturge.

The offer to become Sturge's mistress initially shocks Tabitha, and she returns to Harry. But here she is offered pills to effect a miscarriage, and she leaves, abusing British hypocrisy, narrow-mindedness, and philistinism, and thinking Sturge right about the arts. Sturge's friend Jobson arranges for her to go to Paris to study music. Thus the opportunity to become a concert pianist, denied to Ella, is given to Tabitha. It is given by the kind of men whom John Venn encouraged, but only because they want Tabitha as a mistress – a role Venn also denied Ella, though he kept one himself. To the surprise of these men, Tabitha insists upon having and keeping her baby, and here again she triumphs where Ella failed. Jobson realizes that this will make her ' "safe" ', and tells Sturge: ' "she's a bit of a lady, and that's always the best buy in the end" ' (p. 64). He knows there will be no further talk of giving concerts.

Sturge has been rich, married, and 'utterly respectable' until his conversion to impressionist art, which disgusts his wife. Now Jobson's suggestion of installing Tabitha in a flat haunts Sturge 'like a vision of impossible delight'. Tabitha for her part seems driven by a mysterious energy and purpose, to create a world where her child will be accepted. Manklow shrewdly uses her influence with Sturge to get him to found a new review ' "without the stodginess of the Yellow Book" ' (p. 68). So *The Bankside* is planned, and the first number appears a year later, 'in the spring of '98' (p. 84).

Under Sturge's direction, Tabitha becomes a renowned hostess, and 'several other ladies, perhaps cleverer and more beautiful, but certainly much more blown upon, have in the last ten years established the same kind of salon' (p. 77). Thus Cary invites readers to remember Helen Pynsant, and adds a comment on the effect of South African gold that bears on *Castle Corner* and *To be a Pilgrim* as well as this novel, where he writes: 'It is boredom that has broken the immense fortress of the old Christian society. It is because of boredom that the younger set fly from Windsor and that there are two ruling groups in England; the old, exclusive, high-principled clique dying of age, of lack of imagination; the new, selfish, often vulgar, but full of life. It adores novelty, and is easily penetrated by anyone who can give amusement' (pp. 77–78). In Tabitha, Cary depicts someone judging honestly and forming new values that are not selfish and vulgar, and therefore the opposite of Helen's.

Tabitha frankly condemns the poems of Boole, though Sturge insists that she can have no taste, considering her education and ignorance of the fundamentals. She defends Manklow, for recognizing ' "that rottenness is rotten" ' (p. 81). But always, underlying such arguments, is her impulse to laugh. Sturge's distress leaves her amused, as a nurse might be at a child, ' "making all that fuss about an old poem" ' (p. 82).

'Fundamentals' for Tabitha concern her child John. She calls herself an atheist, but thinks that, if John is not taught to pray, 'she is taking a fearful risk . . . of causing a permanent injury' (p. 90). So she teaches him her childhood prayers – while remaining equally dedicated to '*The Bankside* sphere of revolt and artistic enterprise' (p. 92). Having met Edith, she panics for John: ' "What is going to happen to him in a world full of Harrys and Ediths?" ' (p. 97). She gives all her energy to a more scandalous edition of *The Bankside*. This is in June 1901. But

the number is 'a ruinous failure', because theory is giving way
to practice, in this 'new age of revolution'.

Tabitha's reign in the aesthetic world ends finally, when a
woman claiming to be Bonser's wife appears at one of her
parties, and is thrown downstairs by Boole – so recalling the
famous incident concerning Schopenhauer.[20] The scandal
prompts Sturge's wife to divorce him, and 'respectable people'
regard her as 'a representative of all that is good, vindicating
right against a decadent wickedness.' The judge sums up accordingly. 'He has not noticed that decadence is already out of fashion,
and that the age is not corrupt but primitive and crude' (p. 130).
Tabitha's problems are 'that for John's future she needs a settled
income' (p. 133), and also a standard of values. She feels the
urge to pray, and at this point Harry appears.

Edith is dead, and 'He laughs . . . "My smart little sister . . .
you make me feel like an old buffer" ' (p. 135). Thus Harry himself dismisses his old world.

Tabitha next reigns as wife of Sir James Gollan, an iron master
of sixty-four, who represents the new age. His imagination has
been captured by Tabitha's success as Sturge's hostess. 'She
shudders at the idea of Gollan as a husband' when he proposes.
'But almost at once . . . she is seized with a feeling of smallness;
that self-contempt which rises spontaneously in one who runs
away from a challenge to duty. She perceives that this match will
give her security, a legal position, which is all important for
John's future as well as her own' (p. 148). James understands
John, and Tabitha sighs with relief: ' "At last the boy will have
something like a father to take an interest in him" ' (p. 155).
Thus John, like Ella's child Amanda, gets a substitute father,
named James, a 'supplanter'. Where Groom killed Amanda's
feelings by making her a scientist, Gollan almost kills John by
cultivating the world of machines, and speed. Tabitha herself is
possessed by the idea of progress through motors and planes, but
John becomes interested only when Bonser enters his life, in his
last year at school.

This is just when everyone begins talking of war as inevitable,
and there seems no doubt that Bonser personifies the spirit of
anarchy – or the devil – in which John was begotten, and which
lies behind the wars of our century. His first sight of Bonser
makes John smile, for his very appearance says to all the world
'rejoice with me' (p. 174). His conversation is immediately noth-

ing but lies, then he sweeps John off in 'an immense open two-seater Bentley', and boasts of his possessions and the need for a business man to entertain. He promotes and directs rubber companies, and gambles successfully on the market, he says, by 'a kind of sixth sense, an intuition' (p. 175). He leaves John excited 'as if his experience has been suddenly enlarged by an event which ought to be comic but can't altogether be laughed away' (p. 176). Yet he wonders: ' "But how could that fearful bounder be my father? How could Mother have had anything to do with such a cad?" '

It is after Bonser persuades John to introduce him to Gollan that disaster comes. Tabitha 'feels such fear for the boy, such hatred of Bonser, that she cannot reason. She says, "I *must* make him understand." But what John is to understand is not clear to her.' She knows that what she wants for John is expressed by 'words like wisdom, goodness, sincerity, nobility', but these now seem 'even absurd.' She cannot detect in this compound, says Cary, 'the element that she needs to defend the boy against such as Bonser: security in the spirit' (p. 181). Gollan vies with Bonser for John's affection by sending him to Oxford. Of John's success in the entrance examination, Gollan has said: ' "that'll show 'em at Oxford; that'll cut 'em down." ' Everyone to Gollan is a competitor or enemy, and he competes through John, of whom he now says, ' "He's amusing himself at Oxford. . . . That's the place for spending money" ' (p. 190). To Tabitha it seems that John is surrounded by dangers she cannot save him from. Yet this is the world she has helped to shape.

John 'scrapes a first in classics', then 'demands a road racer of his own' (pp. 192-3). Gollan indulges him, and he is almost killed driving it. Three weeks later World War I is declared. But John opens his eyes, and his injuries will save him from the war. Tabitha feels guilty on thinking this, and her sense of guilt takes her, like many others, to church. She thinks 'Has not the war come upon the world because of man's selfishness and self-seeking?' (p. 195). But she is selfish for her child.

John returns to Oxford, 'and her thankfulness and guilt increase' (p. 198). Following his final examination, he becomes assistant to Gollan, as a leading figure in the Ministry of Supply, and realizes ' "There's a war on" ', when Gollan has a stroke which must be kept secret, to save public morale. Bonser has a flat in Jermyn (German?) Street, which is 'neutral ground, where all meet in a comradeship not of the war but of pleasure, of life. . . . "Chaps tell me I'm a mug to be used as I am," he says to John; . . . But damn it, Johnny, I'm not a hunks. And we've got a tradition, you and me; it's in the blood. We're Hapsburgs on the mother's side; we've got a certain standard . . . it's something I can't help; it's me, that's all" ' (p. 210). These remarks follow Tabitha's realization that Bonser, as one of the profiteers, is like all 'adventurers who have seized a chance of fortune. That mysterious and complex being, the nation, which is fighting for its life, that mother country which they all profess to love, is, like all mothers, a prey' (p. 209). Such remarks invite the reader to see Bonser, Tabitha and John in a universal aspect of the father, mother, child relationship. John almost loves his father in his moments of invention, as in the remarks just quoted. Gollan is the alternative ideal of fatherhood offered him. But he pities his mother, as 'worn out.'

John, 'as a civilian in wartime, and heir to millions, is fair game to the envious' (p. 212). Tabitha reads daily attacks on such people, and feels even more guilty, for she has wanted him protected in this way. She wants John to face this problem with her, as a religious problem, but he is incapable of this – except to think: ' "Probably she's quite right; I am a bit intolerable" ' (p. 214). When the war ends, Gollan is made a Lord, becomes 'an absolute dictator', and then suddenly collapses and dies. To John, Bonser has explained: ' "You don't understand business, Johnny, it's an instinct. I don't mind telling you that me and some of my friends have made a pact to talk up the boom" ' (p. 221). But with Gollan dead, John loses his nerve directing Gollan's enterprises; shares fall, and he and Tabitha lose almost everything. The slump ends this second period of Tabitha's life. 'And this is her song, "The war is over, no one is being killed any more. John was not killed" ' (p. 223). When John and others pity her she laughs. She goes to church, and feels secure in her faith.

Her remaining years test this faith. John becomes a don at a new provincial university, Urrsley. He marries Kit, who, filled with scientific ideas, condemns Tabitha's natural love for their child Nancy, manifest in a desire to kiss her. Kit's different attitude to the upbringing of children, and to Tabitha as a mother-in-law, depicts a major aspect of the women's war. Tabitha lives near them, yet Kit gradually excludes her from their lives. Feeling unjustly treated, 'she finds no happiness in her faith; it turns to anger in her primitive soul, too proud to use religion for escape' (p. 244).

At this point Bonser reappears, and revives her 'primitive soul' by his sheer audacity. He calls himself 'Colonel' and declares that his previous marriage was 'Scotch' and illegal. 'She falls into a chair helpless with giggles' (p. 247). But at fifty-four she actually marries Bonser, with the same feeling of being *'fear-fully'* happy that she had when she first ran off with him (pp. 18, 252). Now she reigns at the 'BEAUSITE HOTEL. GARAGE. DANCING.' (p. 258) as the symbol of the new age. It is Bonser's dream but, as with Sturge and Gollan, it is Tabitha's practical energy that makes the creation of this new world possible. She is horrified at the new morals, unaware apparently that she paved the way for them. Yet again she personifies the viewpoint that is gradually accepted: 'that such places must come and cannot be stopped. .A feeling much more powerful than churches and councils and parents. The sense of a universal force at work, the young imagination seeking a new field, creation itself' (p. 271). By 1934 'Colonel' Bonser owns a select hotel, the Free-masons, and is a highly respected member of Urrsley society. He is proud of his wireless set, which transmits Hitler's speeches. 'He turns a knob and a screaming hysterical voice startles the room. "Hitler!" – with a smile of triumph. It is as though he has commanded the demagogue to do his will' (p. 274). At such times, on the faces of 'smart young people' who have gathered for 'a new story about old Dick Bonser, one sees an expression of wonder which makes the most hard-boiled seem for a moment innocent and foolish' (p. 274). People who have been given no 'security in the spirit', and can admire Bonser, will also admire Hitler, Cary thus says. For Bonser personifies the same spirit in more amiable guise. Beside Bonser, at such times, is John's child Nancy, who thinks him wonderful.

Tabitha is still fighting the battle for other values, but through John. Teaching philosophy at Urrsley, he argues: ' "There's a special feeling in a place like this; it's completely different from Oxford or Cambridge" ' (p. 285). But she despairs. 'And he understands that she can never understand him, or the battle of his life, the tension, the faith, the exciting enterprise of rescuing some young mind, still interested, still curious and sincere, from the enemy, the vast darkness of nihilism, mechanism.' Tabitha knows that John's personal enemy is his wife, who is dominated by Rodwell, in the chemistry department. Kit despises John, whose unhappiness fills Tabitha with a misery that aggravates his. She asks his forgiveness, and he replies: ' "But, my dear mother, you've given me all the happiness I could have" ' (p. 286). Later 'he thinks with surprise, "It is true; she gave me everything that matters, but how can she understand that? You could not get it into her head by an operation." ' This expression of 'life is a gift' directs us to see John's death as the key-point of the novel. Tabitha has always sensed that Kit would achieve it in some way (indeed she soon marries Rodwell). She does so by insisting that they join Rodwell's rock-climbing party; having been 'benighted in fog and wet', John dies of pneumonia. His burial becomes the more symbolic because a bus advertising ' "Holiday Trips" ' stops for the trippers to clamber out and look on.

Tabitha's anger is directed not only against the mob, against the bus and Kit, but against something much larger and more indefinite: against a fundamental injustice which puts the good, the wise, the gentle, simply because of their goodness, for ever at the mercy of the malignant, or simply stupid. "It's not fair," she feels; and the feeling is so intense that she can hardly bear it.

She finds some comfort only in Nancy's grief (p. 289).

Because of her women's war with Tabitha, however, Kit keeps Nancy from her. It is not until the spring of 1938 that Nancy re-enters Tabitha's life. She is like Tabitha re-born: plain and ordinary, but for Tabitha the child of grace, through whom she will find a new sense of purpose. Yet she is highly critical of Nancy, as typical of her generation. 'She feels the mass of youth as a dangerous explosive force; . . . it seems to her that the world is full of youth movements . . . and feeling as if the air itself is full of electric youth, she says, "But of course there must be a war, with all this egotism and recklessness. If Hitler doesn't make war someone else will, or it will simply start by itself" ' (p. 311). This is the spirit of 'old Dick Bonser', which first tempted her, she might have added. Nancy admires the devotion to Hitler in Germany, but Tabitha loathes Hitler.

She can't bear even to hear the voice which has such power over millions. And when she reads in a paper of 'that genius among demagogues', she says angrily, 'I don't call it genius to be a liar and a cheat.'

Yet this is exactly why she trembles with hatred and fear at the name of Hitler, because he has this genius in lying and cheating, and because she feels the immense power of lies and fraud, especially with the innocent. She thinks, "Everyone is telling lies – the communists, the Nazis, all the nationalists – and the young swallow them. They like to swallow them; they'd rather have lies than truth, because lies are more exciting. But it can't go on; it's impossible. If I talked about a judgment they'd laugh at me, but that's what they will get." [The next chapter begins immediately.]

Bonser, like Tabitha, is convinced that there will be a war, and that it will ruin him. He has an immense admiration for Hitler, listens to all his speeches which he cannot understand, reads three or four newspapers a day, and tells everyone, "It's coming all right. He'll beat the lot of 'em, that artist. And he actually wrote in his book that the people are a lot of sheep; and they kiss his arse for it. That's the stuff, that's pretty smart, that's artful. I take off my hat to that bugger; he's spoofed the world, and serve it right for a lot of mugs" (pp. 312–13).

By these passages, Cary has conveyed the feelings that allowed World War II to develop.[21] Bonser's power over Tabitha is exactly similar to Hitler's over young people. He is a Hitler whose only cause is self-indulgence. He dies drunk in a brothel, triumphing that he always tricked Tabitha and everyone else. ' "Spoo-fed 'em – spoooofed 'em – the whole – " which sinks away into a murmur, like a child crooning itself to sleep' (p. 358). He is the Hitler in our midst, and when he praises Hitler, for calling people a lot of sheep, he anticipates Chester Nimmo, who first practises his oratory on sheep, and Joanna Rideout who admires Hitler for saying this very thing (pp. 289, 306 below). By making "spoofed" become "spoo-fed", and ending it as a lullaby, Cary brings "spoon-fed" to mind, and so the danger to youth of being drawn to such men, in 'movements'. The devil as a power of evil must be recognized in his true nature, Cary is saying. For in the very moment that Tabith recalls Bonser's wickedness, she recalls his charms, and 'that danger and burden, has also been the ground and the sky of her life' (p. 359).

Bonser's death coincides with the end of the war, and now Tabitha begins to have 'that air of disorganisation which leads people to say sometimes of an old person that he or she is "going to pieces".' She is surely England at this time, somehow finding the strength to help Nancy to form a family unit with the crudely hard airline pilot, Joey Parkin. To do so she invests in an airline, and raises the money by selling the hotels that represent everything of her life with Bonser. This recalls Ella's sale of Florence Villa (p. 250 above); like Ella, Tabitha is fighting for the next generation. Her brother Harry, by contrast, is to be looked after by his daughter-in-law – a kinder fate than his father's had been, and suggesting that women, in the final analysis, are more independent and readier to shoulder responsibility than men are. For his daughter-in-law, 'old Harry' has 'a harried young woman', who nevertheless belongs to the new generation whom Cary admired. This spirit has been transmitted in some measure by Tabitha to Nancy, with whom she hopes to live.

For Tabitha now, through Nancy – whose son is another John – it is 'as if kindness had been renewed' (p. 376). But then Parkin decides to emigrate to New Zealand, flying as far as possible from Tabitha, by the very invention she has invested in in order to help him. ' "Why should we put up with her?" ' he asks – though she is paying their fares, and giving them an allowance. A month after they leave they have still not cabled or written. Tabitha becomes gradually very ill; she thinks 'Living is not worth while any more, it is nonsense' (p. 386). But 'Apparently her body has a life of its own. . . . And some mysterious warmth rises in Tabitha to meet the warmth of the sun' (p. 387). She is watching children in Kensington Gardens, and the sight of a hideously plain child screaming in misery rouses, in this new primitive life force in Tabitha, 'an irresistible passion of laughter'. It is cruel laughter.

She is terrified that it will kill her, and never has she wished so ardently to live. Her whole being prays to be reprieved this once – for a month, a week, till that letter comes from Nancy.

And the prayer that is torn from her is not to the father or the son or the spirit. It is the primitive cry of the living soul

to the master of life, the creator, the eternal. 'Oh, God,' her
blue lips murmur, 'not quite now.'

Gradually the pain becomes less . . . And as . . . she looks
again . . . at a world remade, she gives a long deep sigh of
gratitude, of happiness (p. 388).

This one God is not the Christian trinity, but the eternal creator
of life in whom Cary believes; in whom laughter, as a power,
has here become almost overwhelmingly manifest in Tabitha.
Her natural 'power of uproarious laughter' which characterized
her as a baby (and now characterizes our age in typical broadcast
programmes?) is here directed with total lack of sympathy at
this child, who seems even less gifted with prospects than Tabitha
had been. It is the power that can become ridicule of Jews and
eventually a willingness to obey a Hitler, in killing them. Just
because Tabitha is so ordinary a person she personifies the age
that let this happen. But the power of love, as another aspect of
this eternal creator, combats this crude aspect, at the moment
when she prays to hear from Nancy. The name signifies that
she gets grace by this power of love – this fearful joy. By it she
is saved, for she will not die in that spirit of despair and cynicism,
which the inane laughter of our time is really expressing.

The ending of this book becomes even more poignant, when
Cary's own battle against cynicism and despair at this time is
remembered. It was published in October 1949, and since April
1948 his wife had been fighting death with all Tabitha's longing
that it would be ' "not quite now".' Enid Starkie tells us:

She died just before Christmas, but the tickets for the evening performance of the pantomime on Boxing Day had been
bought before her death, and everything was carried through
as if she was still there. . . . he laughed uproariously at all
the jokes – even more than they deserved – crossing and un-
crossing his legs, as was his habit in moments of excitement
or nervous tension. When the performance was over he went
back to the house. . . . The Christmas had been as his wife
had always planned it so carefully, it was now his sole responsibility, and he was not going to let down the side, although
his heart was breaking with grief.[22]

The feeling that underlies *A Fearful Joy*, and its message, can thus be understood. When writing of his wife's death, Cary said: 'I never knew anyone with such a genius for life and love'.[23] This gift of life had inspired him, but still he must not 'let down the side'. Enid Starkie continues: 'even after her death, whenever he published a book, he always added a copy first of all to her own shelf of his works, because he wanted, he told me, her collection of his writings to be complete.' This explains his desperate longing to complete the series; for the last book, in its message, is above all a tribute to her. It was the women's war begun by his wife that had made him a major novelist.

The mood of the remaining books is grimmer. Cary was fighting sadness, not only for his wife's death, but also for the betrayal of youth by false values, which mass media was now intensifying. The zest for life, so evident in interviews, seems a conscious effort to combat this feeling.[24] But it is conveyed in the novels. If readers remember Cary's treatment of Hitler in relation to Tabitha and Bonser, they will more readily accept the following interpretation of Nimmo, and then Preedy.

15. The Second Trilogy

Prisoner of Grace
Except the Lord
Not Honour More

Prisoner of Grace is the confession of Nina Latter. She begins: 'I am writing this book because I understand that "revelations" are soon to appear about that great man who was once my husband, attacking his character, and my own.' She establishes herself immediately as sympathetic, fair-minded, and likely to judge others more generously than herself. Indeed, Cary says in the preface that he could make her a credible witness only by the use of brackets. She illustrates Cary's own belief: 'Without this power of sympathy, there is no revelation.'[1] But first she deserves sympathy herself. Her parents both died of cholera in India when she was four. She lived with Mary Latter, a fearsome maiden aunt who did not want her, and slapped her often. They were 'highly incompatible'; so Nina had no experience of love – only the memory of being carried by her mother, with a sense of relief that she had been forgiven some mischief; 'a vast calm peace, which was, in fact, nothing but the sense of being carried by my mother' (pp. 76-77); by comparing this feeling with sailing, Nina recalls similar associations in *A House of Children* (p. 203 above).

But Mary Latter adored Nina's cousin Jim Latter; and 'that passion for Jim which gradually took hold of her and made her rather blind to other peoples dues' is the key to Nina's story. Nina wonders 'if she were simply indulging Jim with me' (p. 15), and by writing immediately after this of love between brothers and sisters in 'rather a strict Low Church household' she hints at Cary's main point; that religion is rooted in human relationships, and can quickly 'roll down hill to primitive naturalism', as he writes in a note for the novel.[2]

266

Jim too had known no love. His mother was dead, and he hated his father, who lived abroad and favoured his older brother Bobby. Another vital clue to the story is that Nina loved Bobby, better than Jim or anyone else, it seems (p. 11). Aunt Latter felt 'the deepest compassion' for Jim, but this grew into a passion which she could not express, except through Nina. As with Rose in *The Moonlight*, others suffer in this novel because Mary Latter's own power to love has been unfulfilled in a husband and children. More daringly here, using the name Mary as a clue, Cary challenges a society that on one hand worships a Virgin Mary as the ideal Mother, and on the other pities a virgin Mary like Aunt Latter who fails to get a husband; who in consequence directs her energy and passions into the management of other people's lives, with a power to love that has turned sour, or evil. As Nina tells us of Aunt Latter: 'she took a very low view of marriage, probably because her own love affair had gone wrong' (p. 43). This trilogy is even more an 'anti-*Kreutzer Sonata*' than *The Moonlight*, and the over-all clue to it is again Tolstoy's split mind.

Regarding Jim, Mary Latter has told Nina: 'If he wants to do things with you, do them willingly' (p. 10). She must have known that Jim, four years older than Nina, teased, terrified and tortured her with his frightening stories, and also with proposals for adventures such as the one when they both swim in a howling gale, and Nina is left wishing herself dead. Yet all their quarrels have ended with his climbing into her bed, vowing they will marry as soon as possible, and sleeping in her arms. Thus Cary answers anyone who believes children should grow up naturally, and form their own moral code (p. 158 above). They do not actually consummate their sexual relationship until Nina is seventeen, and she at the time is more interested in going to a concert. However, she becomes pregnant.

At sixteen she had inherited her fortune of five thousand pounds; she was also beautiful. Cary developed her from Juno, as the archetypal opposite of the plain Hannah. Her situation is thus the opposite of Tabitha's. But Chester Nimmo's approaches are very like Bonser's. He clearly knows about Nina's fortune, for he is a 'pet' of Aunt Latter's. Nina writes: 'He certainly owed much to Aunt Latter. . . . Aunt Latter had got him his first job at Bing's. She had even provided him with suitable clothes' (p. 18). Chester acknowledges no debt to Aunt Latter in his book, and specifically attributes these two acts of kindness to members of his own class.[3] Thus a key point of the trilogy is that Chester's testimony is dishonest. His 'Judas coat' becomes a commentary on the nature of authority, implying that someone like Chester succeeds only through the help of people they label class enemies, and step into a way of life created for them by previous generations of that class – 'it's a gift', as it were.

However, Aunt Latter (like Lucy Wilcher) is disillusioned with her class, and also recognizes Nimmo as a rising radical politician. When, therefore, he begins way-laying Nina and proposing marriage, in romantic terms that Nina finds embarrassing and absurd, Aunt Latter advises: ' "Don't be too unkind to him, Nina; he is much too useful. And, besides, he really has the gift of the gab' (p. 20). This attitude in aristocratic Germany brought Hitler to power, and the power of Hitler's voice is recorded in Cary's notebooks as well as A Fearful Joy – just as his blue eyes are stressed in The Horse's Mouth.[4] So it is the horse's mouth, as the voice of a spellbinder – above all this arch-spellbinder of our age – which dominates this trilogy. When Nina describes the effect of Chester's speeches, she might as easily be describing Hitler's power over millions: 'these speeches, in Chester's "thrilling" voice, had a very strange effect on my nerves. I write "thrill", because as soon as I heard this description (not by a woman, either, but by an enthusiastic young man) I felt how right it was. Chester's voice was one of his great gifts – it made him a power. . . . It seemed that I was two women, one of them quite furious still and watchful of every move by this cunning enemy, and one of them so close and sympathetic to him that she felt all his feelings like her own' (p. 44).

But Chester's gift is a 'gift of the gab', gab meaning originally 'to mock' or 'to tell lies'. Aunt Latter knows this. But her politics are really concerned with the 'Slapton-Latter dynasty to which I owed my position (and several of them had married only to keep up the family)' says Nina (p. 22). When Nina becomes pregnant to Jim, therefore, it is an obvious diplomatic solution for someone of her class, to decide promptly: ' "you'll have to marry Nimmo" ' (p. 23). Jim's regiment forbids marriage for a subaltern, and Aunt Latter cannot consider his resigning. Nor does it occur to her that he has any responsibility. In fact, her diplomacy resembles John Chass Corner's towards Bridget, but in this case a useful member of the rising class is admitted to hers. Nina however is sacrificed to save the family, just as Ella Venn was. Cary directs us to make this comparison, because Lord Slapton has been a character in *The Moonlight*, contrasted with John Venn. Venn's motives regarding Ella are purely selfish, in contrast to Aunt Latter's, which she believes are for the good of wider political issues.

Again Cary seems to be saying that, since ancient times, myths and legends, even of matings with gods, all originated in struggles of certain families to establish power. Nina's book, by its very tone, could be used by later generations of a family, to claim Nimmo as a kind of god – as happened to Alexander, and was already happening with Hitler.[5] When the war ended, the Nuremberg War Crimes Tribunal was set up, and it would be typical of Cary, with his concern to give a 'whole view of life', if his imagination developed the idea already used for his first trilogy, as a trial; as if the Nuremberg trials had produced this confession by Nina, the soul of the world, regarding the world's rulers in our time. Plato's conception of the soul as imprisoned in the body is suggested by the word 'captive' in relation to Nina.[6] But the symbol of the charioteer driving two horses is still relevant to this trilogy.[7] It invites us to see Jim and Chester as universal figures.

As an artist in words, Nimmo can be seen as universal, just as Gulley is. In a story closing with the general strike he recalls Liberal politicians of that time, most obviously Lloyd George. As a personality known and opposed to Cary himself, he is Murry, and also Murry's antipodal self, Lawrence. But in this novel, especially, the universal nature of Cary's characterization enriches the meaning, and it is highly relevant to remember his question: 'But what is an individual?'[8] Thus the men who influenced Murry and Lawrence become incorporated in Chester Nimmo as a universal figure – whom we, the readers, create in our minds from Cary's description, out of our own knowledge of history and human nature. Milton, nicknamed 'The Lady', seems certainly intended to come to mind, when Nina says Chester was nicknamed ' "Pretty boy" ', and ' "The maiden's prayer" ' (p. 18). Nimmo will show that Milton influenced him, and the title of his book is taken from a psalm. Jim's is from Lovelace's Cavalier poem. So Cary invites us to remember the Elizabethan period, when his family went from Devon, where this novel is set, and got land to rule over in Ireland, simply because they accepted the Church of England faith established by Elizabeth. It becomes easy to see that Nina's situation resembles that of the real woman Elizabeth I, who kept peace between Catholics and Puritans by establishing this State Church. For Nina says 'Jim could have been a Jesuit' (p. 74), and Elizabeth might have said of the Puritans, what Nina finally says of Chester: 'I did not love Chester and I had never loved him, but now, more than ever, at the end of his life, I was in his power' (p. 400). It is, after all, only someone with wide knowledge and sympathies who could write as Nina does.

This interpretation of Nina is upheld by the fact that Cary stresses her wide reading and also her strongly sympathetic nature. She – and indeed all women – have been shaped by the women of history, including those known only through reading of them. Nina carries the blood of her Frankish ancestors in her veins. But, just as Cary acknowledges that the great men of England's history had shaped him (p. 24 above); so Nina can be understood from the women of whom Cary had read. Donne's poem 'The Extasie', made him consider 'An Abler Soul' as the title of her book.[9] Robert Graves's *The Story of Mary Powell Wife to Mister Milton*, with its reference to the Carys, points to a strong likeness. She is surely the Countess Tolstoy who was publicly humiliated as a wife by *The Kreutzer Sonata*, after thirty years of marriage – much as happens to Nina, after thirty years with Chester. She is also Kierkegaard's Regina, whose name relates her to the time when this book was published, when another Regina was inspiring Englishmen to hope for a new Elizabethan age. First, ' "Know thyself" ', Cary might be saying through Nina, just as he did in 1941, through Sara.

When Nina writes of 'that great man who was once my husband', she could well be trying to explain, for future generations, how our generation made a Hitler our bedfellow. But Nina has actually to sleep with Chester – just as many women like her, forced to marry to 'keep up the family', had doubtless had to adjust to similar situations. Perhaps this is the chief source for the idea that women should suffer. It was before going to bed with her that Chester's 'thrilling' speeches had the most agonizing effect on Nina, and the passage already quoted actually continues with the suggestion that most women are 'more or less "split personalities" '. Thus Chester's words about his love make Nina increasingly angry; 'yet when I felt his hand tremble as well as his voice this love seemed to fly all through me, so that I was all a tension of anger and pity at the same time, and all my arguments seemed to fall apart into dry dusty fragments which were quite contemptible' (p. 44). It seems that Nina's emotional self can sympathize with Chester, while her conscious self judges him, and belongs, by education and background, to Jim. This interpretation accords with Cary's treatment of Evelyn and Kathy as 'like savages', in contrast to Harry, who here resembles Jim. In fact the words 'noble' and 'savage' echo through the trilogy, as though Cary is using them to contrast the noble savage and savage noble, as these opposites apply to Tolstoy.[10]

What Nina finds most embarrassing is Chester's insistence on praying before sexual relations, 'like grace before a meal' (p. 63). In this sense particularly she is a prisoner of grace. For Chester also prays for 'The lie in the soul' (p. 45). The meaning of this phrase can be understood from the discussion of it, as it occurs in *The Moonlight*. It would accord totally with this interpretation of the novel if Cary's source were indeed Murry's discussion of the story 'La Grâce'.[11]

Why Chester never fathers a child to Nina remains a mystery, as Cary probably intended. The simplest explanation would be that he could not, or that Nina would not allow it, for someone she so much hated. But it seems more likely that Cary is deliberately creating a situation where paternity is a mystery. For the story began as 'Cock Jarvis', when Cary was questioning English Christian institutions in the face of Tolstoy's challenge, and also contemplating a life of Christ: 'shew him born illeg.' (p. 117 above). By making Jim now the irresponsible father, he makes *Not Honour More* appropriate for Jim's story, and also suggests that Christ's divine fatherhood had a similar explanation. On the other hand, Chester, with his chapel background, could probably never escape seeing Nina as a harlot, according to Revelation, for she has been surprised that anyone 'supposed to be so respectable' would marry her (p. 24). So he has had to try to lie to himself that the child is his – as perhaps Joseph did, Cary might be saying, so presenting us with another aspect of 'the lie in the soul'. Since 'virgin', for Jesus' mother, is from a word meaning merely young girl, and Nina is only seventeen, while Chester is thirty-four, Cary may be thought to have created a situation of comparable likelihood. *Tom*, meaning 'twin', for the child's name, fits his double role.[12] It also fits the prophecy of Christ's coming, of which Cary was reading at this time. For he noted 'Prisoners of hope' from Zechariah ix.12,[13] and 'Prisoners of Grace' was the earlier title of the book – by this he meant Nina and Tom,[14] and the title certainly comments upon the messianic message of 'Prisoners of hope' and the notion of grace that it brought, which he is attacking. However, by changing his heroine's name to Nina, and by making her alone the prisoner, he probably thought his point was clearer. In his preface he explains that grace for him was not something 'invoked only by special exercise', but a revelation that comes in ways that, from his description, are intuitions of truth comparable with 'surprise' in Sara's book.

In the preface he also explains that he had to write the key scene of the novel, before he could be sure that the book would work. Nina's chief revelation or moment of grace must therefore occur here, and her entire relationship with Chester builds up to this scene. Cary shows that Chester begins his political career through marrying Nina, yet cannot escape his class hatred (which recalls Gulley's, p. 230 above), even when triumphing in his success: ' "You think me a cad" . . . "No. no, that's not fair . . . You *feel* me a cad" ' (p. 33). But when Nina insists that she does not feel this difference of class, he retorts: ' "Perhaps not – but it's there or I shouldn't have wanted you. None of your back-lane girls for me. I always swore I'd get a lady and I have." ' He raves about the ' "silent conspiracy to keep people like me in our places" ' – even when his place at the moment is in Nina's arms. His resentment against her other 'Aunt Mary', who had brought his mother ' "Christmas dole" ' (p. 35) indicates that with Chester the Christian religious idea of helping the poor has failed as much as the political one. In fact, from the first his propaganda shocks Nina as 'all lies – and also a savage attack on several of my friends' (p. 32).

But Chester's 'real start' in politics has been as a pro-Boer agitator, (at a meeting that could be the very one described in *Castle Corner*, p. 191 above). Lloyd George has organized a meeting in the village, town workers have been brought in to wreck it, and Chester has been injured in the rioting. Lloyd George was generally hated at the time, says Nina:

I should have been glad if he had been lynched; and yet (which is the strange thing about this special hatred) I was also afraid of his getting killed, as if that, too, might make me feel guilty and put God on the enemy's side. And I resented this feeling, too . . .

. . . I felt sure, all the same, that the fact that Lloyd George did risk his life made all these agitators discover in some secret part of their imagination *how people could be tortured and confused in their minds by this tremendous bravery and self-sacrifice.* . . .

they were encouraged by the discovery that governments simply do not know how to deal with martyrs (p. 48).

In the italicized words Cary clearly gives the clue to Chester's hold over Nina. It is aggravated because his best friend is a pro-Boer, Edward Goold, whom Nina detests. But, as Chester's wife, she cannot risk having it said that she ' "deprived him of his friends" ' (p. 50) – though Chester's attacks are calculated to deprive Nina of hers.

Nina's detestation of Edward Goold can be understood from her account, which is also necessary to an understanding of *Except the Lord*. He is a great preacher in the chapel, the son of 'G.' in Chester's novel, who is also 'very religious', says Nina, 'but rather a bad sly old man; he had been fined for some trick with his scales, and also he had been in prison for misbehaving with young girls' (p. 51). When 'G.' retires, Edward buys two more shops, with Nina's money lent by Chester. Chester's first political success delights Goold. He starts a riot by calling 'the Tory gang' 'murderers and cowards'. Chester's politics disgust Nina, whose friends however identify her with them and she becomes too embarrassed to mix with them. For Christian marriage requires her to cleave to Chester. Her devotion to Chester is actually due to fear 'of being a very bad wife; . . . a kind of incantation to make me love' (p. 61).

Then Jim reappears, and an interlude follows when the two male characters (two aspects of one world character) are in harmony. Chester's power of imagination creates a situation where Nina now understands 'what Balzac or perhaps it was what Vauvenargues meant by calling matrimony a political education' (p. 32). Her numerous 'conversions', when she receives grace, have been direct intuitions of the need for sympathy and diplomacy in human relationships. Gradually, however, Nina's affinity with Jim proves too strong, and ends in 'primitive naturalism' symbolized by the setting: dark night in the garden of Chester's house, the Orchard, where Jim suddenly insists on physical union. He employs a technique of love-making he has learnt in India, and the effect on Nina is that 'the physical thing at that moment was so mixed up with the spiritual thing that they could no more have been separated than body and soul' (pp. 85-6). He claims that she belongs to him, not Chester. Thus possessed by Jim, she can think only of joining him. She leaves the house early the next morning – without showing any concern for Tom, whom she hears in the distant nursery. Jim has really won her by a trick, which has made her forget her responsibility as a mother.

The key scene now occurs at the railway station, in the waiting room. The setting shows that here Cary is attacking what he calls 'waiting room religion', in which this world is regarded as a testing place where women especially should be prepared to suffer, in the hope of finding grace in heaven. Chester is more subtle than John Venn was, when Ella wanted to form a family with her child and its father. But he is equally selfish in denying that basic trinity of the true family relationship of Jim, Nina, and Tom, in order to further personal ambitions. These have so far been fulfilled, firstly by taking advantage of Nina's pregnancy, and secondly by working on mankind's capacity for hate and spite, by telling lies.

He has followed Nina, and first tries to make her feel guilty by saying she ' "stooped" ' to him. She cannot argue about class differences, because two market women are listening. When she raises the question of Tom, they have been joined by a man and a child of about four – Tom's age. Chester's spellbinding powers are now winning him a supportive audience, and his argument becomes political. Their marriage has been 'blessed with our work for right and good things' he claims (quite untruly, as shown above); ' "and you might blame yourself if you broke it up" ' (p. 92). God is unlikely to be 'quite so political' says Nina. She doesn't believe in Goold's God, who punishes people with suffering. Chester retorts: ' "we have to fear Him; . . . the consequence of doing wrong – the sin against love" ' (p. 93). The word 'love' makes 'a nerve jump', though Nina knows Chester is really concerned for his career, if she leaves him. He says nothing, but his kiss – surely a kiss of Judas – makes her think: ' "The confidence trick again with a little bit of trust in God added" ' (p. 95). Cary makes it very plain that what really influences Nina in this scene is the word 'love', spoken just before she notices the small boy. He is staring into her face, with his sticky hand on her frock, and when Chester leaves he begins climbing into her lap. When the train comes in, she says 'my feet stopped and turned me aside'. What holds her, surely, is above all the realization, through this child, that her love for Tom must come first. Added to this is the atmosphere created by Chester's supporters in the waiting room, ready to see Chester as a martyr, and so making Nina *'tortured and confused'* in the very way she had remarked of Lloyd George (p. 273 above).

Cary knew that readers would liken Chester to Lloyd George, and took pains to ensure that he could not be identified.[15] But it seems that this key scene comes close to what actually happened with Middleton Murry's third wife, in 1931. She decided, after less than three months of marriage, to leave him. But Murry followed her to the railway station and persuaded her to return to him, which she did, Murry said, ' "as one submitting to Fate" '.[16] It also recalls Mary Powell's situation with Milton, whom Murry so strongly admired. Murry's view of sex appears to be Milton's: 'Hee for God only, shee for God in him'. This view, it is very clear, is what Cary is attacking. The suggestion here offered, then, is that, probably inspired by what Graves wrote in *Wife to Mister Milton* in 1942 – that Milton was a fascist though he claimed to serve freedom – Cary related the idea to Murry and, in creating Chester, wants this identification to be recognized. Murry's conversion to pacifism in 1936 had led to his association with Mary Gamble, with whom he started an experiment in community living, in 1942. This was presumably a development of the dreams Murry shared with Lawrence during World War I. It was a failure, chiefly because Murry proved a dictator – to judge from his account of it in *Community Farm*, published in 1952. This publication could help explain why Cary suddenly decided, in 1952, to write *Except the Lord*, showing Chester's Miltonic upbringing. If so, Cary is likely to have had Murry in mind for Chester in *Prisoner of Grace*.

To be sure of keeping Nina, Chester wins Aunt Latter's support, and also buys her luxuries, against her wishes, by borrowing from Goold. Goold had made a great deal of money in the war by a lucky deal in tinned meat, and had said that 'his money was the gift of God and should be used for God's work' (p. 99). Cary's theme phrase rings ominously here, following Chester's invocation to God in the key scene, and it damns him totally seventeen years later. For, when World War I breaks out, and Chester needs to reject his pacifist doctrine if he is to be in the government, Goold attacks him as 'a turncoat and Judas' (p. 264); so Chester publicizes the fact that the tinned meat that made Goold's fortune during the Boer war was bad, and poisoned some of the troops to whom it was sent. By then Nina could excuse the detestable Goold, who at least had not known the meat was bad, but of Chester she writes: 'It was as though I had never seen before *this* man (to whom I had been married for twenty years) who had suddenly revealed himself capable of a cruel and spiteful plot against an old friend' (p. 276). This is a crime against the basic value of loyalty.

Seventeen years before, however, Goold has been her chief enemy, in persuading people that she has corrupted Chester. In fact, she has wanted to leave him, on discovering that she is again pregnant by Jim. But Aunt Latter forces her to believe that Jim needs a friend in Parliament, and that it will be Nina's fault if Chester loses the current election. So, in order to make life bearable for herself with Chester, Nina shows him 'something of what Jim had revealed to me. And the result was even more surprising . . . For (what I had not foreseen) he took this very natural achievement (just as I had done with Jim) as a sign that we were at last "at one" ' (p. 114). Thus, the act that Jim supposed would make Nina 'belong' to him, makes Chester fall into 'a real passion of love' for '*My* wife', whose every movement is jealously spied upon, chiefly by Goold's nephew Bootham, who becomes Chester's secretary, shortly after Nina's second child, Sally, is born. Sally will later marry Bootham, and will be totally devoted to Chester. She will belong to the generation of the twenties whom Cary thought misled by false theorists. If Jim and Chester are supposed to reveal something about this viewpoint, it seems that the conception of Sally, in Chester's garden, symbolizes the impulse that drew Tolstoy to the peasants, and led eventually to the new attitude to women, following the Russian revolution. But sex is not love, Cary wrote.

By somewhat similar symbolism, Tom becomes the child of promise, born illegitimate, with a message that is misunderstood, and a life that is tragically wasted. Cary devotes a large section of the novel to Tom's career at school and at Oxford, to show that he is doomed by his false position: in truth Jim's son, yet brought up as Chester's; that is, as the son of a leader of the new ruling class, who has reached his position by crying out for the poor against the rich, and now enjoys far greater luxury than those he denounced, without troubling at all, as they did, to help the poor people whom they actually know. At a critical point in boyhood, Tom is driven – 'with an expression on his face exactly like Jim's' – to say that Chester tells lies. He becomes a prisoner to Chester, in the very way Nina is. Mother and son become very close, and Chester fiercely jealous. Nina is driven to such hatred of Chester that she wants to die. But Chester stops her leaping from the window, and leads her back to bed 'like a trojan captive on a rope, with a feeling of submission so acute and complete and sudden that it was comical' (p. 309). The ability to laugh on this occasion gives Nina a ' "conversion" ' – that is, grace; she realizes that she can detest him yet not mind, and thinks 'rather cynically, "It appears that I should have done quite well on the streets." '

Tom goes to the war, and wins the Military Cross. Yet both Jim and Chester fail him. Both are disgusted by the general decline in morals (though who are they to judge?), and quarrel with Tom – Jim because he dislikes the cap Tom chooses to wear. Chester's betrayal is more deadly, and is a total indictment of their relationship. After the armistice Tom has helped Chester in his political campaigning. But Chester does nothing to help Tom get work. Finally he does so as a night-club entertainer. For Chester's 'gift of the gab', which the boy Tom recognized as lies, has developed through his false position, into 'a gift for inventing turns'. These take the form of mimicking politicians. On the occasion when Nina watches him:

he made a face at me so ludicrous, so much more 'like' Chester's when he was using this tone than Chester himself; so wild a caricature, such a picture of everything that was loathsome, of the vulgar false hypocritical demagogue, full of spite and trickery and conceit and an indescribable beastliness, a kind of likerish sensuality; a lustful pleasure in his own nastiness; everything that had been imputed to Chester by his worst enemies (and so cruelly because, of course, there is a trace of all those things in every 'popular' speech) that, to my horror, I was suddenly seized with laughter. I heard myself utter a kind of noise, which was neither a laugh nor a cry, a kind of whinny (p. 342).

This indeed is a horse-laugh, at the generation who made their leader a 'Chester' (owing almost all to the power of his lungs, the name might imply). He has corrupted Tom, who on one hand convinces himself that he is not imitating Chester, and on the other is proud of the fact that, if he does, it has made him better known to people in the West End than Chester himself.

However, the night club is raided, and Tom needs two hundred pounds as bail. Chester refuses to give it to Nina – whose own fortune has dwindled to nothing in Chester's cause. Finally Aunt Latter rallies the 'Slapton-Latter dynasty', who pay up on condition that Tom leaves the country. He goes to Germany, where his mimicking of English politicians is not considered funny, and two months later he shoots himself. Nina writes:

> To me, at the time, this was a tragedy which seemed to break my heart; that is, I didn't know how I could go on living; I blamed everyone for it, including, of course, myself. It seemed to me that Tom had been murdered by a conspiracy of stupid and cruel people, . . . and especially by Chester. I told myself that Chester had never understood or liked the boy; he had been jealous of Tom simply because he was more sensitive, more fine, more subtle, and because he was so good-looking and attractive; and he had always secretly wanted to crush him. At last, out of pure spite, he had taken his opportunity.
>
> Even when I was raving in this way, I think I knew that it was wicked nonsense. I was fighting against a secret wonder if anything or anyone could have saved Tom. For he could never get away from Chester's influence. Somehow Chester had got right inside the boy from his very childhood, so that everything he thought and did was affected (pp. 355-6).

In this sense Tom stands for his generation, just as John Wilcher and John Bonser had done, though in a less powerfully contrived situation.

With Tom's death, Nina has no need to remain with Chester. She returns to the scenes of her childhood; meets Jim and immediately, on the third time they come together – though Nina had thought herself too old – she conceives. Jim's son has been destroyed; his daughter is totally Chester's; now at last he and Nina marry, to form a true family trinity. Once again they are living with Aunt Latter at Palm Cottage, being too poor to own a house. The Aunt is now 'quite mad with drink and fury', and wrathful against Jim, who has called her a busybody. She wanders about the house muttering the word, and wakes Nina in the night to ask 'what would have happened to any of us if she had not been a busybody? It was extraordinary how this word enraged her – it literally drove her mad' (p. 362). So her role in the story is clear. Nina however feels happiness at last. Jim is possessive and domineering, and takes her sailing 'right into the Atlantic, often in the most dangerous seas, so that I had never been so frightened' (p. 364). This implies, symbolically, that he is testing her as a mother.

> But one day, when I was wondering how I endured such a 'life of slavery', it struck me that I was amused at these big words, and that I did not want the life to stop – that I was 'in love' with him. I put the phrase in inverted commas because it was a state so unlike being 'in love' as usually described, . . . For I saw that so far from being Jim's slave, I belonged to myself more intensely than ever in my life before. . . .
> It was from this secret place, the independent calm, as of a private fort, that I found it so easy to submit to his whims. . . . I must not say that I had found out how to laugh at Jim, but there was laughter in the walls of my fort and in my happiness. And as Jim's baby grew in me so did this love grow, so that I, to, wanted to be with him, and, if he was not with me, to know exactly where he was and what he was doing at any moment.
> This, in my private fort, made me laugh at myself (pp. 364-5).

This is the laughter of grace, in contrast to the horse-laugh roused by Tom's caricature of Chester. It is a laughter of acceptance, or grace, and so comparable with the laughter by which Nina suffered Chester (p. 277 above) – and tolerated being treated as 'a trojan captive'. With Jim she also endures a 'life of slavery'. But with him the bond of the child brings grace as happiness, whereas the acceptance of life with Chester had been grace as suffering.

Her child Robert is born. But then Chester appears, saying

that he needs her help in writing his memoirs. The book ends with Chester installed at Palm Cottage. He has come for a visit, but staged a heart attack, so persuading everyone that he cannot me moved; he is sleeping in the drawing-room on Jim's African camp bed, and so comes 'the final "Palm Cottage scandal" ' (p. 384).

Aunt Latter's upbringing of Nina and Jim apparently explains the situation of which Palm Cottage is symbolic: 'with its little wood, its half-tropical garden, its mass of flowers, [it] belonged neither to the fashionable sporting beach just below nor to the bare romantic moor just above; it was like something from a thousand miles away, from the south of France or Italy in Spring' (p. 17). Jim from the sporting beach and Chester from the moor seem to have met here in a situation created by the troubadours and the tradition of courtly love, of Dante, Petrarch, and all poetry in the romantic tradition, including the Arthurian legends by which Cary himself has been so influenced from childhood (p. 21 above) and involving the 'fatal woman' theme, not least in the writings of the Decadent period on which Cary's novels concentrate. The lonely Nina has lived her life in books from childhood, and been ruled by her Aunt's sinister instructions, and by her cousin Jim, who still lives by the cavalier code. What else could you expect of them? Cary might be saying. But Chester too has educated himself by reading, and he thinks of Nina as a 'princess'. This is what he wants of her. But all three romantic young people face the realities of the flesh, and a vital fact about the Palm Cottage situation is that Chester is really turning the tables on Jim. For, when invited by Chester to stay at the Orchard, Jim had won Nina from him by his Indian trick of making love; Nina had taught it to Chester, and now Chester's passion for sex is still so great that he has been accused of assaulting a girl in Kensington Gardens (as Wilcher had been, having been infected by Decadent works of art).

Even the African camp bed seems symbolic of the political situation, as one that had sent Cary himself to Africa, for romantic or religious reasons which he is here exploring in this powerful and profound way. The Palm Cottage situation is that of England and the world in 1926. It was the seed bed that made Hitler possible, and World War II had solved nothing, Cary implies in September 1952, the date of publication. Jim at the

end, aware of Chester's sexual assaults on Nina – the soul of
the world – demands of her ' "What have you been up to?" ',
and she does not know how to answer. He wants the whole
truth. But, in this story of individual complex motives, against
the world politics of our age, it is doubtful whether any reader
could do better.

'*Except the Lord* by Lord Nimmo' sums up the message of
this book. For 'Lord' is now Chester's title. As his memoirs,
which he has supposedly been writing at Palm Cottage, it has
not actually required Nina's help at all, for it concerns his life
before she knew him. Indeed, knowing what we do of Chester,
we should read it with as much attention and scepticism as we
would give to any piece of political propaganda, by an artist as
skilled with words as Chester reputedly is. Above all, we should
remember that Nina has told us what Chester's 'really sacred
causes' are: the Radical Freedom League and the Peace and
Freedom Council.[18] Unaware that we know this, Chester says of the
League of Peace and Freedom: 'This association, if you remember, taught that murder, lies, any trickery whatever, was justified
in order to bring about the collapse of civilization' (p. 135). That
this aim is in his mind is evident from his opening paragraph,
where he says that his story 'throws light upon the crisis that
so fearfully shakes our whole civilization.' The crisis is, surely,
that people with Chester's aims have gained such power, since
they want our civilization to collapse. That this is Cary's meaning seems proved by *Art and Reality*, where he writes of the
'power of the word, of rhetoric, of the demagogue', which makes
'a great many people despair of civilisation as it is. They expect
the world to tumble once more into a thousand years of barbarism' (pp. 24, 25). That Cary himself felt this fear and despair
seems certain.[19]

His decision to write this book came upon him suddenly, he
says in a letter of 5 November 1952, to Harper's: 'I suddenly saw
it gives me the chance to deal with *religion* in a fundamental
manner and make a new kind of trilogy too.' At this very time
he was preparing his lecture on Dostoevsky, which he delivered
on 13 November. In the lecture he describes Dostoevsky's mind
as divided between the 'Satanic self-willed, Byronic', against all
authority, including God's, and the Christ-like, submissive
character whose suffering and non-resistance to evil bring know-

ledge of God'.[20] The split mind of Tolstoy had chiefly inspired *Prisoner of Grace*, but this account of Dostoevsky particularly fits Cary's treatment of Chester and his father, in *Except the Lord*.

What Dostoevsky's viewpoint amounts to in practice (and indeed Tolstoy's, though he put it less dramatically) is that a man like himself can fill the role of Satan, provided that someone else – a woman, or peasant – will accept suffering and non-resistance to evil (notably non-resistance to himself) in order to prove to his own satisfaction that God as goodness does exist. This description goes far to explain all Cary's male characters (except Syson) in his later novels. Milton's doctrine, which influenced both trilogies, can be understood in these terms, and so indeed can Blake's.[21]

Before deciding to write *Except the Lord*, Cary had been working on *Not Honour More*. The new kind of trilogy that he suddenly conceived seems to have been one where this second book forms a kind of 'Pro and Contra' between the other two, highlighting them in a way reminiscent of 'Pro and Contra' in the middle of *The Brothers Karamazov*.

With 'Pro and Contra' Cary inevitably associated Murry and Lawrence, whose plans to bring revolution to England in the twenties must inevitably have brought them to the forefront of his mind when focussing this trilogy on the General Strike. Murry and Lawrence, therefore, seem likely to have contributed to the Nimmos' characters,[22] and the publication of Murry's *Community Farm* seems a direct inspiration for Father Nimmo's farm. Other hints that Chester owes something to Murry have already been given.[23] He resembles Lawrence, too, in being the son of a miner, who married, says Chester, 'above himself'. His mother is a schoolmaster's daughter, and apparently met the father as a soldier (*à rebours* of the pacifist Murry). For 'He came late to farming' and 'her savings had stocked the croft' (p. 5). Chester's own determination to 'get a lady', who also had money, is directly explained by his father's example, though Cary seems to have observed it as a general male principle.

The father was then an independent yeoman under the Duchy, but chapter one establishes the fact that he failed as a farmer because he was dreaming and preaching of the Second Coming of Christ. Chester recalls his mother holding up their empty moneybox, and laughing at his father. As Chester thought his father 'the greatest man in the world', this puzzled him. 'It is impossible to hide anything in a six-room cottage', he continues (p. 7). Later, telling of his first visit to Palm Cottage, he says: 'The very name offended me. This cottage contained ten rooms ... It seemed to me a kind of mockery of my own life in a real cottage to use the name for this mansion' (p. 136). At which point, between six rooms and ten rooms, does a cottage become a mansion, we may wonder. They were evicted from this cottage because the mother became ill, he says. The neighbours would not help because 'They looked upon the Nimmos as proud, our ruin as the just punishment of upstarts. For in such primitive communities, the smallest difference of habit, of education, is enough to bring suspicion and hatred' (p. 9). Chester sensed 'a watchful enemy' behind every window, and their 'gentry' names brought scorn – Georgina from her mother's mother, and Chester from his father's old colonel, his godfather; such names were not gifts. Chester's extreme class hatred, obviously, owes most to the spite of the villagers against their fallen and assumed 'gentry' state. His status in society in fact resembles Gulley's (p. 225 above). Like Gulley, too, he remembers a beautiful higher class mother who told him stories, making him the hero of them. But the real reason for their eviction was clearly that the father never worked on the farm. He spent all his time teaching his adventist faith to the fifteen to twenty believers who worshipped in their kitchen on Sunday, and would 'wait upon him with every kind of problem' there during the week. The mother has had five children in five years. Richard is ten, Ethel has died, Georgina is seven, Chester six, and Ruth five; being 'overworked' and with 'small resources', she fell ill and slowly 'wasted away' until, two years after the eviction, she died, says Chester. Yet she left a baby of eighteen months; so she had been pregnant yet again before the eviction. The baby is Dorothy, whose name, 'gift of God', and also her fate, are commented upon grimly by the father's favourite psalm, which gives the book its title:

Except the Lord build the house, their labour is but lost that build it;
Except the Lord keep the city, the watchman waketh but in vain.
Lo, children and the fruit of the womb are an heritage and gift that cometh of the Lord (p. 284).

In Cary's early books, he showed that in African religions the child is recognized as a gift from the mother. Nimmo's fundamental belief is that it 'cometh of the Lord'. That Nimmo, or 'The Lord', showed such tragic lack of forethought regarding the fruit of the womb is certainly the cause of the mother's death – added to the fact that her labour was certainly lost because her husband failed to 'build the house' or 'keep the city' in any practical terms. For Dorothy too dies.

Having failed her in life, however, Nimmo feels it necessary to honour his wife with an expensive funeral and tombstone. This would accord with primitive fears of the dead as described by Frazer and Freud. However, it is not Nimmo, but Georgina and Ruth, who work 'ten or more hours a day from childhood', and it takes them five years to pay off the debt. Because they are working, Dorothy is neglected, and dies within five months. But 'Richard and I were at school, and when we were not at school we were pursuing eagerly our own lives of exploration and dream' (p. 42). The unjust treatment of the girls is something Chester obviously takes for granted. In fact, what is remarkable, in these memoirs of a liberal politician, is that he says not one word about the suffragette movement, but a great deal about the cruelly unjust treatment of Georgina without a sign of sympathy. Since this book began as the story of Georgina, and the suffragettes,[24] here clearly is the main point.

Chester accepts his father's judgment, that Georgina has 'a devil', and the mother's warning: 'that as she had had a hard birth so she would have a hard mind, "obstinate in evil" ' (p. 258). A cruel revenge, indeed, for a hard birth. Yet it is Georgina who wishes her ailing mother could ' "go to France and be properly warm and drink plenty of wine" ' (p. 39). The father's answer is, 'shortly', 'that wishes never put shoes on a horse or meat in the pot' – though he himself seems to behave as though he expects they will. Now, as on most occasions when he speaks to his hard-working daughter, he has his head in a book. But, he raises it to say sternly: ' "It is not for us to question the work of Providence, the Lord gives and He takes away. You did not earn yourself, Georgy, and you would have no right to cry if you were crooked" ' (p. 39).

Lord Chester Nimmo now explains: 'more than half a century has passed before I have reached again the deeper wisdom of my father in his simplicity. "The Lord provides and the Lord taketh away", and that profound saying, so characteristic of him in its homely penetration, "You did not earn yourself, Georgy, you would have no right to cry if you were crooked" ' (p. 40). Chester has certainly cried out loudly enough for himself – and proved crooked as well, as he is doing in this very instance. That is, he introduces this episode by saying: 'one of the daughters of a local magnate, Lord Slapton, had been sent in the year before, after the birth of her first baby, to Italy' (p. 39). He makes it sound as though it is wicked of Lord Slapton to send his daughter, and in the same context says we must not question Providence, for 'the Lord gives and He takes away'. What he really means is that Georgina must not question her father, because he is her Lord. Chester might of course have added that he himself married a niece of Lord Slapton, and took her to Italy before the birth of her baby – for reasons he would not dream of explaining.

That Cary has Dostoevsky in mind here is clear from his lecture, where he has actually added the words 'crooked or stupid' to his draft; he is making the point that it does seem unfair that some children are born thus, while others have the favours of a Lord Slapton's daughter. The remedy is to see that, by reason, which is God's 'own essential action',[25] men do something about such injustice. It is men's Dostoevskian temptation merely to blame God, when it suits, that must be overcome.

It is vital to get as clear a picture as possible of Chester's father. First he says that he was a soldier and miner who came late to farming. Then he calls him a 'ploughboy' son of illiterate parents. That suggests that he was born to farming; so he had no excuse for failing, when he acquired his own farm. But essentially he is a type common in the imperial army: 'the religious soldier' (p. 15). He has served in India, so recalling Tom Wilcher's grandfather (*Herself Surprised*, p. 190). More particularly he resembles Sergeant Pooley in *Castle Corner*, and actually developed from the same character, created in the thirties. Like Pooley, he is predicting the end of the world, and it is because he claims to be a prophet (as Lawrence did) that he gains power over people – particularly his children. Chester says he was remarkable in that he did not beat them, and that this was one reason for the villagers' dislike of them. They thought he was going against the scriptures. But he did not need to beat them. It gave him a far greater sense of power to force them, by mere words, to their knees, in the fear that the world would soon end, and that he could save them by casting out their devil. So he has Georgina sobbing in the mud and clutching his ankles, while he consoles her by saying the devil has left her. In India he has been a light horseman. So he walks about the village dressed always 'in breeches and leggings of the smartest cut, relic of his yeomanry and last vanity of an old huzzar' (p. 16). He has worn his moustache 'short and waxed at the ends in the style of a smart Troop Sergeant', though he has now allowed it to grow bushy. It is scarcely surprising that the villagers dislike him, and so his family, because of his very appearance, as well as his teaching. They distrust him also for supporting an early form of miners' union, for which he is treasurer and does the accounts. What is unforgivable in him is his treatment of Georgina. From the age of eight she is doing the housework, and working for 'G.', in the shop in the morning and doing his accounts at night – while the father reads a book at home. After the mother's death Ruth does some of Georgina's housework, because Georgina must work on their landlord's farm, and for G.

Chester would no doubt write differently of G., if he knew what Nina had told us about his bad behaviour with young girls, and his imprisonment (p. 273 above). Nevertheless, he conceals the vital fact that his father allowed Georgina to work alone at night for such a man. She worked for such things as 'sugar and tea, my father's tobacco – which we accepted as basic necessities, and of which even my father did not count the expense' (p. 59). One night Georgina, aged eleven, is screaming at Richard that 'it was lies about G.' (p. 49); she has said that Richard does not think how she manages to provide for them, and Richard has said, ' "I think how people say we manage." ' The father asks why she should fear G. 'Georgina hesitated a moment looking up at her father, and then answered that she had said nothing about G. She spoke as a child speaks when suddenly resolved to tell a lie, with a gulp and a rush' (p. 50). The father is shocked that she should lie, and they all pray that Georgina 'should be saved from the lie in her soul' (p. 51).

Now we understand Chester's thoughts, when he prays with Nina for 'the lie in the soul' (p. 271 above). These words apply to the father and to Chester, far more than to Georgina. But he makes it sound as though Georgina fell from grace by this lie, which is in fact the realization of her father's evil; 'from

this time he became to her a person who, like ourselves, sometimes needed to be handled, managed' (p. 52). This is what Nina
has been learning all through her book. It is what Robin Sant
in *The Moonlight* called 'women's religion, the oldest in the
world' (p. 250 above). Georgina is *à rebours* of Nina. Her name
subtly echoes Nina, and derives from Hannah, preceded by
George, meaning 'husbandman'; this symbolizes her role as
supporter of the family – even more cruel and unappreciated
than Rose's in *The Moonlight*.

Georgina now decides to leave 'G.', and work instead for his
wife Bella, who runs the Green Man pub. The father has condemned the pub for years, and implies that service in the pub,
will be 'the service of the devil' (p. 58) whereas service in the
shop is service of G. G. seems like Nimmo's God. In fact, Cary's
notes show G. has a hold over Nimmo, who has been unfaithful
to his wife with Bella, whom G. now rarely sees. Even if Chester
knows nothing of this, which is unlikely, its mere possibility
shows how dangerous it is for anyone to judge the world by
'great confessions', where the confessors will conceal key points,
by ignorance, guile, or personal confusion.

In fact, to give this story its 'whole view', it is necessary to
know that Cary's chief inspiration is Kierkegaard, and the dreadful sin of the father that was supposed to have cursed the whole
family, so that Kierkegaard himself was amazed that he lived
beyond the age of thirty-three, the year in which Christ
supposedly died.[26] That fact relates to Chester's age, thirty-four,
when he marries Nina. In other words, Cary is still exploring
the Existentialist philosophy, of which Nazism is a perversion
(p. 213 above).

A key point in Chester's story concerns Bella's death:

G., driving a fast young horse home from Tarbiton with
Mrs. G. on a dark night, and being somewhat in liquor, went
into the ditch at the Battwell crossroad and wrecked the gig.
Both occupants were thrown out with force, G. was un-
scratched, Mrs. G. was picked up quite dead – her skull was
deeply fractured on a stone, the only stone, so we were told,
for yards about.

That the respected Mrs. G. should die because the dis-
respected G. was drunk, this was a fine subject for the village
philosopher.

But there was another and a deeper point at issue. My father had been denouncing the Green Man for years, was this tragedy God's judgment on Mrs. G.?

You smile with contempt for our primitive religiosity, and it is true that when some months later I happened to notice the site of the crash, it was full of stones, a very dangerous spot (pp. 112-13).

Nimmo apparently makes people believe that he has spoken for God in denouncing Bella, and his increased reputation as a prophet prompts him to predict the Second Coming, for April 15th, 1868.[27] In consequence of his error, his children lose their faith in him, and so in God. By inspecting 'the site of the crash' Chester shows a new critical spirit; by the words 'crossroads' and 'ditch'[28] he suggests that, at this point of the story, he has not only parted from his father with his misguided faith, but also met his downfall.

The false report of one stone, and the discovery of many, gives an undercurrent of meaning that the Christian Church is not a church founded by Peter, the one stone, but by many, who in their simple faith resemble Nimmo; the image also discredits prophecy. In the overturning of Bella in a gig drawn by a fast young horse, we have an image of the spirit of rebellion behind the founding and also the Reformation of the Christian Church, bringing confusion and falsehood as well as some new truth. G. as driver, with Bella as passenger, is also a brilliantly telling variation of Plato's symbol of the soul, as already used in *Castle Corner*. Another symbolic point in this interpretation relates to Nina's account of Chester in Rome on their honeymoon.[29] The fact that Bella looks like 'a Roman empress', 'a woman born to rule' and is absolute ruler of the Green Man, suggests the character of Elizabeth I, while the Green Man, already used in four of Cary's novels, is clearly intended to represent Blake's 'vegetative man'.[30] Since the name Bella does not occur in the source material of 'Hannah' and 'Captive and Free' it has apparently been introduced for a purpose; if interpreted as above, it would link with Chester's significant use, on three occasions, of the name Jezebel, which is the name applied to Queen Elizabeth in Spain and Italy.[31] This interpretation accords with the similar suggestion regarding Elizabeth in *Prisoner of Grace*. It is another example of the way Cary linked his novels.

That we are intended to apply 'crossroads' to Chester in this scene is borne out by the plot. The episode 'central' to his history has occurred shortly before when, watching the play, 'Murder in the Red Barn', he has recognized in the chief actor 'the villian, the devil – and the hero'.[32] In consequence, the 'vision of glory, of power, by means of the spoken word' has led him to address the sheep and rocks on the hillside (p. 111). This scene is followed immediately by the 'crossroad' scene, followed in turn by the failure of the father's prophecy. Next, with his faith 'bleeding to death' (p. 125), Chester begins to drink and 'meditate worse things' (p. 130), and though in the city he runs away from two girls ('known loose characters') he 'resolves not to fall short again in boldness' (pp. 132-3). He runs from the girls into a dark hall, where he is converted to the doctrine of the League of Peace and Freedom, which practises 'murder, lies, any trickery whatever . . .' (p. 135); his feelings for the speaker are that he 'might be able to touch his coat' (p. 142).

Here the coat of authority is clearly the devil's and these three episodes, at the 'crossroads' of Chester's life, show him tempted by the world, the flesh and the devil or, in Dostoevsky's terms, miracle, mystery and authority. 'World Flesh [an]d Devil' in fact appear inside the front cover of the chief file for this novel.[33] The main point about Chester, then, is that, unlike Christ, he has succumbed to Satan's temptations. In this he recalls what Lawrence said of The Grand Inquisitor: that his message is, 'Christ you are inadequate', so that those in authority must serve the devil. And because Lawrence said that the Inquisitor was Ivan, or Dostoevsky in his thinking self, and Murry identified himself with Ivan, it becomes evident why Murry and Lawrence would have been Cary's direct inspiration for this book. For Murry set himself to be the Judas who betrayed Lawrence's real message as a prophet.[34]

Cary's earnest desire for Murry to know his view on the dangers of Lawrence's influence, seems proved by his use of Maria Marten in this novel, as in Gulley's. He could have expected the recurring initials to arrest Murry's attention, though the message he wanted Murry to get would have been his real point. It is the key scene of the novel. Chester says that the true story concerned the murder of a loose-living village girl by a village blackguard. The only reason that it became the most celebrated murder of the century was that the mother claimed to have seen, in a dream, the murderer and the burial place of the body; Corder was wrongly convicted on that evidence. So the danger of human gullibility regarding dreams and prophecies is proved, as with his father, Chester might have added.[35] Moreover, as this play became performed throughout Europe, it took the form that Chester saw at the fair ground. Maria was no longer the village Jezebel, but the virtuous village virgin, forced to yield to rape by Corder, the rich gentleman landlord, who would otherwise evict the poor cottagers, her parents.

> Throughout the play everything possible was done to show the virtue, innocence and helplessness of the poor, and the abandoned cruelty, the heartless self-indulgence of the rich.
> And this was one among hundreds of such plays. I have wondered often how such propaganda failed to bring to England also, as to France, Italy, Germany, almost every other nation, a bloody revolution. For its power was incredible. As I say, it was decisive in my own life (p. 92).

He goes on to explain how, in spite of the horror with which he watched, he felt fascinated admiration for Corder. Then he draws an immediate parallel with the way his father had read Milton to them – warning them that he had made Satan too grand, and so tempting them to emulate Satan.

Cary has thus reminded us that drama in England began in such a way, to teach the Bible to illiterate people. The fair ground audience would readily identify the virgin Maria with the Virgin Mary, and so build on the idea of the poor inheriting the earth, which links directly with the noble savage of Rousseau,[36] in the very way Chester says here. What Chester realized was that he had only to appear as the noble savage and worldly success was assured him; as Lawrence said, 'a natural Lord is the great mystery' (p. 146 above). And to win support from the poor and make the rich feel guilty he had only to campaign in the way we know he did, from Nina, but also, already, from him (pp. 272, 285 above).

Cary drives his point home in the one scene (chapter 32), where Chester mentions Aunt Latter. While writing this chapter, he is actually living in her house, ostensibly (but falsely) to write these memoirs. He has forced himself upon her, and is occupying her drawing-room. Yet he writes here as though he met her this once, and says he had 'a strong dislike to her'. He labours the point that she kept him waiting for twenty minutes, though 'punctual to my time', which he spent watching her last guests, 'the relics of a party gathered to watch the yacht races'. His every word suggests he is mysteriously their victim. Then he brings in the innocent child: Nina, aged five, whose chance entry 'powerfully affected' his destiny. He tells this story, he says, to demonstrate 'that he who founds argument and policy upon our intuition of human goodness will not be disappointed' (p. 140). This is Chester's sure simple recipe for success, and if any reader has been at all moved by his account, he is proved right. Even if there is any truth in this story, Chester's purpose in telling it is purely to make you sympathize with him. He is using Nina's goodness, and the reader's, for his own ends, and this is the trick to be watched in any propagandist, religious or otherwise, Cary implies.

Reference to Chester in Aunt Latter's drawing room recalls the cat in *Castle Corner* who, with the same aim, symbolized Bridget. Chester in fact resembles Bridget in many ways, above all, in his power of imagination, which he has trained his voice to express. He, too, is motivated by having an older brother who is the family favourite. The following recalls the account of Manus (p. 177 above):

Richard was the hope of us all. We thought him a genius, and we were not deceived – many have acknowledged his brilliant quality. . . .

Richard had the best of all we could give him – he was the only one who had a whole suit, unpatched boots. I do not like to think of the sacrifices of my parents to buy him books, but even I understood completely that this was right and necessary. My parents have held it a sin against God's bounty not to cherish this special gift – Richard's light must not be quenched under a bushel (pp. 18–19).

As younger son of a favoured brother, Chester resembles Jim, and his arrogant behaviour may owe something to the jealousy that he is at pains to hide. Richard in fact gets to Oxford, but he ends up working in London in a textile firm, from which he is sacked; he is at home when Chester returns 'like a Napoleon' – or a strike leader. Chester writes: 'I will not say that it was part

W.H.T.—U

of my glory in those days that my admired elder brother should hold the horse for me while I got down' (p. 255). 'The horse's mouth' here says plainly that a sense of injustice begins in the family, simply because God, or nature, is unjust. Therefore, giving poor boys the chance to get to Oxford is no simple solution, because it can drive a Chester, less obviously gifted with brains, to glory in his kind of triumph.

Like Bridget, and then Manus, Chester turns from religion on discovering that his Father, and God, are not Omnipotent, and instead seeks omnipotence in political power. He is converted to membership of the Peace and Freedom League by 'a voice of wonderful tone and flexibility' (p. 135). The speaker is Lanza, who has recently broken with the League and 'taken a position which might be called Tolstoyan, though it anicipated Tolstoy's conversion by several years. He was a nihilist like Tolstoy later'. Thus Cary implies that Tolstoy's conversion, which won him so many followers, was led by these radicals, who led him back to a nihilist position. So we glimpse the way that feelings become attached to names, as symbols, and continue to infect the world, quite apart from the owner of the name, whose feelings have changed. Chester knows the name 'Proudhon' from his father's preaching on perfectibility, but Lanza calls him 'the father of the cause' (p. 145). Towards the end of his book Chester writes of the 'spell of words', as the secret he has learnt as an anarchist spellbinder: 'The world itself is young, we are but little removed from the time when writing was a wonder, when any written speech was magic. Words printed in books – Rousseau, Proudhon, Owen, Marx, what power they can wield. But it is the power of sorcerers – the spell they cast is abracadabra. And the fruit of their sorcery is egotism and madness, war and death' (p. 274). Thus he reveals that in trying to touch Lanza's coat he was turning to serve Satan, rather than Jesus, who was similarly followed by crowds trying to touch his garment. The effect on the reader of calling Chester's own coat a Judas coat is sufficient justification for using name symbolism. But the method, suggested in these pages, is wholly relevant to Cary's theme, by hinting that the power of any individual can almost be measured by the effect and significance of his name.

How Chester is converted is shown by his unfeeling attitude towards the victims of the outrages he plans, in the name of freedom for strikers. He feels himself 'set apart from all those poor fools' (p. 242) – one of Lawrence's élite, in fact. After walking through the wrecked dock quarter he had written a report which found its way into a local paper, and would have ruined him, except that Edward, now Lord Goold, had sworn on oath that Chester was with him, elsewhere, at the time. Thus *Except the Lord* applies cuttingly to this aspect of Chester's career, which was interrupted in any case at this point through his quarrels over personal power.

Georgina saves him from humiliation, by driving him home. There he reflects upon the values of family love, as his father, wrapped in an 'old horse-blanket' (p. 283) quotes the psalm 'Except the Lord'. Its 'musical sounds' tell Chester that, 'not only in his family life but in his political activity' he should 'aim at the life of the soul' (p. 284). Despite these 'musical sounds', however, Chester has built his family life, and so his own soul, on a lie. Already there seems little hope. For, when he goes outside, after hearing the psalm, and Georgina follows him, carrying his Judas coat, he merely feels 'sharp annoyance'. 'But pity held me, Georgina had the privilege of the dying. I waited for her and silently allowed her to help me into the coat.' Her tragic looks are contradicted by her smile, and her remark: ' "Why are you so unhappy. Don't you see how proud we are of you?" ' Chester recognizes 'grief that I knew for love, love that I knew for life, joy that I knew for the joy of the Lord'; that is, out of such grief and love as Georgina's, he could arrive at the joy of being Lord Nimmo. He has illustrated Cary's words, at the close of *Art and Reality*.[37]

The chief character in this book is really Georgina, and the way the mother's death-wish works, through the father, and also Chester, makes almost unbearable reading. But the play Maria Marten, which turned Chester into 'the villain, the devil – and the hero', had affected Georgina as powerfully. In the last scene, Chester describes her thus: 'Georgina then seemed indeed a revenant – her face as she searched, frowning, had the impatient feverish expression of one released only a little while from the grave to do her work on earth' (p. 285). She might indeed have become the ghost of Maria, as Chester remembers her effect upon him at that performance long ago. Of the ghost he writes: 'She represented for him then not only a supernatural being but the Rhadamanthine judgment of Heaven – the inescapable vengeance of the Most High. But did not terror itself bring with it a sense of fearful glory in the man who had defied that vengeance?' (p. 95). It seems then that he has known what he is doing, and has chosen the 'fearful glory' of being 'Satanic, self willed Byronic' rather than the 'fearful joy' that might have been his, if he had been capable of unselfishness and sought some justice for Georgina too.

The book begins: 'Yesterday, an old man nearing my end, I stood by the grave of a noble woman, one of the three noblest I have ever known, my mother, my sister, my wife.' Chester's crime is that he has been willing to let these women suffer, and others like them, in his drive to destroy our civilization. Standing by Georgina's grave, he is apparently moved – by the primitive fear of the dead, typical of all mankind – to write this confession. The last chapter, written almost a year later, ends: 'And my way was made plain. "Here," I said, "the story began and here it shall begin again, in the things I lived with this forgotten one, in the young cruelty of the world, in the making of our souls."' What these high-sounding words mean is revealed in Jim's book: that Chester has suddenly realized how he can make political capital out of Georgina. It is as though he is incapable of a wholly unselfish feeling. He must always turn everything to his own selfish advantage. And that, Cary would say, is the devil.

Not Honour More is written in the style of a true soldier, revealing Jim as Chester's opposite. 'This is my statement, so help me God, as I hope to be hung', he begins. He is careless of the niceties of English. But he is presented as 'honest man among the crooks and time servers'.[38] He is a man facing death fearlessly, but under the strongest emotions. For he has shot Nina, the only woman he has ever loved. People think him a madman; so, before it is too late, he wants to give them the truth, 'the absolute truth', as he sees it. He explains: 'I wish therefore to put on record any errors or omissions are not by my will but due solely to pressure of time. Nor any fault of policewoman Martin taking dictation practically all night' (p. 28). Policewoman Martin could be the avenging angel of Maria Marten and Georgina. Jim takes the trouble to continue: 'She has given every consideration to me and I desire herewith to express my very high appreciation and gratitude for her great patience and courtesy.'

He really has learned to recognize and appreciate the worth of ordinary people, and a great deal of his book is devoted to them.

He reveals himself a true Elizabethan gentleman in the readiness with which tears come into his eyes; and he might be judged sentimental in his sympathies. This is explained largely by his own customary loneliness and need for love, which makes him appreciate any love he is shown, and recognize the need for love in others. He is born of a ruling class, and trained to be 'a guardian of freedom', not only at school but also in his long experience of government as the art of taking responsibility, and of delegating it, according to experience both in judging characters, and in winning respect, by his own worth and integrity.[39] Nina has told us that 'he is fastidious and likes a hard mattress and cold baths' (*Prisoner of Grace*, p. 74). He is in fact the type of soldier-ruler whom Plato had in mind when writing the *Republic,* at a time when the urgent question was, similarly, how a great Empire might be saved. For the British government has been corrupted just as the Athenian was corrupted, by leaders who have seized upon the self-indulgent aspects of Socrates' teaching, and so produced demagogues not unlike Alcibiades. Jim is a fascist in a Platonic sense, also fighting the aspects of Plato that inspired the communists. His demand for absolute truth is platonic, and the impossibility of giving it illustrates the failure of platonism. Even the situation that has obtained at Palm Cottage, for two years now, of a wife in common, finds support in Plato. But Socrates – like Aunt Latter – had 'a very low view of marriage', and the platonic attempt to deny the irrational and ignore marriage as the basis of society is demonstrated in its full falsity in this book.

The events in it cover the period surrounding the General Strike, from 1 May 1926. Aunt Latter has died a year before, but Chester is still encamped on Jim's African bed, in the rear part of their living room (two rooms divided by sliding doors, each with a door opening on to a passage). Jim has learnt to live with this situation by refusing to know of it. But Jim's child Robert, now aged four, has had a Nurse, Amelia Jones, who has been dismissed at a moment's notice, in November 1925, after catching Chester in 'an incriminating situation' with Nina. She is bent on revenge, and goes to Colonel Brightman, in whom Cary is undoubtedly portraying Frank Buchman (allowing Jim to convey his feelings). Brightman believes he is building *New Worlds for Old* (the name of his newspaper, p. 154). He is doing so by probing into people's private lives, and holding house parties. His headquarters are an 'olde Englishe farmhouse' built two years before. Here 'ye old tyme lounge' has a full-length portrait of Brightman as an 'olde Englishe goodchappe' (p. 73); his followers 'went in for open shirts', says Jim, to whom Brightman explains: ' "This is the age of the group" ' (p. 185). After the strike starts, Brightman breaks regulations by going out from the docks to a ship, the Danzig, where volunteers have been quartered. 'These were nearly all students from different colleges', says Jim, who is responsible for their security. They include a 'young fellow in front, in a green jersey which was, I was told, an Oxford fashion' (p. 142). Cary, who had volunteered from Oxford at this time, was greatly concerned about Buchman's influence on its 'green' youth. Through Brightman, Jim's daughter Sally damages his reputation, unwittingly, for they are on very good terms. She is beginning to recognize Chester's failings, as well as those of her husband, now Sir Henry Bootham, whose child she is soon to bear.

The name Henry recalls Henry in *An American Visitor*, as a representative of the new imperialism (p. 164 above). Henry Bootham (Boo them?) is nephew to Goold, whose hold over Chester had brought him into Nina's house, chiefly to spy upon her (p. 276 above). Now, assuming that Jim will be ready to work in with Chester's enemies, Bootham approaches him, revealing his own plot for revolution. He proposes using Chester's name and reputation, and believes he can handle Chester by playing on his conceit, as he now knows well how to do. He hints that Jim can ruin Chester, in the way Parnell was ruined. ' "I don't think I can play in that yard" ', says Jim, calling Bootham 'Fat Boy'. He adds: 'I record this proposal, though hard to believe, without comment on present state of common honesty, not to say loyalty in politics' (p. 110).

Chester is trying to wangle himself into a coalition government, ostensibly to deal with the crisis. He gets himself elected chairman of an Emergency Committee, then forces Jim to take charge of the Special Constables who are directly responsible to it. But he never gives precise instructions, so that if anything goes wrong, Jim will seem to have acted without authority. Yet Jim cannot refuse the post. If he does he will feel disloyal to his country, and people will say that he is guided by spite against his wife's lover. His special duties make it impossible for him to explain the position. Jim says: 'Nimmo had pushed me in the job to close my mouth and it worked like a charm. It split me off even from my old friend Potter' (p. 131); 'the horse's mouth' of the old ruling class is forced shut. Chester's crowning treachery has been to corrupt Nina totally, while staying in Jim's house; besides giving her expensive jewels he has persuaded Aunt Latter to appoint him trustee, for investments left to Nina, and he can juggle these in ways that seem to incriminate Jim. Nina is now so completely in Chester's power that he can use her as his go-between with the communist leader Pincomb. He hopes Jim's feelings for Nina will confuse him.

However, a key point of the book is its title. Although it conveys Cary's usual ambiguity ('There is not honour any more', for example) Jim would (as in Lovelace's poem) put honour in politics above his love for Nina. Moreover, he demonstrates his skill in real government as 'the management of human beings' notably in the scene of Chester's third 'so-called Shagbrook addresses on God in Politics' (p. 6). As anticipated at the close of *Except the Lord,* he has chosen Georgina's grave to make his 'come-back talks' and it is 'just his touch', Jim thinks (p. 6). (The village now has a Nimmo Memorial Cottage.) Chester wants to make his third address quickly on Thursday, 6 May, 'saying anniversary of sister's death. Though Shagbrook people say she died on a Wednesday night in November', says Jim (p. 103). 'The row about the buses was the first charge against me in the Pincomb case.' A 'freeze' of transport had been agreed by strikers on the Tuesday, but Chester has an agreement with Pincomb regarding buses to his meeting. Jim is on duty to keep order, and finds a huge crowd. Chester has made sure people get his message by printing his address, which is plainly an incitement to revolution. Jim sees no difference between it and the Communist manifesto, and asks Bootham: ' "What I want to know is how far Nimmo is actually hooked up with the Bolshies? How did he get this bus permit out of Pincomb? Why shouldn't I tell Whitehall he's double-crossing his own Emergency Committee?" ' (p. 107). Here Bootham makes his proposal for a counter revolution, but Jim writes an official, confidential letter to 'Lord Nimmo' begging to have the 'intolerable position' clarified. Replying informally, Chester congratulates Jim on his 'courage, coolness, patience and discretion' in handling the dangerous situation caused over the buses to his meeting, and adds, 'I hope to get suitable recognition for them' (p. 121). Jim takes this to mean: '(1) Let the Strike Committee and the Bolshies do what they like. . . . (2) If you are a good boy and play our game, we'll see you get a nice little gong, like the Obey Brass Eagerly' (p. 121). Here Cary may be remembering that Murry received an OBE in 1920, in recognition of his services as chief censor for the War Office.

Murry had written to Cary in June 1954, saying that he now realized Cary was the genius, not Murry himself.[40] Cary had responded by arranging a dinner party. But everyone present felt that too much now divided the two men, and Murry wrote in his journal: 'the sadness is: we now just don't understand each other. He reads my books, I read his. I admire his, he likes some at least of mine. But his don't *feed* me, and I'm pretty sure mine don't feed him. It's strange, and disquieting.'[41] He had evidently missed the disquieting, clear reference to Marguéritte in *Herself Surprised*. But they had discussed Marguéritte at length at the dinner party.[42] Therefore, if he had read *Not Honour More* (completed five months later) Murry would surely have sensed that Cary has dramatized in this book something of what they failed to communicate at that last meeting. He puts the words into Chester's mouth, as if allowing him to say what he thought Murry might by now be able to say – regarding themselves as they were when they knew Marguéritte, but more particularly as he understood Cary to be now. Having learnt from that experience and written of it in his books, Cary would surely have wanted Murry, the critic, to see how much his writing owed to it. For Nina, as a universal figure, must include Marguéritte when Nimmo says:

> You were a brute, you say, to that young girl, and I have loved her, let us say, too much. But aren't we forgetting something – something without which we are merely piling up one falsity on another – throwing words about and getting nowhere. The actual situation *at the time*. . . . We were young – that's to say, we wanted everything we could get so long as we didn't despise ourselves. And we weren't sure how bad we could safely be – how selfish – how greedy. . . . I am the last man to say or think evil of Nina, your Nina, my Nina, but she too knows what love is – in every aspect. Jim, if Nina was a feeble thin-blooded creature, should we have loved her – should we have been guilty?

'So you're putting it on her.'

'No, no, no,' he screamed, and then I thought he would fly at me. But he caught his breath and said calmly enough, 'I'm risking the truth with you, Jim – the whole truth. And you're going to have it even if you kill me (pp. 63–64).

. . .

Do you really know Nina, Jim . . . What is her message to us both, forgive and forget. From Nina who is our victim, who has suffered most. She says let us start again here, with hearts renewed in sympathy, in our old tried friendship. Let us start again in truth – the truth of mutual sympathy, the reality of affection, the fact of today and its lesson' (pp. 65–66).

On a later occasion, Jim comes home and finds Chester in his bed, fully clothed, and the situation is so bizarre that the reader senses an underlying meaning. Nimmo screams at Jim to shoot him: ' "Of course we didn't tell you anything. Because we knew you'd get it all wrong, because you are our biggest headache. Because you are a kept man. . . . Now shoot, you kept ass, you hanger-on" ' (p. 164). Jim observes: 'I saw the real Nimmo. . . . A living lie who'd ended by lying himself into looking-glass land.'

This passage comes closest to revealing Jim and Chester as opposite sides of the world's character, with Jim seeing only Chester in that 'looking-glass land'. In order to prove the truth about his lie to Jim, Nimmo insists that they go to the Town Hall. Nina is wearing a white night-dress and Jim's 'Sunday overcoat' (p. 169). Jim does not miss her from his side when he reaches the entrance. But he is told by an observer that 'it was as if she had come up against a door that wasn't there. Then she turned round, rushed down the steps and threw herself in front of the troop carriers' (p. 170). While the doctors work to save her life, the men are taken to a waiting room. They walk 'down the corridor, past the waiting-room door' (p. 172). This could mean that they are escaping from religious 'waiting room' dogma to truth. Nimmo thanks God he has Jim with him, and Jim says: 'Bits of truth came trickling out of the babble' such as:

'Good God, how could anything be too much for Nina who gave us life itself.'

. . . 'You know me, Jim, perhaps better than I do myself. Perhaps better than anyone except Nina, who knows us both too well – too well', . . . I found the tears on my face. Nimmo had said one true thing. My soul could rest on goodness – just one little bit of it – Nina hadn't been able to face that lie.

Jim writes to Nina at once, 'in the hospital waiting room', suggesting that they go away 'far from any town'. But they cannot escape publicity, and so plan to go to Africa, where Jim will find his beloved tribe of Lugas, who are for him nature's gentlemen. But Nina has some correspondence between her and Nimmo, which Jim believes might throw light on the trial of Maufe, one of his constables. He does not want Nina to be incriminated, and says it is for her to decide whether she destroys the letters, or gives them to Nimmo, who wants them for his own purposes. She says Jim may read them, and he discovers that Maufe has been ruined by their collusion. He decides to kill Nimmo who, however, locks himself in the lavatory, and dies there of a heart attack. So Jim turns to Nina. She guesses his intention, and begs him 'not to take her by surprise'. It is for her to know the *reason,* that is. She kneels, but cannot pray, which she does not think would help, and asks Jim's forgiveness, he says, 'because she had truly loved me'. He ends: 'I said it was for her to forgive me and I finished the thing in one stroke. She fell at once and did not struggle at all.'

The book is most obviously Cary's *Kreutzer Sonata.* Jim and Chester, as the two sides of Tolstoy, can also be seen as the old conservative and the new feminist. The message that Chester urges upon Jim is, apparently, that a woman is not a man's property. Nina dressed in white and wearing Jim's Sunday overcoat is the Nina who attempts suicide. Jim thinks merely that she has been unable to face the lie about her involvement with Chester, and therefore has 'goodness'. But a story like Marguéritte's invites the question: why is the woman bad, and the man not, in such a relationship? By introducing the symbol of the waiting room, Cary shows that he is here dealing with a basic religious question.

The moral codes of men like Plato and Tolstoy have been shaped first to suit their personal needs, and have then been widely accepted by the world. But through them women have been 'enslaved in a system that does not suit them'. What nature does require, however, is that a child feels the security of a father and a mother, so that he or she, in turn, can give a child the security it needs. The real tragedy of this book is the fate of the child Robert[43] – which Jim ignores.

Nina felt herself a slave with both Chester and Jim.[44] But with Jim she felt contentment, when at last they formed a unity with their child. Jim's treatment of her was early Victorian, and that attitude had dignity, Cary says, because it valued the woman's place as wife and mother. But it treated the woman as though she had no responsibility and left her at the mercy of people like Aunt Latter. It also failed people like Jim, who adored motherhood and domesticity as ideas, but was otherwise afraid of them. Chester represents the new feminist, who is the Tolstoy who turned to the peasants. He is also Lawrence, who fought against the narrow religious attitude to sex of his upbringing, but preached false notions of the family, largely because of his own inability to have children, and jealousy of his wife's children by her first husband. This could indeed explain why Nina does not have children to Chester, but to Jim. Certainly her relationship to Chester is very much what Lawrence wanted of a woman. Nina's character in this book reveals the confusion of women in the twenties, caught between two codes, as Cary had tried to show in 'Cock Jarvis'.

Jim is without doubt basically Cock Jarvis, as Cary showed by talking of Jarvis soon after completing this trilogy. He said Jarvis feared that civilization would be wrecked for a thousand years, if the British Empire fell, as the Roman Empire fell, before the tribes of nationalist barbarians. Cary generalized that fear in *Art and Reality* in a way that casts light on Chester Nimmo.[45] In 'The Split Mind of the West' he says this collapse into barbarism will come because the west suffers from a state of general neurosis:[46] trying to live by an ancient faith in the absolute power of a supernatural Providence while also believing in the supreme power of science with absolutely strict causal laws. These are the thoughts behind Jim's shooting of Nina. Jim resembles Jarvis, an honest and honourable man who wrongly believed that 'a perfectly just, reasonable, and peaceful world was possible'. It is not possible, Cary says, 'For the simple reason that the majority of human beings are not primarily interested in justice, peace, and reason, but in satisfying their passions and ambitions, good and bad'. This is exactly what this trilogy illustrates. Jim and Chester are ruled by their passions for Nina, and ambitions surrounding her.

Jim demands the absolute truth. But he excludes from his testimony the vital truth that he abandoned Nina and his child to Chester. Jim Latter in fact probably owes a great deal to Conrad's *Lord Jim,* where Jim similarly could never escape from a single act of cowardice. While he was creating Jim Latter, Cary actually discussed *Lord Jim* in a lecture. He said he found the character unconvincing, his main point being that 'very imaginative people are apt to be both wildly brave and unexpectedly timid. But Conrad does not show this ambivalence of the imagination. Not at any rate in the beginning.'[47] Cary shows Jim Latter wildly brave, particularly in relation to the sea which, as a mother symbol, points dramatically to the situation in which he proves unexpectedly timid.

In his confession, Jim Latter shows why this is. 'My mother being dead and my father abroad and not interested, she [Nina] was all I had in the world. And she being an orphan, she also loved me and gave me all my happiness' (p. 11). Lacking parental guidance, he had formed his own moral code, at the age of fourteen, on 'Colonel Lovelace's great poem I'd just discovered. The most beautiful and true of all poems' (p. 126). Jim can thus be thought of as a man of the seventeenth century, judging our world from that point of view. If people think him mad, they should presumably stop teaching such poetry to schoolboys, or at least explain why such a code no longer works. Nina agreed, at ten, to try to live by it 'in case I couldn't go on loving her', says Jim. His earlier account includes: 'in my Hussar regiment no one was allowed to marry under captain.[48] So I was afraid to lose my darling if she would not wait for me, and many were interested in her, being so pretty and having money' (p. 11). 'Juno captive' as a clue to Nina's character is thus made plain – Juno having been the Roman queen of heaven, protectress of marriage and childbirth who, as Juno Moneta, housed the Roman mint, and gave us our word money. Because other men were competing for Nina's money and looks, Jim was moved to make sure of her by giving way to his passion. The rules of his regiment were designed to ensure that the fighting quality of subalterns was not weakened by family ties. Aunt Latter upheld the code, but was left coping with the baby (just as Mother Coker had to do, p. 234 above); so she tried to make the best of the situation.

The moment of union, however, which should have been sacred to Jim and Nina as an expression of their love, had lived in their memories as a silly fiasco: 'we were angry with each other and I accused her of spite against me and spoiling something that should have crowned our great love, and she said I was cruel and tried to make it a punishment to her. We had a great quarrel and the day was spoilt. And this has always been a cause for anger between us' (p. 12).

Cary's moral is clearly that young people should be taught what love really is – not as mere sex and self-indulgence, but the power of creation in God himself, whereby life continues. Jim complains at the close, that the press are turning his 'execution' of Nina into 'just another sex crime'. In fact, it is, because society is based on sex and marriage. Cary has attacked *The Kreutzer Sonata,* as unfair to women, yet simultaneously admitted the falsity in British institutions, by which the Empire is indeed doomed. With Jim as the personification of all that was best in it, as Cary intended for Jarvis, and with Nina as its soul, Jim's execution of her is an admission of guilt, and a kind of suicide pact which is also the suicide of the Empire. The close of *An American Visitor* and of *Mister Johnson* carries a similar message, but far less powerfully. Jim has not understood the situation, but Nina has. When Jim is trying to kill Chester she says he is wrong to be jealous of him, and wrong to accuse her of being the cause, though she supposed 'it was all due to her having given herself to me. "And God knows," she said now, "I only did it because you said it was what you wanted or I should never have done such a wrong thing – and worse than wrong, it was stupid" ' (p. 11).

Here is the key to the book, and the whole trilogy, recalling Cary's use of his theme phrase in *Mister Johnson,* where the woman as 'a gift from God' recalls the Old English meaning of *gift* as 'payment for a wife'. The rot in society of which Jim complains, as Tolstoy did, is primarily the fault of men, who still think of women as marketable possessions. Nina could only feel herself an independent human being by building 'a fort' of feelings around herself (p. 279 above). But she knew that all her troubles had stemmed from that notion of 'giving herself' – which, in the broadest sense, means allowing a totally patriarchal society to prevail.

16. *The Captive and the Free*

The meaning of Cary's title can be understood from this note:

> Captivity and freedom applies only to the mind. Everyone . . .
> is captive to some kind of duty, but he may still be free in his
> general grasp of the whole situation and his attitude towards
> that situation. He can accept the world as he knows it has to
> be. He can understand that any good he gets out of it is a gift;
> that love and beauty which makes life worth living are in-
> separable from the evil of its contingency. He must *know* god,
> he must live *in* god.
>
> The real captivity, that is, is in superstition, hatred, fear
> egotism, jealousy, in all the blind passions good and bad which
> bind men even when they realise that they are being bound
> and driven; and in *ignorance,* in a bad map, a bad idea.[1]

Cary had been using the title, for characterization and plotting,
since around 1931, and this novel seems to confirm that he took
it from *The Brothers Karamazov*. 'Centre is faith Dostoi's child'[2]
shows the death of the child Ilusha in Dostoevsky's novel as his
main point of attack. That is, Cary is attacking the belief that an
Omnipotent God would use a child as a means to an end, because
this denies the child's rights as an individual.[3] The novel he began
as 'Captive and Free' in 1942 centred on the similar denial of
rights to women. From that material he had built his last five
novels, and he was already working on another trilogy from the
same source. He also had plans for a family chronicle, 'The Old
and the Young', from which he developed the character of Kate
Rideout in this novel.[4]

Kate's feelings, as death approaches, give some insight into
Cary's feelings, as it became increasingly clear that his own death
was near. Throughout the writing of this novel, he was having

various forms of medical treatment, much of it experimental and severe, in the hope of curing, or arresting, the paralysis of which he died. His courage required him not only to face the disease, but also to organize his writing so that he could complete his series in one novel, instead of writing three or more. It is evident, therefore, why he decided to concentrate it on the novel from which his theme title grew, so that he actually noted as his aim: ' "To rewrite a masterpiece'/a novel with comment. Novelists novel. What I want to do is'.[5]

Understandably, his thoughts returned to Dostoevsky's direct inspiration for *Charley is my Darling*; so the fate of Liz, pregnant to Charley at fourteen and punished for it in a remand home, is recalled in Alice Rodker, sent to a remand home at fourteen, because pregnant to Walter Preedy, who was then twenty-eight. From Charley's story Cary had gone on to plot 'He Must Die. Again', attacking Dostoevsky's belief in the suffering Christ. Alice Rodker can be recognized there in Daisy Collett, who had meanwhile become the narrator of the third book of the proposed trilogy, where the husband is called Marcus Ball, but is recognizably Preedy.[6] Preedy is also recognizable in Canon Bronson of 'He Must Die Again', who had meanwhile contributed to Tom Wilcher of *To be a Pilgrim,* and now divides also into the Anglican curate Tom Syson, opposed to Preedy. Harry Hooper, the author and journalist of *The Captive and the Free,* owes something to both the detective (Babbage) and the writer-artist (variously named) of 'He Must Die Again'.

If it is also remembered that Cary was writing 'The Forgotten Women' when he began *Charley,* the general background of this novel can be understood. For Joanna, daughter of Kate Rideout, is another variation on the archetypal Hannah; she resembles Nina in being an heiress – she is shortly to inherit a large block of press shares in her family's newspaper, the *Argus.* But, where Nina was beautiful, Joanna is 'a tall rather mannish figure, with a plain, pug face', and has 'no charm' (p. 16). She is 'known to have had affairs', is now twenty-eight, and shows no inclination to marry. But she is going about with Harry Hooper, an editor on the *Argus,* 'said to be a complete egotist in all his dealings with women', and assumed to be pursuing Joanna for her wealth. He is also thought to be giving publicity to Preedy, now a faith healer, in order to win favour with Joanna's mother, whom Preedy claims he can 'save'. Nevertheless, like Nina, she has the capacity to receive grace, for to Joanna, the fundamental question concerns Hooper's honesty. 'Did he really mean what he said – did he really *feel* what he said? For this seemed to her the only thing in the world you could depend on, sincerity, personal truth, in someone you liked. She liked it even in people who repelled her in every other way, whom she hated – so that her hatred even for Hitler had been mixed with admiration for his honesty when he had said openly that the German people were sheep to be driven' (pp. 21–22; cf. p. 262 above). This same 'ruthless sincerity' draws Joanna to Hooper. In other words, Hitler taught the world to admire men of his type.

Preedy is described thus:

Preedy has been taken to pieces by experts. They say, 'The typical schizoid – a little Hitler. You find him everywhere – the village boy who goes from Mass to do murder is the basic type. And it works both ways. Sudden conversions are nearly all schizoid – St Augustine, St Francis, all the young men who commit every kind of crime or folly, even extreme cruelties, and then suddenly turn to religion, where they are equally violent and equally indifferent to authority, prudence or common sense.'

But what is the good of calling St Francis an egotist and an anarchist. True, he was the kind of saint that the Church might have burnt had he not, more by luck than anything else, happened to choose a policy that the Pope could approve – even if his immediate superior could not. Yet he was a saint, he sacrificed his comforts, his peace to do good as he conceived it. If he went his own way, if he sought power, then it was power for good. It's no good asking whether in doing so he made peace with his own nature, whether he had to be a devil or a saint, because no one knows what his nature was, least of all himself (p. 57).

Hooper and Preedy, then, both bear some resemblance to Hitler. But it has been argued that they are based on Murry and Lawrence, in their relation to Dostoevsky.[7] It is then this self-willed Satanic spirit of our time that has infected these characters, owing most perhaps to Napoleon;[8] Lawrence rejected Christ and said England longed for a despot, and Murry followed him (p. 146 above). Anyone who has lost faith in a supernatural

Providence, and acknowledges no other ruler or god, must inevitably have made a god of themselves, it seems. But they need to believe in goodness, the suffering Christ, and can know it only in a human being. Hence Preedy needs Alice Rodker, though he clings to belief in an Omnipotent God.

Alice in fact seems to be based chiefly on Dostoevsky's wife, Anna Snitkina. Her diary was ' "a masterpiece, both for the picture of D. and even more, the unconscious revelation of the girl Anna" ', Cary said.[9] She was not interested in Dostoevsky's ideas, but she protected him from his enemies, ordered his affairs, and gave him comfort and peace. We should not have Dostoevsky's masterpieces, but for her.[10] She was to him then, the proof of goodness, the suffering Christ, as Preedy wanted it in Alice, and Hooper in Joanna. Hooper's rudeness to Joanna proves her willingness to suffer. And Hitler has increased that willingness. Cary had already described 'a little Hitler' in Manus Foy and Philip of *Castle Corner,* and also in Dick Bonser and Chester Nimmo. Our only basis for judging someone a devil or a saint, he implies in his analysis of Preedy, is by his willingness to sacrifice 'his comfort, his peace to do good as he conceived it'. But a devil may at any time experience a conversion, thus making it unfair to judge him by past actions. The moral is clearly to distrust the power of names, and to judge every immediate situation as unique.

A dominant idea of this novel is the power of the word, especially as a proper name; and especially the name of users of words. This is developed from Chester's remarks on names of power, and from Jim's on the power of the press to distort the truth.[11] *The Captive and the Free* is written in a reporter's style, with the dialogue reflecting the debasement of language, in a world ruled by the ideas Cary is attacking. He makes sure that his positive message takes precedence over this theme, however, by making the book a flashback to the opening chapter, which concerns Syson. Syson's final viewpoint is Cary's own, and it is actually the culmination of the women's war; it shows Syson accepting the truth of the religious experience that inspired Cary's first novel. Moreover, what Cary called the creative imagination is shown working through the women of this novel, to make theirs the first generation in our society to have recognized freedom as responsibility, and to have chosen that role for themselves, as Cary explained in *The Moonlight* (p. 7). Responsibility is the key word of *The Captive and the Free*; it is preached by Hooper, but practised by the women. Thus the women of this novel contrast with those in Cary's previous novels, and have, as it were, his farewell blessing. Apart from this, it is a powerful denunciation of a world likely to collapse into a thousand years of barbarism, through captivity to 'blind passions', and above all, 'a bad map, a bad idea'. The name Harry indicates that for Cary Hooper represents the ruling power in this world.

The story begins in May 1955, when the election is the excuse for a press party 'consisting largely of what might be called still the ruling class. Almost all present, from cabinet ministers to civil servants, professors, pressmen, and simply big business men, were deeply aware of the importance of popular ideas, popular obsessions . . . were everlastingly aware of how they depended for any influence or position they had on some form of propaganda' (p. 18). Hooper's propaganda to promote Preedy recalls Billy Graham, who proved religion to be ' "a good stunt" '. Through advertisements, says a judge, ' "the whole world knows that name" '. A name of power, one says ironically, and ' "Names make news, names and pictures" ', say others. Photographs can hypnotize, as Mussolini and Hitler ' "taught us" '; so ' "now all the papers are giving us photographs of their columnists" '.

Hooper as a 'go-getter' resembles all the men in Joanna's world; so his manners do not shock her. She to him represents the typical product of English education for girls: ' "you don't even know what you feel" ' (p. 26). Is there anything 'she would die for?' he asks (so trying to make her into a saint, in Cary's terms). He complains that she has been taught ' "never to give yourself away" ' (p. 27) – in contrast to Nina, who had 'given herself' to Jim. When he suddenly attacks her, 'pulling at her clothes', she fends him off easily, but angrily, and he retaliates by asking, ' "why shouldn't I want to – well, to use a word that won't shock the British magistrates – have you?" ' (p. 29). This verb 'have', which can equally mean 'cheat', recurs in this novel, in contrast to 'give', to express the modern male attitude to sex, it seems.

Hooper goes to Preedy's Pant's Road Mission to attend a healing service, because, 'if the old woman [Kate] fell into Preedy's hands', the vote on the Board might go against Ackroyd'

(Hooper's enemy). His journalist's eye recognizes there 'every variety of class; much more varied, for instance, than the Buchmanites' (p. 42). These Hooper recalls as chiefly 'county and their cooks' – though including a Cambridge don – and having two accents: 'that of smart society, and that of rural Oxfordshire' (p. 43). The sight of their faces, in rows, with closed eyes, waiting for God's voice, as instructed, had brought from Hooper an involuntary 'snort of laughter'. Thus Cary takes this last opportunity to denounce the Buchmanites by name. When Hooper reflects that faith healing has a wider appeal than Buchmanism, Cary is probably making this observation, too, from personal experience. For all this time he was receiving an increasing number of letters, advising him to try faith healing for his own illness. Another personal touch occurs when the hymn at Preedy's meeting causes 'a constriction in Hooper's throat'. Cary writes as though a hymn learnt in childhood has this effect universally, for he used it in his first novel; he means, presumably, that this would be an almost infallible trick for winning converts at such a meeting. Hooper is pleased that Preedy's 'actual laying on of hands . . . did not excite any emotion except curiosity' (p. 44). However, he declares himself 'greatly impressed' when he meets Allday, chairman of Preedy's advisory committee, who clearly wants Hooper's publicity just as Hooper wants something to write about. Preedy has been high-handed with Hooper, refusing to help sell his paper by modifying his message, which is: " 'that God can cure all disease" ' (p. 46). He marches off with three disciples; 'the effect was that of the chief, the leader, surrounded by his thugs'.

Hooper next visits Tom Syson. A night fighter pilot during the war, he has left a good job at the Ministry to minister in the church. As curate at St Enoch's, he has been rashly out-spoken against Preedy, who has won converts in consequence by large notices all over the parish: ' "Faith Healing. Where Does the Church Stand?" ' Syson has received letters from writers 'obsessed with adoration of Preedy, or with violent hatred against him' (p. 50). That is, Preedy rouses feelings at the price of reason. Several have accused Preedy of causing the deaths of children, by persuading parents not to call the doctor. One is Fred Rodker, brother to Alice, whose baby by Preedy had died. Another is Rollwright, whose wife has left St Enoch's for Preedy and has left her husband because he has wanted to call a doctor to their only child, Ada. Rollwright has appealed to Syson, whose vicar has told him not to interfere, since neither Mr nor Mrs Rollwright is now a parishioner. Rollwright has observed that this 'didn't seem much like common decency, much less Christianity'; so Syson has explained to Mrs Rollwright that if Ada dies, there will be an inquest, and she will be held responsible. Preedy retaliates with a new notice, 'God or the Church'.

The vicar has reprimanded Syson. Now Hooper confronts him with Preedy's message: ' "Either God has power to abolish evil or he hasn't, and if he hasn't then he isn't God, in fact there isn't any God. . . . It's the belief that works, that makes the contact so that the power can flow in" ' (p. 54). Syson can only answer that Preedy has ' "a horrible record" '.

In fact, Preedy admits to being drunk and violent in youth, and to seducing Alice; it dramatizes his conversion, which has been at Hyde Park Corner, kneeling in the dirt to an anarchist, pacifist, faith-healer named Jackman. ' "I went forward that day to give myself up to God . . . and felt within a voice that said, " Come to me – and I will give you peace" ' (p. 58). Chester's conversion by the actor playing Corder comes to mind (p. 290 above). For Preedy has become Jackman's successful rival, supported financially by Allday. Preedy attracts rich converts, being himself middle-class: the brilliant only son of a parson, who intended him for the church, he has been expelled from his public school for corrupting younger boys. He has delighted in terrifying and humiliating his widowed mother, 'whose only fault was that she loved him to distraction'. Then, until his conversion, his practice has been to 'do casual labour, spend the proceeds on drink and live on the dole' (p. 59). Kate Rideout is typical of the converts he cultivates. She has power on the *Argus*.

Hooper wants to present the *Argus* in a new popular style, he tells Joanna:

'I want to do something to this bloody world – and I want to do it to the *Argus* first. As a start. And I do believe in something. I believe in freedom. Don't laugh. I not only believe in it, I want to do something about it. Before it's too late. Before there isn't any left. I know, of course, most people don't give a damn for it. . . . They don't even want responsibility. Have you read this article in the *News Cronk,* "Teenagers"? Not one of 'em wants any responsibility. . . . No, it's the one cry among the lot. Feed me, keep me comfortable but don't ask me to believe in anything, stand up for anything, defend anything. . . . Straight out of Dusty Evsky' (p. 79).

So Cary makes his attack on Dostoevsky quite plain, and shows Hooper as one of the self-appointed elect, in service to Satan.

When Fred Rodker shows responsibility, by trying to protect his sister against Preedy, Hooper ridicules him. He has, 'like many of his type, a great contempt for the class from which he had sprung', and 'could not understand the Rodkers, and especially Alice Rodker, because he did not want to do so' (pp. 84–85). Here is the real problem for advocates of freedom like Harry Hooper, Cary argues. He implies also that Alice will teach Christ's spirit of freedom, which Hooper denies, as he proves by his service to Preedy, as Satan. Preedy, as the devil, is the one who inevitably recognizes the spirit of Christ, of goodness, in Alice. For: 'It was as if some devil had possessed her', the mother has thought, when Alice first comes under Preedy's influence (p. 86). But Alice thinks: 'Who else had lain in Preedy's arms and felt his love, heard him speak it in that voice which could make her tremble and weep in happiness?' (p. 87). We understand Alice, from Nina's account of Chester. The world, it seems, must understand the devil as a power of enjoyment in themselves, which is evil, if entirely selfish.

However, Hooper's plan to publicize her story is not justice, says Alice. She has no doubt about Preedy: ' "he murdered my kid, and he nearly murdered me. He doesn't care for anybody but himself and his old God, which is the same thing. It's not as though he even believes in that old God. He just wants to think he's saved; him saved! Well, all I can say is, he needs it" ' (p. 90). But public concern should be for the truth of his preaching and its consequences, not for her own private life. She insists: ' "my life's my own" '. She states this on other occasions, and it is Cary's final key to his theme: that life is a gift to each individual. If Nina's notion of 'giving herself' to Jim was 'stupid and wrong' (p. 303 above) then Preedy is surely wrong when he claims of Alice, ' "she's given herself to love, she's lived with God" ' (p. 93). For it is Preedy's faith in himself that depends on this belief. When he begins pestering her, reminding her how much she was previously prepared to suffer for his sake, he shows a Dostoevskian love of suffering. He has returned ' "to see how

much I can take" ', Alice accuses. Yet their mutual excitement
makes her 'lost in a confusion of motives' (p. 99); she pulls him
into an embrace, then thrusts him away with loathing. Fred is
heard in the flat, and she wants to force Preedy to hide. But he
walks out grandly, giving Fred and Syson the evidence they want.
Alice finds herself kneeling, in prayer against Preedy's God,
' "beast and murderer, and you're not going to get me again" '
(p. 101). The beast in him has aroused the beast in her, and she
repents, in the manner she has learnt as a child. Instead of
'giving herself to love', she now learns to 'Trust love working in
liberty by reason' as Cary advocates.[12]

This incident leads Fred to write letters to the newspaper
about Preedy, which Syson supports. 'His sense of honour
would oblige him to make such a statement' his vicar realizes,
yet thinks Syson unwise. *Not Honour More* is thus commented
upon. Preedy brings an action for slander. It makes headlines,
for a minister accusing a parson of immorality with a young
girl appeals to people's 'deepest, most primitive feelings' (p. 121).
Both men are inundated with malicious letters, but Syson is
'worse than Judas' to church supporters, as well as to Preedy's
followers. Preedy testifies that Alice herself, now nineteen, had
instigated sex on the occasion in question, and he had thought
that, ' "as one especially gifted to do God's work" ', she might
thus be brought back to the Mission. He is testifying now according 'to guidance, to God's will' (p. 124). It was by such guidance,
in open confession, that Buchmanites had worked off private
jealousies, according to Cary's notes.[13] Preedy's 'overwhelming
appetite for the dramatic gesture' explains his behaviour at his
trial. Cary's aim is obviously to show how easily people's moral
standards can be challenged, being all created for a particular
society. The only universal code is one of loyalty, courage, truth.
Preedy, enjoying his sense of glory, and twisting the truth, is not
admirable. His stated conviction, 'that the child Alice had been
sent to save his soul by the revelation of her unselfish love' strikes
Hooper as magnificent. He will fail to see that the same could be
said of Joanna and himself. But why should either be 'sent'?

Syson in the witness box has been 'not only trying to give the
truth, but one favourable to Preedy. He was using, deliberately,
a Christian charity towards the man' (p. 132). When this annoys
the judge, Preedy's counsel is encouraged to make this a trial of
Syson's religious convictions. Cary observes: 'it is very doubtful

if any Bishop would have done better.' Preedy is seen to believe what he professes, as Syson does not, notably regarding God's power to perform miracles. Alice has sworn she will not answer, if cross-examined as a witness, as though she were again on trial for having had a baby. Her silence and her evasive answers seem intended to recall Christ's silence at his trial, and more particularly to suggest how Mary his mother might have answered, in the same circumstances. For, if a Bishop could not have explained miracles, how would Mary have answered to:

'You had a child, I believe?'

Alice was silent, and continued to stare at the judge's box. . . . Counsel repeated his question and Alice was seen to move her lips. The judge asked her to speak up, whereupon she turned scarlet and said in an unexpectedly loud voice, 'Yes, I had, and they sent me to a home.'

'Was that Preedy's child?'

Alice was silent and again the judge interposed. 'I'm afraid you will have to answer counsel's questions. You can be sure that we sympathise with you in your painful position, but it is absolutely necessary that we should know the facts.'. . .

[Alice is thinking of herself] as a thin ugly child with a swollen belly, standing before the four magistrates . . .

The counsel repeated his question. 'I'm sorry, Miss Rodker, but I must have an answer. Was your child Preedy's child?'

Alice was silent.

'I'm afraid you must answer.'

Alice did not reply. . . . She felt such hatred of everybody in the court, in the world, that she did not even think of what she would say.

Again the counsel repeated his question, and she answered promptly, 'Just as you like.'

'I'm afraid it's not as I like, but as it happened. I must ask you again to answer my questions .'. . .

. . . Alice was understood to answer, 'Yes.' . . .

. . . 'Do you mean that you will answer my questions or that Preedy was not the father of your child?'

'Yes, that's it.'

This lie was quite unpremeditated. . . . But the moment she had uttered this lie it seemed to her that lying was just what these people had asked for (pp. 136–9).

Cary's life of Christ is thus finally fulfilled in this trial of Alice, who has already been cleared of her 'sin', so that here Christian dogma is really on trial. Since Syson is found guilty, the public can be said to have accepted Preedy's God who, capable of miracles, killed Alice's child by Preedy. This God is then the cruel Jehovah of the Old Testament.

Alice is now watched wherever she goes, and asks Joanna for help. At Joanna's house, she meets Kate, who has been a magistrate, but now, facing death, believes she is talking more sense than ever before. She thinks Preedy ' "either a crook or a lunatic" '. But she advises Alice that he will ' "give her a character" ', being ' "a flourishing prophet already – a real power" ' (pp. 148–9). He does not propose marriage. ' "But so much the better – if Alice can't run him she can leave him." ' Kate's questions regarding Preedy's Indian blood give a strong hint that Cary is thinking of Lawrence – on whom he was writing and making notes at this time.[14]

Kate is now anxious to see Preedy perform an act of healing, and it is arranged for her to watch a private service for a rich American girl Nona Clench. But because this girl is supposed to have no expectation of being cured, Hooper persuades Kate to leave before the service begins. Thus Hooper wants to manipulate truth to suit his ends. But Nona is cured, and Cary clearly intends her cure to be symbolic of the kind of miracle that could take place in Western society, to cure the split mind that Nona so plainly suffers from. She has distinguished herself at Oxford, but then been crippled in a riding accident. Like her family, she is an American liberal, sympathetic to communism and so 'fundamentally an anarchist, who believed in ' "freedom," in an anarchist's mystical sense of the word' (p. 166). It was 'a law of nature' for Nona, who did not believe in God. That is, she believed in a power working for truth, beauty, and goodness, but she could not believe in a God capable of miracles, for 'a miracle would ruin my whole belief'. Her physical paralysis reflects her mental state. Because she is so keyed up to resist a miracle, Preedy's cold hard hand lying on her forehead shatters her resistance and she does ' "rise and walk" ', as Preedy instructs ' "in the name of Jesus" '. Such a cure is not beyond any of us, Cary implies. The symbolism of Nona's circumstances suggests that he is thinking of Oxford as a place where many people lose their established faith, so suffering a 'riding accident' from which someone like Lawrence can seem to cure them, by offering an alternative faith by which to live.

Nona's 'miracle' cure wins Preedy many converts, including Kate – though she did not witness it. Kate believes herself physically cured also, and supports any publicity Preedy wants. Hooper and Joanna therefore give Preedy wholehearted support. Joanna becomes a 'scrubwoman' at the Mission, where Preedy's staff delight in giving her the most unpleasant jobs, as proof of the power of conversion. Living thus, 'a life almost without reflection', she becomes pregnant to Hooper. He wonders whether she did it on purpose but adds: ' "However, it's your own business; you promised to take care; it's nothing to do with me" ' (p. 193). He volunteers, as an afterthought, that he can give her the name of an abortionist in Paris. 'But Joanna, to her own surprise, shook her head. She perceived that this was something she could not do. That course of events into which she had thrown herself was apparently stronger than any consideration of prudence, or even of kindness to her mother [whom Hooper has said her news will kill]. . . . She belonged to a process, a movement of life, which seemed to be stronger than her will' (p. 194). Hooper therefore reacts as Harry Dawbarn and Bonser did (pp. 249, 255), though his 'punch on the nose' takes the form of words: ' "Don't you realise that I'd rather shoot myself than marry you?" ' He can make enough money out of her parents' newspaper without being troubled to marry Joanna for money. For her part, she realizes that he has reacted as she expected, and she does not really mind (p. 195).

Cary is apparently suggesting that the creative imagination has freed women from the terror of illegitimate pregnancy by working through a woman like Joanna, who has rejected the code of her class. She now becomes cut off from it almost entirely because her mother dies, leaving her no money. Having believed herself healed by Preedy, Kate has given him large sums of money, and her financial affairs are in chaos. The *Argus* is to be rescued by Hooper, who hopes to do so through Preedy.

Hooper launches a campaign in the Albert Hall: 'The "Pant's Road Battle of Britain" . . . As he said, "Of course it's shocking bad taste, but that's what we want – to give 'em a shock . . . The early Christians hadn't much taste either – they were all for smashing those nice, domesticated Roman gods. But they won out – they gave people something to live for" ' (p. 211). Hooper's idea of 'life is a gift' in this context recalls 'Juno captive', as an inspiration in part for Joanna as well as Nina (p. 302 above). This goddess of marriage and childbirth, whose temple became the mint, is the most likely of the domesticated Roman Gods to be attacked by early Christians, for reasons not dissimilar to Hooper's. 'Pant's Road' suggests various sarcastic and vulgar associations, such as 'kick in the pants' for people like Syson, who probably fought in the Battle of Britain. Thus Cary urges recognition of Britain's real needs. Hooper has indeed given Joanna something to live for – a child – but disowned it. Whereas early Christians attacked Roman gods, Hooper's Christians are attacking Victorian gods, at the Albert Hall. Fred Rodker realizes this, and plans to wreck the meeting.

Alice feels she cannot bear more publicity. Gazing at photographs of girls who have suffered similarly, she wonders how they feel when recognized as, for example, ' "the girl who was had by those Teddy boys" ' (p. 212). Preedy now regularly 'has' Alice, who cannot stop him without more publicity. She contemplates suicide, yet 'the very power to kill herself, enraged her against those who were making her life impossible' (p. 212). She therefore telephones Joanna, hoping she can persuade Hooper to keep her name out of the papers, since it will wreck his campaign if Preedy is exposed.

Joanna confronts Alice as 'a primitive creature'. Alice, frowning at Joanna's lovely mink coat, wonders, ' "Can I trust this lady" ' (p. 214). Joanna's mink coat makes her the primitive creature, symbolic of her world.

Alice asks whether Joanna would like her life exposed:

'Does he have you – your chap?'
'That's my own business.'
'Well, it's my own business too ——' (p. 215).

But Alice needs a confidant. She begins confessing her situation, and ends hysterically by (truthfully) accusing Joanna – ' "you'd sell me for a cuddle" '. Joanna, furious, is leaving, but Alice seizes her coat. ' "I've told you, you tell me – he has you?" ' '

'Yes, of course he does. Why not, what of it? Go and tell if you like.'

And to her surprise, the girl suddenly fell against her and began to sob.

Joanna is the daughter of a magistrate who might indeed have been one who sentenced Alice to a remand home; yet it would ' "kill" ' her to know Joanna was having an illegitimate child, Hooper has warned, when advocating abortion. Society's unjust, cruel hypocrisy is thus exposed.

Yet Joanna, shocked by Alice's tears, but secure against her, merely (and untruthfully) promises, ' "I shan't tell on you" '. Alice says:

'I thought you were nice first time I saw you, with that chap. I thought he was giving you a bad time too – and you were hating it like me. It's awful to have to do with a beast. You can't get on and you can't get off.'

'I know – I know.'

'Bossing you about – sending you here to worm it out of me. And why, why? But you like it, do you? He's got you.'

And Joanna, to her own surprise, as if this question had found its own answer in a reaction deeper than her mind, answered, 'Yes, he's got me.'

'You love him?'

'I don't know – sometimes.'

'That's what it is – and then you hate him. You wish he was dead – you wish you'd never seen him. He has you and you do it to spite him and make him feel like dirt and then you feel like dirt and what does he care. He's up in the air again as soon as his thing is flat. He's the great man – he's the great big name and if you spat in his face he'd only laugh at you. He'd only say, poor kid, what does she know – that's what she's for but of course you mustn't tell her. She's got to take it, so what. Or she don't get nothing at all' (p. 217).

This scene, with its extraordinary insight, is answered at the end of the book. Alice is convinced that Preedy's God has made him evil and mad, but she cannot escape him, because Harry, manipulating her world to suit himself, has chosen to support him. He advertises himself on posters for his ' "Battle of Britain Mission of Healing" ': ' "Harry Hooper, Chairman of the Campaign Committee." ' Joanna's first reaction to this 'self-display, and back-slapping appeal' is 'disgust; but the disgust instantly produced a reaction', partly because she has been conditioned, like all of us, to accept such public values; also because she must accept them, for her private happiness. So the leaders of this world get the confidence they need primarily from their women, Cary signifies, through Hooper as well as Preedy.

Preedy's only Albert Hall meeting is a failure, chiefly because Syson's pamphlets denouncing him are backed by the Truth Society. This society is controlled by Sir Robert Tinney, who is Hooper's personal enemy. Bertrand Russell as the prototype of Tinney is strong evidence for regarding Murry and Lawrence as the prototypes of Hooper and Preedy. Indeed, since Lawrence and also Huxley recognized a fruitful source for characterization in Murry, it should not be surprising if Cary used him also. In fact, in this book, Cary seems to invite readers to recognize characters as real people. Syson is essentially Cary, a serviceman who decided that churchmen do not strictly believe what they still preach, notably regarding miracles. Like Cary, Syson has then turned to scientists, whose arguments he finds unconvincing. Tinney has backed him against Preedy because he is now 'a monomaniac, on this subject of the return of superstition' (p. 226). His monomania accords with Cary's attack on superstition (a characteristic of Murry as well as Dostoevsky).[15] Syson's Truth Society pamphlet does 'immense damage' to Preedy's Mission, which now hinges totally on the name 'Preedy', as Preedy knows. But Hooper is now finding Preedy a burden.

Hooper has married Joanna. He lets people think he has done so purely to get control of the *Argus*. This suits his public image. But in truth he had come to depend on her, and then suddenly found that she was planning to go abroad. She had decided not only to have the child there, but to remain for a minimum of five years, as a widow, to ensure that it could not suffer the stigma of illegitimacy. Because of his attitude to the child, she was no longer thinking of him at all. 'And this realisation shook him so deeply that something cracked in his idea of things. For a moment he was aware of a realm beyond from which blew a wind so cold that it made him freeze. He had a glimpse of a solitude like that of an arctic waste where man is alone, not only physically, but spiritually, where he does not belong at all, where his existence is simply an anomaly (p. 232).

Thus the creative imagination, working through women of this new generation, is bringing the truth to men: that the primitive family is mother and child, though the quality of a society depends on the way a man accepts his responsibility as the physical father of the child, whose very soul depends on the nature of his acceptance. As the only one of Cary's characters to marry in these circumstances, Hooper brings the series to the close that Cary clearly wanted. For a key note for the novel reads: 'Clue in family relations must be re-established.'[16] Though Hooper's proposal of marriage is typically egotistical, Joanna would have married him, simply to establish 'a normal situation' for herself and their child. But she has also come to care for Hooper, and proof that he now needs her moves her almost to tears, so that Hooper too is moved 'in an extraordinary manner' (p. 234). He feels for the moment that he loves her, wants to show it, and to make her happy, 'even if she did not thank him for it. He was, of course, sure of her gratitude, but he recognized in himself the unselfishness of his intention and it pleased him to think of it. In fact, during this weekend Hooper enjoyed an extraordinary happiness, something he had never known before' (p. 234). So Cary shows the power of unselfish love. Even when Hooper reflects of Joanna, 'it was very likely that she'd caught him by a trick', he realizes it proves she loves him. ' "A woman's trick," he thought, "but what could she do?" He felt an immense indulgence towards women because Joanna was a woman.' Thus Cary ends his series, as a counter to *The Kreutzer Sonata*.

Hooper, Preedy, and Syson are drawn together through Ada Rollwright. Syson persuades her father to kidnap her, so that she can be examined by a doctor. Because Cary is arguing against Dostoevsky, he makes a point of stressing that people dealing with 'children even younger than twelve in such circumstances are always struck in the same way, with their poise of mind and body' (p. 249). They are individuals and, in Ada's case, deserving of considerably more respect than any of the adults. In this situation Cary also answers Tolstoy's attitude to 'women's work'. For, from the moment she arrives at her father's hiding-place for her, Ada spends her time sewing a skirt which she says must be ready for a school examination. Her father and Syson think this shows her childish incomprehension of her situation. But Cary says it 'was much more likely the ordinary tactics of much older women in the same predicament. This work was always her excuse for not answering questions, or seeming not to notice what was going on' (p. 250).

Ada and her mother have greatly influenced Preedy: 'at the mere sight of mother and child together he had felt again that mysterious movement of feeling which he called power. From the love on one side completely selfless, from the trust of the child, something flashed into him; something like those discoveries made by the pure contact of sense – a glimpse of the sea, . . . which yet bring a shock of recognition' (pp. 252–3). This is Cary's definition of grace,[17] and for Preedy 'it was through this mother and child, especially the child'. Thus Preedy has received grace, in Cary's sense, and it is with a feeling of love for Ada that he now goes to her with her mother. The doctor has already arrived, and it is when Preedy hears him spelling out Ada's name, to arrange an X-ray appointment, that he suddenly believes he has received grace in the sense that Cary has been attacking since his first novel. One of his disciples (Brank), has already pointed out to him that Ada Rollwright and Alice Rodker have the same initials. Brank is a bachelor, who has lived in the East. 'He was writing a book about revelations and was exploring the Bible for what he called signs. So the letters of the first words of a certain psalm, added together, gave the date of the next war, which would also be the last, Armageddon, the end of the material world' (p. 259). This account (ironically) invites readers to recognize initial letters as signs. Preedy has despised such practices. But at this time he is suffering from a state of total dejection, due to the feeling that, by Hooper's campaign, he has been turned into 'a piece of magic', 'a dynamo'. Desperately needing a renewal of grace himself, Preedy is moved to believe that the initials 'A. R.' are indeed a sign: 'Brank's words came to him with a force of shock which broke the whole fabric of that solid construction which was his idea of things – the construction which, at that moment, stood over him like a prison or a convent cell' (p. 260). Suddenly he is back in the world of his earliest childhood:

> of old stories, terrifying, mysterious, of murderous kings, savage prophets, a turmoil of cruelty and war. And over all the presence of Jehovah . . . who gave the sign to and tested Abraham with the demand that he should cut the throat of his

only son as an offering. And Abraham was loyal; he proved himself. And Isaac lived.

Was this world today any different from that one of the Old Testament? . . .

And what were the people, the mass? Were they any wiser, better, than the tribes of Israel – any less greedy and self-seeking, . . . less responsible for themselves or anyone else? . . .

. . . How did they know their leader and maintain their faith? By revelation only. . . .

. . . Here was a sign of the plainest kind given to him personally. Saved by one childish messenger, he was to be retrieved by another. A sign made threefold sure by an actual signature – by a repetition of letters which was by itself beyond expectation or plan.

Conviction broke upon Preedy with such force that . . . He was panic-struck with fear that he would be too late, that he had already failed his test, that Ada Rollwright would die (p. 261).

When Ada dies six weeks later the mother's 'superstitious blindness' and Preedy's 'disastrous teaching' are deplored by the coroner. Cary has ensured that Preedy's good intentions are clear. But Syson distributes more leaflets, denouncing him, and Hooper decides that Preedy must go. Hooper is 'very angry, but also frightened', because Preedy's failure may mean his own ruin. Then Alice comes to his mind as his possible saviour. She is now very upset over Ada, and so over Syson, whose efforts to save Ada had been thwarted by Alice's failure as a witness in Syson's defence. To Joanna's amazement, Hooper is now ready to set Alice against Preedy, to save himself.

Alice detests Hooper, but thinks him a friend to Preedy, whom she also hates, while knowing that he is 'not responsible for her baby's death or the Rollwright child's. She knew that on this matter of religion he was mad. Perhaps he was mad all through. But this did not entitle him to be a murderer. And when she thought that, she was quite sure that she must help Syson, to stop him from murdering more children. Grown-ups could take care of themselves, most of them were mad too, but children had to be protected' (p. 273). She therefore agrees to go to the Mission with Hooper. Preedy is confronting his committee, and Alice interrupts, pointing at Preedy: ' "Perhaps he is a murderer, but if he is he doesn't know it. He doesn't know anything straight. He doesn't really believe anything either, he just tries. He's a fraud" ' (p. 279). Now Syson enters. Preedy is ready to debate with him, and Syson begins to realize why people cling to a faith: ' "Yes, he's got to believe all this. It would be better for me if I could have gone on believing my own nonsense. I can see now what a difference it makes. It's not just between lies and truth, it's between life and death. He's alive and I'm dead" ' (p. 281). Syson is now arguing mechanically, to the point of saying that a God who allows misery would be a devil.

'If you're going to speak blasphemy,' said Preedy, 'we won't get any further.'
And at this point, Syson's brain suddenly moved and he perceived that Preedy was afraid, and promptly he said, 'Yes, you don't like that because you know he is a devil, your God' (p. 282).

Now everyone begins behaving irrationally, and all three men are at their lowest ebb together, as if their lives are aspects of each other. Syson already realizes 'that in the sphere where Preedy operated, this foggy element, it was impossible to say how much he served God, and how much he served the devil'. Yet he hits him, calling him a devil, and gets himself arrested. Preedy disappears, and Hooper, losing the backing for the Mission, loses his job on the *Argus*. 'Hooper and Fleet Street were confident . . . that the *Argus* was done for' (p. 286). This fact comments upon Hooper's ambition to 'do something to the world' and 'do it to the *Argus* first'.[18] However, he becomes an editor on the *Dispatch* (on the day his daughter is born).
Publicity surrounding Syson's arrest brings Alice back into the news. 'All her pictures had had exciting character; the first, with the enormous terrified eyes, and the half-open mouth, like that of some animal which is at once frightened out of its senses, and ready to bite, had been acclaimed by experts' (p. 293). As these 'experts' know, her pictures hypnotize the public who, with the photographers, hunt her out in increasing numbers wherever she goes. Even Preedy rings Joanna for her address. As society's quarry, Alice realizes that her only refuge will be the Mission. With two of his supporters, she finds Preedy, 'back on the stump',

at Hyde Park Corner. The gist of Preedy's address is what Hooper has supposedly told him: that preachers like himself ' "preach God because you are devils. You preach the life of sacrifice because you need the kick of suffering. You take to Christ as drunkards take to drink, because your batteries are flat, and without juice you're dead" ' (p. 295). It is the devil, then, who knows God. Knowing that he will always be forgiven, he can continue to be a devil. This is Dostoevsky's message, given by the Grand Inquisitor. It makes Christ inadequate, Lawrence said. The difference between Hooper and Preedy is that Preedy admits he is evil and needs goodness, in the person of Alice, to keep alive his assurance of the willingness to suffer and forgive. Yet Hooper had experienced a happiness he had never known before, when he momentarily felt unselfish love for Joanna. That is the secret of the happiness men seek, not an obsession like Preedy's to be saved by suffering, says Cary. Yet Preedy is a better man than Hooper, because he believes in God and admits the reality of evil.[19]

When Alice realizes that Preedy must be denounced as a fraud and above all prevented from murdering any more children, she is recognizing the right priorities – assuming 'murder' to mean, also, destroying children with false doctrines. In doing what she sees needs to be done she becomes a martyr, an innocent victim of injustice. But she is not doing it with that in mind – any more, presumably, than Christ denounced the evils of his society with that in mind. But Christ was hounded down and destroyed, because men did not want their evil recognized. They did recognize it by witnessing his suffering, but they wanted that 'kick'. So it is with Alice, who is answering Nature's demands of her, as a woman, who knows, by the actual experience of giving birth, that women bear children to live, not to be sacrificed to a notion of fatherhood like Preedy's, which has always threatened humanity – as Cary shows dramatically in Preedy's vision of Abraham and Isaac – (doubtless influenced by Kierkegaard, p. 213 above).

Alice accepts her role as Georgina accepted hers. She brings Preedy's coat, for he has been preaching in the rain; he has thus become ill, and will need nursing. As they arrive at his lodging, where there are already two cameramen, the sun comes out, and Preedy says laughing: ' "Yes, just in time for the camera. Cover your face, Rodker" ' (p. 302). His laugh is from the horse's

mouth, heralding the sun, symbol of God and the devil, a sign
and symbol of the elect in all Cary's novels.

The whole scene now becomes highly symbolic and almost
uncanny. It is vital to Hooper's future that he gets an interview
with Alice, and he can do so only through Joanna, who is
embraced warmly by Alice when they arrive, and thereafter fills
the role of Judas. The address is 19 Murden Street. 'Hooper had
expected a crowd at the house but he was astonished when he
saw the street. A crowd queued as if for church, a long train,
four deep, of quiet, decent-looking people of both sexes, but
mostly young, and gazed at all that could be seen from a distance,
the upper windows of 19' (pp. 305–6). Alice is only 19 and the
photographs of her that have hypnotized the public have convinced them that murder will be done at this address – which
many would read as 'a sign'. As at the close of *The Horse's
Mouth* they resemble the crowd at Christ's crucifixion, but also
those watching the murder of Maria Marten in *Except the Lord*.
While Hooper is trying to get a statement from Alice, Preedy's
supporter, Colonel Marris, says: ' "I think the Missioner is asking for you." ' This is untrue. He has said it 'to get the girl away
from the dangerous presence of Hooper'. Alice is now locked in
the more dangerous presence of Preedy who, 'in a fever of anger
and despair, had forgotten about Rodker' (p. 311). He asks what
she wants: ' "*You* wanted *me*." ' She begins helping him remove
his wet clothes, while he accuses her of calling him a fraud, or
at least a fool. ' "I know what a doctor would say – have you
any dry things here?" ' . . . He was exhausted and he enjoyed
this mothering, by a woman who was now completely his in body
and soul.' The whole scene becomes a dramatization of the evil
at the heart of a society that treats mother love as an evil, as
Cary was concurrently writing of it in *Art and Reality* (p. 172;
below, p. 338).

Preedy starts accusing Alice of ' "The Hooper disease. You
had no faith. You didn't believe in God." "Have you any
pyjamas here?" ' As she struggles to help him, his abuse of her
becomes a denunciation of society, for which she is now the
scapegoat. She ' "whored after a lie" ', instead of believing in
his God, ' "who judges, who punishes, who saves – the king of
the world – the omnipotent – you believe in him now" '
(pp. 312–13). He accuses her of coming to make a fool of him.
' "You can't sit there naked." ' Yelling in rage, he gives her that

pathological blow that is a protest against the world, a violent 'punch on the nose' that flings her across the room: ' "Go away – get out – whore – bitch." ' She is the whore of the Revelation, 'THE MOTHER OF HARLOTS' present in all Cary's novels. She also stands for Preedy's mother, for he has publicly con- fessed, regarding her, 'that he was a great deal worse than a murderer; he had killed his mother with despair, he had counted on her death to get her money' (p. 176). Preedy here directly recalls *Fantasia of the Unconscious,* as Lawrence's attack on 'Woman, wife and mother'. For, of this preoccupation Lawrence writes: 'Batter her out of it till she's stunned. . . . Reduce her once more to the naked Eve.'[20] Alice is battered, but Preedy is naked. At this moment his disciples burst into the room, and the scene dramatically exposes the myth of man as a noble savage – if the papers are intent, as Hooper says, on printing the truth. Moreover, Alice, a woman under great stress, has proved far more rational than the man. Asked what happened, she replies: ' "Nothing. He didn't want to go to bed." ' But her face is bleed- ing, and swollen, and Joanna urges her to leave. ' "But I came to look after him. I've got to look after him – no one else is doing it. And he's really ill" ' (p. 313). Hooper says it is unsafe. ' "Oh, I can manage. He's like that. He won't kill me." She looked at the pair with a new expression, a new realisation came into her face, that is to say on the undamaged side. "You needn't worry about me," she said. "I'm all right. I can take it. I've got straight again and I can take anything" ' (p. 313).

Thus Alice gets grace, the intuition that frees her. At that moment, the window is broken, and she is photographed. Joanna realizes the depth of her treachery, and even Hooper says, ' "I didn't arrange that ." ' But Alice interrupts:

'It's all right, I don't mind. Let him shoot. I don't care now. You'd better go and print it all. I don't care for anything you say – or anything you do.'

She tossed her head at them, with the universal gesture of the person who defies the world, the glance of a free soul (p. 314).

Hooper is elated; pays a high price to the free-lance photo- grapher, who says: ' "she was right in the bull's-eye." ' Hooper imagines the photograph in the paper: 'what an easy job for the retouchers'. This brings a final memory of Lawrence, who preached that we have 'lost touch'. Still Cary probably agreed with Joanna, that the picture was ' "a wicked cruel lie against that poor man." ' For he mirrors society. So of Hooper, Joanna sighs: ' "you can't really help yourself." ' As his wife, she expresses society's basic dilemma. Preedy's disciple Gomm (meaning 'man') says loudly enough to be heard 'by the staring crowd above. "Mr Hooper – look at him – the millionaire who sucks the public bum – the dirtiest man on earth." ' But Hooper insists that he serves and understands the public, whose ' "pleasure is the truth" '.

Hooper's first impulse has been to publish the truth revealed to him by Alice: 'My God, human nature was a wonderful thing. You couldn't beat it. A little floozy like that out of some slum, or worse, some evangelical terrace, and she throws off phrases like that'. Perhaps the words 'My God', and 'beat' work their deadly poison on him. He considers presenting Alice 'as really the stronger party; as a person of remarkable character who had come back to Preedy simply because it seemed to be the right thing to do . . . He could emphasize Preedy's cruel, or at least thoughtless and irresponsible action in allowing a girl of that age and that reckless character to sacrifice herself' (p. 316). But reporters would blame him for suppressing the photograph, and what did readers want: 'a piece of psychological analysis? A complicated story of mixed motives leaving them to make out their own judgments? It was crazy even to imagine it.' Thus Cary makes clear what he has been doing himself, in this novel most obviously, but in fact throughout the series. That this is not what the public wants – or at least the reviewers – has been proved by their incomprehension of his work; so his final paragraph reads like a bitter personal reflection, as well as a denunciation of Hooper:

No, there was only one story here – the poor little girl seduced and ruined by a parson who then proceeds to murder her baby, who has such power over her still that he recalls her to his side and beats her up as a reward. And the poor little victim, besotted with love or terror, takes it. One could suggest perhaps that she likes being beaten; always a popular line. Really, whatever Joanna might think, there was no choice. And a good thing too. Yes, the story of the year.

However, the essential message of the book is one of hope. Cary prepares the reader for it, as usual, on his first page. Syson is 'smiling in the most cheerful manner'. This so angers 'some true believer' that he throws a bottle and cuts Syson's eye. The crowd are enraged because, having been sentenced to six months in jail (for attacking Preedy), Syson seems unrepentant. Moreover, the police have tried to spare him their abuse, by smuggling him out by a back way.

The reason for Syson's smile is not revealed until chapter 62, following the scene where he attacks Preedy as a 'devil', and is arrested (p. 322 above). During his imprisonment Syson has written *A Sure and Certain Faith,* which can be taken as a statement of faith by Cary in a dramatized, fictional form. He was himself ' "the devil's prisoner" ' at that time, says Syson, hating Preedy (and all the prophets he stands for) because he had shown him that his own faith was 'a muddle of wish-fulfilment and time-serving' (p. 282). But he was made to realize that anyone who argues in such vague terms as ' "It's all a mystery -- the thing is too big for human intelligence" ', has 'no right to any reasonable faith at all. You could defend any faith in those terms. Hitlerism, communism.' The Churches' ruling regarding disease required him 'to ask the doctors first if God would be any good in this case.' This convinced him 'that the Churches did not really believe in this power of God to do miracles'. Having thus lost faith in the Omnipotent God of the Churches, he hated life and sought imprisonment to escape from it.

' "But God saved me in the very nick" ', he writes (Nick being the devil, who tempts belief in luck in such cases). While waiting to be smuggled out the back way, Syson is taken to a waiting room, which again signifies the religious view of this world as a testing place. Here he is handed a note from Mrs Rollwright, who wants to thank him for his efforts to save Ada. She admits she was wrong about Preedy, but wants Syson to forgive him, because he had not meant to do evil. The following passage sums up 'life as a gift' as the message of all Cary's novels. Syson says:

' "I know now," she wrote, "that you were right, and God could not save my poor child. But still you were wrong too for he can do miracles. He has done one with me, for he has given me forgiveness and peace. I am all alone in the world now, for my husband has left me, and once I wanted to die. But

now I am glad to be alive to remember that happiness when I
had my child and to thank God for all the love in the world."

'I remembered this woman . . . And when I read her letter,
I was suddenly moved to understand . . . the miracle of God's
love in the world.

'And so I found my truth where I had left it, and I wanted
to go out and tell the people. It seemed to me that the truth
was so great, so obvious that I had only to speak it and all
should know that great joy, all should be free' (p. 284).

But then he realized he was a prisoner, and laughed, and the true
believer threw the bottle.

This laughter contrasts with Preedy's when the sun shines, for
the final scene of the book; it might be called laughter on 'the
other side of the mouth'. It is not devilish, as Preedy's is. Nevertheless, both are expressing the world as Cary had realized, by
1927–8, that we must accept it. For he noted then (giving a clue
to a major influence): 'the world results from the labouring
efforts of one growing spirit, or spirit in process of revelation to
itself. Look up Spinoza. Good is absolute and eternal, so is evil,
and they are parts of one thing like day and night – the climate
in which the spirit breathes and can breathe nowhere else.'
These words appear in the notebook, where he also recognized a
quality of life in his mother and Aunt Doll, which he has
portrayed, in a modern context, in Alice.[21]

He might indeed have consulted this notebook as an inspiration for this novel. Syson's laughter, as a prisoner, might well
have been Cary's, reflecting on his high hopes for his first novel,
for which this had already been the message. But he had been a
prisoner to words, to conventions, to habits of mind in readers
and reviewers. He had been sustained by his wife's love, but now,
like Syson (and Mrs Rollwright too) he was alone. Syson's wife
Clarinda ('brightly fair') could be a portrait of Gertrude Ogilvie,
and through her Cary again conveys his belief that it is in a
beloved landscape that we most readily know God, as the Being
of the World. For Clarry Syson, at her home village of Brownhill,
'Fields, cottages, people, cows, even tractors were at one in an
existence which was simply the larger aspects of family life where
everything and every person is part of a remembered and continuing story' (p. 239). In Clarry's fears for her husband 'with
his material worries, his humiliation', Cary is surely showing his

understanding of what it had been like for his wife, through the years when he could not write, because he did not have a clear picture of the world.

Now, in this book, with its author's commentary, he had made his meaning plainer. But the final 'horse-laugh' was that he felt it a duty to complete *Art and Reality,* and so had insufficient time for the novel. ' "I shall die, if I don't finish this book" ', he had said to Winifred Davin. As Dan Davin comments, 'there was grimness in the jest'.[22] That was in December 1955. But he was fortunate in that year that Edith Millen came to him as secretary, for she was a trained nurse. Mrs Lightburne was his devoted housekeeper and, as his strength failed rapidly, Winifred Davin helped with the preparation of manuscripts. He stated his essential theme at the end of *Art and Reality* thus: 'that what makes life worth living are such common things as family love, ordinary goodness and truth, the duty and self-sacrifice which we know every day in the smallest as well as the greatest actions' (pp. 172–3). He was sustained to the end in this faith, because he had daily proof of it.

We are indeed indebted to Winifred Davin for editing *The Captive and the Free,* which Cary had discussed with her, and which was more nearly finished than he realized, she says.[23] He had repeated, ' "It will break my heart if I don't finish this." ' Let us hope, then, that he knew in his heart it would be published. It lacks his final revision, yet its power is unmistakable, and it ends his series as a challenge to us all.

17. Conclusion

'I look upon life as a gift from God. I did nothing to earn it.
Now the time is coming to give it back I have no right to
complain.'[1]

Cary spoke these words in August 1956, and they were quoted
in his obituary notices around the world, seven months later.

They express his faith in a God who had given him life continually, from birth to death, in forms that he intuited as freedom and grace. Because life is in truth a gift, we can all say – as
Alice Rodker did: ' "My life's my own" '. But we must concede
this same right even to the smallest child – and not imagine that
God would make a gift of someone else's life to us as well, either
in the way Preedy imagined, or in the way many people regard
their wives or children. Having done nothing to earn it, we should
certainly not complain that God is not just. For justice is manmade, and depends on each of us to make it a part of Reality.
What we give back, at death, is the sum of good and evil that
marks our time on earth. We were lucky to be born, should be
glad to have lived, and have no reason to expect rewards, punishments, or an extension of life, hereafter.

Some such statement underlies this final message, according to
the foregoing interpretation of Cary's life and writing. If he
could have known that it would be circulated so widely in this
way, he might have supposed that the mysterious power in which
he so fervently believed was, at this last opportunity, urging men,
through him, to consider what these words do indeed mean, for
them.

What they would have meant to Tolstoy can be judged from
his play, 'The Light that Shines in Darkness' – as it seems Cary
wanted us to see. For the words ' "My life's my own" ', as spoken
by Alice Rodker, both echo and challenge what Nicholas says

330

in the play: ' "I had believed that my life was my own . . . as soon as I realized that my life was not my own, that I was sent into the world to do the work of God [I realized] . . . our whole life is not a fulfilment of this will, but, on the contrary, is in perpetual contradiction to it." ' Here Tolstoy has summed up the crisis in liberalism of which Cary wrote. It divided Tolstoy's own soul, his own family, his country, and finally the world. It divided Tolstoy the moralist from Tolstoy the artist. For in real life Tolstoy felt bound to give the peasants anything they demanded. But Tolstoy the artist knew this would not persuade an audience, whose sympathies might therefore turn to the wife. In the play, therefore, Nicholas proposes keeping some land for his family. What frightened Tolstoy's wife was that she was being asked to manage a household in which there should be no limit to the giving up. And the artist and moralist cannot be separated, Cary insisted, when lecturing on Tolstoy. Art should express the view of a 'whole' man. *Except the Lord* depicts the sufferings of a family whose head tried to follow Christ's doctrine, in the way Tolstoy advocates. In *The Captive and the Free* Cary drives the lesson home. By the simple device of making Tolstoy's key words the key to his own book, but spoken by Alice, he gives the vital clue to his reader's subconscious, urging him to consider what is finally the basic metaphysical problem facing us all. Whether Cary gave the clue consciously or unconsciously can be judged only by studying his annotations in his copy of Tolstoy's play, together with other notes for his novel. In either case he would have been acting upon an intuition.

This mysterious power, which works through all of us, was for Cary the creative imagination. Walter Allen called him 'its novelist and its celebrant'.[2] It defines the life of the world, at the very point where man and God meet, and part. The early chapters of *Art and Reality* show how this is so.

In Cary's view, we begin life as a nexus of feelings in one common personality – God – and only gradually become individuals. Infants *react* to impressions, through intuitions, and gradually gain the power to *act*, which is imagination. By imagination we form images, or symbols, of experience which record a 'feeling about the fact'.[3] This is Cary's definition of Art. In this power to form symbols we are all artists. The symbol is always unique, and stands for a particular experience – of seeing a bird, for example. But, as the power of reason develops, it analyses such an experience into two parts: feeling and fact. At this point the individual really creates himself. Out of the symbol of a unique experience he forms the concept of, say, birds, as a class of things objective to himself. In building up a private world of concepts, he forms a 'map', or guide, with which to comprehend the world. The power to do so is vital for human beings. For reason develops in them at the price of instincts, by which lower animals are able to survive. Yet this individual power of reason is God's 'own essential action' (p. 285 above). It is the highest expression of freedom. For the laws of Nature are the laws of God's own Being; God is defined by them, just as a species of bird, or tree, or a human being, is defined by certain unalterable characteristics. To ask God to perform miracles is to ask Him to change His very Nature. This is not only presumptuous, but also absurd. For freedom in men can be effective only if the laws of Nature are strict and predictable. By reason these laws can be modified, and that is its purpose. The strict causal chains of events, by which one child is born gifted in every way, and another has every disadvantage, can be modified by men's intelligence, working in such fields as medicine, science, or education. The power is God's, but it must work through men. For only as an individual, standing momentarily as it were outside the chain of being, can the individual make a judgement or form an idea, which, becoming a new link in the causal chain, can modify it.

Man is wholly free in mind in such moments, and in that sense alone. He must be independent, if his power is to be effective. But in becoming free to do good he inevitably becomes free to do evil, for selfish ends. Thus evil is of two kinds: the evil due to Nature's strict laws, and evil due to man's selfish will. Man needs to realize that he is part of a living whole, and this he does only by feelings – feelings being the source from which his world of concepts actually grew. 'We are not alone in feeling, in sympathy, but we are alone in mind'; so art is 'the bridge between souls', says Cary.[4]

A great artist is someone who retains into adult life, and to an exceptional degree, the powers of intuition and imagination shared universally in childhood. His art begins with an intuition that 'surprises' him, Cary says, using this key word most strikingly in the opening of *Art and Reality*. But his greatness will depend also on his conceptual powers, and for these to have developed he will need to have been given a 'map' that his reason can accept or revolt against. Great art is the symbolic world, created from the conflict between reason and the new intuition (cf. p. 52 above). But in speaking of 'works' of art we are remembering that they result from the real labours of individuals, striving to give form to 'some personal and compelling experience'. Intuitions come from God himself, eternally urging men through sounds, colours, forms, to co-operate in realizing truth, beauty, and goodness in this world. Having grasped his intuition, the artist will be 'great' only if he succeeds in giving it a form that communicates it to other people. For art is indeed an 'infection', as Tolstoy said. The great artist's symbol of Reality may be 'fantastic, evil or mad, according to the form laid upon the complex of personal feeling'.[5] In this statement Cary doubtless includes 'Artist Hitler'.[6] For greatness in art is primarily the power to infect others with a strongly felt intuition. Whether we judge it good or evil depends on our moral code, which is manmade – though Cary insisted that there are basic values of 'Courage, duty, affection, loyalty, self-discipline, truth' (p. 82 above), and we 'differ only about their relative importance'. Hitler infected a new generation with a new arrangement of these values, and proved the significance of Cary's basic tenet: that every child begins life at the level of his stone-age ancestors, and learns the world anew. The spirit of goodness, or God's grace, as well as freedom, is reborn in every child, but must be educated. In a world ruled by Hitlers every child can readily be infected by such ideas.

As a symbol of Reality, a work of art can take many forms, and Cary realized that his own idea of life, as a 'metaphysical construction', was itself a work of art. He ends chapter 1 of *Art and Reality*:

It may be said that all works of art, all ideas of life, all philosophies are 'As if', but I am suggesting that they can be checked with an objective reality. They might be called propositions for truth and their truth can be decided by their correspondence with the real. Man can't change the elemental characters. If you could, the world would probably vanish into nothing. But because of their permanence, you can assemble them into new forms. . . . The creative soul needs the machine, as the living world needs a fixed character, or it could not exist at all. It would be merely an idea. But by a paradox we have to accept, part of this fixed character is the free mind, the creative imagination, in everlasting conflict with facts, including its own machinery, its own tools' (p. 7).

The creative imagination, as here defined, is the meeting point of artists, God and men.

An unpublished essay on the imagination, written by Cary on completing *The Horse's Mouth,* includes:

> Imaginative creation lays a pattern upon memory and the real by reassembly of physical elements, which are however only gateways to the imaginative act. . . .
> The activity is that of a creative imagination, all shot through with creativity beating against its characteristic limitations . . .
> We see the living earth as a branching forest of light . . .
> And Spinoza's attributes which he tells us come together only in the being of god, obstinately refuse to converge . . . .
> They are not in short seen to be necessary parts of the same being, which, without their conjunction, their complete fusing, could not be at all.[7]

It is on such terms that Cary is a philosophical novelist, and also a religious one, basing his convictions on aesthetic experience. Of the more traditional view of philosophy, he writes:

> The forms were invented to explain the world's order, for experience presented an order, a uniformity; as well as diversity; and both had to be explained. They can be explained only as aspects of a living whole, free and therefore diverse and unpredictable; but whole and therefore possessing relation between its attributes. But this wholeness and self consistency is that of a living character, which cannot be represented or imagined by any mathematical figure or logical construction. The mother knows her child and the child the mother, throughout life, but what formula can describe a relation between two free beings in continuous growth and change. . . .[8]

Of the creation of human societies, as the supreme creative, co-operative act of God and men, he writes:

We derive from elemental emotions in the elemental society of father, mother and child. In these elemental relations and this elemental society lie the roots of all our complex arts and law, authority and liberty. What changes everywhere and every day is the local convention, the social system, the imaginative construction in which these elemental affections and ambitions have to realize themselves . . . They produce the triumphs of science and art, the immense delights of life and also the everlasting revolution in which we are compelled to live.[9]

These quotations together suggest that the quality of a civilization depends on the way the father assumes his role. They suggest also that, for Cary, the new religious symbol so badly needed in our time (p. 38 above), is a symbol in which 'life is a gift' represents this trinity in a new way. The power to create it will derive from the creative imagination.

Cary's first published reference to the creative imagination is in *Power in Men,* which has as its theme: 'Because liberty is a certain kind of free power in men, governments and peoples must do certain things or be broken' (p. 241). A state will be broken, for example, if people cease to produce children. Therefore:

What can it answer to people who say, 'Why should we consider the future condition of any state?'?
The only possible answer by the state is this: 'Because I stand for something – for traditions, ideals which are worth preserving.'
190 [no. of para.]. The problem must be solved, of course, like all those raised by liberty, in liberty itself. The creative imagination will deal with its details as they arise. It is already beginning to see that having children is in itself a service to society and that the mother of a family carries an unequal burden (p. 158).

These words suggest that the creative imagination itself is evolving. Cary continues with practical suggestions for aid to mothers and families, which were very advanced in 1938, though now generally accepted. He then writes:

A democratic state which fails to solve this problem will disappear and be replaced not by servile states or brave new worlds but by another form of the democratic state in which a different social plan will give women the power to realize their natural creative liberty without the artificial restraints which now prevent it.

The misery, boredom, and waste of kindness which we see everywhere, especially among women, is not the necessary product of liberty, but of anarchy and tyranny, of atomism, of egotistic thought and a bad social education.

192 [no. of para.]. In some parts of Africa, women possess already this liberty denied in European states. She can always, if she choose, marry and bear children (p. 159).

The creative imagination appears again in *Power in Men,* and again with reference to motherhood. Cary is arguing against nationalism, yet recognizing that nationhood is rooted, finally, in the mother-child relation. This relates to his treatment of the 'real nature of the liberal crisis (p. 9 above). He says that it was wrong to condemn liberal leaders for supporting nationalism. For they knew:

that the real folly was to defy or ignore a passion which roots in the strongest instinct of man and moves his deepest feeling. For a nationalist, patriotism unites the natural law which is the strongest emotion of the heart with religious devotion which is the passion of a soul. It is not for nothing that men speak of the mother country and give to their ideals the names of women. Even when they speak of the father-land, they give it a woman's name and worship it as a woman. Thus they die for her literally as lovers and as worshippers in a passion of devotion far greater and richer than anything known to lovers of real women, or to any but those few lovers of God whose mystical power has been able to bring them the ecstasy of vision.

. . .

Love and the creative imagination of poets can do great evil and great good, but they are the very springs of man's life. To say to a man 'You shall not love' is to say 'You shall not live like a man, but like a machine.' It is either useless or it destroys the man as a man (pp. 168–9).

Love and the creative imagination in the greatest of men have thus chiefly shaped our world, according to this deepest feeling, which explains everything written in this study about the place of the mother in religious and political thinking – above all in Cary's own life. It was in this relation that he traced his convictions back to Raffalovich, who is understandably, therefore, the key to *Castle Corner*, which Cary wrote concurrently with *Power in Men*. Like Nussbaum in that novel, Raffalovich's real mother found him too ugly to love. In *Castle Corner*, too, Cary showed his understanding of his imperialist self: Cock Jarvis performed an incredible feat of patriotic heroism, for love of a mother country whom he was serving the more fervently, because his love for Stella, his real 'star', had been thwarted. This had happened as a result of the key debate between Mary and Helen, on the very subject discussed in our last paragraph.[10]

It was with regard to *Castle Corner* that Cary wrote of his conviction: that we have reached a turning point in time, when men have at last realized that there is no supernatural providence, and man is responsible for his own fate (p. 140 above). This too suggests that, in creating a new religious symbol, what is particularly needed is a more realistic, responsible notion of fatherhood.

Any doubts regarding Cary's intentions are dispelled by the close of *Art and Reality*. 'The churches use all the arts', he says, 'to give us back only one single piece of real knowledge, the experience of goodness, of the good man, as an ultimate fact, something we cannot dodge, and something that, when we know it, changes the whole nature of things for our feeling, and gives a new meaning to our world' (p. 170). This expression of 'life is a gift' is immediately illustrated by Cary, with reference to *Tess of the D'Urbervilles*, where Tess christens her illegitimate dying baby in the washbasin, and gets her little brothers and sisters out of bed to act as congregation. Her education tells her that she has been wicked to bring the child into the world ' "without any father to look after it" ', and that now it will go to Hell. 'But she says "perhaps God will forgive it if it has some kind of christening." ' This scene 'never loses its power and significance for us', says Cary. For 'Hardy takes that oldest relation of mother and child and gives it a new aspect for us. He shows Tess as responsible for the child's soul, and he shows it in a dramatic form. He renews for us also the christening service, because it is

Tess, the mother, with all her obsessive anxiety for that child's salvation, who performs it' (pp. 171–2). Cary immediately opens the next and final chapter with:

> What is commoner than mother-love? It is a platitude, vulgarised, a joke in the music-halls. It is, as symbol, such a bore that the modern fashion, at least among writers who are afraid to deal with a fundamental real because it seems to them too ordinary, too trite, who seek not the new expression but some new concept, is to represent it as an evil. But Hardy, as a great writer, deals only with great and simple issues.

This relates directly to Cary's own intuition, that we know unselfish goodness in the relationship of mothers and children. It is this intuition that dominates his series of novels. But he could not have written of it as he did if he had not been given a new insight into his own role as a father.

Cary thought Hardy a great writer because he reveals 'that what makes life worth living are such common things as family love'. He says also of Hardy: 'The more we recede from him in time, the greater he seems. . . . He is master, like Shakespeare, of the great dramatic scene . . . such scenes of which we can hardly put the meaning into words, and, like Shakespeare, he goes to great lengths to contrive them' (*Art and Reality*, pp. 168–9). Here is Cary's clue to his own standard of greatness. His general method was to give a clear hint of his theme on his opening page, and to build up to a final dramatic scene, to which indeed 'we can hardly put the meaning into words'. Understandably, therefore, full meaning of these scenes has by no means been conveyed in this book. But enough has been said, and illustrated, to show that Cary deserves to be read beside any other English writer of our century, to whom the epithet 'great' has been applied. His books give a new, and richer, experience at each re-reading, especially if read as 'chapters of one work', and they reflect a 'whole view of life'. Cary's final comment regarding the artist is that he achieves 'education of the whole man again', by means of 'the charged symbol'. He does so 'as teacher or expositor, as creator of meanings'.[11] Cary can achieve that in his readers.

He was aware himself that his unorthodox views would not readily win converts, as his letter to Schorer shows (p. 4 above).

But the following note, expressing a viewpoint, surely also expresses a private wish: 'Why does the original artist i.e. Manet, Joyce finally make his way against prejudice – because people are looking for the new sensation and when someone shews them how to get it they seize it".[12] Perhaps readers will recognize from this study that Cary too offers 'the new sensation'.

He would indeed have been heartened by Bernard Levin's recent articles, putting him 'in the very next rank to the greatest of them all' – here naming with others, Dostoevsky, Tolstoy and Balzac.[13] Levin praises Cary's 'understanding of the complexity of the human soul', his capacity to enter into the mind and heart of characters, and his mastery of dialogue. He calls Cary a *'for* man', in 'the cause of yes against no', and says he is 'a life-enhancer' because he conveys the feeling that the universe makes 'glorious sense'. All these statements are borne out by this study.

Though Cary appears to have suffered eclipse in recent years, and has never won recognition as a great writer in the highest academic circles in England, nevertheless his influence may have been far greater than is realized. Public libraries are well stocked with his books, which are always being read, in any part of England, librarians report. Certainly the world, for women especially, has changed a good deal since he wrote, and no one can say what his influence has been, because it is the nature of his art to influence readers subconsciously.

This may be true also of his influence on African politics. His new and enlarged edition of *The Case for African Freedom* was written because the first had received 'so much support in many different circles', and 'established itself as an indispensable guide to the intricacies of the problems of African development'.[14] Certainly his forecasts regarding Africa, and its vital place in the post-war world, have been largely fulfilled. In his foreword to the first edition George Orwell wrote: 'He has an unusually independent mind, and many readers will feel a certain relief in reading a book on a political subject by a man who has thought deeply over the problems of our time, and has been above current political movements and their characteristic jargon.'

Cary's independent mind made him appreciated in other fields outside the purely literary. Thus Lord Brain, the eminent neurologist, an authority on the imagination from this viewpoint, found inspiration in *Art and Reality,* saying: 'his book is full of pregnant insights into the part played by what he calls the symbol, but I should prefer to term the image, in art.'[15]

As a religious broadcaster, Douglas Stewart regarded Cary as 'not simply the great Protestant, but the great Christian novelist of our time'. He stated this view in a series of lectures on great modern novelists,[16] his theme being 'that the authors here studied are living voices who have a message not simply for the world but for the Church, and that the Church in all her forms is impoverished by her deafness'.[17] His judgement of Cary deserves a place in Cary criticism, because he so fully understood that: 'What we have in these books is indeed a gospel vision of humanity. All the characters are seen through a charity, a compassion, which is vaster than their sin. It is a Christ's-eye view we are sharing . . . of the whole race of types and characters who crowd these pages.'[18]

Regarding his religious views, Cary told John Fischer that he was essentially 'a hot gospeller', whose books were his pulpit, because a soap box was unsuitable for his truth. He also told him, in connexion with the proposed book on religion, that he had discussed his ideas with David Cecil, who found them very interesting and original too.[19] In his introduction to *The Captive and the Free,* David Cecil has written: 'Cary did not identify God with Christ or with any kind of personal spirit. But experience had convinced him that man's apprehension of beauty and of human love was inexplicable on any purely rational or materialist terms. It was proof of some transcendental spiritual reality with which a man must relate himself harmoniously if he is to find satisfaction.'[20] It is difficult to reconcile these words with Cary's belief in God 'as a person', 'the person of the universe', in whom he felt 'my being as part of his being', and beauty, goodness and love as personal feelings, known 'by his grace', since 'the life of the world is the nature of God'. Clearly it is not easy to explain Cary's faith. But its effect is unmistakable when Lord David continues: 'It burned within him, an intuitive conviction . . . strengthening his spirit and directing his actions. To be often in his company was to be aware of its presence.'

It seems evident that Cary did succeed in uniting greatness and goodness – freedom and grace – in his own person, as both man and writer. Of course he had faults. In his writing they stem chiefly from an over-creative imagination, and perhaps an over-eagerness to preach his creed. But these are the kinds of faults recognizable in the greatest. They have not been stressed in this study, because its object has been to make Cary's theme and view of life understood. As a man he had ordinary human failings. Enid Starkie describes him as 'one of the most lovable people I have ever known . . . utterly genuine and good'.[21] Yet interviews with many other people revealed that he could be selfish, thoughtless, and unsympathetic, at least, in earlier years. He could adopt a superior tone that made him seem a snob. His compassion and understanding, particularly towards children, apparently grew as his theme became absorbed into his personality. With his illness, his appreciation of kindness indeed became one with his theme.

How far 'life is a gift' became his 'whole view' can be judged from Lord David Cecil's tribute in *The Times* of 4 April 1957:

Joyce Cary combined a courage to face the harshest facts without flinching with a deep spiritual wisdom and a chivalrous tenderness of heart that made him immediately forget any trouble of his own in his quick, ardent understanding sympathy for others. . . . He was unself-pitying and apparently even cheerful; he went on working to within a week of his death; he never seemed to lose his responsive, affectionate interest in the outside world. So that even when he was wholly paralysed and expecting to die at any moment it was he who gave faith in life to his friends, rather than they who gave it to him. With awe and humility and grateful love, they remember him.

Bibliography 1:
Chronology of Joyce Cary's Published Writings within a Framework of his Life

---

The following list contains all the published writings of Joyce Cary that I have so far traced, and includes published interviews. It is an expansion of the list published in the *Bodleian Library Record*, Vol. VIII, No. 4 (April 1970), from which all items appear here by permission of the Bodleian Library. Additional material has necessitated the changes made to that list.

The order of published items follows the order of first publication, as nearly as this could be ascertained. A subsequent first publication in the United Kingdom or America is also listed. But later publications elsewhere are not listed, except to show changes of title or content.

The right-hand marginal letters classify the writing thus: P (Poem), S (Story), N (Novel), T (Treatise and memoir, a monograph), E (Essay, article or review), L (Letter), Q (Interview, talk, or quoted broadcast). The numbers following these letters give the chronology within each classification. For the significance of the asterisks, see *Spring Song and Other Stories* (item S.49–53 below); for the daggers, see *Joyce Cary Selected Essays* (E.80–82).

The chronological arrangement draws attention to Cary's development and concurrent use of different literary forms, and the relation of his non-fiction to his fiction. The biographical framework gives an idea of the private and public worlds from which the writing grew. Of necessity it omits much – notably annual holidays, and the many occasions, from 1942, when Cary lectured, by invitation, to audiences in universities, British Council gatherings, his own school, and cultural and political groups throughout the UK. Only overseas lectures are mentioned, to affirm his world-wide reputation.[1]

Unless otherwise stated, the name used for authorship was *Joyce Cary*. For the pseudonym *Thomas Joyce*, see p. 57 above.

1888	Arthur Joyce Lunel Cary, first child of Arthur and Charlotte Cary, born at the home of his maternal grandparents, James and Helen Joyce, in Londonderry, Dec. 7.
1892	His brother John born, Jan. 28.
1898	His mother dies at home, 41 Kitto Rd, London, Oct. 1.
1900	His father marries Dora Stevenson, a cousin.
	The family moves to 70 Duke's Avenue, Chiswick.
	Enters Hurstleigh prep. school, Tunbridge Wells, as a boarder, with his brother, Sept.
1902	His half-brother Anthony born, Oct. 30.
1903	Enters Clifton College, Sept.
1904	His half-sister Shiela born, Jan. 15.
	His stepmother dies, May 8.
	His brother John leaves Hurstleigh to enter the Royal Naval College, Dartmouth.
	He spends a sketching holiday in Normandy, summer.
	Is confirmed in the Anglican faith, autumn.

1906   'A Lawn, and in the midst a Silken Pool' [anon.].   P.1
The Cliftonian, XIX (June 1906), 194, 195.
Leaves Clifton to study art in Paris, July.

1907   Enters School of Art (soon to become the College of Art), Edinburgh, Jan.
His father marries Mary Agar, Jan.
The family move to 42 Grosvenor Road, Gunnersbury, ca. March.

1908   *Verse* by Arthur Cary. Edinburgh: Robert Grant,   P.2–
July 1908.   P.14

1909   Enters Trinity College, Oxford University, Oct.

1910   'Thus Crime is Punished by Thomas Joyce.[2]   S.1
Idler, XXXVII (May 1910), 895–8.
In Paris with John Middleton Murry, Dec. 27 to mid-Jan.

1912   Leaves Oxford for 10 Store St, London, to write.
Arrives in Antivari, Montenegro, Nov. 20.
Joins Red Cross; writing 'Memoir of the Bobotes'.

1913   Returns to England, May.

Receives Oxford degree in law, June.

Joins Sir Horace Plunkett's Cooperative Society in Ireland, but finds services unwanted, Aug.

1914   Enters the Imperial Institute, Jan. 12.

Appointed Assistant District Officer, Northern Nigerian Political Service, April 29.

1915   Appointed 2nd Lieut. in the West African Field Force.

Wounded in attack on Mora Mountain, Sept. 1.

1916   Granted leave in England, March 26.

Marries Gertrude Margaret Ogilvie, June 1.

Sails from Liverpool for Lagos, Aug. 9.

1917   Returns to civilian rank, Asst. District Officer, Jan.

First son, Arthur Lucius Michael (known as Michael), born April 3.

1918   Arrives in Liverpool on leave, Feb. 1.

Commences twelve months' tour of Borgu, Aug. 24.

Second son, Peter, born Dec. 9.

1919   Returns record of his Borgu tour, Dec. 10.

1920   Medical exam. 'proceeding on leave', Jan. 6.

Retires from Nigerian Service; buys 12 Parks Rd, Oxford, April.

'Bussa History' [by] Authorities, Mr Harry Kemble,   E.1
Police Officer, and Mr A. J. L. Cary, ADO.
Gazetteer of the Kontagora Province. Compiled by Mr E. C. Duff from Provincial Records. Revised by Major W. Hamilton, DSO, with Additional Notes. Printed London: Waterlow & Sons, 1920, pp. 23–24.

'Variant' by Mr Carey [sic] and Mr P. R. Diggle,   E.2
ADO. Ibid, pp. 24–26.

'Borgu Languages, Etc.' [by] Authority, .   E.3
Mr A. J. L. Cary, ADO. Ibid, pp. 70–72.

'Lombrosine' by Thomas Joyce. *Saturday Evening*   S.2
Post (31 Jan. 1920), 30, 32, 62; [published as] 'Experimental Love' by Thomas Joyce. *Pearson's Magazine,* L (July 1920), 41–47.

'The Springs of Youth' by Thomas Joyce. *Saturday*   S.3
Evening Post (6 March 1920), 30, 32, 189, 190.

'The Idealist' by Thomas Joyce. *Saturday Evening*   S.4
Post (13 March 1920), 40, 42.

'The Cure' by Thomas Joyce.[3] *Saturday Evening*   S.5
Post (1 May 1920), 30, 99.

'The Reformation' by Thomas Joyce. *Saturday*   S.6
Evening Post (22 May 1920), 20, 21, 124;
[published as] 'The Sins of the Mothers' by
Thomas Joyce. *Grand Magazine,* XXXVII
(July 1920), 439–46.

'A Piece of Honesty' by Thomas Joyce. *Saturday*   S.7
Evening Post (26 June 1920), 66, 69, 70.

'The Bad Samaritan' by Thomas Joyce.[4] *Saturday*   S.8
Evening Post (3 July 1920), 40, 42, 44, 46.

'A Consistent Woman' by Thomas Joyce. *Saturday*   S.9
Evening Post (21 Aug. 1920), 30, 32, 81, 82.

'None but the Brave' by Thomas Joyce. *Saturday*   S.10
Evening Post (11 Sept. 1920), 18, 19, 100, 104,
107, 110.

'Salute to Propriety' by Thomas Joyce. *Saturday*   S.11
Evening Post (9 Oct. 1920), 40, 42, 45, 46;
Hutchinson's Magazine, IV (Jan. 1921), 54–65.

1921   ' "On the Line" An Academy Story' by T. Joyce.[5]   S.12
Strand Magazine, LXI (May 1921), 454–60.

'The Uncle' by Thomas Joyce. *Hutchinson's*   S.13
Magazine, IV (June 1921), 601–15.

'The Failure' by T. Joyce. *Strand Magazine,* LXII   S.14
(Oct. 1921), 369–77.

1922   Visits Hungary with members of Oxford Univ.,
July.

1923   'Not Wholly Matrimony' by Thomas Joyce. *Strand*   S.15
Magazine, LXVI (Dec. 1923), 655–65.

1925   Third son, Tristram, born May 14.

1926   Works on Hays Wharf London during General
Strike, May.

1927   Fourth son, George, born Aug. 12.

1932   *Aissa Saved.*[6] London: Ernest Benn, 1932 [Jan.];   N.1
New York: Harper, 1962. [See E.26.]

1933   *An American Visitor.* London: Ernest Benn, 1933   N.2
[Aug.]; New York: Harper, 1961.
[See E.31.]

1936 [Criticism of Gilbert Spencer's wall painting at   E.4
Holywell Manor, anonymous; under 'A Spectator's
Notebook'.] *Spectator* (20 March 1936), 502.

The African Witch. London: Victor Gollancz, 1936   N.3
[May; a Book Society choice]; New York:
William Morrow, 1936. [See E.24.]

1937 His father dies, at Wadeford, Somerset, Nov. 23.

1938 *Castle Corner.* London: Victor Gollancz, 1938   N.4
[Jan.; a Book Society recommendation]; New
York: Harper, 1963. [See E.32.]

1939 'The Foundation of Liberalism.' *Spectator*   L.1
(17 March 1939), 450

Power in Men. London: Nicholson & Watson, for   T.1
the Liberal Book Club, 1939 [May]; Seattle:
University of Washington Press, 1963.
Declines invitation to be a Liberal Parliamentary
candidate, May.

Mister Johnson. London: Victor Gollancz, 1939   N.5
[July]; New York: Harper, 1951. [See E.27.]
Serves as an air-raid warden, from Sept. to 1945.

1940 *Charley is my Darling.* London: Michael Joseph,   N.6
1940 [April; a Book Society recommendation];
New York: Harper, 1960. [See E.23.]

1941 *A House of Children.* London: Michael Joseph,   N.7
1941 [Feb.; awarded the James Tait Black
Memorial Prize, 1941]; New York: Harper, 1956.
[See E.22.]

The Case for African Freedom. London: Secker   T.2
and Warburg, 1941 [July]; revised and enlarged
edition, 1944 [revised text, without the introduction
written by George Orwell for the first version].
*The Case for African Freedom and other writings
on Africa by Joyce Cary,* University of Texas Press
(1962), 1–136; 'Co-ops for Africa?' [condensed
from *The Case for African Freedom*]. *World
Digest* (May 1945), 44–47.

Herself Surprised. London: Michael Joseph, 1941   N.8
[Nov.; a Book Society recommendation]; New
York: Harper, 1948. [1st book of 1st tril.; see
also E.15, E.78.]

1942   Attends Civil Defence Course in Bournemouth,
        April 27 to May 2.

      'Britain's Colonial Record.' *Bulletins from Britain*,   E.5
        no. 104 (26 Aug. 1942), 7–10.

      To be a Pilgrim. London: Michael Joseph, 1942   N.9
        [Oct.]; New York: Harper, 1949. [2nd book of
        1st tril.; see also E.16, E.78.]

      'Joyce Cary or What is Freedom?' [interview   Q.1
        conducted by Stanley Parker]. *Oxford Mail*
        (15 Dec. 1942), 3.

1943   Sails for Freetown as script writer with
        Thorold Dickinson, to make film *Men of Two
        Worlds*, Jan. 17.

      Flies in stages to Dar es Salaam; home on May 20.

      'Tolstoy's Theory of Art' [from a lecture entitled   E.6†
        'Tolstoy on Art and Morals' delivered at the Univ.
        of Edinburgh on 27 Nov. 1942]. *University of
        Edinburgh Journal*, XII (Summer 1943), 91–96.

      'African Politics.' *London Calling*, no. 209   E.7
        (1943), 15.

      Process of Real Freedom. London: Michael Joseph,   T.3
        1943 [Nov.].
        Revises *The Case for African Freedom*,
        with a new introduction as first chapter.[7]

1944   *The Horse's Mouth*. London: Michael Joseph,   N.10
        1944 [Aug.; a Book Society recommendation];
        New York: Harper, 1950 [a Book-of-the-Month
        Club selection]. [3rd book of 1st tril.; see also
        E.17, E.78.]

1945   *Marching Soldier*. London: Michael Joseph, 1945   P.15
        [March].

      'Bush River.' *Windmill*, 1, no. 2 (1945), 120–5;   S.16**
        [revised for publication in] *Esquire* (US), XLII
        (July 1954), 40, 106–7 [British edn., vol. I].

      'Sonnet.' *Modern Reading No. 13*. Ed. Reginald   P.16
        Moore. London: Wells, Gardner, Darton
        (1945), 19.

      Finally revises script of *Men of Two Worlds*,
        June 19.[8]

1946   Tours India on film project with Thorold Dickinson,
        Jan. 3 to mid-April.

The Moonlight. London: Michael Joseph, 1946   N.11
[May; a Book Society recommendation]; New
York: Harper, 1947. [See E.33.]

Britain and West Africa. London: Longmans,   T.4
Green, 1946 [Aug.]; rev. edn, 1947; [revised text].
*The Case for African Freedom and other writings
on Africa by Joyce Cary,* University of Texas
Press (1962), 137–200.

1947 *The Drunken Sailor: A Ballad-Epic.* London: P.17
Michael Joseph, 1947 [Nov.].

1948 His wife has an operation for cancer, April 28.
Spends a holiday in Switzerland with his wife,
Aug. 15 to Sept. 1.

1949 'Dinner at the Beeders' [excerpt from *The Horse's*   S.17
Mouth]. *Harper's Magazine,* CXCIX (Sept. 1949),
38–46.

A Fearful Joy. London: Michael Joseph, 1949   N.12
[Oct.]; New York: Harper, 1950. [See E.28.]

'On the Function of the Novelist.' *New York*   E.8†
Times Book Review (30 Oct. 1949), 1, 52;
Joyce Cary Selected Essays. Ed. A. G. Bishop.
London, Michael Joseph (1976), 150–3.

Declines the award of a CBE, Dec. 5.

His wife dies, Dec. 13.

1950 'The Way a Novel Gets Written.' *Harper's*   E.9†
Magazine, CC (Feb. 1950), 87–93; *Adam
International Review,* XVIII, nos. 212–13
(November–December 1950), 3–11.

'Introduction.' *Man in Ebony* by Denys Craig.   E.10
London, Victor Gollancz (1950), 9–12.

'L'Art.' *New York Times Book Review*   E.11
(12 March 1950), 8.

'A Novel is a Novel is a Novel.' *New York Times*   E.12†
Book Review (30 April 1950), 1, 34; *Adam
International Review,* XVIII, nos. 212–13
(November- December 1950), 1–3; [abridged as]
'This Age of Labels.' *Books and Authors*
(September–October 1950), 15–17; [adapted as]
'Lust und Leid des Definierens.' Trans.
H. J. Hansen. *Die Welt* (30 Jan. 1951), 5.

'Introduction. The Old Strife at Plant's.'   E.13
[See S.18.]

'The Old Strife at Plant's' [a discarded chapter of   S.18
The Horse's Mouth]. With an Introduction by the
author. *Harper's Magazine*, CCI (Aug. 1950),
80–96; *World Review* (Feb. 1951), 45–62; [the
introduction appears as 'Author's Note' on
pp. 43–44 of] 100 copies with illustrations by the
author, at the New Bodleian, Oxford, 1956
[which differs slightly from the first version].

'Joyce Cary' [in] 'Important Authors of the Fall,   E.14†
Speaking for Themselves'. *New York Herald
Tribune Book Review* (8 Oct. 1950), 10;
[published as] 'Speaking for Myself.' *Joyce Cary
Selected Essays*. Ed. A. G. Bishop. London:
Michael Joseph (1976), 19–20.

'Umaru.' *Cornhill Magazine*, CLXV (Winter   S.19**
1950/1951), 50–54.

'Three New Prefaces' [subtitled] *Herself Surprised,*   E.15
To be a Pilgrim, The Horse's Mouth'. Adam   E.16
International Review, XVIII, nos. 212–13   E.17
(November–December 1950), 11–14. [Published
separately as:] 'Prefatory Essay'. *Herself
Surprised*, Carfax ed., London, Michael Joseph
(1951), 7–8; 'Prefatory Essay'. *To be a Pilgrim,*
Carfax ed. (1951), 7–8; 'Prefatory Essay'. *The
Horse's Mouth,* Carfax ed. (1951), 7–10.

'The Novelist at Work: a Conversation between   Q.2
Joyce Cary and Lord David Cecil.' Transcribed
from a Telediphone Recording made on 7 July
1950 (by courtesy of the BBC). *Adam
International Review*, XVIII, nos. 212–13
(November–December 1950), 15–25.

1951   Tours the United States, lecturing, Jan. 2 to
April 21.

'A Talk with Joyce Cary' [conducted by Harvey   Q.3
Breit]. *New York Times Book Review* (18 Feb.
1951), 14.

'The Revolution of the Women.' *Vogue* (US),   E.18
CXVII (15 March 1951), 99, 100, 149.

['Young Writers Reply . . . points of view' on   L.2
'Is there a future for young writers?' by Stephen
Spender.] *News Chronicle* (1 April 1952), 2.

'Including Mr Micawber.' *New York Times Book*   E.19†
Review (15 April 1951), 4, 21; *Joyce Cary
Selected Essays.* Ed. A. G. Bishop. London,
Michael Joseph (1976), 172–5.

'Africa Yesterday: One Ruler's Burden.'   E.20†
Reporter (15 May 1951), 21–24; *The Case for
African Freedom and other writings by Joyce
Cary,* University of Texas Press (1962), 201–9.

'What Does Art Create?' *Literature and Life,* II,   E.21
Addresses to the English Association by
Margaret Willy [et al.] London, Harrap (1951),
32–45.

'A Special Occasion.' *Harper's Magazine,* CCIII   S.20**
(Sept. 1951), 97–98; *Cornhill Magazine,* CLXV
(Winter 1951/1952), 387–9.

'Prefatory Essay.' *A House of Children,* Carfax ed.   E.22
([Oct.] 1951), 5–8.

'Prefatory Essay.' *Charley is my Darling,* Carfax   E.23
ed. ([Oct.] 1951), 5–10.

'Prefatory Essay.' *The African Witch,* Carfax   E.24
ed. ([Oct.] 1951), 9–13.

1952   'The Front Line Feeling.' *Listener* (17 Jan. 1952),   E.25
92–93.

Gives a course of three lectures entitled 'The
Novel as Truth' at Oxford University, Jan. 27
to Feb. 10.

'Prefatory Essay.' *Aissa Saved,* Carfax ed.   E.26
([Feb.] 1952), 5–11.

'Prefatory Essay.' *Mister Johnson,* Carfax ed.   E.27
([Feb.] 1952), 5–10.

'Prefatory Essay.' *A Fearful Joy,* Carfax ed.   E.28
([Feb.] 1952), 5–8

'The Mass Mind: Our Favourite Folly.' *Harper's*   E.29
Magazine, CCIV (March 1952), 25–27;
[published as] 'Myth of the Mass Mind: a
Modern Catchword'. *Cornhill Magazine,* CLXVI
(Summer 1952), 138–42; [published as] 'Myth of
the Mass Mind'. *Reader's Digest,* LXII (Feb.

1953), 135–6; [condensed and translated as] 'Le mythe
de "l'homme robot" '. *Sélection du Reader's
Digest*, XIII (Sept. 1953), 150, 152, 154.

'Personality' [on Sir A. P. Herbert; anon.]. *Time*,   E.30
LIX (10 March 1952), 45 [Atlantic ed., p. 25].

'Prefatory Essay.' *An American Visitor*, Carfax   E.31
ed. ([May] 1952), 7–11.

'Prefatory Essay.' *Castle Corner*, Carfax ed.   E.32
([May] 1952), 5–8.

'Prefatory Essay.' *The Moonlight*, Carfax ed.   E.33
([May] 1952), 5–11.

'A Message from Joyce Cary.' . . . from the talk   Q.4
which he gave as Guest of Honour at the
League's At-Home on March 18. *Books.
Journal of the National Book League*, no. 270
(April–May 1952), 33–34.

'Success Story.' *Harper's Magazine*, CCIV   S.21**
(June 1952), 74–76.

'The Ugliest Trend' [comments on censorship by   E.34
several authors], Joyce Cary. *Author*, LXII
(Summer 1952), 84–85.

'The Sources of Tension in America.' *Saturday   E.35†
Review* (23 Aug. 1952), 6, 7, 35; *Joyce Cary
Selected Essays*. Ed. A. G. Bishop. London,
Michael Joseph (1976), 220–6.

Prisoner of Grace. London: Michael Joseph, 1952   N.13
[Sept.]; New York: Harper, 1952 [Oct.].
[1st book of 2nd tril.; see also E.46.]

'Joyce Cary puts a tumult into the words of one   Q.5
woman' [interview conducted by Nancy Spain,
with a review of *Prisoner of Grace*]. *Daily
Express* (15 Sept. 1952), 4; *Winnipeg Tribune*
(4 Oct. 1952).

'Romance.' *Time* (20 Oct. 1952, 119 [Atlantic   S.22**
ed., p. 47].

'Joyce Cary Replies' [to a letter of 20 Sept.,   L.3
criticizing 'The Sources of Tension in America'].
Saturday Review (1 Nov. 1952), 21.

'Evangelist.' *Harper's Magazine*, CCV (Nov.   S.23*
1952), 88–89; *Harper's Bazaar* (British), LI
(May 1954), 68–69.

'The Period Novel.' *Spectator* (21 Nov. 1952), 684.   E.36†

1953   'Look Out for Labels.' *This Week Magazine*   E.37
       (4 Jan. 1953), 2.

His youngest son, George, dies, Jan. 9.

'Revolutionary Leaders' [a brief quotation from a   Q.6
broadcast, 'Freedom and Power', BBC European
Service].[9] *Valetta Bulletin,* Malta (10 Jan. 1953).

'Proposals for Peace – III.' *Nation* (10 Jan.   E.38
1953), 28.

'Introduction' [from a MS. entitled 'On the Little   E.39
Magazine']'. *Chance,* 2nd (Jan. 1953), 8-9.

'My First Novel.' *Listener* (16 April 1953), 637-8.   E.40

'The Oxford Scholar.' *Holiday,* XIII (June 1953),   E.41
96, 98, 100, 132, 134, 136, 137, 139–43.

'Babes in the Wood.' *Evening News* (28 May   S.24**
1953), 9.

'Why They Say "God Save the Queen".' *New*   E.42
York Times Magazine (31 May 1953), 7.

Receives honorary degree, Doctor of Laws,
Edinburgh University, July 3.

'A Date.' *New Yorker* (1 Aug. 1953), 56–58;   S.25*
[published as] 'Red Letter Day.' *Punch*
(21 Oct. 1953), 478–80.

Tours the United States, lecturing, Aug. 10 to
Dec. 8.

Except the Lord. New York: Harper, 1953   N.14
[12 Nov.]; London: Michael Joseph, 1953
[16 Nov.] [2nd book of 2nd tril.]

'A Child's Religion.' *Vogue* (US), CXXII   E.43†
(Dec. 1953), 86–87; *Family Doctor,* IV
(Aug. 1954), 440, 442.

'Buying a Horse.' *Punch* (2 Dec. 1953), 654–6.   S.26**

'Christmas in Africa.' *Esquire,* XL (Dec. 1953),   E.44†
101, 208; *The Case for African Freedom and*
other writings on Africa by Joyce Cary (1962),
211–17.

1954   'Spring Song.' *London Magazine,* I (March 1954),   S.27**
       29–31.

'Is the World Getting Anywhere?' *Vogue* (US),   E.45
CXXIII (15 March 1954), 68–71; [published as]

'The Idea of Progress.' *Cornhill Magazine,*
CLXVII (Summer 1954), 331–7.

Lectures in Turin, Genoa, Milan, Rome,
March 19–23.

Stays in Nice and Menton, March 25 to April 1.

'Prefatory Essay.' *Prisoner of Grace,* Carfax ed.   E.46
([22 March] 1954), 5–8.

'Glorious Expectations' [excerpt from the novel   S.28
Except the Lord]. *World Digest* (April 1954), 3–6.

'The Limit.' *Esquire* (US) XLI (June 1954), 43;   S.29*
Esquire (British) I (June 1954), 43.

'Speaking of Books' [from a MS. entitled   E.47
'Character on the Manhattan Boat']. *New York
Times Book Review* (6 June 1954), 2; [published
as] 'Character on a Manhattan Steamboat:
Inspiration and the Subconscious.' *Irish Writing,*
no. 30 (March 1955), 34–37.

'Barney Magonagel.' *New Yorker* (19 June 1954),   E.48†
27–31; *Joyce Cary Selected Essays.* Ed. A. G.
Bishop. London, Michael Joseph (1976), 32–42.

Lectures in Cologne, Frankfurt, Marburg, Mainz,
Freiburg, Stuttgart, Tübingen, Munich, Berlin,
June 29 to July 14.

'Switzerland.' *Holiday,* XVI (Aug. 1954), 27–29,   E.49
32–33, 36–37.

'Notes sur l'art et la liberté.' Trans.   E.50
A. Proudhommeaux. *Preuves, XLII* (Aug. 1954),
28–32.

[On the Censorship of Boccaccio.] *Times* (London)   L.4
(2 Aug. 1954), 7.

'A Novelist and his Public.' *Listener* (30 Sept.   E.51†
1954), 521, 522; *Saturday Review* (27 Nov. 1954),
11, 36, 37.

'On this Side of the Channel.' *Adam International*   L.5
Review, XXII, nos. 241–242–243 (1954), 18–19.

'Catching up with History' [a review of Richard   E.52
Wright's *Black Power*]. *Nation* (16 Oct. 1954,
332, 333; *The Case for African Freedom and
other writings on Africa by Joyce Cary* (1962),
219–24.

Lectures at the British Institute, Paris, Oct. 27.

'Party of One [subtitled on the contents page] –   E.53
Anglo–American Relations.' *Holiday*, XVI
(Nov. 1954), 6, 8, 11, 12, 97.

Lectures in Stockholm, Uppsala, Helsinki, Malmo,
and Copenhagen, Nov. 30–Dec. 8.

'An Interview with Joyce Cary' [conducted by   Q.7†
John Burrows and Alex. Hamilton]. *Paris
Review*, II, 7 (Winter 1954–5), 63–78; *Writers at
Work: The Paris Review Interviews*. Ed. Malcolm
Cowley. London, Secker & Warburg (1958),
47–62; New York, Viking (1958), 51–67.

'A Good Investment.' *Harper's Magazine*, CCIX   S.30*
(Dec. 1954), 64–72.

1955 'The Heart of England.' *Holiday*, XVII   E.54†
(Jan. 1955), 27, 28, 30, 76, 78, 79, 81; *Joyce Cary
Selected Essays*. Ed. A. G. Bishop. London,
Michael Joseph (1976), 189–203.

Aboard a plane that crashes at take-off, but boards
next flight for Athens, Jan. 16; gives 9 lectures –
in Athens, Corfu, Salonica, Nicosia, Limassol,
Famagusta; returns Feb. 4.

'Auktoritet och Upror' [translator not named].   E.55
Dagens Nyheter (30 Jan. 1955), 5.

'Religionen Friketens Forsvar' [translator not   E.56
named]. *Dagens Nyheter* (1 Feb. 1955), 3.

Becomes a hospital out-patient, treated for
paralysis developing in his leg, Feb. 11.

'Carmagnole.' *London Magazine*, II (Feb. 1955),   S.31**
37–39.

'Horror Comics.' *Spectator* (18 Feb. 1955), 177.   E.57†

'The Censorship Plot.' *Spectator* (11 March 1955),   E.58
275–6.

[In reply to Mr Cotton, on 'Horror Comics'].   L.6
Spectator (1 April 1955), 390–1.

Not Honour More. London: Michael Joseph, 1955   N.15
[April; a Book Society recommendation];
New York: Harper, 1955 [May]. [3rd book of
2nd tril.]

'A Glory of the Moon.' *Mademoiselle* (US), XLI   S.32**
(May 1955), 101, 156.

'L'Influence britannique dans la révolution   E.59†

libérale.' Trans. M. Bouvier. *Comprendre,*
nos. 13–14 (June 1955), 45–51; [published as]
'Britain's Liberal Influence.' *Joyce Cary Selected
Essays.* Ed. A. G. Bishop. London, Michael
Joseph (1976), 210–19.

'Speaking of Books' [from a MS. entitled 'Form   E.60
and Meaning (A Slice of Life)']. *New York
Times Book Review* (26 June 1955), 2.

'Out of Hand.' *Vogue* (US), CXXVI (July 1955),   S.33**
60–62; *She* (Sept. 1956), 28–29.

'Notes on the Way. Can Western Values Survive   E.61
Without Religion?' *Time and Tide* (9 June
1955), 901–2.

'Notes on the Way. Faith in Liberty.' *Time and   E.62
Tide* (16 July 1955), 933–4.

'Le roman à thèse.' Trans. Christine Lalou. *Les   E.63†
nouvelles littéraires* (11 Aug. 1955), 1, 2;
[published as] 'Morality and the Novelist'.
Joyce Cary Selected Essays. Ed. A. G. Bishop.
London, Michael Joseph (1976), 154–64.

'Policy for Aid.' *Confluence,* IV, 3 (1955),   E.64†
292–301; *Joyce Cary Slected Essays.* Ed.
A. G. Bishop. London, Michael Joseph (1976),
97–106.

Learns that his illness is amyotrophic lateral
sclerosis, a form of paralysis that will steadily
extend from his limbs to the rest of his body;
he can live for five years at most, and will more
probably die within two years; Nov.

'The Jubilee Christmas' [excerpt from the novel   S.34
A House of Children]. *Mademoiselle* (US), XLII
(Dec. 1955), 62, 63, 127, 128.

'Political and Personal Morality.' *Saturday Review* E.65†
(31 Dec. 1955), 5, 6, 31, 32; *Joyce Cary Selected
Essays.* Ed. A. G. Bishop. London, Michael
Joseph (1976), 227–32.

1956   [Correspondence headed 'The Christian Hope and   L.7
Physical Evil'.] *Listener* (12 Jan. 1956), 65.

[Correspondence headed 'The Christian Hope and   L.8
Physical Evil'.] *Listener* (26 Jan. 1956), 149.

'A Mysterious Affair.' *New Yorker* (28 Jan. 1956),   S.35*
28–34.

'The Period Novel.' *New Epoch*. Ruskin College   E.66
Magazine, Oxford (1956), 4–5. [A different
essay from E.36.]

'Westminster Abbey.' *Holiday*, XIX (April 1956),   E.67†
62, 63; *Joyce Cary Selected Essays*. Ed. A. G.
Bishop. London, Michael Joseph (1976), 204–9.

'Britain is Strong in Herself.' *New York Times*   E.68
Magazine (22 April 1956), 12, 32, 33.

'Growing Up.' *Vogue* (US), CXXVII (1 May   S.36*
1956), 122, 123, 160.

'A Slight Case of Demolition.' *Sunday Times*   E.69†
(20 May 1956), 6.

'Gerald Wilde.' *Nimbus*, III, 2 (1955), 47–54.   E.70

'A Hot Day.' *Time and Tide* (16 June 1956), 710.   S.37*

'If You Could Face Your Problems Today as This   Q.8
Man Faces His . . .' [interview conducted by
Merrick Winn]. *Daily Express* (27 Aug. 1956), 4.

'Party of One [subtitled on the contents page] –   E.71†
Of Novels and Novelists.' *Holiday*, XX (Sept.
1956), 6, 8, 9; [published as] 'Travels in a
Mind'. *Joyce Cary Selected Essays*. Ed. A. G.
Bishop. London, Michael Joseph (1976), 165–71.

'You're Only Young Once.' *Encounter*, VII   S.38*
(Sept. 1956), 24–26.

His six Clark Lectures read on his behalf by his
nephew Robert Ogilvie, at Trinity College,
Cambridge, between Oct. 19 and Nov. 23; by
now Joyce Cary cannot stand, and his failing
voice makes dictation difficult; he writes with
his hand supported by a sling from above, and
the pen fastened to his fingers; the paper is on
a bed-desk invented by himself, on spools that
move it automatically when his wrist drops on
to an electrically-controlled button.

'Cromwell House.' *New Yorker* (3 Nov. 1956),   E.72†
45–52, 54, 56, 58, 61, 62, 64, 67; *Joyce Cary
Selected Essays*. Ed. A. G. Bishop. London,
Michael Joseph (1976), 43–65.

'A Private Ghost.' *New Yorker* (10 Nov. 1956),   S.39*
121–30.

[Review of *Henry James, The Untried Years*, by   E.73
Leon Edel.] *Sunday Times* (23 Dec. 1956), 6.

As always since he has lived at 12 Parks Road,
his family and friends gather for Christmas and
New Year.

1957   Realizes he cannot revise 'The Captive and the
Free' for publication, as well as the Clark
lectures; so works on the lectures, stories (S.44,
45, 47) and letters (L.9, 10), Jan.

'A Great Author Faces up to Death' [interview   Q.9†
conducted by Graham Fisher in Aug. 1956].
Coronet, XLI (Jan. 1957), 41–44; *Joyce Cary
Selected Essays*. Ed. A. G. Bishop. London,
Michael Joseph (1976), 251–5.

['What is religion About?'] *Listener* (24 Jan.   L.9
1957), 157, 159.

'The Breakout.' *New Yorker* (2 Feb. 1957), 28–36.   S.40*

['What is Religion About?'] *Listener* (7 Feb.   L.10
1957), 235.

'New Boots.' *Harper's Bazaar* (British), LV   S.41**
(March 1957), 92–93, 117, 126.

Sends manuscript of lectures, as 'Art and Reality',
to the publisher, and polishes his last short story,
by mid-March; can no longer write, but remains
mentally clear and alert to the end.

'A Conversation with Joyce Cary' [interview   Q.10
conducted by Nathan Cohen, in Sept. 1956;
broadcast on CBC in Jan. 1957]. *Tamarack
Review*, no. 3 (Spring 1957), 5–15.

'A Valedictory of a Great Writer' [based on   Q.11
Cary's written answers to questions sent in
Dec. 1956]. *Life* (25 March 1957), 105, 106, 108.

Dies in his sleep, at home, at 10 a.m., March 29.

'The Tough World of Surtees.' *Sunday Times*   E.74†
(14 April 1957), 8; [with the omission of the
first sentence and slight alteration of the
second, published as an introduction to]
Mr Sponge's Sporting Tour by R. S. Surtees

(London: Oxford University Press, 1958), pp. vii–xii.

'Psychologist.' *Harper's Bazaar* (US), XC (May 1957), 140–2, 175–80, 182, 185.   S.42*

'The Most Exciting Sport in the World.' *Holiday,* XXI (June 1957), 42, 44, 47, 48, 155, 157; *Joyce Cary Selected Essays.* Ed. A. G. Bishop. London, Michael Joseph (1976), 74–82.   E.75†

'Joyce Cary's Last Look at his Worlds.' *Vogue* (US), CXXX (15 Aug. 1957), 96, 97, 150, 151, 153; *Joyce Cary Selected Essays.* Ed. A. G. Bishop. London, Michael Joseph (1976), 239–47.   E.76†

['What Christ has Taught Me.' Sent 10 Jan. 1955 for a symposium in volume form; translator not named.] *Vart Kristus lärt mig,* Stockholm, Bokförlaget Natur och Kultur (1957), 34–38.   E.77

'The Tunnel.' *Vogue* (US), CXXX (1 Oct. 1957), 186, 187, 226.   S.43*

1958   'Preface.' *First Trilogy.* New York, Harper (1958), pp. ix–xv.   E.78

Art and Reality. The Clark Lectures, 1956. Cambridge: Cambridge University Press, 1958 [7 March]; New York: Harper, 1958.   T.5

'The Meaning of England.' *Holiday,* XXIII (April 1958), 117; *Joyce Cary Selected Essays.* Ed. A. G. Bishop. London, Michael Joseph (1976), 71–73.   E.79†

'Happy Marriage.' *Harper's Magazine,* CCXVI (April 1958), 65–68; [republished under Joyce Cary's original title] 'New Women.' *Spring Song and Other Stories,* London, Michael Joseph (1960), 189–95.   S.44*

'Period Piece.' *Harper's Bazaar* (US) (April 1958), 110, 111, 208.   S.45*

'A Hero of Our Time.' *London Magazine,* V (Sept. 1958), 13–18.   S.46**

'The Sheep.' *Texas Quarterly,* 1, no. 4 (Winter 1958), 23–37.   S.47*

1959   *The Captive and the Free.* New York: Harper, 1959 [Jan.]; London: Michael Joseph, 1959 [March].   N.16

'A Government Baby.' *Lilliput,* XLIV (July   S.48**
1959), 13, 14, 18, 62–65.

1960 *Spring Song and Other Stories.* London: Michael   S.49
Joseph, 1960 [Feb.]; New York: Harper, 1960.   –53
[Contains all stories marked with an asterisk;
a 2nd asterisk gives the additional information
that, from the evidence of paper and handwriting used, the story was completed in
substantially its final form between 1935 and
1940.] The last five pieces in the volume are
hitherto unpublished [so giving its designation
to the collection].

'A Touch of Genius.' . . . pp. 240–70.   S.49**
'The Rebel.' . . . pp. 271–4.   S.50*
'First Love.' . . . pp. 275–7.   S.51**
'Taste of Glory.' . . . pp. 278–82.   S.52*
'The Explorers.' . .. pp. 283–5.   S.53**

Memoir of the Bobotes. Austin: University of   T.6
Texas Press, 1960; [also issued as a Supplement
with *Texas Quarterly* III, no. I (Spring 1960)];
London: Michael Joseph, 1964.

1961 'The Ball' [a discarded opening for *A Fearful*   S.54
Joy]. *Texas Quarterly,* IV, no. 3 (Autumn
1961), 74–83.

1971 His brother John dies, March 23.

1974 *Cock Jarvis An unfinished novel.* Ed. A. G.   N.17?
Bishop. London: Michael Joseph. 1974.

1976 His eldest son, now Sir Michael Cary, dies,
March 6.

Selected Essays. Ed. A. G. Bishop. London: E.80
Michael Joseph, 1976. [Contains all items   –82
marked with a dagger; the following, hitherto
unpublished, give the collection its designation.]

'Carrig Cnoc.' . . . pp. 29–31.   E.80†
'Unfinished Novels.' . . . pp. 109–16.   E.81†
'Clothes as Expression.' . . . pp. 233–8.   E.82†

Bibliography II:
Other Works Cited

(1) *Works in which Cary is discussed*

Allen, Walter Ernest. *Joyce Cary.* Writers and their Work:
no. 41. Revised ed. London: for the British Council and
National Book League by Longmans, Green & Co., 1963.
——. 'Foreword.' *Memoir of the Bobotes.* London: Michael
Joseph (1964), 7–12.
Bloom, Robert. *The Indeterminate World: A Study of the
Novels of Joyce Cary.* Philadelphia: University of Penn-
sylvania Press, 1962.
Brain, Walter Russell, 1st *baron. The Nature of Experience.*
Riddell mem. lects, ser. 30 (University of Durham).
London: Oxford University Press, 1959.
Cecil, *Lord* David. 'Tenderness of Heart.' *Times* (4 April 1957),
14.
——. 'Introduction.' *The Captive and the Free.* London:
Michael Joseph (1964), 5–7.
'Cheerful Protestant.' *Time* (20 Oct. 1952), 118–30.
Courlander, Alphonse. 'The Man Who Was Blown Up.' *Daily
Express* (8 Nov. 1912), 6.
Davin, Dan. 'Five Windows Darken.' *Closing Times: Recollec-
tions of Julian Maclaren-Ross, W. R. Rodgers, Louis
MacNeice, Enid Starkie, Joyce Cary, Dylan Thomas,
Itzik Manger.* London: Oxford University Press (1975),
91–120.
Davin, Winifred. 'Editorial Note.' *The Captive and the Free.*
London: Michael Joseph (1959), 9–10.
Fisher, Barbara. 'Files and Notebooks in the Manuscript Col-
lection of Joyce Cary: a Classification and Analysis.'
Unpublished Ph.D. dissertation, 1965. University of
London Library.

——. 'Joyce Cary's Published Writings.' *Bodleian Library Record,* VIII, no. 4 (April 1970), 213–28.

——. 'Two Joycean Novelists.' *Canadian Journal of Irish Studies,* IV, no. 2 (Dec. 1978), 5–22.

Foster, Malcolm. *Joyce Cary: A Biography.* Boston: Houghton Mifflin, 1968.

Hoffmann, Charles G. *Joyce Cary: The Comedy of Freedom.* Pittsburgh: University of Pittsburgh Press, 1964.

Johnson, Pamela Hansford. 'Joyce Cary's Later Manner.' *John O'London's Weekly* (14 Sept. 1952), 895.

Levin, Bernard. 'A pilgrim's progress to Joyce Cary.' *Times* (11 May 1977), 18.

——. 'Don't take my word, just read it.' *Times* (22 Sept. 1978), 14.

Mahood, M. M. *Joyce Cary's Africa.* London: Camelot Press, 1964.

Meriwether, James B. 'The Books of Joyce Cary: A Preliminary Bibliography of English and American Editions.' *Texas Studies in Literature and Language,* I, no. 2 (Summer 1959), 300–10.

Orwell, George. 'Foreword.' *The Case for African Freedom.* Searchlight Book No. 11. London: Secker & Warburg (1941), 5–6.

Pritchett, V. S. 'Books in General.' *New Statesman and Nation,* XLII, no. 1077 (27 Oct. 1951), 464, 465.

Schorer, Mark. 'The Socially Extensive Novel.' *Adam International Review,* XVIII, nos. 212–13 (Nov.–Dec. 1950), 31–32.

——. 'Native Boy in Patent Leather Shoes.' *New York Times Book Review* (7 Oct. 1951), 1.

Starkie, Enid. 'Joyce Cary, A Portrait.' Tredegar Memorial Lecture. Read 24 Oct. 1957. *Essays by Divers Hands* Being the Transactions of the Royal Society of Literature, n.s., XXXII. Ed. Joanna Richardson. London: Oxford University Press (1963), 125–44.

Stevenson, Lionel. 'Joyce Cary and the Anglo–Irish Tradition.' *Modern Fiction Studies,* IX (Autumn 1963), 210–16.

——. 'The Cary Family of Inishowen.' Unpublished typescript photocopy, 1963. Privately distributed.

Stewart, Douglas. 'Joyce Cary – Protestantism.' *The Ark of God:* Studies in Five Modern Novelists. W. T. Whitley Lectures for 1960. London: Carey Kingsgate Press, 1961.

Wright, Andrew. *Joyce Cary: A Preface to his Novels.* London: Chatto & Windus, 1959.

(2) *Works that influenced Cary*

Evidence of their influence has generally been given in the text of this study, chiefly from notebooks. Those items marked with an asterisk were owned by Cary in the editions named, and his copies are now in the Bodleian. Many are annotated by him. But his family received several of his books; his Withycombe's Dictionary is not in Bodley, for example. Even so, the 2,000 odd items in the Library's Cary Collection are but thinly represented here. Having been cited to illustrate his theme, they fairly illustrate Cary's thought and taste, however.

Items marked with a dagger are of likely, but not proven, influence.

*Alexander, Samuel. 'Theism and Pantheism.' *Hibbert Journal,* XXV, no. 2 (Jan. 1927), 251–264.

Balzac, Honoré de Balzac. *Old Goriot.* Trans. Ellen Marriage. Everyman ed. 1907; rpt. London: J. M. Dent, 1970 [exemplifying the influence of *La Comédie humaine*].

*Baudelaire, Charles. *Les Fleurs du Mal.* Ed. Enid Starkie. Oxford: Basil Blackwell, 1942.

*Blake, William. *Poems and Prophecies.* Everyman ed., 1927; rpt. London: J. M. Dent, 1942.

†Burney, Frances. *Evelina, or, a Young Lady's Entrance into the World.* London: T. Lowndes, 1778.

*Carlyle, Thomas. *Sartor Resartus: The Life and Opinions of Herr Teufelsdröckh.* London: Chapman and Hall, 1831.

*Cary, Robert *Earl of Monmouth. Memoirs of Robert Cary Earl of Monmouth.* Ed. G. H. Powell. London: Alexander Moring, 1905.

*Corrie, Joan. *A B C of Jung's Psychology.* 1927; rpt. London: Kegan Paul, 1928.

*Dostoevsky, Fyodor. *The Brothers Karamazov.* Trans. Constance Garnett. 1912; rpt. London: Heinemann, 1930.
*——. *Letters from the Underworld.* Trans. C. J. Hogarth. Everyman ed. 1913; rpt. London: J. M. Dent, 1915.
*Dostoevskaya, Anna Grigoryevna. *The Diary of Dostoevsky's Wife.* Ed. René Fülöp-Miller & Dr Fr Eckstein. Trans. Madge Pemberton. London: Victor Gollancz, 1928.

†Eliot, T. S. *The Waste Land.* New York: Boni and Liveright, 1922.
Emmet, Dorothy M. 'Kierkegaard and the "Existential" Philosophy.' *Philosophy,* XVI (1941), 257–71.
Empson, William. *Seven Types of Ambiguity.* London: Chatto & Windus, 1930.

†Fergusson, John Duncan. *Modern Scottish Painting.* Glasgow: William MacLellan, 1943.
Frazer, Sir James. *The Golden Bough.* Abridged ed. London: Macmillan & Co., 1922.
Freud, Sigmund. *Totem and Taboo:* resemblances between the psychic lives of savages and neurotics. Trans. A. A. Brill. London: G. Routledge & Sons, 1919.

*Goodyear, Frederick. 'The New Thelema.' *Rhythm,* I, no. 1 (Summer 1911), 1–3.
†Graves, Robert. *The Story of Mary Powell, Wife to Mr Milton.* London: Cassell & Co., 1943.
†Gray, John. 'The Redemption of Durtal.' *Dial,* no. IV (1896 and 1897), 7–11.
†Gray, Thomas. 'Ode on a Distant Prospect of Eton College.' *Poems by Mr Gray.* Drawings by William Blake. London: J. Murray, 1790.

*Haecker, Theodor. *Søren Kierkegaard.* Trans. Alexander Dru. London: Oxford University Press, 1937.
*Hardy, Thomas. *Far From the Madding Crowd.* London: Macmillan, 1916.
*——. *Tess of the D'Urbervilles:* A Pure Woman. 1st pocket ed. 1906; rpt. London: Macmillan & Co., 1916.

*Hitschmann, Eduard. *Freud's Theories of the Neuroses.* Trans. C. R. Payne. New York, 1917; rpt. London: Kegan Paul & Co., 1921.

*Hobbes, Thomas. *Leviathan.* Everyman ed. 1914; rpt. London: J. M. Dent, 1924.

Holy Bible. Containing Old and New Testament. Authorized Version.

Huysmans, J. K. *À Rebours.* Trans. anon. *Against the Grain,* with Huysmans' Preface to ed. 1903. London: Fortune Press, 1926.

*——. *Là-Bas.* Trans. anon. London: Fortune Press, 1943?

*James, Henry. *The Spoils of Poynton.* London: William Heinemann, 1897.

*James, William. *The Varieties of Religious Experience: A Study in Human Nature.* Gifford Lectures 1901–1902. 36th Impression. London: Longmans, Green & Co., 1928.

Joyce, James. *Ulysses.* Paris: Shakespeare and Co., 1922; 1st unlimited ed. London: Bodley Head, 1937.

*——. *Finnegans Wake.* London: Faber & Faber, 1939.

†Jung, C. G. *Psychology of the Unconscious.* Trans. Beatrice M. Hinkle. London: Kegan Paul, 1921.

*Kant, Immanuel. *Critique of Pure Reason.* London: George Bell, 1893.

Kierkegaard, Søren. *Philosophical Fragments . . .* Trans. David F. Swenson. New York: American Scandinavian Society, 1936.

——. *The Journals of Søren Kierkegaard.* A Selection edited and translated by Alexander Dru. London: Oxford University Press, 1938.

†Lawrence, D. H. *Sons and Lovers.* London: Duckworth & Co., 1913; Penguin Books, 1948.

——. *The Rainbow.* London: Methuen & Co. Ltd, 1915; rev. ed. 1926; rpt. London: Martin Secker, 1929.

†——. *Women in Love.* London: Martin Secker, 1921.

*——. *Fantasia of the Unconscious.* London: Martin Secker, 1923.

†——. *The Escaped Cock.* Paris, 1929; re-entitled *The Man Who Died.* London: Martin Secker, 1931.

†——. 'Introduction.' *The Grand Inquisitor.* Trans. S. S. Koteliansky. London: Elkin Mathews & Marrot (1930), iii–xvi ; *Selected Literary Criticism.* Ed. Anthony Beal. Mercury Books. London: Heinemann (1961), 233–41.

†——. *Apocalypse.* Florence, 1931; London: Martin Secker, 1932.

Lewis, Percy Wyndham. *Paleface: The Philosophy of the 'Melting-Pot'.* London: Chatto & Windus, 1929.

†Macmurray, John. *Creative Society: a study of the relation of Christianity and Communism.* London: Student Christian Movement Press, 1935.

Malinowski, Bronislaw. *Sex and Repression in Savage Society.* London: Kegan Paul, 1927.

†Marett, R. R. *Threshold of Religion.* London: Methuen & Co., 1909.

Martin du Gard, Roger. *Jean Barois.* Trans. Stuart Gilbert. London: Bodley Head, 1950.

*Moore, George. *Confessions of a Young Man by George Moore 1886.* Ed. George Moore 1916. London: William Heinemann, 1917.

Murry, John Middleton: *Fyodor Dostoevsky: A Critical Study.* London: Martin Secker, 1916.

——. *Still Life.* London: Constable & Co., 1916.

——. *The Evolution of an Intellectual.* London: R. Cobden-Sanderson, 1920.

——. *Aspects of Literature.* London: W. Collins Sons & Co., 1920.

——. *The Life of Jesus.* London: Jonathan Cape, 1926; [as] *Jesus, Man of Genius.* New York: Harper, 1926.

——. *Son of Woman: The Story of D. H. Lawrence.* London: Jonathan Cape, 1931; *D. H. Lawrence: Son of woman,* issued with a new introduction. London: Jonathan Cape, 1954.

——. *William Blake.* London: Jonathan Cape, 1933.

——. *Between Two Worlds.* London, Jonathan Cape, 1935.

——. *Adam and Eve.* London: Andrew Dakers, 1944.

——. *Community Farm.* London: Peter Nevill, 1952.

——. *Jonathan Swift.* London: Jonathan Cape, 1954.

†Otto, Rudolf. *Das Heilige. The Idea of the Holy.* Trans. John W. Harvey. 1923; 4th impression. London: Humphrey Mitford, 1926.

Paul, Maurice Eden and Cedar. *Creative Revolution: A Study of Communist Ergatocracy.* London: George Allen & Unwin, 1920.

*Perry, W. J. 'The Drama of Death and Resurrection.' *Hibbert Journal,* XXV, no. 2 (Jan. 1927), 237–50.

†Plato. 'Phaedrus.' Trans. J. Wright. *Five Dialogues.* Everyman ed. 1910; rpt. London: J. M. Dent (1947), 215–87.

——. *Republic.* Trans. B. Jowett. The *Dialogues of Plato,* vol. II. 1871; 4th ed. Oxford: at the Clarendon Press. 1953.

*Rimbaud, Jean-Arthur. *Oeuvres de Jean-Arthur Rimbaud.* Paris: Societé du Mercure de France, 1907.

*Robinson, C. H. *Dictionary of the Hausa Language.* 2 vols. Cambridge: at the University Press, 1913, 1914.

*Roth, Leon. 'The Goodness of God.' *Journal of Philosophical Studies,* II, no. 8 (Oct. 1927), 503–15.

*Rousseau, Jean Jacques. *Confessions.* London: Wliliam Glaisher, 1923.

Sainte-Beuve, Charles-Augustin. *Causeries du Lundi.* Selected and edited G. Saintsbury. Oxford: The Clarendon Press, 1885; *8 vols. Trans. E. J. Trenchmann. London: George Routledge, n.d.

*Shakespeare, William. *Sonnets.* Guildford: A. C. Curtis, 1902.

*Schopenhauer, Arthur. *Selected Essays.* Ed. with an Introd. Ernest Belfort Bax. London: G. Bell, 1914.

Sheean, Vincent. *In Search of Hisory.* London: Hamish Hamilton, 1935.

Spinoza, Benedict de. *The Chief Works of Benedict de Spinoza.* 2 vols. Trans. R. H. M. Elwes. London: George Bell & Sons, 1883.

Stone, Irving. *Lust for Life. The novel of Vincent Van Gogh.* London: John Lane, 1934.

*Swift, Jonathan. *The Works of D. Jonathan Swift.* 9 vols. 7th ed. Dublin: G. Hamilton & J. Balfour, 1752.

*Symons, Arthur. *The Symbolist Movement in Literature.* 2nd ed. rev. London: Constable & Co., 1908.

*Tolstoy, Count Leo. *Childhood, Boyhood, & Youth.* Trans. C. J. Hogarth. Everyman ed. 1912; rpt. London: J. M. Dent, 1921.

*——. *War and Peace.* 3 vols. [vol. I not in Cary Collection]. Everyman ed. 1911; rpt. London: J. M. Dent, 1915.

*——. 'What Men Live By.' *Twenty-three Tales.* Trans. L. and A. Maude. London: Oxford University Press (1906), 50–74.

*——. *Anna Karenina.* Trans. Constance Garnett. 2 vols. London: William Heinemann, 1901.

*——. *A Confession and What I Believe.* Trans. with an introduction Aylmer Maude. World's Classics ed. 1921; rpt. London: Oxford University Press, 1931.

*——. *The Kreutzer Sonata and Other Tales.* Trans. J. D. Duff and Aylmer Maude. World's Classics ed. 1924; rpt. London: Oxford University Press, 1926.

*——. 'The Light That Shines In Darkness.' *Father Sergius and other stories and plays.* Ed. Hagberg Wright. London: Thomas Nelson (1911), 113–283.

*——. *Resurrection.* Trans. Louise Maude. World's Classics ed. 1916; rpt. London: Oxford University Press, 1926.

——. *What Is Art? and Essays on Art.* Trans. A. Maude. London: Oxford University Press, 1904.

——. *New Light on Tolstoy.* Literary fragments, letters and reminiscences not previously published. Ed. René Fülöp-Miller. Trans. Paul England. London: G. G. Harrap & Co., 1931.

*Tolstoy, Countess. *The Diary of Tolstoy's Wife 1860–1891.* Trans. Alexander Werth. London: Victor Gollancz. 1928.

*——. *The Countess Tolstoy's Later Diary 1891–1897.*

*Twain, Mark. *A Yankee at the Court of King Arthur.* London: Chatto and Windus, 1889.

*Whitehead, Alfred North. *Religion in the Making.* Lowell Lectures 1926. Cambridge: at the University Press, 1927.

*——. *Process and Reality: An Essay in Cosmology.* Gifford Lectures 1927–28. Cambridge: at the University Press, 1929.

Wilson, Edmund. *Axël's Castle: A Study in the Imaginative Literature of 1870–1930*. New York, London: Charles Scribner's Sons, 1931.

*Wilson, John Dover. *The Fortunes of Falstaff*. The Clark Lectures of May 1943. Cambridge: at the University Press, 1944.

Withycombe, E. G. *The Oxford Dictionary of English Christian Names*. Oxford: Clarendon Press, 1945.

*Yeats, W. B. *Where There is Nothing. Being Volume One of Plays for an Irish Theatre*. London: A. H. Bullen, 1903.

†Yonge, Charlotte M. *A History of Christian Names*. 2 vols. London: Parker, Son, and Bourn, 1863; rev. ed. 1884, 1 vol.

(3) *Works providing general background evidence*

Baldick, Robert. *The Life of J. K. Huysmans*. Oxford: Clarendon Press, 1955.

Bardsley, C. W. *English Surnames*. 5th ed. London: Chatto & Windus, 1897.

Boak, Denis. *Roger Martin du Gard*. Oxford: Clarendon Press, 1963.

Carswell, John. *Lives and Letters. A. R. Orage Beatrice Hastings Katherine Mansfield John Middleton Murry S. S. Koteliansky 1906-1957*. London: Faber & Faber, 1978.

Cazamian, Louis. *A History of English Literature. Modern Times (1660-1963)*. Revised ed. London: J. M. Dent, 1964.

Cottle, Basil: *The Penguin Dictionary of Surnames*. London, 1967.

Descaves, Lucien. *Deux amis. J. K. Huysmans et l'abbé Mugnier*. Documents inédits. Paris: Librairie Plon, 1946.

Dodds, E. R. *The Greeks and the Irrational*. 5th printing. Berkeley: University of California Press, 1966.

Driberg, Tom. *The Mystery of Moral Re-Armament*. London: Martin Secker & Warburg, 1964.

Ellmann, Richard. *James Joyce*. London: Oxford University Press, 1966.

Fraser, G. S. 'Proper Names in Poetry.' Correspondence. *Times Literary Supplement* (11 June 1970), 638.

Freud, Sigmund: *Psychopathology of Everyday Life.* Trans. A. A. Brill. London: Benn, 1960.

Garland, Hamlin. 'The Reformer Tolstoy.' Introduction. *Recollections and Essays* by Leo Tolstoy. Centenary ed. Trans. Louise and Aylmer Maude. London: Oxford University Press, 1937.

Garnett, David. 'Frieda and Lawrence.' *D. H. Lawrence: Novelist, Poet, Prophet.* Ed. Stephen Spender. London: Wiedenfeld and Nicholson (1973), 37–41.

Gathorne-Hardy, Jonathan. *The Rise and Fall of the British Nanny.* London: Hodder and Stoughton, 1972.

Jeffares, A. Norman. *A Commentary on the Collected Poems of W. B. Yeats.* London: Macmillan, 1968.

Joyce, James. *Daniel Defoe.* Ed. and Trans. Joseph Prescott. Buffalo: State University of New York, 1964.

——. *The Critical Writings of James Joyce.* Eds. Ellsworth Mason and Richard Ellmann. New York: Viking Press, 1964.

——. Letters of James Joyce, II. Ed. Richard Ellmann. New York: Viking Press, 1966.

Jung, C. G. *Psychology and Alchemy.* Trans. R. F. C. Hull. London: Routledge & Kegan Paul, 1953.

Laver, James. *The First Decadent: Being the strange life of J. K. Huysmans.* London: Faber and Faber, 1954.

Lea, F. A. *The Life of John Middleton Murry.* London: Methuen, 1969.

Maclysaght, Edward. *Guide to Irish Surnames.* Dublin: Helicon, 1964.

——. *Irish Families: Their Names, Arms and Origins.* Dublin: Allen Figgis, 1972.

Macmurray, John. *Search for Reality in Religion.* Swarthmore Lecture, 1965. London: George Allen & Unwin, 1965.

Meyers, Jeffrey. 'D. H. Lawrence and Homosexuality.' *D. H. Lawrence: Novelist, Poet, Prophet.* Ed. Stephen Spender. London: Weidenfeld and Nicholson (1973), 135–46.

Meyerstein, E. H. W. *Of My Early Life (1889–1918)*. Ed. Rowland Watson. London: Neville Spearman, 1957.

——. *Some Letters of E. H. W. Meyerstein*. Ed. Rowland Watson. London: Neville Spearman, 1959.

Montgomery, A. C. *Acronyms and Abbreviations in Library and Information Work:* a reference handbook of British usage. Compiled and edited by A. C. Montgomery. London: Library Association, 1975.

Moore, Harry T. *The Life and Works of D. H. Lawrence*. Revised ed. London: George Allen & Unwin, 1963.

Raine, Kathleen. *Blake and Tradition*. 2 vols. London: Routledge & Kegan Paul, 1969.

Schorer, Mark. 'Fiction and the "Matrix of Analogy".' *Kenyon Review,* IX (1949), 539–60.

——. *William Blake: the politics of vision*. New York: Henry Holt, 1946.

Sewell, Father Brocard (Ed.). *Two Friends: John Gray and André Raffalovich*. Aylesford: St Albert's Press, 1963.

Tonge, John. *The Arts of Scotland*. London: Kegan Paul, 1938.

'T. S. Eliot and the "out there".' Review of *The Waste Land: A facsimile and transcript of the original drafts including the annotations of Ezra Pound*. Ed. Valerie Eliot. *Times Literary Supplement* (10 Dec. 1971), 1551, 1552.

Notes

Chapter One

1 Joyce Cary, *Art and Reality* (Cambridge, 1958), p. 105.
2 From a photocopy kindly given by M. M. Mahood; MS. Cary 302/2, fols. 293-6, are identical, but lack the date, salutation, final paragraph, and signature, all in Cary's hand; Charles G. Hoffmann, *Joyce Cary: The Comedy of Freedom* (Pittsburgh, 1964), p. 1, quotes from the Bodleian copy, and rightly stresses the significance of *change* to his title.
3 MS. Cary 238.
4 MS. Cary 250/N.16, fol. 2^r; cf. p. 338 below.
5 (London, 1921), p. xii.
6 See his 'Prefatory Essay', *Aissa Saved*, Carfax ed. (1952), pp. 9-11; discussed in ch. 7, para. 1, below.
7 *The African Witch*, Carfax ed. (1951), pp. 9-10.
8 William James, *The Varieties of Religious Experience* (London, 1904), p. 187.
9 'My Religious History', MS. Cary 331, fol. 11; for a good intuition of Cary's meaning, but a denial of its consequences, see Robert Bloom, *The Indeterminate World* (Philadelphia, 1962).
10 Andrew Wright, *Joyce Cary: A Preface to his Novels* (London, 1959), p. 28; hereafter cited as Wright, *Preface*.
11 'A Conversation with Joyce Cary' [interview conducted by Nathan Cohen], *Tamarack Review*, no. 3 (Spring 1957), p. 15.
12 *The Case for African Freedom*, new and enlarged ed. (London, 1944), p. 12.
13 *Aissa Saved*, p. 159; quoted below, p. 151.
14 MS. Cary 293, file S.22.J.
15 'Travels in a Mind', *Joyce Cary Selected Essays*, ed. A. G. Bishop (London, 1976), p. 166; essay previously published as 'Party of One— Of Novels and Novelists', *Holiday*, XX (Sept. 1956), 6. 8. 9.
16 *Joyce Cary*, Writers and their Work, no. 41; revised ed. (London, 1963). p. 5; Shakespeare's influence on Cary will be shown in the following pages.
17 'Books in General', *New Statesman and Nation* (27 Oct. 1951), p. 464.
18 'Joyce Cary or What is Freedom?' [interview conducted by Stanley Parker], *Oxford Mail* (15 Dec. 1942), p. 3.
19 MS. Cary 239, fol. 46, is the original, which includes deletions, besides errors in punctuation and spelling; Cary never attempted to compose in typescript before his wife died, and here haste is added to inexperience.

20 *Process and Reality* (Cambridge, 1929); ch. vii 'The Subjectivist Principle' and ch. viii 'Symbolic Reference' are particularly relevant; as is *Religion in the Making* (Cambridge, 1927); his own copies of both are much annotated.

21 MS. Cary 292/N.132.

22 MS. Cary 258/S.5.E.*a*; this rough draft beginning 'Dear Mr. Hughes', evidently to his publisher, or agent, is cited hereafter as 'Hughes' MS.

23 The reference book chiefly used will be *The Oxford Dictionary of English Christian Names*, by E. G. Withycombe, 2nd ed. reprinted with corrections, 1963, hereafter cited as Withycombe; Cary consulted the first edition of 1945, Michael Cary confirmed. Withycombe quotes as the standard work from which all other works have drawn: Charlotte M. Yonge, *A History of Christian Names*, 2 vols. 1863; revised ed. 1884. Therefore Yonge will be cited also. For Cary, Miss Yonge was the novelist who best revealed the Victorian period (*Selected Essays*, p. 176), and Sara describes her influence in *Herself Surprised* (pp. 13-14, 144). It would be untypical, therefore, if Cary had not familiarized himself with this book, which grew out of articles in *The Monthly Packet*, a magazine edited by Miss Yonge to educate girls like Sara. It could indeed be the old book described below, p. 103.

24 MS. Cary 284/P.123 fol. 2^r; for his article on A. P. Herbert, 'Personality', *Time*, LIX (10 March 1952), p. 45 [Atlantic ed. p. 25].

Chapter Two

1 The chief source for family history in this chapter is a chronicle by Lionel Stevenson, 'The Cary Family of Inishowen' privately distributed, unpublished typescript photocopy, 1963.

2 Information from Cecilia Dick and Winifred Davin.

3 MS. Cary 244, fol. 166.

4 MS. Cary 252/S.3.D; for the significance of the name, see below, p. 30.

5 *Charley is my Darling*, Carfax ed. (London, 1952), pp. 5-6.

6 *Except the Lord* (London, 1953), p. 8.

7 'What Christ has Taught Me', MS. Cary 249, fol. 238.

8 *Prisoner of Grace*, Carfax ed. (London 1954), p. 88.

9 In the first trilogy, the main protagonists do not lose their mothers young, but learn from them rather the opposite lesson—that they must not hate, in a cruel, unjust world; see *Herself Surprised*, Carfax ed. (London, 1951), p. 14; *To be a Pilgrim*, Carfax ed. (London, 1951), p. 334; *The Horse's Mouth*, Carfax ed. (London, 1951), p. 20.

10 *Except the Lord*, p. 11; cf. *To be a Pilgrim*, p. 288, which also describes a child praying in his mother's lap.

11 *Selected Essays*, p. 21.

12 *To be a Pilgrim,* p. 24, tells how Robert Brown fought with his mother; *A House of Children,* Carfax ed. (London, 1951), p. 196, describes the horse also.

13 'Prefatory Essay', *A House of Children,* pp. 5-8.

14 Ibid., p. 166; the boat trip is recounted more fully here than in the preface.

15 See *Art and Reality,* ch. 3; outlined below, p. 331.

16 'Cromwell House', *Selected Essays,* p. 57, first published in the *New Yorker* (3 Nov. 1956). The title etc. is explained below, p. 26.

17 So John Fischer writes in MS. Cary Adds. 1, fol. 264; *The Drunken Sailor* (London, 1947).

18 Cary's study of Jung, who describes such sea symbolism, is evident from notebooks of 1928—(e.g. MS. Cary, 251/P.6); he can therefore be assumed to use the symbol with conscious intention.

19 *A House of Children,* p. 224; 'Canon P.' was Canon Joseph Potter, who had officiated at the marriage and funeral of Cary's mother.

20 *Power in Men* (London, 1939), p. 156; cf. p. 237 below.

21 Information from Dorothy Heard, daughter of Helen Beasley, described below, p. 21; as a doctor specializing in child psychology, and as a member of Cary's family, she believes the early death of his mother to be of vital importance.

22 Metaphorically speaking, they expect to be beaten, he told Cecilia Dick.

23 Information from Dorothy Heard.

24 Discussed below, p. 203; the stress laid on Plato in this study is justified by the testimony of Sir Michael Cary, that his father discussed Plato with him from the time he was seven years old.

25 *Art and Reality,* p. 17: 'as a moralistic dictator, hating and fearing the power of art, he wished to put art in the humblest possible place'.

26 'Speaking for Myself', *Selected Essays,* pp. 19-20; 'should have' implies that family affection overcame tensions.

27 Edward MacLysaght, *Irish Families* (Dublin, 1972), p. 189; *Guide to Irish Surnames* (Dublin, 1964), p. 122.

28 Letter of 29 Aug. 1904, to Nora Barnacle, Richard Ellmann, ed., *Letters of James Joyce,* II (New York, 1966), p. 243.

29 French *Aveline* means 'hazel-nut', and 'The Normans introduced *Aveline* into England . . . giving rise to the surnames . . . *Evelyn*', writes Withycombe; *Harry* derives from Old German *Haimirich,* meaning 'Home ruler', which has several relevant associations in Cary's writing; Yonge gives the same meanings.

30 A Norman Jeffares, *A Commentary on the Collected Poems of W. B. Yeats* (London, 1968), p. 62.

31 *Holiday,* XXIII (April, 1958), 117; checked from MS. Cary 236.

32 'The Novelist at Work', *Adam International Review,* XVIII, nos. 212-13 (Nov.–Dec., 1950), p. 21; that Cary linked his theme with James's, is suggested by the fact that his wife gave him a first edition of *The Spoils of Poynton* just after he completed *Castle Corner.*

33 *Castle Corner,* Carfax ed. (London, 1952), p. 184.

34 'Cromwell House', *Selected Essays,* p. 65.

35 'Barney Magonagel', *Selected Essays,* p. 33.

36 'Cromwell House', p. 55.

37 'Joyce Cary and the Anglo-Irish Tradition', *Modern Fiction Studies*, IX (Autumn 1963), 210.
38 'The Cary Family of Inishowen', p. 2.
39 Discussed below, p. 143.

Chapter Three

1 MS. Cary 256/S.4.C; many cancellations; developed in Cary's typescript of 'Tottenham', MS. Cary 180/1, fol. 142, where a mother remarks: "I'm sure if I was a nurse, I should preach the highest morals. Its the only way to secure any peace and comfort for oneself".' For 'Its' see ch. 9, n. 2.
2 MS. Cary 180/2, fol. 56ᵛ.
3 E.g. 'Tottenham', MS. Cary 180/1, fol. 83, shows prefects behaving like fascists, and also remarking to each other: ' "What's all this silly rot about, what do you call 'em—" "Do you mean the fascists?" '
4 Ibid., fol. 108 ff. shows prefects competing for sleeping partners amongst small boys who, like Johnny, are anxious to 'give satisfaction', but also able to feel security and gain advice.
5 *The Story of Mary Powell, Wife to Mr. Milton* (London, 1943) has a foreword by Graves, dated June 1942, to which Cary's attention is likely to have been drawn, since Graves refers to his illustrious ancestor, Lucius Cary, who died in Charles I's cause, and also to another Lucius Cary, the 13th Viscount who, as his neighbour in Devon, had helped Graves with the MSS. for this book; but the essential point is that Graves refers to Milton's politics and marriage in terms with which Cary would wholly have agreed, as his second trilogy especially shows; to quote 'Milton! thou shouldst be living at this hour', as a solution to problems in 1942, says Graves, is to forget that Milton endorsed the Cromwellian solution to political questions, which was 'undisguised Fascism'; after World War I Chester Nimmo similarly agrees to killing a king (*Prisoner of Grace*, p. 325).
6 By Jonathan Gathorne-Hardy (London, 1972).
7 Cf. *Power in Men*, pp. 157-9.
8 *A House of Children*, pp. 169-70; the idea is developed below, p. 80.
9 MS. Cary 259/N.42 shows this as Cary's ideal; see below, p. 382.
10 *Power in Men*, p. 93.
11 'Joyce Cary, A Portrait', Tregedar Memorial Lecture, read on 24 Oct. 1957, *Essays by Divers Hands*, ed. J. Richardson, being the transactions of the Royal Society of Literature, n.s. XXXII (1963), p. 126.
12 See below, pp. 125, 195.
13 For Tolstoy as the Russian Socrates, see below, p. 156.
14 MS. Cary 271/N.98, fol. 23.
15 E.g. in 'A Conversation with Joyce Cary'.
16 *A House of Children*, p. 169; his father's letter is MS. Cary 321, dated 11 May.

17 *Art and Reality*, p. 104; the personal background of this statement lends weight to the key quotation of this study, to which it directly leads.

18 *A House of Children*, pp. 186-7; like a 'punch on the nose', 'blue eyes' have apparent symbolic significance, since it was traditionally through the blue-eyed Athena and Poseidon that authority came to the tall fair races of Europe; these would include Cary's own Frankish ancestors; see below p. 229.

19 *The Horse's Mouth*, pp. 61, 62; the idea of art as an infection, which Cary took from Tolstoy, is here illustrated; 'Gee and Jay' are the initials of God and Jesus, but also of Gulley and Jimson.

20 Ibid., 'Prefatory Essay', p. 10.

21 'Cheerful Protestant', *Time*, Atlantic ed. (20 Oct., 1952), pp. 48, 50.

22 'A Lawn, and in the midst a Silken Pool', *The Cliftonian*, XIX (June 1906), 194, 195.

23 *Herself Surprised*, p. 97.

Chapter Four

1 MS. Cary Adds 4e, fol. 105; MS. Cary 272/P.52, fol. 4.

2 Wright, *Preface*, p. 21.

3 MS. Cary 272/P.52, fol. 2.

4 Information from Dr Melville Clark, in a letter of 5 Sept. 1968 to B. Fisher; these words add meaning to *Herself Surprised*, p. 130, where Sara describes words in balloons floating from the mouths of figures in Gulley's paintings.

5 *A History of English Literature*, rev. ed. (London, 1960), pp. 1279, 1280.

6 *The Symbolist Movement in Literature*, 2nd ed. rev. (London, 1908), pp. 3, 5, 7, 2.

7 MS. Cary 271/N.85 *h*; typescript draft of a lecture.

8 *Seven Types of Ambiguity* (London, 1930), p. 312; see ch. 6, n. 37; for the censor and symbolism, see ch. 10, n. 24.

9 See 'A Portrait', p. 129.

10 MS. Cary 268/S.10. D.*e*; cf. *Castle Corner*, pp. 235-7.

11 MS. Cary 259/N.44.

12 *Confessions of a Young Man by George Moore 1886* (London, 1917), pp. xi, 6.

13 Cazamian, op. cit., p. 1289.

14 Wright, *Preface*, p. 42.

15 John Tonge, *The Arts of Scotland* (London, 1938), p. 93.

16 Information in a letter of 13 Sept. 1968, to B. Fisher from Miss C. Kirkwood, whose home Cary visited 'very often' while in Edinburgh.

17 MS. Cary 331, fols. 4-5; the script has 'Reffallovitch'; this quotation exemplifies the way Cary often confused his memories, for he says the church was in Torphicen Street, whereas the studio was there.

18 John Fischer of Harper's proposed the book.

19 The typical expression of the Symbolist spirit is *Axël*, says Edmund Wilson, *Axël's Castle* (London, 1931), possibly guiding Cary's interest; for Cary's views on Wilson, see ch. 5, n. 40; for *Axël* see p. 212 below.

20 *A Fearful Joy*, Carfax ed. (London, 1952), pp. 47, 76; since Sturge Moore was also a regular contributor to the *Dial*, the name is possibly another clue to Cary's inspiration, for he names the founder of these reviews, Sturge.

21 'The Redemption of Durtal', *Dial*, no. IV (MDCCCXCVI and MDCCCXCVII), pp. 7-11.

22 MS. Cary 255/N.38; 'cf. Rossetti' links with the quotation on p. 41 above; it appears to have been added in c. 1942.

23 *The Symbolist Movement*, p. 22; the sonnet is quoted on p. 23, as Cary noted.

24 Ibid., p. 33.

25 *Phaedrus*, 244, as translated by E. R. Dodds, *The Greeks and the Irrational* (Berkeley, 1951), p. 64.

26 Cf. the titles: *Deux Amis J. K. Huysmans et L'Abbé Mugnier*, by Lucien Descaves (Paris, 1946); *Two Friends John Gray and André Raffalovich*, ed. Father Brocard Sewell (St. Albert's Press, Aylesford, 1963); the latter is the chief source of information above; both Raffalovich and Huysmans became oblates.

27 MS. Cary 253/N.9, fol. 1.

28 John Middleton Murry, *Between Two Worlds* (London, 1935), p. 144.

29 From Huysmans' 1903 preface to *À Rebours*, as it appears on p. xi of an anonymous English translation, *Against the Grain* (London, 1926), which has on the frontispiece: 'The Book that Dorian Gray loved and that inspired Oscar Wilde'; the Bodleian Library copy is stamped 7 Dec. 1931; for Cary's use of the Bodleian, see p. 107.

30 *The Horse's Mouth*, p. 241.

31 'Hughes' MS.

32 See pp. 225-6 below.

33 *The Horse's Mouth*, pp. 64, 87.

34 *Là-Bas*, trans. anon. (London, n.d.), p. 200; introduction dated 1943; Cary owned a copy, and marked it; possibly he had already read an anon. trans. *Down There* (London, 1930), in Bodley from 15 Nov. 1938; and also a French copy (cf. p. 27 above); notes on Huysmans in *The Symbolist Movement* appear, from handwriting, to belong to 1942.

35 Gulley denies the devil (see p. 238 below).

36 *The Symbolist Movement*, pp. 137, 138, 141.

37 Ibid., p. 139.

38 James Laver's title (London, 1954).

39 *The Life of J. K. Huysmans* (Oxford, 1955), p. 82.

40 Ibid., p. 83.

41 M. M. Mahood develops this description of himself in *Joyce Cary's Africa* (London, 1964), p. 3ff.

42 MS. Cary 280/N.113.

43 MS. Cary 283/N.153; the quotation is on separate leaves.

44 MS. Cary 283/N.134 shows Boole's inspiration as 'the Baudelairean, embracing suffering [an]d contempt'; MS. Cary 283/N.137 contains the drafts, entitled 'Boole The King of the World'.

45 *A Fearful Joy*, p. 128, where (*à rebours* of Schopenhauer?) Boole says: ' "I was born a man of the renaissance. Violence follows me, events cling to me. Yes, that is why I, who adore women, had to throw a woman downstairs." ' In his case, Schopenhauer was forced to pay a pension to the woman, whose long life prompted Ernest Bax to say that she 'might have furnished Schopenhauer with the theme of a dissertation . . . on the strength of . . . "the Will-to-live" enshrined in the female body'; these words appear on p. xxi of Bax's introduction to his edition of *Selected Essays of Schopenhauer* (London 1914), which Cary owned (Cary B.337) and inscribed '1918', and had annotated with other works of Schopenhauer by the end of the twenties.

46 'Preface', *Against the Grain*, p. xiv.

47 Baldick, *Huysmans*, p. 179.

48 Ibid., p. 215; on p. 214 Baldick says Huysmans was thus persuaded by Léon Bloy, one of the 'apostles of pain', so indicating why Cary spoke of Bloy's fears and passions in the essay referred to in n. 50 below.

49 Ibid., p. 5.

50 *Selected Essays*, p. 164, under the changed title, 'Morality and the Novelist'; a comparison of the manuscripts shows that MS. Cary 301, fols. 141-4, also concerns 'Conflict and Contradiction', is on foolscap of identical water-mark, in similar typescript, with similar ink for Cary's handwritten additions, including 'Souvent homme varie'; it leaves me in no doubt that this is a draft discarded from 'Le Roman à thèse', which appears in *Les Nouvelles Littéraires* (11 Aug. 1955), pp. 1, 2, translated by Christine Lalou.

51 Cary echoes these words at the end of his last novel, showing this is to be his basis for characterization: *The Captive and the Free*, Carfax ed. (London, 1963), pp. 316-7.

52 MS. Cary 301, fol. 144; several cancellations.

53 *Selected Essays*, pp. 154-5; 'Le Roman à thèse' has: '. . . leur athéisme était une conviction, une morale.'

54 *The Horse's Mouth*, p. 114, developed below, p. 213.

55 Thomas Higham (April 1968), said Clifton had a separate house for Jewish boys, who were pelted with cheese etc. in good-humoured scorn as they passed other Houses to get to school, including Cary's House (Tait's).

56 Information in a letter of 29 Sept. 1968, to B. Fisher from C. Kirkwood.

57 Denis Boak, *Roger Martin du Gard* (Oxford, 1963), is the chief source for all references to Martin du Gard in this study.

58 *Dédoublement* was the depiction of contradictory tendencies in the author's own nature, as he explained was his plan for the brothers in *Les Tibault*; cf. Harry and Evelyn Corner, and Cary's second trilogy, with *dédoublement* not only of Chester and Jim, but also of each with an older, favoured brother; Huysmans' *à rebours*, which is similar, seems to inspire the first trilogy.

59 *Jean Barois*, trans. Stuart Gilbert (London, 1950), pp. 47-49; Cary referred to it in 'My Religious History', MS. Cary 290/P.144, P.147, P.159, and most forcefully in a letter to the *Listener* (12 Jan. 1956), p. 65.

60 Cf. pp. 24 above and 55 below.

61 *Art and Reality*, p. 9; discussed further below, p. 331.

62 Martin du Gard was much influenced by the writings of Félix le Dantec, and Raffalovich's interest in such subjects is shown by the contents of his library, according to Ian Grant, of Grant's Bookshop, Edinburgh, who handled many of Raffalovich's books (which Cary may well have seen on his shelves); he was interested in anthropology, abnormal psychology, and crime, as well as in art—and obscure artists of about 1900, so being an appropriate model for Gulley's patron.

63 See p. 122 below; Cary's most notable evangelical Americans are Marie in *An American Visitor*, Professor Ponting in *The Horse's Mouth*, ch. 15, and Nona Clench, in *The Captive and the Free*, ch. 39.

64 For the 'chestnut' with similar meanings see pp. 230, 251 below.

65 MS. Cary 271/N.95.

66 MS. Cary Adds 4e, fol. 108 (undated; c. March 1909).

67 MS. Cary Adds. 4e, fol. 100; letter of 26 Feb. 1909 (see envelope).

68 MS. Cary 259/N.42 has a note of the mid-thirties showing that Cary held to this sentiment: 'The highest type of each country is a self-conscious and all-round master—a Sydney [sic], the supreme type, the poet-philosopher-warrior, is international only in fundamentals—in the arts of life, he is national, i.e. his poetry and feelings have a national form'; Yeats's sentiments are well known from his poem, 'In Memory of Major Robert Gregory': 'Our Sidney and our perfect man'.

69 See above, p. 23.

70 MS. Cary 329, fol. 20.

71 *Idler*, XXXVII (May, 1910), 895-8.

Chapter Five

1 MS. Cary 271/N.82, written around Oct. 1944, but drawing on the autobiographical essay in 272/P.52, begun around Christmas 1941 (judging by handwriting).

2 *Sunday Times* (20 May 1956), p. 6; *Selected Essays*, pp. 66-70, from which quotations below are taken.

3 Cf. 'Tottenham', p. 29 above, who could not 'perform a cheeky action'.

4 MS. Cary Adds. 1, letter dated 17 Dec. 1947, concerning the publication of *Herself Surprised* in America.

5 Dodds, *The Greeks and the Irrational*, p. 18.

6 'Five Windows Darken', *Closing Times* (London, 2975), p. 110.

7 MS. Cary 271/N.82; the general feeling in this passage underlies the closing pages of Cary's article 'The Oxford Scholar', *Holiday,* XIII (June, 1953), 141-3.

8 MS. Cary 265/N.73.

9 'My Religious History', fols. 5-6.

10 Ibid.; Cary's much-annotated copy of Kant's *Critique of Pure Reason* (London, 1893), has this early note for p. 125, showing its influence on his thought: 'object of sense phenomena *must* depend on subjective intuition of space and time'.

11 *The Symbolist Movement,* pp. 65, 66.

12 p. 121; he goes on to refer to Cary only as 'my Oxford friend' who 'had been at an art-school some time before' (p. 144), but no acquaintance could mistake whom he meant.

13 E. H. W. Meyerstein, *Of My Early Life* (London, 1957), p. 70.

14 In *Between Two Worlds,* p. 34, Murry praises his aunt (Mrs Parkhouse) with his mother and grandmother, the only three women he knew as a child, much as Cary praises his Aunt Doll and his two grandmothers in 'Cromwell House'; cf. Chester's opening in *Except the Lord,* regarding 'the three noblest' women he has known—his mother, sister, and wife.

15 Ibid., p. 30.

16 Ibid., pp. 50-51.

17 See pp. 66, 98 below.

18 *Between Two Worlds,* p. 125.

19 *Not Honour More,* Carfax ed. (London, 1966), p. 16; for 'Slapton-Latter dynasty, see *Prisoner of Grace,* p. 22.

20 *The Life of John Middleton Murry* (London, 1959), p. 16.

21 Ibid., p. 25.

22 *Between Two Worlds,* pp. 182-3; John Carswell, Lives and Letters 1906-1957 (London, 1978), p. 72, says Murry went with Hugh Kingsmill to a brothel, and contracted gonorrhea. He may have confused Murry's reference to Kingsmill on p. 181, with 'my friend' on p. 182; otherwise, if Murry's report is untrue, Cary had every reason to be offended.

23 Lea, *Murry,* p. 28.

24 'My Religious History', fols. 7-8.

25 N.9; these sketches could represent the book he speaks of.

26 MS. Cary 253/N.8.

27 *Murry,* p. 20.

28 For confirmation of Gulley's identity I am indebted to Professor M. K. Joseph, University of Auckland, in a report to the Auckland University Press, 2 March 1976: 'In one case I can confirm the truth of Mrs Fisher's carefully supported conjectures: I once heard Cary say, in answer to a question, that the Scottish painter Ferguson [sic] was the original of Gulley Jimson'; that Fergusson knew and admired Cary is confirmed by his widow Margaret Morris Fergusson, in a letter of 29 Aug. 1971 to B. Fisher.

29 *Herself Surprised,* p. 94; it should be understood that no *portrait* of Fergusson in Gulley is here suggested. Gulley is a universal figure, to whom all artists of Cary's acquaintance, in person or in books, probably contributed, and in whom many artists have recognized themselves, as did Gerald Wilde (on whom Cary wrote an article, published in

Nimbus, III, 2, 1955). The best clue to Gulley, as a painter, is an obituary notice (in MS. Cary 82, fol. 57), which was evidently discarded for the italicised passage in *The Horse's Mouth,* p. 271. It includes (with much illegibility and cancellation): 'famous twenty years ago for his nudes. Afterwards . . . changed his style . . . for allegorical works in a [?slight] style [?compounded] of W. Blake and the extreme modern school represented by the Spencers', the last name being changed, with much apparent hesitation, to 'Stanley Spencer'. Gulley's biography, the note ends, 'should establish this great painter in his rightful position which belongs rather to European and especially French art, than the English school'. In terms of painting, the reference to early nudes and French art certainly suggests Fergusson; in terms of Cary's own written art, the description supports suggestions of European, and especially French, influence made in this study.

30   *The Horse's Mouth,* p. 276; cf. *Modern Scottish Painting* (Glasgow, 1943), pp. 142-3.
31   'A Conversation with Joyce Cary', *Tamarack Review,* p. 5.
32   See pp. 70, 71 below regarding the strict Calvinist upbringing of Cary's wife; his letters to her include such remarks as: 'Blackmore has been bullying me about Art exactly like Mother & Father' (23 Aug. 1916).
33   It is reproduced in The Leicester Galleries Catalogue of an exhibition of 'Nudes and Bathers' by J. D. Fergusson, Exhibition No. 1373, May 5-30, 1970.
34   *Between Two Worlds,* p. 155.
35   *Between Two Worlds,* pp. 152, 153.
36   *Between Two Worlds,* p. 193.
37   Information from D. M. Davin.
38   Meyerstein's *Of My Early Life* (London, 1957) describes the great influence of two platonists as tutors: E. D. Lee, who introduced him to Jowett's *Plato,* and J. A. Stewart, who showed an 'aperçu foreshadowed by Schopenhauer' in relating the *Symposium* and *Phaedrus* to music and poetry. Meyerstein's sufferings as a Jew at Harrow, resembling those discussed above in 'Tottenham' and *A House of Children,* give insight into the way Jewish boys at Clifton might have felt, as described by Thomas Higham (ch. 4, n. 55 above).
39   *Some Letters of E. H. W. Meyerstein* (London, 1959), pp. 44-45; cf. Murry's reaction against Rossetti with Cary's, noted above, p. 41.
40   E.g., MS. Cary 238, fol. 8 is an envelope, postmarked 24 Aug. 1948, with notes reading 'Lit. Clubs . . . I learnt a lot at old MILTON'; the envelope exemplifies Cary's method of lecturing, intended to give the impression of being 'unscripted', says Enid Starkie ('A Portrait', p. 137), as she assumed they were, though MSS. show that Cary also wrote his lectures out; MS. Cary 240, fols. 135-6 (Cary's typescript) outline a talk to the Beaumont Club, describing his membership of Oxford clubs, implying that he held some office in the Milton, since he says he owns a box labelled Milton which he now uses for family papers. Cary's theme in this lecture is noteworthy: that the criticism of literary clubs as the centre of English study is that they are too critical, pigeon-holing and studying works from the outside, so that papers criticizing

critics should be encouraged: 'Edmund Wilson for instance with his theory . . . that all that matters to a writer is to have an unhappy childhood dickens and the blacking factory I don't altogether believe this . . . but it makes a good there is something perhaps in it to explain wilson [sic]'; the remark proves Cary's familiarity with Wilson, and possibly a previous acceptance—in view of his own background.

41 Letter of 1 Dec. 1911.

42 Recalled in a letter of Joyce Cary to his wife, 7 Nov. 1916.

43 See below p. 99.

44 That Cary was conscious of such a reason seems evident from Cary C.1360, his copy of Joan Corrie, *A B C of Jung's Psychology* (London, 1927; reprinted Aug. 1928); p. 67 concerns the projection of unconscious complexes: 'a man may project the image of his mother into his wife'. Cary has marked: 'such a man when choosing a wife is unconsciously looking for a mother. She must be the kind of woman his mother was.'

45 MS. Cary 322, fol. 8; stamped July 5 1912.

Chapter Six

1 E.g. p. 49 above, and Cary's marginal gloss on Byron in *The Drunken Sailor*, p. 23; 'He will always be a model for those who hide self-mistrust with a defiant gesture.' 'Byronic' is an early conception of Jim Latter in MS. Cary 288/S.20.D.

2 As in his poem to Tolstoy, and *The Evolution of an Intellectual* (London, 1920)—discussed below, p. 101.

3 MS. Cary 252/S.2.B.

4 MS. Cary 256/S.4.F.*a*, a bundle of loose notes; 'Like an . . .', on a different leaf from the previous lines, may be influenced by Whitehead, for whom God is a poet, and through Whitehead, by Plato's *Timaeus* or *Phaedrus*.

5 E.g. MS. Cary 271/N.98, fol. 7.

6 MS. Cary 271/N.96, 98, 99, 100 contain Cary's notes on Tolstoy, preparatory to his lecture in Edinburgh, delivered immediately before he began *The Horse's Mouth*.

7 In MS. Cary 251/P.3, fol 28ᵛ (dated 1927-8); and 296/P.172 (dated May 1955) where it appears on the cover and as a general title on the theme of 'the fight to reconcile oneself with death' (fol. 22ʳ).

8 *Daily Express* (8 Nov. 1912), p. 6.

9 *Memoir of the Bobotes* (London, 1964), p. 14.

10 Ibid., p. 9.

11 Wright, *Preface*, p. 23.

12 *Bobotes*, p. 154; the influence of Thomas Hardy, which Cary acknowledged, may here be discerned.

13 See below, pp. 83, 175.

14   Discussed below, p. 143.

15   Wright, *Preface*, pp. 23-24; the medal is the equivalent of the Military Cross.

16   'Five Windows Darken', p. 100.

17   See *Aissa Saved*, pp. 159, 169; *The African Witch*, pp. 35, 281; *Castle Corner*, p. 156; *Charley is my Darling*, pp. 159, 177; *Herself Surprised*, p. 81; *To be a Pilgrim*, pp. 23, 261; *The Horse's Mouth*, pp. 30, 67, 117, 151, 156; *A Fearful Joy*, 215, 219, 222, 315; *Except the Lord*, p. 241; *The Captive and the Free*, pp. 31, 57, 130.

18   *A House of Children*, p. 136.

19   Cf. p. 56 above.

20   MS. 255/N.35; 251/P.12, fol. 1ᵛ has a note for *An American Visitor*: 'Bewsher enjoys life at the moment and understands that life is an art—that 'progress' etc. beside the point—that men and society are constructions—works of art'.

21   MS. 252/S.3.G; 'Bush River', *Windmill*, no. 2 (1945), 120-5; *Spring Song and other stories* (London, 1960), pp. 9-18.

22   Confirmed by MS. Cary 290/P.147, fol. 4.

23   For Jung, see ch. 2, n. 18. This symbolism appears in *The African Witch*, pp. 42, 54, 72.

24   Dodds, *The Greeks and the Irrational*, p. 8 ff., gives an account which illuminates this story.

25   Most strikingly in *To be a Pilgrim*, ch. 9.

26   *Cornhill Magazine*, CLXV (Winter 1950/1951), 50-54; *Spring Song*, pp. 19-24.

27   *Art and Reality*, p. 153.

28   Cf. pp. 142, 222 below.

29   Malcolm Foster, *A Biography* (Boston, 1968), p. 105 (not in 'Cheerful Protestant', Atlantic ed.); this elucidates Cary's key word *surprise* e.g. in *An American Visitor*, Carfax ed. (London, 1952), p. 229; Murry describes death similarly (*Between Two Worlds*, pp. 57-58).

30   *Reporter* (15 May 1951), pp. 21-24; *Selected Essays*, pp. 83-90.

31   Wright, *Preface*, p. 7.

32   Letter from Cary to his wife; discussed by Mahood, *Joyce Cary's Africa*, p. 89.

33   This is Cary's essential point, as the close of *Art and Reality* makes plain.

34   Some of the writing surrounding Jarvis has been published as *Cock Jarvis an unfinished novel*, edited by A. G. Bishop (London, 1974); the text of this study had been completed before its publication, being based on a direct study of the MSS.; Bishop's thesis was also read.

35   *Castle Corner*, p. 365; p. 188 below.

36   *Fyodor Dostoevsky* (London, 1916), pp. 79, 44.

37   Cf. 'Cheerful Protestant', p. 52: 'Personal salvation, Cary would say, is too selfish a business to bother about'.

Chapter Seven

1 In 'A Conversation', *Tamarack Review,* and 'The Novelist at Work'.
2 E.g. Pamela Hansford Johnson, 'Joyce Cary's Later Manner', *John O'London's Weekly* (26 Sept. 1952), p. 895.
3 Letter of 4 April 1952, to Harper's.
4 MS. Cary 240, fol. 50; fol. 20 reads: 'Dosto. English club Oxf. 1952/ English club Camb. 1952.'
5 MS. Cary 268/S.10.D.*e*; see below, pp. 139-40.
6 However, the name is almost certainly derived from *Carré,* the name Cary was known by in France.
7 MS. Cary 259/N.44, fol. 21 (c. 1934).
8 'The Novelist at Work', p. 24.
9 John Middleton Murry, *D. H. Lawrence: Son of Woman,* with a new introduction (London, 1954), p. xvii; Murry also quotes Lawrence's final rejection of him in May 1929: ' "even as immortal spirits, we shall dwell in different Hades".'
10 Harry T. Moore, *The Life and Work of D. H. Lawrence,* 2nd ed. (London, 1963), p. 103, letter of Jan. 1915 from Lawrence to W. E. Hopkin.
11 Ibid., p. 104; letter to Lady Cynthia Asquith.
12 Ibid., p. 116.
13 Ibid., pp. 245-6.
14 (London, 1923); Cary's copy was given to him by his wife on their wedding anniversary, June 1927, but he is likely to have read it earlier (see p. 107 below).
15 Cf. this paragraph with *The Horse's Mouth,* p. 255.
16 Expressed in *Women in Love,* and discussed by Moore, *Lawrence,* p. 139.
17 Discussed further below, p. 121.
18 MS. Cary 266/S.9.C; a valuable clue to the *à rebours* nature of Gulley and Tom Wilcher lies here; quotations are from *Fantasia of the Unconscious,* pp. 138, 159.
19 *Fantasia,* p. 172; *Charley is my Darling,* p. 316.
20 *The Brothers Karamazov,* trans. Constance Garnett (London, 1912, reprinted 1930), p. 245; beating as a British institution is most clearly depicted in *Charley is my Darling,* where, p. 175, ' "I'll stick to facts" ' seems a deliberate echo of *Karamazov,* p. 249; ' "I want to stick to the fact".'
21 MS. Cary 255/N.33.
22 See Tolstoy's letter to Nikolai Strachov, dated 19 March 1870, which answers Strachov's article 'John Stuart Mill on Women', and ends: 'Just think of London without its 70,000 prostitutes! . . . No, I believe the prostitute is necessary for the maintenance of the family.' In view

of Cary's interest in Mill (evident in *Power in Men* and notebooks surrounding it), this surely underlies Cary's theme, particularly in *The Horse's Mouth;* for on 4 Nov. 1942 he ordered, in the Bodleian Library, *Tolstoy: New Light on his Life and Genius,* ed. R. Fülöp-Miller, trans. Paul England (London, 1931), where the letter appears, pp. 249-51; MS. Cary 271/N.98 contains Cary's notes from this work.

23 See Jeffrey Meyers, 'D. H. Lawrence and Homosexuality', *D. H. Lawrence Novelist, Poet, Prophet,* ed. Stephen Spender (London, 1973), pp. 135-46.

24 Ibid., p. 41, in 'Frieda and Lawrence', David Garnett reveals Lawrence's shocking, spiteful jealousy of Frieda's love and distress for her children.

25 'Travels in a Mind', *Selected Essays,* p. 165.

26 'Tolstoy's Theory of Art and Morals', the subject of his talk, was published as 'Tolstoy's Theory of Art', *University of Edinburgh Journal,* XII (Summer 1943), 91-96; thus his message appears to have been resisted.

27 As suggested on p. 70 above.

28 MS. Cary 312, fol. 220.

29 He offered Eliot the assistant editorship of the *Athenaeum;* as editor, he praised Lawrence's *Sons and Lovers,* to 'give him a leg-up', and also upheld reprinting *The Rainbow* (Lea, *Murry,* p. 66).

30 'Five Windows Darken', p. 111; I had not noted the letter, or its significance, at the time that I read a draft of Dan Davin's memoir (as he kindly acknowledges on p. xxii).

31 MS. Cary 312, fol. 218; Cary always wrote *dependance.*

32 Interview, 23 Aug. 1968.

33 'Five Windows Darken', p. 112.

34 Mrs Helena Bret-Smith, 3 Oct. 1967, kindly filled in this background.

35 Michael Cary confirmed that he remained bitter.

36 Wright, *Preface,* p. 107, remarks on Cary's use of 'drunk'; for Murry, see *The Evolution of an Intellectual,* p. 20.

37 'The Sign-Seekers', pp. 8, 9-10; first published in Oct. 1916.

38 Lea, *Murry,* p. 92, p. 183: ' "I follow the sign".'

39 By Thomas Joyce, *Strand Magazine,* LXVI (Dec. 1923), 655-65.

40 By Thomas Joyce, *Hutchinson's Magazine,* IV (June 1921), 601-15.

41 MS. Cary 250/N.16, fol. 82.

42 MS. Cary 253/N.14; others include 251/P.9, 274/P.37; in 258/S.5.G.*b,* under 'Plan of campaign', is 'Notebook for names' (c. 1933).

43 MS. Cary 254/N.18; 'old book' is deleted; see ch. 1, n. 23.

44 Sir James Frazer, *The Golden Bough,* abridged ed. (London, November 1922) followed publication of *The Waste Land;* ch. XXII, deals with superstitions attaching to personal names.

45 See below, pp. 292, 307; also his long poems: *Marching Soldier* which, first called 'Tell Me the Name', repeats this theme throughout, and *The Drunken Sailor,* which warns against names like Dante, now used to serve authority, or Marx, in itself a formula for hate and war; any inhibitions regarding names in Cary's writing can be understood from Freud's *Psychopathology of Everyday Life,* ch. III.

46 *Acronyms and Abbreviations* . . . handbook of British usage, complied A. C. Montgomery (London, 1975).

47 MS. Cary 254/N.17, bundle 2.

48 *Maurice* 'has been used in Ireland to render the native *Moriertagh* (Moriarty)' Withycombe says; *Moody* is from the Old English, meaning 'bold, proud, passionate', says Basil Cottle, *The Penguin Dictionary of English Surnames* (London, 1967).

49 So interpreted below, ch. 11; for a fuller comparison of James Joyce and Joyce Cary see Barbara Fisher, 'Two Joycean Novelists', *The Canadian Journal of Irish Studies*, IV, no. 2 (Dec. 1978), pp. 5-22.

50 'James Clarence Morgan', *The Critical Writings of James Joyce*, Ellsworth Mason and Richard Ellmann, eds. (New York, 1964), p. 83.

51 MS. Cary 238, fol. 45.

52 'The Way a Novel Gets Written', *Selected Essays*, p. 120.

53 *Finnegans Wake* (London, 1939), p. 55.

54 MS. Cary 271/N.85 *h.*

55 Richard Ellmann, *James Joyce* (London, 1966), pp. 3, 4.

56 MS. Cary 254/N.21, fol. 28, contains notes in French on Scott and Rabelais from *Causeries du Lundi;* L. P. Entry Book 20/7 records that Cary ordered relevant volumes on 13 and 15 Feb. 1923; such evidence as handwriting and paper supports this dating, from which notes for 'Maurice Moody' can be dated—in N.17 also.

57 E.g., it seems evident from p. 47 above, that he had recently read *Là-Bas,* before buying his copy.

58 E.g., MS. Cary 257/N.37, fol. 11, dated 1930, records Tristram's saying ' "Its Brownade—and when its full its a skemeton"; *A House of Children,* p. 54, attributes almost identical words to Anketel.

59 MS. Cary 312, fol. 216; notes in M.S. Cary 254/N.17, bundle 1.

60 MS. 254/N.20, fol. 8: Maurice Eden & Cedar Paul, *Creative Revolution* (London, 1920).

61 MS. Cary 254/N.18.

62 MS. Cary 254/N.17, bundle 4.

63 MS. Cary 252/S.3.B; cancelled by Cary from the word 'asked'.

64 Thus a likely inspiration, for this political trilogy, would be Blake's lines: ' "What is a Wife & what is a Harlot? What is a Church & What/ "Is a Theatre? are they Two & not One? can they Exist Separate?/"Are not Religion & Politics the Same Thing? Brotherhood is Religion".' (*Jerusalem*: III, 57); cf. p. 178 below.

65 See MS. Cary 162, fol. 88; it will be argued that Gulley Jimson owes much to Lawrence, with whom Cary evidently tried to identify Jarvis (as shown immediately below); possibly therefore Cary was here attempting an *à rebours* treatment of character—which he was in fact using at this time for his first novel, for Bradgate and Carr for example.

66 MS. Cary 162, fol. 121 ff.; quotations appear in *Cock Jarvis,* pp. 185-197, see also pp. 85, 188 of this study.

67 See *Murry,* p. 129, where Lea also shows how Murry calls Jesus a poet endowed with the gift of 'imaged speech' who taught 'not goodness, but *wholeness';* Cock Jarvis supposedly has great gifts as a storyteller, and is an autocrat, as 'proved by the mob of tradesmen, snobs, cranks, prostitutes, thieves . . . who gathered round him everywhere' (MS. Cary 163, fol. 114); since other references to Jesus are so evident,

a comparison here too can be assumed, both Jesus and Jarvis in their ways exemplifying Cary's idea of a 'spellbinder'.

68 For Platonism, and Murry, see ch. 5; regarding women, Murry noted in his journal, on 16 Sept. 1931 : 'This looks like being my baptism into direct knowledge of the Female—the thing I have always eluded'—he refers to the episode described below, p. 275; for Lawrence as a platonist, see Moore, *Lawrence*, p. 142.

69 But a 'Nancy' is also a Jezebel; for, in 'The Revolution of the Women', Cary writes that women of the twenties began to paint themselves like a 'Nancy'; *Vogue* (U. S.), CXVII (15 March 1951), 99; checked from MS.

70 MS. Cary 165, words quoted in this para. being on fols. 81, 83, 136, 137.

71 MS. Cary 167/1, fol. 122; MS. Cary 167/2, fol. 42 has 'When N. finds that Jimson would have married her she hates Jarvis, or Jimson says that he would.' The situation hints at the 2nd trilogy, and the names suggest the first; for Sara is a variant of Nancy in the Jarvis story, and mother and daughter are so named in the first trilogy, which concerns Jimson.

72 MS. Cary 165, fol. 202; *Cock Jarvis*, p. 31.

73 MS. Cary 167/1, fol. 177; here the young lovers' names are Kate and Rory Thompson.

74 Information from Mr Tristram Cary, 1962.

75 'Unfinished Novels', MS. Cary 249, fol. 170; *Selected Essays*, p. 109; unfortunately, on this page, the editor has given Cary a false viewpoint by repeating a typist's error, and omitting the words 'hope of' in : 'He believed in the Empire, in fact, as the only hope of liberal civilisation in the world.' Of this, Cary says : 'Though Jarvis was right in principle he was wrong in fact because the Empire couldn't last.'

Chapter Eight

1 MS. Cary 254/N.26, fol. 3.

2 MS. Cary 251/P.4, fols. 1-3.

3 MS. Cary 251/P.11, fol. 7, and 256/S.4.E.*b*.

4 MS. Cary 251/P.3, fol. 20.

5 MS. Cary 251/P.5, fols. 15, 16.

6 MS. Cary 254/N.30, fols, 75, 80.

7 'Hughes' MS.

8 Letter to B. Fisher of 10 Nov. 1967; Cary's interest in John Macmurray would have been fostered during the thirties by the latter's association with Middleton Murry's political activities; see Lea, *Murry*, p. 233.

9 *Search for Reality in Religion* (London, 1965), p. 9.

10 MS. Cary 265/N.73; Hausa, as well as European, names appear to have been used symbolically by Cary; but the use was poetic, rather than scientific, and based on his practice of the language between 1914

and 1920, with reference to C. H. Robinson, *Dictionary of the Hausa Language*, 2 vols. (Cambridge, 1913, 1914), which he owned, and inscribed '1914'.

11 Cary owned an Authorized Version of the Bible inscribed '1935', with passages from Romans noted on the inside cover.

12 *Prisoner of Grace*, chs. 31-33; discussed below, p. 274; *The African Witch*, p. 178, contrasts 'the religion of the waiting-room' of Mohammedans 'waiting for paradise', with the 'purposeful activity' of a pagan for whom 'there was only one world'.

13 *What I Believe*, p. 375.

14 Introduction, *Recollections and Essays*, Tolstoy Centenary ed., trans. Louise and Aylmer Maude, vol. 21 (London, 1937), pp. vii, viii, x; records of the earlier publication of Garland's essay were destroyed during the war.

15 MS. Cary 255/N.36.

16 MS. Cary 255/N.33.

17 See Ch. 1, n. 24.

18 MS. Cary 258/S.5.N.

19 Dodds, *The Greeks and the Irrational*, p. 218.

20 *Totem and Taboo*, trans. A. A. Brill (London, 1919), pp. 267, 235-6.

21 Ibid, pp. 255, 256, 257.

22 On p. 227, the lines arrest the eye; for 'Eating the God', see *An American Visitor*, p. 154: ' "as if she could eat him" ' describes the way Marie looks at Bewsher, who is then actually eaten, in a pagan ritual incited by her.

23 MS. Cary 270/S.11.B; these quotations are on separate leaves.

24 A letter from Michael Joseph Ltd., dated 3 Sept. 1947, refers to the undated attached announcement; 'A State of Nature' could owe something to Hobbes and Spinoza also, judging from notes on both in MS. Cary 271/N.95.

25 P. 18 gives the key to the novel in the aunt's 'passion for Jim', which she indulges through Nina; reference next to love between a brother and sister possibly owes something to Cary's wife, who wrote to him on 5 Nov. 1916 regarding her brother Frederick: 'I know if he hadnt been my brother I should have fallen in love with him, & wanted to marry him!' For the novel describes how a certain brother and sister were 'encouraged to love each other', though belonging to 'rather a strict low Church household' called 'Legh Boles', which is almost an anagram for Ogilvies, and certainly an odd name; moreover, a letter of 3 April 1915 from Mrs Ogilvie to this daughter, regarding Frederick, says she is 'full of my mother's love for you both—that he has written as he has and of your love for each other . . . So take heart darling about *all* our dear human love that God has given us—make the most of it'. Martin du Gard's 'Confidence Africaine' could have stimulated Cary's interest in incest.

26 See below, p. 213.

27 MS. Cary 258/S.5.N.

28 MS. Cary 251/P.9, fol. 9, entitled 'Hor. Mou.' is a loose leaf of pencil notes resembling those on *Totem and Taboo* in S.5.N, where the paper and the ink notes match S.4.F (quoted below).

29 'A Conversation . . .' *Tamarack Review*, p. 9.
30 MS. Cary 251/P.8, fol. 3^r.
31 MS. Cary 251/P.9, fol. 2^r.
32 MS. Cary 256/S.4.F.*a*.
33 MS. Cary 255/N.35.
34 MS. Cary 258/S.5.C.
35 E.g. in both novels the sun appears in key scenes (pp. 165, 172 below), accord with Jung's view, that it 'is adapted as is nothing else to represent the visible God of this world. That is to say, that driving strength of our own soul, which we call libido, and whose nature it is to allow the useful and injurious,' the good and the bad to proceed' (*Psychology of the Unconscious*, trans. B. Hinkle (London, 1918), p. 128); *The African Witch* depicts the Jungian rider on horseback mastering his *libido* on pp. 43, 54, 72; Bewsher has 'jockey's legs' and the air of a 'parson' (p. 38) implying that his libido is mastered; for Freud, see ch. 8, n. 34, above.
36 *Totem and Taboo*, p. vii; 'My Religious History', fol. 5, records Cary's familiarity with Kant's Categorical Imperative from Oxford student days; he condemns allegory, 'because it lays down categorical imperatives' (*Art and Reality*, p. 163).
37 Freud quotes Wundt, that the most primitive human impulse originates ' "*in the fear of the effect of demonic powers*" ' (p. 40); thus Evelyn's wish for his horse, in *A House of Children*, would signify fear of demonic powers that could overcome the God of love he had known from his mother; Evelyn and little Hans are plainly comparable.
38 For Jung, see MS. Cary 258/S.5.C; for Whitehead, notes on *Process and Reality*, e.g. in MS. Cary 267/N.64, which relates to MS. Cary 265/N.63 regarding 'Creative imagination'.
39 *Phaedrus* (254), trans. J. Wright.
40 Ibid. (246).
41 *Power in Men*, p. 259; markings also signify Cary's reading of Alexander's article 'Theism and Pantheism', *The Hibbert Journal*, XXV, no. 2 (Jan. 1927), 251-64; Alexander is recognized as the precursor of Whitehead.
42 MS. Cary 258/S.5.E.*b*.
43 Ibid., cancellations are 'intelligence' after 'natural'; 'dev' after 'easily'.
44 Ibid.
45 *Power in Men*, pp. 3-6.
46 MS. Cary 258/S.5.D.
47 MS. Cary 256/S.4.G.
48 MS. Cary 257/N.41, fol. 5.
49 E.g. *Psychology and Alchemy*, trans. R. F. C. Hull (London, 1953), Part I; for Cary see below, p. 335.
50 MS. Cary 251/P.7, fol. 4.
51 *Journal of Philosophical Studies*, II, no. 8 (Oct. 1927), 503-15; Roth is assessing psychological and anthropological evidence, chiefly from Rudolf Otto's *The Idea of the Holy*, trans. John W. Harvey (1923; 4th impression, London, 1926); and R. R. Marett's *Threshold of Religion* (London, 1909); Cary's notes are in MS. Cary 251/P.6, fol. 10.

52 The annotations are in pencil, which is more difficult, than ink, to date. But the suggestion here offered is that the note 'Goodness used ambiguously . . .' was added after 1940, as discussed in our next para.; those on pp. 506-7 of the journal, with vowels omitted, seem certainly of the late twenties, as are those in 251/P.6.

53 MS. Cary 271/N.82.

54 MS. Cary 272/P.59, fol. 1.

Chapter Nine

1 MS. Cary 268/S.5.E.*a* (Hughes MS.); many cancellations.

2 MS. Cary 268/S.10.D.*e*; the passage is in Mrs Cary's typescript, recognizable by the (corrected) mis-use of 'it's'; she may have misread Cary's handwriting, to type Edmunden for Edmondson, the name of a preacher and religious writer of the early 19th century.

3 'Proper Names in Poetry', *Times Literary Supplement* (11 June 1970), pp. 638, 639.

4 *Lawrence*, p. 127.

5 *Kenyon Review*, IX (1949), 539-60.

6 See pp. 18, 218, 337 of this study.

7 MS. Cary 250/N.16, fol. 9.

8 MS. Cary 265/N.63, fol. 5 (using horse symbolism).

9 Scala cinema, March 1938; Cary admired Fields from the 30s as (with Chaplin) the greatest modern comic, and saw many Fields films again in USA with Irene Laune, she reports (2 Oct. 1979).

10 'An Interview with Joyce Cary', *Selected Essays*, p. 7.

11 MS. Cary 265/N.63, fol. 1.

12 Written on a letter of 22 Sept. 1949, from T. Tornquist.

13 'The Novelist at Work', pp. 16-17.

14 MS. Cary 247, fol. 224.

15 *D. H. Lawrence: Selected Literary Criticism,* ed. Anthony Beal (London: Mercury Books, 1961). p. 233, shows that Lawrence named Murry, but that the name of Katherine Mansfield was substituted for Murry's, when this introduction was published in *The Grand Inquisitor,* trans. S. S. Koteliansky (London, 1930), pp. iii-xv; 'Pro and Contra' includes this story in a broader argument.

16 MS. Cary 265/N.70.

17 MS. Cary 274/P.61, fol. 43.

18 Lea, *Murry*, p. 340.

19 'A Portrait', p. 143.

20 Ibid., p. 133.

21 These ideas are presented in *Power in Men*. It was much altered by another hand before publication; so the God of Cary's vision appears only in '*Notes II*, but is unmistakable—and not anthropomorphic, he shows. For *Art and Reality* see below, p. 331.

22 MS. Cary 272/P.82, fol. 1.

23 'My First Novel', *Listener* (16 April 1953), p. 638.

24 By closing his essay on Tolstoy thus (p. 97 above), Cary indicates that it was the sentiment closest to his own aims as a writer.

Chapter Ten

1   For advice on the meaning of African and Arabic words, I am indebted to Mr F. W. Parsons, of London University, and Mr A. H. M. Kirk-Greene, of Oxford University.

2   Dodds, *The Greeks and the Irrational*, p. 8.

3   The name Abba perfectly symbolizes the theme; though not a normal Hausa name, it is a Kanouri title meaning 'Prince', while sounding like the common nickname for a Hausa child, *A bar* [*shi*], meaning 'let it be spared'. As this is an invocation, to ward off the evil eye, it clearly fits Aissa's baby, who escapes being destroyed at birth as a witch, only to be sacrificed by 'Christians', his mother having become known as the Christian witch.

4   *The Brothers Karamazov*, p. 265.

5   James, *The Varieties of Religious Experience*, p. 78, says that laughter and happiness may produce the sort of religion which is the grateful admiration of the gift of happy existence, and that complex religions point the way to supernatural happiness, 'when the first gift of natural existence is unhappy'.

6   'My First Novel'; see ch. 9, n. 23.

7   MS. Cary 255/N. 36 shows 'The Buchmanite' and this novel plotted for simultaneously; other evidence below.

8   *Paleface: The Philosophy of the 'Melting Pot'* (London, 1929), p. 289.

9   Ibid., pp. 296-7.

10 MS. Cary 12.

11 *Week End Review*, 9 Sept. 1933; reviewers in *Manchester Guardian*, 25 Aug. 1933, *Sunday Times*, 25 Aug. 1933 were similarly obtuse.

12 *Paleface*, pp. 146-8, 271.

13 Letter of 4 Dec. 1956 from the office of Curtis Brown.

14 MS. in A. Wright Box 5; not yet located in reclassification.

15 'T. S. Eliot and the "out there",' *Times Literary Supplement* (10 Dec. 1971), pp. 1551-2.

16 See Tom Driberg, *The Mystery of Moral Re-Armament* [later name for the movement] (London, 1964), p. 52.

17 MS. Cary 258/S.5.S, to his publisher Ernest Benn.

18 'The Grand Inquisitor', *Selected Literary Criticism*, p. 241.

19 MS. Cary 8.

20 W. J. Perry, *Hibbert Journal*, XXV, no. 2 (Jan. 1927), 237-50.

21 Manuscripts show that she was to have thought herself pregnant before marrying Bewsher, whose offer therefore becomes more in character, and accords with 'Cock Jarvis' plotting; remarks in ch. XVII suggest

that Marie is believed to be involved already with Gore, who is likely in any case to become known as the child's father; the situation thus anticipates the 2nd trilogy, and fulfils the idea of a parallel life of Christ, which Cary was already planning.

22 Cottle, *Surnames*, pp. 47, 256.
23 MS. Cary 251/P. 12; MS. Cary 254/N.31, fol. 95, has 'Search for happiness. Begin with the song I want to be happy. . . .'
24 Eduard Hitschmann, *Freud's Theories of the Neuroses*, trans. C. R. Payne (London, 1921), pp. 65-67; Cary's symbolism can be understood from Hitschmann's discussion of the censor, which compels the use of wit rather than plain words, or the symbolism most obvious in dreams; this bears on p. 39 above.
25 *The Golden Bough*, abridged ed., pp. 331, 347, 350.
26 See ch. 8, n. 35.
27 MS. Cary 251/P.11, fol. 2.
28 Jung, pp. 281-3; Cary's horse symbolism is illuminated by: 'The horse is a libido symbol, partly of phallic, partly of maternal significance, like the tree. It represents the libido . . . repressed through the incest prohibition' (p. 316).
29 Ibid., p. 62.
30 *Art and Reality*, p. 170; p. 337 below.
31 MS. Cary 255/N.35.
32 Cottle, *Surnames*, gives the meaning 'singer' chorister', which accords with the idea of the mouth transformed by art, as attributed to Judy Coote, p. 173 below; his 'blue eyes' (pp. 190, 191) signify his skill as a ruler (cf. ch. 3, n. 18).
33 E.g. Lepper, p. 186, appears in *Cock Jarvis*, p. 58 ff.
34 MS. Cary 259/N.44.
35 *Ju-ju*, as printed in this novel, is more eye-catching than 'juju', in the previous novels.
36 As in *Aissa*, the swamps are near the mission; Bewsher escapes the sacred crocodiles (*Amer. Vis.* p. 190). much as Rackham does (p. 172 below).
37 MS. Cary 255/N.33.

Chapter Eleven

1 MS. Cary 251/P.21, fol. 1.
2 MS. Cary 257/N.46.
3 See *Power in Men*, pp. 158-9; pp. 335-6 below.
4 Lea, *Murry*, p. 241.
5 Mary 'knew all his sermons by heart' (p. 96), and they had some influence on her trusting that an Omnipotent God would not let Shon die.
6 *Power in Men*, p. 158; discussed below, p. 337.
7 Jarvis has 'the true Napoleonic nose and chin' (p. 366) when hailed as 'conqueror'; Felix too, as a 'Napoleon', can be understood by this note

(which continues the quotation on p. 91 above): 'The war itself was a culmination of nationalist and vulgar forces, arising with Napoleon.'

8   *Power in Men*, pp. 158, 169.

9   MS. Cary 297, fol. 207; MS. Cary 256/S.4.K.

10 *Power in Men*, pp. 154-7 argues the case, with particular reference to Tolstoy, and states the theme of the book as Cary's answer to Tolstoy; it is presented on p. 237 below, being relevant to Gulley Jimson.

11 MS. Cary 263/N.54; cf. ch. 10, n. 23. *A House of Children* and *Charley is My Darling* grew from plans for another Irish novel (see MS. Cary 270//S.11.A etc.) which had the tentative titles 'It's a Gift They Want to be Happy'.

Chapter Twelve

1   MS. Cary 265/N.73; Gollup's unorthodox habits include wearing 'pale blue socks with green suspenders' (p. 122); cf. ' "your greens and your blues" ' of Gulley, p. 229 below.

2   Cf. ch. 10, n. 5, and Jung's *Psychology of the Unconscious,* p. 261: 'Not only is heaven no father and earth no mother, but they represent hostile destroying powers.'

3   As a university graduate, candidate for the vacant chieftancy, and involved in riots, Isa has developed from Aladai; that Johnson too is to be compared with Jesus is shown by this discarded ending: ' "O Jesus, you didn't want to die neither . . . they kill you. They break your heart—you good, I bad . . ." ' MS. Cary 265/N.73.

4   Ibid.

5   The Green Man represents Blake's vegetative man, and appears as the pub in drafts of the 1930s and so in other novels developing from that material, from *Castle Corner* (p 272) to *Not Honour More* (p. 38), with special emphasis in *Except the Lord* (p. 52 ff.).

6   References to this novel in chs. 2 and 3 supplement this analysis.

7   MSS. Cary 269/N.81; 270/S.11.I.

8   *'teach me how to live'* trans. Rosemary Edmonds, Penguin ed. (London, 1964), p. 44; ' "Teach me to know what thou wouldst have done",' is less convincing as a source, in Cary's copy, trans. C. J. Hogarth (London, 1912), p. 32; but is is difficult not to think that Cary was inspired by Tolstoy, who also begins by describing the tutor, just after the tenth birthday of Nikolai, whose father takes him on a hunt, and whose first love is named Katya—the Russian form of Kathy.

9   MS. Cary 266/S.9.E.

10 E.g. as *catel* meaning 'movable property'; 'divine kettle or cauldron, probably connected with creation' (Yonge), extends the idea imaginatively; that Christ was an 'ass traveller' on Palm Sunday implies that most Christians are taking a long time to catch up.

11 See ch. 7, n. 58.

Chapter Thirteen

1 By Gilbert Murray; discussed by Dodds, *The Greeks and the Irrational,* p. 179 ff.
2 MS. Cary 265/N.73; referred to above, p. 119.
3 *The Symbolist Movement*, p. 46.
4 Genesis xvii 15, 16, shows *Sarai*, 'contentious', changed to Sarah; the hellenized form *Sara* avoids the distinction.
5 See pp. 44, and 190.
6 C. W. Bardsley *English Surnames*, 5th ed. (London, 1897), p. 82, gives this derivation for Hickson, as does Yonge, in 1863.
7 *Herself Surprised*, pp. 38, 66.
8 *The Horse's Mouth*, p. 71; see below, p. 333.
9 D. M. Emmet, *Philosophy*, XVI (1941), 257-8.
10 MS. Cary 271/N.97.
11 *Herself Surprised*, p. 214.
12 MS. Cary 81.
13 Cf. *Between Two Worlds*, p. 136; *Herself Surprised*, p. 10.
14 MS. Cary 281/N.92.
15 As all Cary's characters named James can be thought of as supplanters, they can be called sons of Jacob who supplanted Esau (Gen. xxv. 26), giving the name its popular meaning; for *Jimson* as also a son of St James, see below, n. 39.
16 *Varieties of Religious Experience*, p. 155.
17 MS. Cary 270/S.11.F.
18 *The Brothers Karamazov*, pp. 52, 53; cf. *Herself Surprised*, p. 149: 'Jimson had said . . . I was born servant', and p. 212 above.
19 Letters of May 1933 show that 'Tod' grew from 'The Jew story' incorporating 'Brant' material (cf. p. 127 above), and that on 'May 3rd '33' Cary 'disentangled a third out of the other two'; the latter became the earliest 'Captive and Free' material which Cary set aside to write *Castle Corner*, intending to make it the sequel; it became incorporated instead in *To be a Pilgrim* (then becoming the basis for later 'Captive and Free' material). Cary's method of writing novels concurrently began at this time.
20 See p. 121 above.
21 *Sons and Lovers*, Penguin ed. (London, 1948), p. 87.
22 MS. Cary 266/S.9.C.
23 In *Childhood, Boyhood, Youth*, pp. 144-7, Tolstoy (as author) is older when locked in the box room, but the time is equally decisive, for here he first felt religious doubts; pp. 120-4 show his sense of ugliness and awkwardness with an admired elder brother, regarding the maid; the relationship resembles Tom's with Edward, and possibly contributed to Evelyn and Harry (cf. ch. 12, n. 8).

24 Cf. *Art and Reality*, pp. 150-1.

25 P. 159; see below, p. 336.

26 MS. Cary 251/P.22, fol. 1, has: 'Theme/Rise of Rankins and fall of Basketts'; so Rankin is probably the pro-Boer agitator of *Castle Corner* (p. 391), transferred to this trilogy (p. 237 below); the Basketts appear in *A Fearful Joy*; see n. 49 below.

27 *The Golden Bough*, p. 109.

28 Letter of 17 June 1953 to Ruth Van Horn: 'Defoe has had no influence upon me whatsoever. The thing was invented by one of those stiff-minded persons who must find a pigeon-hole for a book before he can understand it'.

29 See James Joyce, *Daniel Defoe*, ed. and trans. Joseph Prescott (Buffalo, 1964), pp. 21, 22; Joyce says Defoe presents 'the eternal feminine in an unexpected light', Moll being 'the unique, the incomparable woman'.

30 Professor John Dover Wilson emphasised this fact, in an interview of 23 Aug. 1968.

31 Interview Dec. 1967.

32 *Power in Men*, note to p. 42.

33 *Art and Reality*, p. 169.

34 So he told John Fischer; notes confirm it; cf. n. 37 below.

35 See pp. 46-49.

36 *The Fortunes of Falstaff* (Cambridge, 1944); Prof. Dover Wilson agreed that Gulley is a Falstaffian character (23.8.68).

37 See p. 178 above; Lea, p. 216, also shows Murry reverting to Spinoza more and more, as the greatest Jew after Jesus; Murry's epitaph might have been Samuel Alexander's *Erravit cum Spinoza*, and his Shakespeare is Coleridge's, 'The Spinozistic deity—an omnipresent creativeness'; in all these respects Murry's and Cary's thinking agrees.

38 MS. Cary 274/P.60, fol. 21.

39 *What I Believe*, p. 451 quotes James ii. 14-22, 24, 26; p. 459 quotes John i 9-12; this explains why Gulley was conceived as a character in *Mister Johnson;* that Cary intended using *What I Believe* in his religious book is proved by MS. Cary 293/S.22.K.

40 *Power in Men*, pp. 42-43, concerns *Leviathan;* Gulley's whale, as his Judas, with Hitler's blue eyes, may symbolize the betrayal of democracy (see p. 262 below).

41 See ch. 7, n. 26.

42 MS. Cary 271/N.98, fol. 23; cf. *Herself Surprised*, p. 72.

43 *Power in Men*, pp. 89-90; a footnote reads: 'So, of course, is everybody else, according to his powers'; a note of the mid-thirties in MS. Cary 255/N.36 reads: 'Novel about William Blake—like the van gogh.' Irving Stone's *Lust for Life*, on Van Gogh, appeared in 1934; Murry's study of Blake appeared in 1933.

44 Trans. C. J. Hogarth (London, 1913); Cary has marked passages on pp. 12-17, concerning a man wanting vengeance whom 'only a wall will stop' (cf. p. 147 above); 'one may be at fault even in regard to a stone wall' comments directly on the wall demolished as Gulley painted on it.

45 *The Horse's Mouth*, p. 271, explains this in a footnote, in italics.

46 But the prison symbol dominating the trilogy recalls Plato's view of the soul as imprisoned in the body; cf. *Art and Reality*, p. 165: 'We

have to have conceptual knowledge . . . to engage in any activity at all, but that knowledge, like the walls we put up to keep out the weather, shuts out the real world and the sky. It is a narrow little house which becomes a prison to those who can't get out of it.'

47 *The Horse's Mouth*, p. 190; cf. pp. 104, 228 above.

48 *The Horse's Mouth*, p. 255; cf. pp. 94, 282 of this study.

49 An illegitimate child is Ella Venn's error, and Tabitha Baskett's glory; the word 'basket' occurs in *An American Visitor* p. 194), and *The Moonlight* (p. 68), with sexual connotations; Jung, *Psychology of the Unconscious*, p. 236, gives 'basket' with 'chest' and 'box', as a typical symbol of the mother's womb.

50 MS. Cary 279/S.16.B.*b*; the original is in TS., with the exception' of the following, which are in Cary's longhand; [in 3rd line] conflict . . . as Gulley tells himself; [in 7th line] taking his own advice; [in 8th line] resentful.

51 *Power in Men*, p. 267; below, p. 332.

52 See ch. 11, n. 10.

53 *The Horse's Mouth*, p. 241; discussed above, p. 46.

Chapter Fourteen

1 MS. Cary 280/N.112, fols. 20-22; notes from B. Malinowski, *Sex and Repression in Savage Society* (London, 1927).

2 MS. Cary 280/N.110, p. 65.

3 Ibid., p. 4.

4 MSS. Cary 259/N.42; 270/S.11.A; see also ch. 13, n. 19.

5 MS. Cary 281/N.92.

6 MS. Cary 255/N.33.

7 MS. Cary 82.

8 *Castle Corner*, p. 273.

9 Cf. Tolstoy's view of women, ch. 7, n. 22, above.

10 Pp. 271, 286 below; Murry's use of 'lie in the soul' occurs in a highly relevant essay 'The Discovery of Pain', *The Evolution of An Intellectual, pp.* 39-49. Speaking of French writers, during World War I, he says: 'The war has cauterised the lie in the soul', whereas the English seem blind in their literature. He is reviewing *Vie des Martyrs* by Georges Duhamel, and concentrates on the story 'La Grâce'; it concerns suffering, which makes Augur popular, because he has mastered it. Murry says that unless we receive the vision of this truth into our hearts the lie in the soul which has made its manifestation possible will be indurated for ever.

11 P. 225; this view appears in 'Cock Jarvis', p. 111 above, and is finally commented upon by Harry Hooper, p. 319 below.

12 The 'tears' signify the collapse of this age; similar horse symbolism recurs in Cary's novels; e.g. *The Horse's Mouth*, where Plant's 'Back

room' has 'Horsehair chairs' (p. 73); his 'hobby-horse is Spinoza' (p. 86); cf. p. 293 below.

13 Pp. 55, 230 above.
14 MS. Cary 174.
15 MS. Cary 272/P.82, fol. 1.
16 Edn. Printed for J. Murray (No. 32). Fleet-MDCCLXXXX; I am indebted to Dr Ruth Christiani Brown for suggesting this possible source.
17 'The Novelist at Work', p. 19; *Art and Reality*, p. 9.
18 MS. Cary 283/N.134; for the bicycle, cf. *Selected Essays*, p. 244.
19 The slang term 'bonzer' is equally descriptive.
20 See ch. 4, n. 45.
21 See 'The Novelist at Work', p. 18, where he discusses Hitler in this novel in these terms.
22 'A Portrait', p. 132.
23 Letter of 22 Dec. 1949, to Elizabeth Lawrence.
24 Enid Starkie thought his 'gusto for life' was 'a deliberate attitude of courage', and that 'he had a very sad view of life' ('A Portrait', p. 126).

Chapter Fifteen

1 *Art and Reality*, p. 133.
2 MS. Cary 281/N.131.
3 *Except the Lord*, pp. 225, 278.
4 E.g. MS. Cary 274/P.31; pp. 229, 260 above.
5 See 'The Novelist at Work' (p. 18): 'people wouldn't believe Hitler was dead'; see also ch. 10, n. 20.
6 This relates to the prison theme of the first trilogy; see ch. 13, n. 46.
7 See p. 288 of this study.
8 P. 213 above; discussed on pp. 331-2.
9 MS. Cary 287/N.145 (cancelled); beside this title, amongst drafts, Cary noted of Nina: 'interested in Donne and the 17th cent.'.
10 Cf. pp. 78, 90; Tolstoy is discussed by name on p. 388.
11 See ch. 14, n. 10.
12 He is as it were two sons; the guilt connected with paternity relates also to Kierkegaard (p. 287 below).
13 MS. Cary 290/P.142, fol. 39.
14 MS. Cary 287/N.145; the final 's' of 'Prisoners' is doubly underlined, followed by the initials 'N & T'; this follows alternative titles, all cancelled.
15 Cecilia Dick did research for him, to secure that Chester held no similar post, or similar opinion on a specific policy at a given time.
16 Lea, *Murry*, p. 187.
17 See ch. 3, n. 5, above.
18 *Prisoner of Grace*, p. 140.

19 *Art and Reality*, pp. 24, 25; in 'Unfinished Novels' (p. 110) he says that the problem regarding the British Empire was 'to dissolve or transform it in such a way that it wouldn't be succeeded by a thousand years of barbarism, war, and misery'. See p. 301 below.

20 Date in MS. Cary 292/N.155; lecture in MS. Cary 240.

21 In Blake's view of the crucifixion, it is through the 'mother' that Jesus inherited all the evils of human nature, and was 'in the state of humiliation': 'He was in the state of glorification so far as, and when, He was in the Human from the Father . . . for the Divine could not be tempted, still less could it suffer on the cross' (*Doctrine of the New Jerusalem concerning the Lord*, p. 35); quoted by Kathleen Raine, *Blake & Tradition*, vol. II (London, 1969), p. 234.

22 *Adam and Eve* (London, 1944), chapter 3, 'On the Significance of D. H. Lawrence', is particularly relevant; in Murry's view, 'right marriage depends upon the man serving God, and the woman serving through the man the same God, in whom she also believes' (p. 100).

23 Pp. 64, 66, 275; some readers may see a resemblance between the prose style of Chester's book and *Between Two Worlds*.

24 As in the notes quoted from N. 92, p. 242 above; Georgina is essentially Hannah—plain, with a pretty sister Ruth, developed from Leila in N. 92.

25 *Power in Men*, p. 267.

26 The sin of Kierkegaard's father was that he had cursed God when a peasant boy keeping sheep; thus Cary's imagination has worked 'in reverse'; he owned and annotated *Søren Kierkegaard*, by Theodor Haecker, trans. Alexander Dru (London, 1937).

27 *Except the Lord*, p. 113; Pooley's belief in the 'toes of the prophet Daniel', noted in MS. 262/S.7.I (and p. 180 above) is developed in MS. Cary 290/P.146, containing notes from 'Signs of the Times 1872', a monthly magazine with which is concerned 'Rev. Sir W. Tilson Marsh, M.A./of Oriel College Oxford', and 'The Coming Battle [?et.] 1866 and 1875/price 3 half-pence'; this would presumably be Pooley's *Christian Intelligencer;* notes include: 'Duke of Manchester. The Times of Daniel which fix the end of the world [?within] 10 years of 1868. Louis Napoleon the antichrist is the man of papacy d is destined to be cast with the Pope into the burning lake abt 1868.'

28 MS. Cary 290/P.147 (close in date to P. 146 in n. 27 above) has notes on symbolism, including 'ditch——double meaning' (fol. 4); ditch appears symbolically in *Charley* (p. 106) as well as *The Moonlight* (p. 248 above).

29 *Prisoner of Grace*, p. 28.

30 See ch. 12, n. 5 above.

31 Yonge, vol. 1, p. 89, with the meaning 'oath of Baal'.

32 *Except the Lord*, p. 95; cf. Jung, *Psychology of the Unconscious*, p. 191: 'we approach the personification of the libido in the form of a conqueror, a hero or a demon' (p. 191).

33 MS. Cary 289/N.154.

34 *Son of Woman;* final para.

35 The stepmother had invented the dream from reading a romance, *The Old English Baron;* her involvement in the murder was probably

through jealousy of Maria; this murder, in May 1827, is still a powerful tourist attraction of Polstead village, near Ipswich.

36 *Power in Men*, pp. 57-58; he attributes five major revolutions to Rousseau, and continues: 'Both sides, the Hegelian absolutists, the anarchists, have taken inspiration from him. He has not solved any problems, but increased them'. On the publication of *Between Two Worlds*, many critics compared it with Rousseau's *Confessions*; Murry's article 'The Religion of Rousseau', *Aspects of Literature* (London, 1920), pp. 15-28, shows that he understood Rousseau very much in terms of himself.

37 Cary says all men believe in goodness. 'Their particular difference is in their reaction to it, the use they make of it in pursuit of some personal achievement, good or bad.'

38 MS. Cary 289/N.154.

39 Cary's view seems evident from an essay written concurrently, 'Policy for Aid', which he ends with reference to a confidence from 'A high European official' regarding the troubles in his country: ' "our adminis-trative class had only two generations behind it. You, in Britain, have had such a class for centuries and your public schools continually support its ideals' "; such a class, ready to serve, with little pay or recognition, has been 'but one step in the complex and difficult advance of a nation towards real democracy', says Cary. Twenty British genera-tions have not produced 'any very dignified or rational polity', he admits. 'But it is the freest yet known to the world' (*Selected Essays*, pp. 105-6).

40 'Five Windows Darken', p. 111.

41 Lea, *Murry*, p. 338; journal entry of 10 June 1954.

42 Information from Winifred Davin.

43 MS. Cary 381/P.149, fol. 1, shows that Cary considered making Nina's last thought for 'Poor Robert'.

44 *Prisoner of Grace*, pp. 309, 364.

45 See n. 19 above.

46 MS. Cary 247.

47 MS. Cary 238.

48 P. 11; that Chester's father served in this regiment, in India, provides a link between him and Jim, of possible significance to Chester.

Chapter Sixteen

1 MS. Cary 294/N.162; in typescript with longhand additions.

2 Ibid.

3 See p. 144 above.

4 MSS. Cary 296/P. 171-3.

5 MS. Cary 296/P. 170, fol. 11.

6 MS. Cary 281/N.131.

7 P. 145 above.

8   See ch. 11, n. 7.
9   From a letter to Dan Davin, quoted in 'Five Windows Darken', p. 111.
10 MS. Cary 240, fol. 50.
11 *Except the Lord*, p. 274; *Not Honour More*, ch. 5, and p. 223.
12 See ch. 11, n. 10, and p. 237 above.
13 E.g. in MS. Cary 259/N.42; 251/P. 15.
14 MS. Cary 293/S.22. J.
15 Wholly relevant to this study is Murry's experience of tumbler turning,
    when he asked ' "the only question which truly concerned me. What
    shall I do to be saved? . . . The answer was "Christ's Coat" ' (Lea,
    Murry, p. 92). Murry interpreted this to mean that he must become
    'whole', and kept the paper bearing this answer in his pocket-book
    for twenty years. His account of the experience was published in *The
    Aryan Path*, Jan. 1938.
16 MS. Cary 146.
17 Cf. *Prisoner of Grace*, p. 7: 'It operates . . . every time we see the
    meaning of a poem, grasp the beauty of a picture, recognise and
    respond to kindness or feel sympathy. Grace is so ordinary and
    common that it is not noticed in its true quality.'
18 Quoted above, p. 310; contrary to Hooper's expectations, a northern
    carpet manufacturer revives the *Argus*.
19 In MS. Cary 293/S.22.J.c Cary states that Christian values 'Put at the
    shortest' are 'the value of the individual soul as an autonomous moral
    self and the reality of evil'.
20 Quoted above, pp. 94, 95.
21 Ch. 8, n. 5.
22 'Five Windows Darken', p. 114.
23 'Editorial Note', *The Captive and the Free*, p. 9.

Chapter Seventeen

1   'If You Could Face Your Problems Today as This Man Faces
    His . . .' [interview conducted by Merrick Winn], *Daily Express* (27
    August 1956), p. 4.
2   *Joyce Cary*, p. 9.
3   *Art and Reality*, p. 11.
4   Ibid., pp. 9, 10.
5   Ibid., p. 174.
6   Ibid., p. 148: 'Hitler, with his art of the demagogue, did immense evil';
    cf. *The Horse's Mouth*, p. 71, and p. 213 above.
7   MS. Cary 271/N.82.
8   MS. Cary 272/P.52, fol. 22.
9   'On His Own Method', MS. Cary 237, fol. 4; published as 'Notes sur
    l'art et la liberté', translated by A. Proudhommeaux, *Preuves*, XLII
    (Aug. 1954), 28-32.

10   *Castle Corner*, p. 308; see p. 187 above.
11   *Art and Reality*, p. 174; cf. p. 6 above.
12   MS. 269/N.78, fol. 39 Cary wrote *sieze* for seize, as he did regularly.
13   'Don't take my word, just read it', *Times* (22 Sept. 1978), p. 14; 'A pilgrim's progress to Joyce Cary' appeared in *Times* (11 May 1977), p. 18.
14   Publisher's jacket announcement and Cary's introductory words; his correspondence confirms these statements.
15   *The Nature of Experience* (London, 1959), p. 72, note.
16   *The Ark of God: Studies in Five Modern Novelists* (London, 1961), p. 158; appropriately for Cary, the title is from William Blake: 'Man is either the ark of God or a phantom of the earth and of the water'; Stewart was Assistant Head of Religious Broadcasting, B.B.C.
17   Ibid., on the jacket cover.
18   Ibid., pp. 157-8.
19   Information from John Fischer, July 1967.
20   P. 7.
21   'A Portrait', p. 125.

Notes to Bibliography I

1   The full record is in the files of the Joyce Cary Collection in the Bodleian Library, where most of the facts here quoted can be checked. For the more personal details, I am indebted to Shiela Cary, Edith Stapleton (née Millen); Dan and Winifred Davin.
2   I am indebted to Peter Shillingsburg for knowledge of this story, and of the first English publication of S.18 and E.13.
3   The records of A. P. Watt & Son, Cary's first literary agents, show that 'The Cure' was published in *Nash's Weekly* of 5 June 1920, but I have been unable to find a copy of this issue. I am grateful to Patricia Butler for all information from her firm's records.
4   A play version of this story was offered to Charles Hawtrey, the actor-manager, with the right to produce, but clearly nothing came of it.
5   This is evidently the story originally entitled 'The Connoisseurs', which the *Strand* bought on 25 April 1921.
6   I here acknowledge, as a valuable check in the early stages of compiling this bibliography, James B. Meriwether's 'The Books of Joyce Cary', *Texas Studies in Literature and Language,* I (Summer 1959), 300-10.
7   It would otherwise be classed as a separate essay; see T.2.
8   The script was adapted by E. Fisher, and published by World Film Publications, London, 1946.
9   The script is in MS. Cary 236; the published item scarcely warrants inclusion, which I can justify only because of the subject-matter, and because it would have been published fully in the *Listener* had it been on the Home Service.

Index